FABRIC FOR THE
Designed INTERIOR

FABRIC FOR THE

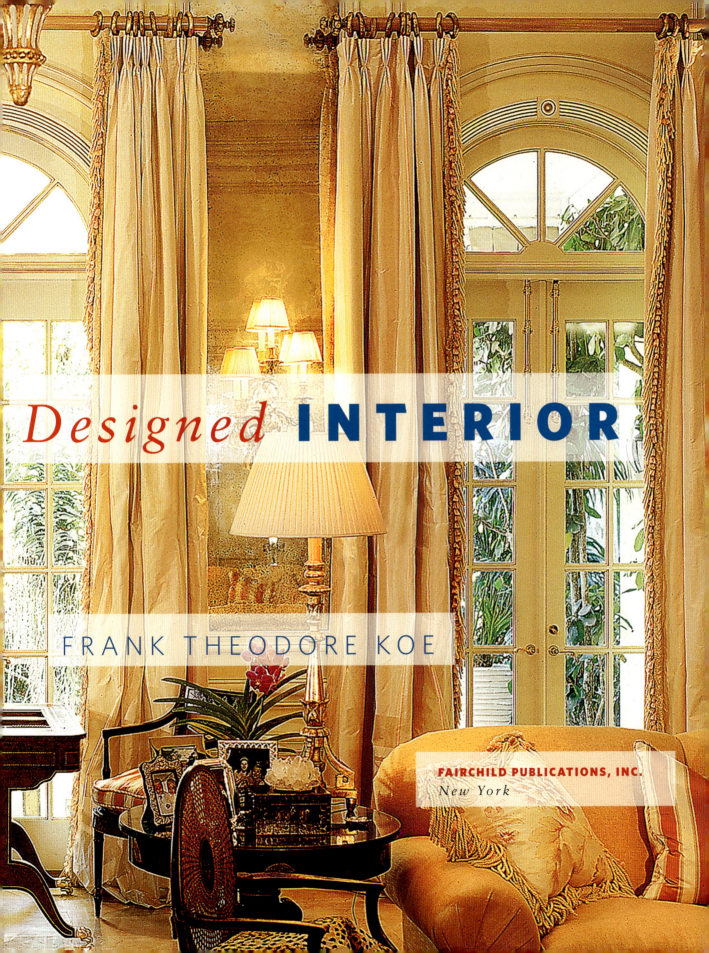

Designed INTERIOR

FRANK THEODORE KOE

FAIRCHILD PUBLICATIONS, INC.
New York

Director of Sales and Acquisitions: Dana Meltzer-Berkowitz
Executive Editor: Olga T. Kontzias
Acquisitions Editor: Joe Miranda
Senior Development Editor: Jennifer Crane
Development Editor: Sylvia L. Weber
Art Director: Adam B. Bohannon
Production Manager: Ginger Hillman
Production Editors: Beth Cohen and Jessica Rozler
Cover Design: Adam B. Bohannon
Cover Art: Photograph by Ren Dittfield of private residence of Mr. and Mrs. James Keenan,
designed by William R. Eubanks and D. Mitchell Brown
Text Design: Renato Stanisic
Page Composition: MidAtlantic Books & Journals, Inc.
Illustrator: Ron Carboni
Photo Researchers: Erin Fitzsimmons and Photosearch
DVD Developer: High Noon Productions
DVD Manufacturer: Rainbow Multimedia, Inc.

Copyright © 2007
Fairchild Publications, Inc.

Library of Congress Catalog Card Number: 2007926727

ISBN: 978-1-56367-407-5

GST R 13304424

Printed in China
TP11, DVD01

Contents

Extended Contents

Chapter 12 Learning from the Professionals 226

'Tis to create, and in creating live
A being more intense, that we endow
With form our fancy, gaining as we give
The life we image, even as I do now.
—Lord Byron, *Childe Harold's Pilgrimage, canto III*

Acknowledgments

If life can be expressed as an ongoing travelogue, the journey becomes richer with each person we meet along the way.

I am indebted to the following individuals, who offered support, encouragement, time, and knowledge to give *Fabric for the Designed Interior* life and purpose.

A manuscript becomes a book only when it is published. I would like to thank my friends at Fairchild Books, who had faith early on that this project would take form. In particular, Olga Kontzias, executive editor, and Joseph Miranda, acquisitions editor, enthusiastically supported the concept from the start and took on the additional commitment of filming and producing the DVD. I would also like to acknowledge Sylvia Weber, development editor, for her insightful and thoughtful editing and for coordinating and facilitating the steps necessary to keep the project on track. Adam Bohannon, art director, gave the book its distinctive appearance.

One of the truly great design resources in the United States is the library at the Cooper-Hewitt National Design Museum in New York City. I would like to thank Stephen H. Van Dyk, chief librarian, and Elizabeth Broman, reference librarian, for their assistance and for considering me their writer-in-residence.

Mary Beth Rembold assisted in locating illustrations and preparing the art program. Without colorful illustrations lighting the way, a book of this nature would be less instructive and would dull the nature and intent of fabric.

One special feature of this text is the DVD, which reveals the inner workings of the 110,000-square-foot Scalamandré mill, which operated in Long Island City, New York, for more than seventy years. In particular, I would like to express my appreciation to Adriana Scalamandré Bitter, Edwin Bitter, and their son, Robert, who opened the doors to their historic vertical mill, allowing us to view the remarkable process of manufacturing fine quality fabrics and trimmings. The DVD features studio design professionals and dedicated artisans who devoted years of their life to achieve their specialized knowledge and abilities. I would like to thank them for their patience and willingness to appear on camera and share their expertise.

Helping the uninitiated learn what to expect when obtaining fabric from a to-the-trade showroom is an important aspect of becoming a professional interior designer. Karen R. Rodgers, manager of Lee Jofa, played a lead role in the DVD and clarified how a design center showroom works through an instructional tour of the showroom.

The number of fabric qualities, colors, and designs available to satisfy any application are vast. I would like to acknowledge Elizabeth Searl of Rogers & Goffigon, Carly Maready of Zimmer & Rohde, and Heather Pitzen of Knoll Textiles for generously allowing us to tour their showrooms and taking time from their busy schedules to share their impressive range of products for both residential and commercial spaces.

High Noon Productions of New York City filmed and edited the showroom tours. I would like to thank Shari Smith Dunaif and her assistant, Melissa Kelly, for their excellent work.

I am indebted to Michael Hillebrand, president of Material, Technology & Logistics (MTL), whose considerable knowledge of weaving and modern weaving technology influenced Chapter 3, "Fabric Construction: Wovens and Nonwovens."

Designers must understand the applicable codes and compliance issues in order to specify the safest fabric. Lives depend on it. Marty Gurian, director of technical services at the Association for Contract Textiles, was most helpful in clarifying language and reviewing content related to codes and safety.

I thank Bill Elliott, senior manager, contract sales, at the Robert Allen Group, who provided useful information regarding contract fabric and trends. Heather Kane was instrumental in sharing the resource library of Perkins Eastman and revealing how interior designers utilize the resource. And Stephanie Ebeyer, senior associate at Gensler, facilitated the illustrations of the Design Library seen in Chapter 8.

Without competent craftspeople to convert fabric into functional and beautiful creations, cloth would have little use for interiors. I thank Lana Lawrence and Joe Lawrence of Anthony Lawrence-Belfair of New York City, whose 5,000-square-foot workroom maintains the highest standards for producing upholstered furnishings and fabric treatments. Likewise, I wish to acknowledge Vincent Suppa of Mount Vernon, New York, who has successfully demonstrated for decades the skillful art of upholstery. Contributions by Lana, Joe, and Vincent are evident in Chapter 10, "Inside the Workroom."

I am grateful to Colette Marsicano of Nice, France, who assisted in the research and translation of French resources for the book.

A book of this nature would not be complete without contributions from designers and suppliers of fabric. I would like to thank the following interior designers, who took time from their exceptionally demanding workloads and worldwide travel schedules to share their views: Albert Hadley, Carl D'Aquino, William R. Eubanks, Joe Nye, Frank Guner, Greg Jordan, Eric Cohler, Rita Yan, Susan DiMotta, Paul Wiseman, Michelle Nassopoulos, Tom Britt, and Harvey Herman. Thanks also to the following fabric manufacturers and suppliers, who were equally generous with their time and willingness to share their expertise: Nina Butkins, S. Harris & Fabricut; Lorraine Lang, Old World Weavers; Robert Bitter, Scalamandré; Christopher Hyland, Christopher Hyland, Inc.; and Scott Kravet and Tony Amplo, Kravet, Inc.

I consider myself fortunate to know Mindy Derketsch of S. Harris & Fabricut, whose working knowledge of color, trends, and design, both technically and aesthetically, is evident in her work. I acknowledge Mindy for making insightful comments along the way and offering support and encouragement.

The following reviewers, commissioned by the publisher, provided helpful recommendations: Wendy Beckwith, La Roche College; Elizabeth Easter, University of Kentucky; Nann Miller, University of Arkansas; Maureen Mitton, University of Wisconsin–Stout; Kathleen Mores, IADT–Chicago; and Patricia Williams, University of Wisconsin–Stevens Point. Rodney Berger of Lees Carpets, a division of Mohawk Industries, provided an industry perspective on the sections of the text that discuss carpeting.

Family always influences outcomes. I would like to thank my father, Frank, and mother, Kerstin, for their understanding throughout the process of writing this text. I am most appreciative of their support and their expressions of care and concern. I would also like to acknowledge my brother Frederick, an accomplished architect, for ongoing design discussions, ranging from the functions of various components of Formula 1 racing cars to an analysis and preservation of the Rembrandt Lodge and its interiors.

Preface

Fabric for the Designed Interior examines fabric as a potent contributor to the overall design and practical expression that defines interior spaces, both private and public. The information is presented in a logical sequence, and the chapters fall into two major areas: a foundation for designing with fabric and the practical application of this knowledge.

The first six chapters discuss the production and properties of fabric, providing a basis from which interior designers can make informed recommendations to their clients. Chapter 1 places fabric in a historical context and recognizes that, through the ages, few creations have contributed as much to civilizing and expanding the geographic boundaries of humankind as fabric. Fabric permitted early civilizations to extend their range to the cold regions of the world, and fabric has been credited with contributing to the evolution of cultures, as seen through archaeology, anthropology, sociology, religion, politics, and economics.

Chapters 2 and 3 review fiber and yarn construction, challenges in managing a modern American fabric mill and its technology, and woven and nonwoven structures. Chapter 4 discusses how the functional and aesthetic qualities of fabric can be enhanced through coloring, printing, and finishing.

Most interiors contain carpeting or rugs, and the importance of floor coverings is emphasized in Chapter 5. Because people spend so much time indoors, Chapter 6 was written to highlight environmental and fabric safety issues.

Interior designers must know a project intimately, communicate with the people involved, understand the fabric capabilities, and source the product. The second six chapters of this text are practical in nature. Chapters 7 and 8 explain the issues related to specifying commercial and residential fabrics and floor coverings. Sourcing fabric products is the topic of Chapter 9, and the operations of one prominent resource, the design center showroom, are detailed.

While interior designers must understand every aspect of a project in order to design a desirable space, they must also know what to do with the fabric after it is purchased. Chapter 10 provides this additional knowledge, taking the reader inside the workroom to show how fabric is transformed into something useful and aesthetically pleasing. The chapter examines the components of specifying and selecting fabric, placing an order, shipping the fabric to a workroom, and producing, delivering, and installing the window treatment or upholstered piece. The chapter underscores the importance of careful management of each phase involved in converting the ordered product into its final form. After it has been installed, fabric should be properly cared for. Chapter 11 discusses the proper maintenance of fabrics and floor coverings.

To expand on the practical orientation of the second half of this text, prominent interior designers and fabric providers working in the United States were interviewed. Chapter 12 records their responses, which provide a realistic analysis and synthesis of issues related to specifying fabric and carpeting. Readers who learn from these combined experiences will be better prepared to specify fabric appropriately, thereby enhancing opportunities for success.

This text presents fabric in a relatively uncomplicated way and addresses topics that relate to the use of fabrics in interiors.

Technological changes and world economic shifts are affecting the very definition of "fabric," in terms of both yarn composition and manufacturing methods. This text, however, focuses on the impact of these changes on interior design and does not presume to cover all categories of fabric. Clothing and home furnishings such as towels, sheets, and tablecloths are mentioned only to place fabrics for interiors in a broader context.

To support and reinforce aspects of the text, several aids broaden and clarify the content. For example, each chapter contains a list of suggested Activities. The Expand Your Knowledge section challenges readers to apply what they have learned toward the discovery of new information beyond the scope of the text. The Read On section and the appendix to Chapter 12 provide starting points for further research. An Instructor's Guide accompanies the text to assist in planning, teaching, and evaluating the content presented.

In addition, *Fabric for the Designed Interior* is accompanied by a DVD that guides the viewer through the 110,000-square-foot Scalamandre mill, formerly located in Long Island City, New York. The tour demonstrates fundamentals in manufacturing fabric and producing passementerie or trimming. The process begins in the design studio and ends with fabric inspection. A second part of the DVD illustrates how to navigate through a New York City design center and showroom. Topics include the duties of showroom personnel, establishing an account, and reading product labels. To provide insight into the range of fabric choices available worldwide, three additional showrooms were filmed, including one showroom that focuses on contract or commercial fabrics.

Throughout the text an effort is made to use the word "fabric" instead of "textile" as a reference to interiors. For me, "fabric" has several meanings. One definition implies inclusion as well as an underlying structure or construction, as in the "fabric of society," where people cluster in unique, colorful, and complementary or discordant ways. Fabric in this sense is textural and humanizing, broad. Fabric also means what results after a product has been woven, printed, *and* finished; something more akin to cloth. Fabric implies process, the process of making as well as using. In contrast, the word "textile" originates from the Latin *textilis* and the French *texere*, meaning "to weave." The literal translation of textile has broadened over time from its basic roots, but remains limiting and does not allow for knitting or felting, where fibers are matted together using one of several techniques. Furthermore, the common term borrowed from the textile industry, "mill mentality," carries a pejorative tone implying a restrictive or lockstep way of thinking or behaving.

Fabric for the Designed Interior was written for interior design and architecture students and practicing design professionals, but the text can be useful for fabric editors, converters, sales representatives, business owners and their employees, and members of the general public who wish to know more about fabric and its influence on transforming, humanizing, and stimulating aesthetic sensibilities for interior spaces.

FABRIC FOR THE
Designed INTERIOR

Origins of Fabric: A Primer

The discovery of cloth by humans contributed to their survival and the rise of civilization. Fabric is inexorably tied to the study of archaeology, anthropology, sociology, religion and symbolism, politics, and economics. And, of course, the aesthetic value of fabric deserves consideration as well. Tracing the origins of cloth provides a trail that reaches into the distant past, revealing primitive life and early civilizations while offering clues as to how fabric helped advance culture and civilization as we have come to know it.

IN THE BEGINNING ...

Speculation abounds as to where, why, and when fabric made its first appearance on earth. Exposure to the natural elements over time was responsible for consuming much of the early evidence, with the exception of fragments that were frozen or submerged in water absent of air. Nevertheless, one "theory" suggests that the origin of cloth emanated from the need to fulfill the basics of life: food, clothing, and shelter.

Long before cloth was made, there are references to Adam and Eve (Figure 1.1) who "sewed fig leaves together and made themselves aprons" (Genesis 3:7). And in Genesis 3:21, "unto Adam and to his wife did the Lord God make coats of skins [possibly held together by bones or thorns] and clothed them." Having "clothes" created warmth, especially when fur was placed next to the skin. This basic attire provided early humans, who were losing their coat of body hair, protection from the elements and gave them the ability to explore and migrate to cooler climates. If mankind was not endowed with the intellectual capacity and the wherewithal to protect itself from ranging temperatures, the growth of civilization would have been restricted to warm places. "The saying that 'clothes make *a* man' ... is too narrow in scope. We should say 'clothes make mankind,' for without them civilization, as we know it, simply would not be."[1]

CHAPTER 1

Opposite: Silk weaver, plate from Japanese women, late eighteenth century.

Figure 1-1 References to Adam and Eve's "clothing" may have contributed to the start of protecting skin from cold temperatures and encouraging early human exploration.

Whether the need was to increase physical mobility or comfort or to strive toward a more interesting "look" by distinguishing oneself from others through added embellishment, larger furs gave way to many smaller ones connected together. In Oirotia, Siberia, a fur robe dis-covered in a tomb was made of hundreds of strips of ermine, squirrel, and reindeer hides arranged to simulate a colorfully dyed reindeer gut.[2]

The early humans were consumers of their environment. They used vines, reeds, and quills as ropes and twine. They may have also used these and other materials in the creation of basket-like structures (Figure 1.2) to assist them in carrying objects as they migrated, or possibly to aid in the capture of fish. In warm regions, where the bark of trees was used for tents and other purposes, the glutinous inner bark was pounded to produce the tough yet thin **tapa cloth** of the South Seas Islands.[3] In addition to using grasses and bark, the early humans heated animal hair by pounding it, creating a substance similar to **felt** that may have served as bedding.

NEOLITHIC DEVELOPMENTS

Evidence gathered from the Neolithic period demonstrates major advances made by the early humans. The Neolithic period, or late Stone Age, which began in Western Europe around 10,000 B.C.E. and lasted nearly 7,000 years, was a remarkable period in human evolution. During this time many advances were made, including the invention of the wheel and the discovery of how to grind stone and bone, create pottery, use the bow and arrow, cultivate grain and fruit, and weave linen. The Neolithic period was also marked by people living together in families and villages as a way of establishing social order and enhancing safety. Many of these villages were later discovered in Switzerland, where people congregated around lakes. Slowly the division of labor evolved: Men gravitated to hunting, fishing, and food gathering while women remained near the fire and tended to children and the camp. Many of these findings did not surface until 1854, when a drought significantly lowered the water level of a Swiss lake.

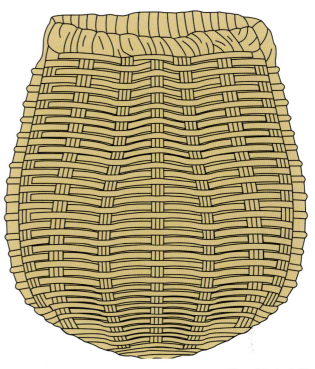

Figure 1-2 A primitive basket showing a basic woven structure.

FIRST FIBERS

Plants, animals, and minerals from the earth provided the ingredients for early fabric. Throughout the world and at different times **fiber**, the smallest unit of fabric capable of being spun into yarn, made its appearance. Perhaps the most important fiber consisted of plant material, such as flax, hemp, jute, ramie, and cotton. Evidence also suggests that, during the early development of civilization, humans used animal fibers, such as wool and silk, and the **sericulture** process by which raw silk is produced. They used reflective threads made of precious metals and minerals, which had their own unique properties. Here, we explore the early uses of these fibers. In Chapter 2, we will consider the processing of fibers to produce fabrics in more modern times.

TAPA CLOTH: Bark cloth made from beating the fibrous inner bark of certain trees, particularly the paper mulberry tree.

FELT: A nonwoven sheet of matted material made from wool, hair, or certain manufactured fibers by applying heat, moisture, and pressure.

FIBER: The smallest unit of fabric capable of being spun into yarn.

SERICULTURE: The cultivation of caterpillars more commonly known as silkworms to produce raw silk.

Figure 1-3 (top) The flax plant was used in the production of an early fabric alleged to have special powers.

Figure 1-4 (bottom) Cotton grows naturally in an array of colors.

VEGETABLE DYE: Class of natural dyes including woad, madder, and indigo that originate from roots, bark, and berries.

SISAL: A hard leaf fiber obtained from the sisal plant found in Java, East and West Africa, and Haiti.

Flax (*Linum usitatissimum*)

Linen originates from the flax plant (Figure 1.3). Evidence of linen nets and garments dating from 8000 to 7000 B.C.E. was discovered in Switzerland, and linen remnants discovered in the Mediterranean, Iraq, and Iran date about 6000 B.C.E. In the Nile Valley of Egypt, linen fragments treated with **vegetable dye** survived from about 5000 B.C.E. in tombs because of the controlled temperature, the arid climate of the region, and the absence of light. After careful study of the linen used to wrap mummies, some strips 300 yards in length, it can be determined that the higher the deceased's place on the social scale, the finer the weave of the cloth used to wrap them. The fine linen used to wrap one mummy had more than 500 threads per inch.[4]

In ancient Egypt, linen allegedly was endowed with special medicinal powers and capable of warding off leprosy for those fortunate enough to own linen garments. Linen was also quite popular among the Coptics, a Christian religious sect in Egypt dating from around the first century, C.E. Flax grew in many places, and it was cultivated in Mexico by the Aztecs, as well as in Belgium, the Netherlands, England, and Ireland, where it grows today.

Hemp (*Cannabis sativa*)

Some evidence suggests that hemp was widely cultivated as early as 4500 B.C.E. in Southeast Asia and China. Hemp was used in floor coverings, baskets, cloth, and rope. **Sisal**, another fiber that originates from the leaves of a woody stem plant, replicates the texture and appearance of hemp. The hemp fiber is extremely durable and resists rotting as well as the effects of salt water, which is one of the reasons it lasts for so many years.

Cotton (*Gossypium*)

The history of cotton dates from around 3500 B.C.E. in India, the ancient world's "cradle of cotton," and around 3000 B.C.E. in Peru. Cotton is native to Asia, Africa, the Middle East, and North and South America. Cotton has been raised in natural colors such as brown, yellow, and blue since about 2700 B.C.E. in Egypt, India, Pakistan, and Peru (Figure 1.4), and naturally colored cotton is now being grown in the United States as well.[5]

The first written reference to cotton was made between 445 and 425 B.C.E. by Herodotus: "There are trees which grow wild there [India], the fruit of which is wool exceeding in beauty and goodness that of sheep. The Indians make their clothes of this tree-wool."[6] However, it appears that at one point there was confusion in Egypt between the terms "flax" and "cotton." Herodotus states that the "Egyptian priests wore linen cloths, but Pliny (the naturalist) refers to them as wearing cotton material,"[7] which seems to have been worn by many individuals across the social spectrum. Perhaps they wore both. In 350 B.C.E. Theophastus wrote about cultivating cotton, apparently around the Tigris and Euphrates rivers, and in 71 B.C.E. it was recorded that the Romans used cotton for tenting material.

Wool

The Second Stone Age, about 4000 B.C.E., was the period when wool fibers were first used. In "Jericho [Palestine] which is near ... the Cave of Treasure at Nahal Mishmar ... thirty-seven pieces of undyed linen and eight pieces of wool, some (dyed) in different colors (red, green, black, and tan) were discovered in about 4000 to 3000 B.C.E."[8] Wool was discovered among early civilizations in the Near East, and "Pliny devotes an entire chapter to sheep raising and wool culture (*Historia naturalis, vii, 48*). He tells that in early times the sheep were plucked or combed, later shorn."[9] Shear-like instruments did not appear until the Iron Age, or about 1000 B.C.E.

Wool is excellent for matting as well as spinning due to its interlocking scales. And within the irregular shapes of the wool fibers many air pockets exist, sustaining an even temperature and making wool useful where warmth is desired. Wool also holds dye well; hence, the expression "dyed in the wool."

Additional evidence of wool can be traced to the tablets of Ur, a city that was near the Tigris and Euphrates rivers. Around 2000 B.C.E. the tablets describe very large flocks of white and black sheep. The tablets tell of wool being sold and the prices received. The tablets further mention 127 slave girls and 30 children working the wool and 165 women and girls weaving.[10] Wool is the oldest of the fibers to be spun, and the word "wool" is found in all European tongues. The Greeks call it "lenas," the Gauls called it "laine," and the Germanic tribes and Saxons of England named it "woll" or "wolle."[11]

Before long, selective sheep breeding became commonplace, and the early coarse hairs were replaced by softer, finer ones.

Wool was popular for its warmth and readily available to the classes of society who were able to sustain the animals and process the fibers. Wool can be made into extended lengths rather easily, especially when the **lanolin** oils, dried perspiration, and dirt that collects on the sheep during grazing are removed by washing. Both long and short wool fibers were used, providing they were sufficiently aligned and separated, a process that was facilitated early on by combing the wool with thistles.

Through the ages, various specialty hairs, or specialty wool, became prominent in addition to sheep's wool. Silky white mohair, for example, was first discovered several thousand years ago in Anatolia, located in Asia Minor, East of the Bosporus or Istanbul Strait near Turkey.

The alpaca, llama, and vicuña first roamed the altitudes of the Andes in South America at about the same time, covering an area that includes Ecuador, Peru, Bolivia, and Argentina. The llama, larger than the alpaca, originated in the Old World, as evidenced by fossil remains. All three animals may have descended from the guanaco, a distant member of the dromedary, or one-humped camel, family. The alpaca and llama have been domesticated for about 1,200 years and prefer grazing Andean tussock grasses at heights ranging from 13,000 to 16,000 feet. Llama fibers tend to be somewhat coarse, but llama fleece is soft and valuable. The alpaca, a close relative of the llama and vicuña, is said to be a crossbreed of the two and was domesticated by the Incas around 500 B.C.E. Fibers from the vicuña (Figure 1.5), the smallest of the species at approximately 2 feet, 8 inches

LANOLIN: Wool grease sometimes used in the production of ointments and cosmetics.

Figure 1-5 The vicuña produces fine woolen hairs.

to 3 feet, 7 inches tall, produce a very fine grade of wool. The vicuña has not been fully domesticated, making its fibers difficult to obtain. The vicuña traverse the rocky mountain peaks and breathe the thin air at roughly the same altitudes as the alpaca and llama, about 13,000 to 15,000 feet.

Cashmere is *generally known* to come from many breeds of these animals, commonly called goats. They are located in roughly 12 countries, with most in Central Asia and China. Technically, there is not one particular animal registered for producing cashmere; however, the goat that originates from the Kashmir mountain region and traverses India and Pak-

istan and is known as the Cashmere goat, produces what many agree is the only source of cashmere. Cashmere also comes from cashmere goats bred in captivity in Australia and other countries, where the quality of hair relates to both genetics and the environment.

Other animal fibers that have been used throughout history include hairs from the camel, rabbit (especially the Angora rabbit), horse, cow, muskrat, and various rodents.

Silk

It is difficult to imagine how much high drama has been associated with "one of the usefullest creeping things or insects upon the whole earth."[12] The silkworm and its thread have been traced to China and the year approximately 2640 B.C.E., during the reign of Emperor Huang Ti. His wife, Empress Hsi-ling-shi, whether rightly or wrongly, has been celebrated as the Patroness of the Silkworm and was known in some circles as the spirit of the mulberry tree and the silkworm. Allegedly, as the empress was sitting in her garden having hot tea one day, she looked up and discovered a number of cocoons clinging to a mulberry tree. She picked one and, as she examined it, the fuzzy ball fell into her tea. With her assistance, the cocoon began unraveling. As a result, her province of Shantung was celebrated as the "cradle of silk weaving."

For centuries, China kept sericulture a secret. Anyone who attempted to divulge the connection between the silkworm and mulberry leaves or any aspect of silk farming was put to death. But it was impossible to keep the luxurious fiber a secret from the West forever. One story that explained how silk was discovered by the rest of the world involved two trusted Persian monks who frequently visited China and quietly observed the entire silk production process. They traveled to Constantinople (Istanbul) and told the emperor, Justinian the Great, what they had seen. The emperor was impressed, and he made an arrangement with the monks to return to China and secretly secure some silkworm eggs (seeds). In 552 C.E., the emperor was presented with the stolen eggs, which had been tucked inside the monks' hollow cane. The monks collected a reward for their efforts.

Much has been written about the production and migration of silk throughout the world, as well as the best methods of cultivating mulberry bushes and trees. Even Aristotle, in *History of Animals*, written in the fourth century B.C.E., was aware of the silk-producing worm; he described it as "the worm which has horns."[13] It was not long before the association between worms and silk fabric spread throughout the Byzantine (Eastern Roman) Empire and, around the twelfth century, from Spain to Italy, where high-quality woolen fabrics were already well established. Even today, the desire for the silk fabrics used in interiors, as well as clothing, continues to be strong.

Metallics

Both gold and silver threads dating to about 2000 B.C.E. were used to enhance the appearance of fabric, typically through embroidery (Figure 1.6). In Exodus 39: 2–3, Moses refers to the metallic threads used in a richly embroidered garment called an ephod, usually made for a high official, which was woven for Aaron: "And they did beat the gold into thin plates, and cut it into wires, to work it in the blue, and in the purple, with cunning work."[14]

Metallic threads were sometimes produced by hammering pure gold into thin, flat sheets and then cutting the sheets into narrow strips about 5 millimeters (0.197 of an inch) in width. These strips would be wrapped around a core of linen or sometimes cotton or silk. Often the core was dyed to complement the color of the metal, as was done in China. This method of creating gold and silver

Figure 1-6 This silk brocade caftan with gilt metal threads originates from sixteenth-century Turkey.

king in 5th century Rome, appeared in a golden tunic. Josephus had a similar tale about Herod Agrippa, who wore a mantle woven of silver. Both men were eventually assassinated."[15]

Minerals

Early civilizations appear to have had a keen eye for searching out fibers. Mineral crystals that originated in India were used in Chinese garments. Brittle strands of **asbestos** were extracted from the crystals and carefully woven into flame-resistant material. Additionally, Arabs used the fiber to construct protective clothing that could be worn during battle. Supposedly, Charlemagne awed an army of barbarians into retreat by throwing a tablecloth made of asbestos into the fire and retrieving it undamaged.[16]

SPINNING THROUGH HISTORY

The remarkable achievement of learning how to extend fibers into something longer through twisting expanded construction possibilities and variety in fabric.

Spinning

Before humans appeared on earth, spiders made use of spinning, as did the silkworm. But the ability to collect fibers, understand their value, and find a way to twine them into continuous thread is one of the most significant developments of humankind.

Spinning is the process of straightening out and twisting fibers into yarn or thread. A **yarn**, or the less specific term **thread**, is the result of combining many

threads was used until about the thirteenth century.

There is evidence of the use of metallic embroidery in places such as southern Russia; however, few examples have survived from these ancient times because invading armies and others burned or unraveled the fabric to obtain the valuable metals. One drawback of this sort of metallic attire was that its weight made it uncomfortable to wear and strained other fibers adjacent to the metallic threads. Also, metallic threads tarnished over time. The response to this problem was to create a lighter imitation, and one method was to gild an animal gut with gold and silver that eventually wore off and appeared a dull brown or gray color. It was fashionable in the Early Roman Empire to wear garments that reflected such richness, although some evidence would suggest that it was socially segregating and not conducive to living a long life: "Vertius told how Tarquinius Priscus, a legendary

ASBESTOS: A mineral that easily separates into long, flexible fibers used in noncombustible, nonconducting, or chemically resistant material.

SPINNING: The process of straightening out and twisting fibers into yarn or thread.

YARN: Two or more fibers of varying lengths, twisted together.

THREAD: A thin, continuous cord, especially strands of cotton, linen, silk, wool, or manufactured fibers often used in sewing.

short or long fibers through the twisting process. **Carding** is the first process in spinning. After cleaning the fibers, the bunched cotton or wool material passes through rows of stiff metal wires that are attached to a board, separating the yarns. It was not until the eighteenth century that the process was mechanized.

The earliest implements to facilitate the spinning process were the distaff and the spindle. The **distaff** was a long stick that could be placed between the legs or under an arm, permitting the spinner to keep both hands free for twisting fibers. The **spindle** was a shorter stick that held the hand-twisted yarn after it was wound. The spindle was weighted down with a **whorl**, a small flywheel often made of terra-cotta that kept the wound yarn from sliding off the spindle (Figure 1.7). Ancient whorls have been found in ruins of Asia Minor, Africa, Italy, and India. "Distaffs were occasionally made of costly materials. Homer mentions one of gold that was given to Helen of Troy by Alexandre of Egypt, and Theocritus relates how he presented one carved of ivory to the wife of his friend Nikias of Milesia (a city in Asia Minor)."[17]

It appears that in India, sometime between 750 and 1000 C.E., a spindle was attached to a frame and rotated by turning a wheel. The result was the spinning wheel. Improvements on the spinning process were slow to evolve, but in the sixteenth century the Brunswick Wheel increased the speed of spinning. With the invention of the spinning jenny during the Industrial Revolution, rapid spinning could be done effectively by filling more than one spindle at a time.

Figure 1-7 The distaff, spindle, and whorl are ancient implements used in the production of thread.

Early Weaving

It is difficult to date the first act of **weaving**, but early evidence taken from mats and baskets seems to point to about 6000 B.C.E. in Jarmo, Iraq. The weaving process was, arguably, the most civilizing accomplishment of early civilizations. The main difference between weaving and knitting, or net making, is that weaving uses more than one yarn to make a product.

The system of interlacing vertical and horizontal material has significantly advanced over the years, but the central idea of weaving has remained the same for centuries. The first visual reference of a weaving apparatus appears on an Egyptian dish depicting Penelope's warp-weighted loom from about 4400 B.C.E.[18]

The progression from laying plant material on the ground and interconnecting the strips to create a mat to weaving with

CARDING: the process of separating, distributing, and equalizing fibers to remove most impurities and some broken, short, or immature fibers.

DISTAFF: A wooden stick about 3 feet long that holds fibers while they are twisted by hand.

SPINDLE: A round wooden stick or rod used to twist yarn in spinning.

WHORL: Small flywheel weight at the base of the spindle that keeps thread in place.

WEAVING: The method or process of interlacing two or more sets of yarns or similar materials so that they cross each other, usually at right angles.

Figure 1-8 (above) An example of an early woven, flat structure.

Figure 1-9 (right) A framed loom apparatus was used to facilitate weaving.

WARP: Set of threads or yarns traveling lengthwise on the loom. Also known as ends. Warp ends interlace with weft yarns.

WEFT: Set of threads or yarns traveling horizontally to the warp yarns. Individual yarns are also known as picks or filling yarns and interlace with warp yarns.

SHUTTLE: A boat-shaped device that carries weft yarns through the warp shed in the weaving process.

SHED: The raising of some warp yarns by the harness so the shuttle can pass through.

HEDDLES: Cord, wire, or flat steel strip through which one or more warp threads are connected. Heddles are supported by the harness.

HARNESS: A wood or metal frame that holds the heddles in position during weaving.

TREADLES: Foot pedals used to control the opening and closing of the shed in hand-weaving.

spun fibers was a major development. In the case of the vertical loom, weaving required weighting down the **warp** threads that were attached to a frame with stones or clay. The weaver then passed the spindle by hand, separating the odd **weft** yarns from the even warp yarns, and packing them tightly together, creating cloth (Figure 1.8). The spindle was eventually replaced by the **shuttle**. Over time, modifications to the early loom made the weaving process more

efficient. For example, instead of opening up the **shed** with his or her fingers to introduce the weft yarns, the weaver used a paddle or "sword" that permitted several weft yarns to be selected and held open in a predetermined manner, allowing for the creation of different weaves. Later on, looms used **heddles** to lift the even warp yarns. The frame that holds the heddles is the **harness**.

Looms with **treadles** were an advancement over early looming but permitted only a limited number of sheds to be formed. The draw loom, however, appearing about 2500 B.C.E. in Syria or perhaps China, was important because it had many heddles gathered together to form cords and could be lifted in any arrangement, creating never-before-seen patterns. The cords occupied much less space than shafts actuated by treadles (Figure 1.9). The invention of the draw loom was significant and can be attributed to economic growth in regions of the world where it was used.

In order to create an elaborate fabric design, a weaver must be able to raise warp yarns in a seemingly random and individual way, independently controlling each yarn. This was accomplished by attaching individual warp yarns to a string, then attaching all of the strings to a board connected to the top of the loom. Children positioned themselves on the loom, high above the weaving floor, and, at the appointed moment, pulled up a coded harness in a particular sequence that corresponded to a shape in the design. These "draw boys," who performed the monotonous work prior to 1801 in France, were always in danger of falling off or modifying the pattern of the weave by forgetting the "lifting" sequence of the cords. Needless to say, mistakes were made. It appears that Leonardo da Vinci (1452–1519) made a serious but unsuccessful attempt to create a mechanical device that would relieve the draw boys from their tedium.

Jacquard Technique

Joseph-Marie Jacquard (1752–1834), an experienced draw boy himself, combined and improved upon three components that led to the development of the **jacquard mechanism** or jacquard head (Figure 1.10). The first invention was by Basile

Figure 1-10 The jacquard mechanism was the forerunner of the present-day computer, capable of weaving complex structures.

Bouchon, who used perforated paper and needles to raise and lower warp yarns. And in 1728, Jean Falcon, another Frenchman, strung perforated, rectangular "hard" cards to communicate to the loom which yarns should be lifted. These two developments, in addition to Jacques de Vaucanson's mechanical cylinder and an early version of a mechanical loom he developed, led to the improved jacquard mechanism and loom that was eventually adopted. These early techniques of punching holes in cards that corresponded to a fabric pattern were the first steps toward programming a language, in this instance a "design language," and eventually led to the present-day computer. Jacquard first demonstrated his dependable loom mechanism at the Paris International Exhibition in 1801, and "by 1812 it had been fitted to eighteen thousand looms in Lyon."[19]

Throughout the jacquard loom's development, there were, however, violent protests from workers who were going to lose their jobs or be forced to learn a new skill. Protesters discovered that the loom's guiding system could be made inoperable if a wooden shoe, known as a *sabot*, were dropped into the mechanism. This act may have been the first recorded instance of industrial "sabotage."

Through the years, modifications on the jacquard weaving technique and other methods of creating fabric have evolved—to a great extent due to advances made in technology and through the discovery of new ways to solve old problems. Space exploration, for example, has been partially responsible for the development of the manufactured fibers that have kept space explorers warm. Some of these same technologies have been applied to the outdoor clothing available today. Other technologies have used specialized woven materials for boat building, such as the Vanguard Vector sailboat (Figure 1.11),

Figure 1-11 Advanced glass and polyester resins produce fabric for specialized uses, such as the sails for this sailboat. Photo courtesy of Vanguard Sailboats.

in which unidirectional meshed glass fibers and polyester resins form the hull. Early weaving techniques have yielded to advanced technologies to improve the quality of living.

SUMMARY

Throughout the ages, humans have worked to invent, improve, and advance their culture. Few examples demonstrate with such clarity the march of civilization as fabric. The early humans, as hunters and gatherers, found ways to extend their reach beyond warm or comfortable climates by using fabric to protect themselves from harsh weather. They modified what they found in nature to increase their chances of survival. Today cloth is not limited by how well it can protect. Like interior design in the modern age, what matters most is not survival, but how well one is surviving. From the roots of the early flax plant to modern, chemically produced products, the search continues for new fibers that complement contemporary lifestyles brought on by technology, the need to have more for less, and the competition that motivates individuals to a strive for comfort, convenience, and aesthetically pleasing surroundings.

ACTIVITIES

1. Visit a museum or historic house. Interview a curator about the oldest fabrics in the collection. Determine and describe the historic period. What furnishings were used in conjunction with the fabrics?

2. Create a spindle, distaff, and whorl.

3. Acquire raw cotton. Pull the fibers out and twist them together by hand to simulate the creation of a continuous fiber strand.

4. Contact a weaving organization, such as the Handweavers Guild of America. Interview a weaver. Ask how his or her loom works and why he or she weaves.

EXPAND YOUR KNOWLEDGE

1. Trace the origins of wool in North America. Determine the influence Native Americans had on this fiber.

2. Compare and contrast the four different kinds of silk thread. What makes silk more flame resistant than cotton or other natural fibers?

3. Naturally colored cotton is not new, but it is grown commercially in different parts of the world. Where is it being grown now? How is it being used in today's market, and what might be the profile of a contemporary consumer?

4. Trace the evolution of the spinning wheel to the high-speed spinning used today.

5. Research the influence and economic importance of the draw loom. Trace the improvements made to the loom that led to high-speed Jacquard looms.

6. Explain how early jacquard cards were punched and attached to the Jacquard mechanism. How does the loom "read" the cards to create complex patterns?

7. In the eighteenth century, one of the centers of weaving was located in Lyon, France. Research the rise of Jacquard weaving in Lyon. What fabrics were

produced there? Where were they sold, and for what purpose were they produced?

8. What are the methods of dating ancient fabrics? Which technique(s) are most effective, and why? Within what range of years can researchers date fabric?

9. How can the economics of a region be changed by increasing fabric production methods and decreasing labor costs? Offer present-day examples.

READ ON

Alisa Baginski and Amalia Tidhar, *Textiles from Egypt, 4th–13th C.E.*, Jerusalem: Los Angeles Mayer Memorial Institute for Islamic Art, 1980.

E.J.W. Barber, *Pre-Historic Textiles: The Development of Cloth in the Neolithic and Bronze Ages*, Princeton, N.J.: Princeton University Press, 1991.

Rene Batigue and Louisa Bellinger, "The Significance and Technical Analysis of Ancient Textiles as Historic Documents," *American Philosophical Society Proceedings* 6 (1953), pp. 670–80.

Lousia Bellinger, "The Bible as a Source for the Study of Textiles," The Textile Museum paper no. 18, Washington, D.C.: The Textile Museum, November, 1958.

CIBA Review, "The Early History of Silk" No.11 (July 1938).

Collectif *"Soies tissues, soies brodees chez I'Imoeratrice Josephine"* from Musee national des chateaux de Rueil-Malmaison et de Bois-Preau de November, 1002 a fevirer 2003. Editor, Réunion des Musées Nationaux.

Grace Crawfoot, "Textiles, Basketry, and Mats," in *A History of Technology*, ed. Charles Singer, et al., Oxford: Clarendon Books, 1954–1958.

M.D.C. Crawford, *The Heritage of Cotton*, New York: Grosset & Dunlap, 1924.

Helen C. Evans and William D. Wixom, eds., *The Glory of Byzantium: Art and Culture of the Middle Byzantine Era*, A.D. 843–1261, New York: Metropolitan Museum of Art and Harry N. Abrams, 1997.

R.J. Forbes, *Studies in Ancient Technology*, vol. 4, Leiden, the Netherlands: E.J. Brill, 1964.

K.T. Freshly, "Archaeological and Ethnographic Looms: A Bibliography," I. Emory Roundtable on Museum Textiles, Washington, D.C.: The Textile Museum, 1977, pp. 269–314.

H.W. Haussig, *A History of Byzantine Civilization*, New York: Praeger Publishers, 1971.

Norma Hollen et al., *Textiles*, 6th ed., New York: Macmillan, 1988.

William F. Leggett, *The Story of Linen*, Brooklyn: Chemical Publishing, Co., 1945.

William F. Leggett, *The Story of Silk*, New York: Lifetime Editions, 1949.

Jean Paulet and the Academie des sciences, *L'art du fabriquant d'étoffes de sole*, Paris: s.n., 1773–78.

Walter Perry, *The Story of Textiles*, New York: Tudor, 1925.

Peru Naturtex Partners (on naturally colored cotton), James M. Vreeland, Jr., Director, http://www.perunaturtex.com/textile.htm.

Pliny the Elder, *Natural History: A Selection*, trans. John F. Healy, London: Penguin, 1991.

K.G. Ponting, *Discovering Textile History and Design*, Great Britain: C.I. Thames & Sons, 1981.

Elizabeth Riefstahl, *Pattern Textiles in Pharaonic Egypt*, New York: The Brooklyn Museum, 1944.

Mary Schenck Woolman and Ellen Beers McGowan, *Textiles: A Handbook for the Student and the Consumer*, rev. ed., New York: Macmillan, 1926.

Annemarie Seiler-Baldinger, *Textiles: A Classification of Technique*, Washington, D.C.: Smithsonian Institute Press, 1994.

W. Fritz Volbach, *Early Decorative Textiles*, New York and London: Paul Hamlyn, 1969.

Annette B. Weiner and Jane Schneider, eds., *Cloth and Human Experience*, Washington, D.C., and London: Smithsonian Institution Press, 1965.

Klaus Wessel, *Coptic Art*, New York: McGraw-Hill, 1965.

Structure and Content of Fiber and Yarn

Our exploration into the nature of fibers begins beneath the surface. The history and identity of animal and plant fibers reflect the development of civilization. Not only do their origins correspond with humans living thousands of years ago, but their usage can be charted throughout the world. Moreover, many of these same fibers and fabrics remain in high demand today, providing personal comfort as well as practical and aesthetically pleasing solutions for daily life. Scientific analysis can explain why natural fibers are so useful, and various surface applications (finishes) can be applied to extend this usefulness. Manufactured fibers, with their various chemical compositions, also contribute significantly to the list of fibers currently available. In fact, today nearly two-thirds of all fibers are manufactured.

IDENTITY OF FIBERS

The fabric selection process usually begins with the senses: sight followed by touch. But even the most accomplished designer can be more than a little confused about the identity or preferred use of an unmarked or unidentified fabric. Unmarked fabrics should not be used; however, there are methods for distinguishing one fabric from another, and it is usually best to employ more than one test to make an accurate identification. For example, an effective method for testing the composition of some natural fibers involves burning the fibers and observing their response to the flame while smelling the aroma and noting the burnt ash. The composition of various manufactured fiber blends may go undetected unless the fibers are examined under a microscope. When a designer knows the properties and capabilities of fibers, he or she can direct a client toward a purposeful choice (Figure 2.1).

Extensive information about the composition and molecular arrangements of a vast number of fibers is available. This chapter highlights some general identifiable

CHAPTER 2

Opposite: Ball of wool, close-up.

Figure 2.1 Knowledge of fabric composition helps to narrow choices.

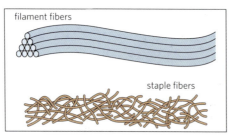

Figure 2.2 Filament and staple are two types of thread.

STAPLE: Short fibers. Staple fibers require spinning and twisting to create a yarn. In manufactured fibers, staple fibers are cut in lengths from about 1 inch to 1 ½ inches from the extruded material.

FILAMENT: A fiber of extreme or indefinite length. The length permits a yarn to be made with little or no twist.

characteristics of fibers found in fabrics widely specified for use in interiors.

CATEGORIZING FIBERS

The process of classifying and describing fibers equips a designer to understand their sources and uses. Performance and appeal are two essential ingredients in the selection of one fabric over another. Performance characteristics relate to function and versatility. Appeal refers to qualities related to how a fiber feels (hand), fabric texture, luster, cost, availability, and the aesthetics associated with the overall de-

sign, as well as appropriateness for placement of fabric in an interior space. In order for a fiber to be considered for use, it must be spun, readily available, priced competitively, and desired by the end user.

Fibers fall into four basic categories: plant (cellulose), animal (protein), mineral, and manufactured. Fibers can appear in their initial form as staple or filament (Figure 2.2). **Staple** fibers are short in length and usually need to be straightened through spinning. **Filament** fibers are considerably longer than staple. New fiber compositions are being researched, tested, and marketed on a regular basis that has led to remarkably high-tech fabrics that frequently find their way into clothing as well as interiors.

Each fiber has its own signature shape and structure, making it discernable and offering clues to the designer, and consequently the client, about how and where it should be used. For example, wool would be preferred over linen for theatre seats because of its elasticity, soft hand, and resiliency. Examination of the composition and qualities of common yarns used in interiors can lead to better fabric choices. Characteristics of both natural and manufactured fibers and filaments are listed in Tables 2.1 and 2.2.

PLANT FIBERS (CELLULOSE)

Plant material is the source of the earliest fibers on record and remains important today. Linen and cotton are the most commonly used plant fibers. Hemp, jute, ramie, and sisal also have applications in interiors. The inner bark of some plants produces a woody material that is the source of **bast** fibers. This section describes the plant fibers used in interiors.

Flax (Staple)

One of the most important bast fibers used in interiors is linen, which originates from the flax plant (Figure 2.3). Flax, from which linen is made, looks similar to bamboo under a microscope. A cross section appears as small, differently shaped, smooth stones with markings. Flax grows well in acidic soil and reaches heights from 2 to 4 feet. Flax is planted in the spring and harvested by pulling the roots

and stems out of the ground, not by cutting. The stocks are bundled and retted. **Retting** is the process of separating bast fibers from the natural gum and wooden matter of the plant stalk. In modern times, retting is accomplished by using water that is sometimes diluted with sodium hydroxide, sodium carbonate, or a tincture of sulfuric acid to facilitate the process. If the flax remains in the liquid too long, the filaments will weaken. And if they are not left in the chemical mixture long enough, the filaments will not separate properly. Another method of separating the flax from the stem is to pass it through fluted metal rollers. Other bast fibers, such as hemp, jute, ramie, and sisal, can be processed using similar methods.

Hemp

Hemp can grow to 10 feet tall and is used for rope, cord, and fishing line. The strongest hemp comes from a tree-like plant stem in Manila related to the banana family. Because it is also related to marijuana, industrial hemp cannot be grown legally in the United States; however, industrial hemp does not have the psychotropic properties of the plant grown for illegal drug use, and efforts to lift the ban eventually may prove effective. Much like

BAST: Woody material such as flax, hemp, jute, or ramie obtained from the inner cortex of the bark.

RETTING: Process of separating bast fibers from the natural gum and wooden matter of the plant stalk.

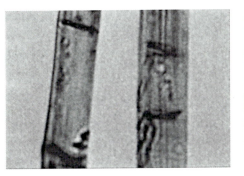

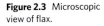
Figure 2.3 Microscopic view of flax.

Table 2.1 Characteristics of Natural Fibers/Filaments

CHARACTERISTICS	LINEN	COTTON	WOOL	SILK
Fiber length	2 to 40 inches	$\frac{1}{2}$ inch to 2 inches	$1\frac{1}{2}$ to 15 inches depending on breed of animal	300 to 1,600 yards and from rare cocoons up to 3,000 yards
Luster	High	No or low luster if untreated	Low or matte depending on breed of animal	High
Effect of heat on fabric	Withstands high heat	Resists heat at high temperatures	Resists heat well	Sensitive to heat and scorches easily
Pilling	No	No	Yes, but not to a great degree; shorter fibers tend to break off	No
Sensitivity to light	Resists sunlight	Fair; slowly deteriorates and yellows over time	Fair to good; resists sunlight	Very sensitive when exposed over long periods of time
Ability to accept dyes	Fair; not as good as cotton	Good but less than silk	Very good	Very good dyed in yarn form; prints well
Strength	High; increases when wet; stronger than cotton	Strong but less than silk or wool in untreated form	Fair; loses about 25% of strength when wet	Strong when dry but loses about 15% of strength when wet
Abrasion resistance	Fair	Good	Fair	Fair
Flame test results	Burns on contact; continues burning when removed; aroma of burning paper; produces a light, feathery ash	Burns on contact; continues burning when removed; aroma of burning paper; produces a gray, feathery ash	Burns on contact; self-extinguishes when removed from flame; aroma like burnt hair; produces brittle, black ash	Burns when exposed to flame but self-extinguishes when removed; aroma of burnt hair; produces crushable black ash
Care	Steam or dry clean; sheds oil well; resistant to moths	Withstands many washings; may be steam cleaned	Fibers weaker when washed with strong soap; must be steam cleaned	Steam clean and may be laundered by hand or machine depending on finish
Resiliency	Poor	Poor	Very good when dry; resists wrinkles	Fair to good
Draping ability	Fair	Very good but can be stiff depending on finish	Good	Very good; thinnest of all fibers
Uses in interiors	Window treatments; pillows	Window treatments; pillows; some upholstery, depending upon treatment; upholstered walls; trimming	Upholstery, some wall applications; pillows; trimming	Window treatments when lined; pillows; upholstery, especially when blended with other yarns; trimming; upholstered walls

Table 2.2 Characteristics of Manufactured Fibers/Filaments

CHARACTERISTICS	RAYON	ACETATE	NYLON	POLYESTER	ACRYLIC	OLEFIN®
Fiber length	Filament or staple	Filament or staple	Filament or staple	Filament or staple	Filament or staple	Filament or staple
Luster	High	High	High	High	High	High
Effect of heat on fabric	Melts under high temperatures	Poor	Melts under high temperatures; can be heat formed	Retains heat and pleats well	Melts under high temperatures; pleats well	Low resistance
Pilling	No	No	Yes and is capable of building up static	Yes; produces static	Yes	No
Sensitivity to light	Good but not over extended periods of time; weathers well but can yellow	Poor	Poor, especially during prolonged exposure	Resists sun and weathering	Resists sun and weather	Resists sun and weather well
Ability to accept dyes	Very good; absorbs dyes evenly	Very good	Good	Good	Fair	Good
Strength	Weak to fair; loses about 40% to 50% of strength when wet	Weak; about 25% weaker when wet	High; only loses about 10% when wet	Very good	Fair; becomes about 20% weaker when wet	Very good
Abrasion resistance	Poor	Poor	Very good	Very good	Fair	Very good
Flame test results	Burns rapidly when exposed to flame, sometimes faster than cotton; burns after exposure to flame; aroma like burnt paper; produces small amounts of light, fluffy ash	Burns rapidly and sparks; aroma like vinegar; produces hard, shiny black ash	Melts and drips; aroma like celery; produces hard, black ash	Melts before burning; emits black smoke and forms hard, black mass	Melts when in flame; small amount of black smoke with little aroma; produces black, sticky ash	Burns slowly and shrinks from flame; creates a waxy soot; aroma like burning asphalt and produces a hard tan ash
Care	Launder or dry clean	Dry clean	Launder or dry clean	Launder or dry clean	Dry clean	Dry clean
Resiliency	Poor; wrinkles easily and shrinks when washed	Fair	Very good	Very good	Very good	Very good
Draping ability	Very good	Very good	Good	Very good	Very good	Very good
Uses in interiors	Window treatments and upholstery, especially when blended with other yarns; trimming	Commercial grade upholstery; carpets; window treatments, interlinings	Upholstery and window treatments when blended with other yarns; carpeting and rugs	Window treatments; upholstery, especially when blended with other yarns; substitute for down in cushions; carpeting	Outdoor furniture cushions; when blended with other yarns, indoor upholstery	Outdoor furniture cushions and seating; carpeting; interlining; carpet backings

linen, fine Italian hemp can be used in the manufacturing of clothing and rustic window treatments. Hemp is an especially good choice for open-air interiors located near saltwater, due to its ability to resist decomposition while exposed to the salty air.

Jute

Jute, also known as burlap, is used for rope, twine, and matting and originates mostly in Bengal, India. Jute is very inexpensive. Some finer qualities of jute can be combined with wool, flax, or cotton to make inexpensive clothing and curtains. Jute rots readily when exposed to moisture but resists the invasion of microorganisms and insects, making it a good choice for carpet backing. Jute can also be used in interior wall hangings and rustic window treatments.

Ramie

Ramie, also known as China grass, is typically softer than hemp or jute. Ramie fibers are about 2 to 18 inches in length, but the plant can reach 8 feet in height. Its white fibers have a high sheen with a silk-like appearance, very fine yet stiff. Ramie accepts dyes readily, and its fibers are strong and capable of resisting alkalis and mildew. Ramie is almost three times stronger than cotton. Sometimes mixed with wool in the weaving process, it can be used as a substitute for flax. Some evidence suggests that ramie was used to wrap mummies before linen.

Sisal

Sisal, or henequen, comes from agave plant leaves common to Mexico and the Yucatan peninsula. The fiber is cultivated in Africa, Java, and South America. Sisal is used to make rope but is also popular in brightly dyed colors and used as indoor or outdoor floor covering or mats, particularly when interconnected in a variety of patterns. Saltwater can destroy the fibers rather easily, so sisal must be used sparingly in areas exposed to salty air.

Cotton (Staple)

Cotton is unusual because of its elongated cell structure and natural twists, a combination that enhances its ability to be spun easily (Figure 2.4). Because of varying temperatures and soil and water conditions, many varieties of cotton and staple lengths exist. For example, the cotton grown in Korea is a longer staple, about

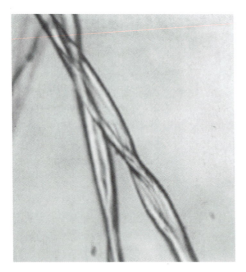

Figure 2.4 Microscopic view of cotton.

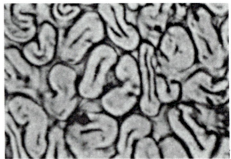

2.5 inches in length, and a higher quality than the cotton grown in China.

All cotton carries seeds and dirt from the field. These were removed by hand until the roller gin was invented in India during the Middle Ages. To straighten out the fibers (lint), they must be carded, as shown in Figure 2.5. Modern machinery cards cotton and other fibers.

Under a microscope, cotton is rather complex and generally appears as a flat, twisted ribbon with the outer casing containing a wax-like coating. The cross section looks like a kidney bean with a long, narrow sliver of a fading moon. The twist of the ribbon can range from 150 to 300 turns per inch, and the coating facilitates its ability to be spun. Sea Island cotton, grown primarily in Georgia as well as the western United States, and American-Egyptian cotton (pima, registered as Supima), raised in Arizona, California, and New Mexico, are both of excellent quality. Cotton has been grown throughout the world, with Egypt producing a fine, long staple of 2 inches or more.

Cotton fiber is actually "hair" growing off the cotton seed, which is planted in March and matures after about 45 days. The cotton **bolls** must be picked when they first bloom to prevent discoloration of the fibers. If cotton is picked before it has matured, the length of the fibers will be short and immature, creating spinning problems.

ANIMAL FIBERS (PROTEIN)

Fibers from animals, including wool and silk, provide lustrous choices for interiors. Some of these fibers are reviewed next.

Figure 2-5 Cotton seeds were removed by hand before carding methods were developed.

Wool (Staple)

Wool is composed of keratin, which is the same protein found in human hair and fingernails. Under a microscope, wool fibers are crimped yet round and have large scales (Figure 2.6). A cross section of wool appears like small, irregular circles with specks. Fine or smooth qualities of wool have more crimp and much smaller scales. The consistency of wool and crimp depends on the breed of sheep. For example, Merino sheep produce fibers that range in length from 1.5 to 5 inches.

Wool that is shorn from live sheep is *clipped* wool. *Pulled* wool is the wool that is removed from the hide of dead sheep. The best grade of wool is shorn from the sheep's back and shoulders, while wool from the legs and stomach region is less desirable.

The distinction between *woolen* and *worsted* relates to the length of the fibers,

BOLL: The seed pod of the cotton plant. The seeds vary in number and are covered with staple fibers.

Figure 2.6 Microscopic views of wool.

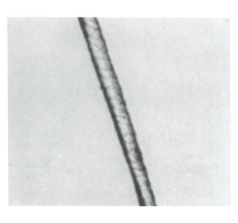
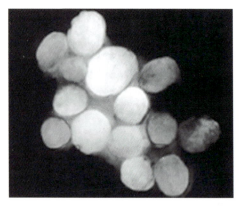

how the fibers are converted into yarn and woven, and how they are finished. Worsted fibers are longer, have a tighter twist that reduces the amount of surface fuzz or **nap**, and are combed so the fibers lie parallel, creating a softer, smoother surface than plain wool. Some wool fibers are identified as specialty wool. This wool comes from different animals and includes the following:

- *Mohair* originates from the Angora goat—not the Angora rabbit—which is raised throughout the world. For the U.S. market, the goat is raised primarily in Texas. Mohair has a high sheen, resists fading, and is perhaps the most durable of the animal fibers.

- *Cashmere* is very soft with high napability and **loft**, or springiness, allowing it to be constructed into fine or coarse yarns. Cashmere hair is collected by hand during the spring molt or by brushing the domesticated goats. The finest of fibers are the long ones found under and around the neck and chest of the goat and protected by coarse, outer guard hairs. In the West, cashmere is sometimes known as pashmina (from the Persian word for

wool, *pashm*), but rarely is a pashmina product woven 100 percent from the prized underfur of the goats. The pashmina blend usually includes silk or other fibers. Cashmere is often difficult to distinguish from other fine animal hairs, such as those originating from the Chiru or Tibetan antelope. Further confusion can arise when fibers of different animals are combined, such as crossing an Angora with a Cashmere goat, which results in "cashgora."

- Camel's hair descends from the two-humped or Bactrian camel. This hair varies in quality according to the geographic range of the animal and can be fine but coarser than cashmere.

- The domesticated llama and alpaca produce hair somewhat weaker than camel's hair. Alpaca fibers are approximately 8 to 15 inches long. There are two types of alpaca: the huacaya, which produces longer, coarser fibers, and the suri, whose fleece is thicker and more refined.

- Fibers from both the vicuña and guanaco are exceptionally rare and finer than cashmere. Both drape very well. Efforts to raise these animals in

NAP: Protruding fiber ends from the surface of one or both sides of a fabric, giving a fuzzy appearance and produced by brushing and elevating the fibers.

LOFT: The quality of rebound or springiness in a natural or manufactured yarn.

the United States in sufficient numbers to make the hair economically viable have been unsuccessful.

Silk (Filament)

There are more than 200 species of worms (caterpillars) that secrete something resembling silk filament, but only the *Bombyx mori* silkworm produces sufficient volume and quality of silk to be commercially viable.

Under a microscope, cultivated silk looks similar to a smooth, transparent rod (Figure 2.7). The cross section resembles many small, smooth pebbles. Silk remains in high demand, especially for residential interiors, and has many qualities that draw individuals to it, including its luxurious hand and reflective capabilities. This natural protein fiber produced from hard-working caterpillars is comparable in strength to steel yet highly elastic.

Most silk is cultivated with worms that are raised in controlled conditions. In its freshly extruded or reeled form, which is accomplished mechanically more often than by hand, the silk appears gray or yellow. The color comes from the **sercin**,

which must be boiled off, making the fibers white or cream in color and less prone to water spotting in a finished state. When silk is uncultivated or produced in uncontrolled conditions, it is called *tussah* silk. Tussah, which is light brown in color, produces fibers that are thicker, rougher, flatter, and generally irregular in shape. When two silk worms pair together to make one cocoon they produce *dupioni* silk. This interlocking, double filament appears as irregularities, causing the filament to be thicker in places along the filament shaft. These thicker areas are called **slubs**.

Although silk is unusually strong, the filaments must be prepared for the stressful weaving or knitting process by **throwing**. In the throwing process, four types of silk threads are produced: organzine, crepe, tram, and thrown singles. Organzine thread is made by twisting the raw silk in one direction and then twisting two threads together in the opposite direction. Crepe is made the same way but not twisted quite as much. Tram thread is made by twisting

SERCIN: Gum produced by the silk worm's gland.

SLUB: An uneven, elongated, and somewhat thick section of a yarn considered a flaw in some fabrics such as finished satin but valued for adding texture in other fabrics.

THROWING: The process of making a twisted yarn from reeled silk or adding an additional twist into manufactured filament.

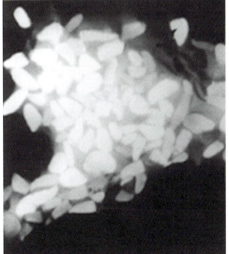
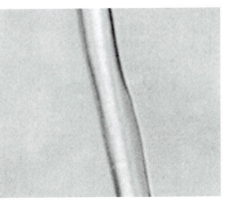

Figure 2.7 Microscopic views of silk.

two or more filaments in the same direction. Thrown singles are individual filaments twisted in one direction. Organzine is typically laid lengthwise on a loom, and the tram interconnects widthwise. Crepe threads are used for weaving crinkly fabrics, and thrown singles are used to create sheer cloth.

The silkworm appears to be a sensitive creature. It is a productive and cooperative silk producer as long as it is not distracted by loud noises or foul odors. Some evidence suggests that the worms enjoy music.

MINERAL FIBERS

From hard surfaces come many useful fibers. Fibrous, inorganic substances found in nature have been used throughout history. These materials come from clay, rock, or glass. One of the best-known fibrous minerals is asbestos. Asbestos fibers lie parallel to each other and can be easily parted. The thicker the vein of asbestos, the longer the fibers will be. The families of asbestos are serpentine and amphibole. Within serpentine there is chrysotile asbestos, and within amphibole there are amosite, crocidolite, tremolite, actinolite, and anthophyllite. Not all forms of asbestos contain the same potency in causing cancer; although, amphibole appears to be the most toxic.

For nearly a century, asbestos has been used in fire-resistant material such as fire-smothering blankets, mitts to protect hands in the kitchen, insulation, and heat-resistant fabrics for theatre curtains. In the United States, new uses of asbestos have been strictly regulated by the **Environ-**mental Protection Agency (EPA) since the 1970s. Because many old houses and factories are being restored for new uses, the designer should be alert to signs of asbestos and, if it is discovered, contact a reputable service to have it properly removed.

In 2000 there was a strong reaction to the discovery of minute traces of harmless asbestos in three popular brands of crayons. However, serious health problems from asbestos result almost exclusively from the inhalation of airborne fiber particles associated with the more dangerous family of asbestos. This inorganic fiber is rarely used today—in part because of the public's perception that all forms of asbestos are harmful.

MANUFACTURED FIBERS

The intervention of chemistry as a complement to nature, or as an independent source of new product development, provides an ever-increasing array of fiber and fabric choices. The desire to experiment and innovate by producing fibers that go beyond raising animals and growing plant material, as well as the need to expand the functional qualities and production capabilities of fibers, led to two basic classifications of manufactured fibers: **regenerated** or *reformed* **fibers** that originate from natural cellulose, a substance common to plant fibers, and fibers that are **synthetic** or synthesized exclusively from chemical **polymers**, large molecules consisting of repeated chemical units.

The first written reference to the concept of providing manufactured fibers is found in Robert Hook's *Micrographia*, a book published in 1664, when its author

ENVIRONMENTAL PROTECTION AGENCY (EPA): A government agency responsible for control and abatement of pollution of air and water by solid waste, pesticides, and radioactive and toxic substances.

REGENERATED FIBERS: Fibers that are chemically processed from cellulose using, for example, wood chips.

SYNTHETIC: A term applied to any manufactured fiber other than rayon, acetate, or regenerated protein (azlon) fiber.

POLYMERS: Substances created by the reaction of two or more monomers (simple molecular compounds) that have reactive groups allowing them to join, forming long, chain-like molecules.

was 29. Hook theorized that there might be a way to duplicate the "excrement" of the silkworm through mechanical means. Hook's observation of silkworm activity stimulated the design of the **spinneret**, a device for producing strands of manufactured fibers by extruding the material through a hole or holes (Figure 2.8). The spinneret was refined by the Frenchman M. Ozanam in 1862; however, before the spinneret was fully developed for use, Swiss chemist Georges Audemars experimented with dissolving the inner bark of the mulberry tree, eventually producing cellulose. He formed threads by inserting needles into the substance and was able to lift strands of the material. Audemars was granted a patent in 1855 for "artificial silk" but was unable to conceive a way to convert his discovery into practical use.

The most significant feature of fiber manufacturing is the ability to control the number of fibers extruded at one time, predetermine their thickness, and have the capability of producing an endless flow of product measured on a daily basis in miles. Because of this control, the length of manufactured fibers can be either staple or filament. To increase the number of fibers, one simply increases the number of holes in the spinneret. It is also possible to vary the size of the holes, thereby increasing or decreasing the thickness of the fibers. The diameter of extruded fibers is measured in terms of **denier**. The finer the fiber, the lower the denier.

Sir Joseph Wilson Swan, the English chemist and electrician and, according to the U.S. Patent Office, inventor of the electric light carbon for the incandescent lamp (not Edison), was the first to use the

Figure 2.8 Extruding filament through a spinneret.

spinneret effectively. He successfully pressured a solution of cellulose nitrate in glacial acetic acid through the small holes of a spinneret in 1883. These early beginnings signaled the start of rayon—the first regenerated, manufactured, cellulose-based fiber. Other *cellulosic* manufactured fibers include acetate, triacetate, and lyocell, a relative of rayon.

Cellulosic Fibers

Natural fibers treated with chemical intervention increase their applications. Some of the cellulosic fibers are reviewed below.

Rayon

Under a microscope, rayon looks like a series of compact, vertical striations adhering to one another (Figure 2.9). The cross section looks like a cluster of irregular clouds with abstract circle markings inside.

Rayon was patented in 1884 by Hilaire Bernigaud, count de Chardonnet, a French student of Louis Pasteur who combined an interest in chemistry with finding a cure for silkworm diseases that threat-

SPINNERET: A nozzle with 1 to more than 1,000 holes, through which manufactured fiber material is forced, then appears as a coagulated strand. The holes are usually from 0.002 to 0.005 inch in diameter.

DENIER: An international numbering system for describing linear densities of silk and manufactured filament.

Figure 2.9 Microscopic views of rayon.

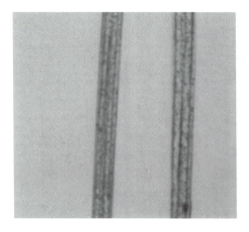

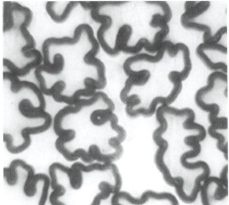

ened silk production in Europe. After some experimentation, Chardonnet produced a volatile cocktail consisting of raw cotton treated with nitric and sulphuric acid and dissolved the mixture in alcohol and ether. This solvent mixture was then evaporated and transformed into a solid filament.

The name "rayon" was conceived in 1924 by Kenneth Lord, Sr., in response to a contest to name the substance known as "artificial silk." Manufacturers wanted to increase sales by moving away from the word "artificial" and toward a more descriptive reference to the fiber based on its appearance and feel. The new name singled out the product's reflective properties, as in the sun's "rays" (sheen), and its soft feel, as in cotton "on."

Three enduring methods of manufacturing rayon evolved that enhanced the fiber's qualities of suppleness, evenness, luster, strength, absorbency, and ability to be cleaned. The first and most common is the *viscose* process. Viscose rayon was developed in 1881 in England by Charles Frederick Cross, Edward John Bevan, and Clayton Beadle and made by treating purified cellulose with sodium hydroxide

and then carbon disulfide. The commercial success of producing rayon did not materialize until Samuel Courtaulds formed the American Viscose Company in 1910.

In 1890 French chemist L.H. Despaissis pioneered and patented the *cupramonium* process for making rayon fibers but died before he put it to use. Later, German scientists perfected this eight-step method, and J.P. Bemberg made it commercially viable. In the cupramonium process, purified cellulose of wood or cotton **liners,** lengths of fibrous tissue, are dissolved in an ammoniac copper oxide solution. One form of nylon has been named Bemberg, in honor of one of rayon's early developers.

The third method of creating a form of rayon is by the lyocell process. While the fiber Lyocell, named for the process from which it stems, seems different from what is commonly understood as rayon, it is technically a subclassification of rayon, as defined by the Federal Trade Commission. Lyocell was initially produced in the United States by Acordis Cellulosic Fibers in 1992. The fiber's only U.S. manufacturer is Tencel, Ltd. The fiber, also known as Lenzing Lyocell R or Tencel R. Lyocell rayon, is produced by dissolving cellulose

LINERS: Lengths of fibrous plant tissue.

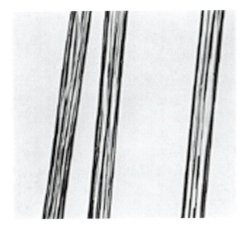

Figure 2.10 Microscopic views of acetate.

found in wood pulp in a water bath diluted with amine oxide, then coagulating and extruding the fiber. Lyocell has many of the same characteristics as rayon. All three processes for producing rayon are used in rayon produced for interior fabrics.

Acetate

Under a microscope, acetate appears striated, with three or more rounded columns (Figure 2.10). The cross section of the fiber resembles kernels of popcorn with rounded edges.

The Swiss brothers Camille and Henri Dreyfus created the first commercial process to manufacture acetate in 1904. The first uses were for toilet articles and film for the motion picture industry. Acetate burns more slowly than celluloid and was, therefore, safer for the film industry. The Dreyfuses also sold a liquefied version that was used to coat, stretch, and strengthen airplane wings during World War I. In 1917, Camille Dreyfus founded the American Cellulose and Chemical Manufacturing Company (Amcelle), which eventually became the Celanese Corporation. The name Celanese was created by combining the words "cel(lulose)" and "ease," as in easy care.

Triacetate, a form of acetate, is derived from wood fibers (cellulose) mixed with an acetic compound derived from acetic acid and acetic anhydride. The cellulose acetate is dissolved in a mixture of methylene chloride and metethanol so it can be spun. Acetate and triacetate fibers were first produced in 1924 by the Hoechst Celanese Company and more recently by Celanese AG; however, in October 2004 Celanese AG announced an end to producing acetate fibers.

Noncellulosic Fibers

Years of chemical experimentation have led to the discovery of a host of fibers. Synthetic, *noncellulosic* fibers are made exclusively from chemical resins. The fibers are polymeric amides with a chemical structure originating from coal and other petrochemicals. Synthetic and regenerated forms of acetate are **thermoplastic**, meaning the fibers can be shaped by exposure to high temperature. One advantage of this capability is that the fabric can be heat-creased with lasting results.

THERMOPLASTIC: The capability of a yarn or filament to be softened with heat after it has hardened and cooled.

One drawback of synthetic fibers is that they can melt if they become too hot. Nylon and acrylic are examples of products formed by polymers.

Nylon (Polymide)

Nylon can be produced in various forms, thereby influencing its performance and its appearance when it is magnified (Figure 2.11). Basically, nylon appears as a round, smooth cylinder or rod. A cross section of the fiber resembles rounded equilateral triangles.

Wallace Hume Carothers, Julian Hill, and their team of organic chemists at E.I. Du Pont de Nemours (DuPont) announced in 1935 that they had developed nylon (Fiber 66), the first totally synthetic fiber, using the petrochemical toluene. The first product to be made of nylon was the toothbrush. The first commercial success of nylon occurred when nylon stockings were introduced to New York stores on "N-Day," May 15, 1940. It is estimated that five million pairs of stockings were sold that day! Numerous advertisements soon appeared promoting nylon stockings.

Nylon was first called the "coal-air-water" filament. There is no agreed upon story as to how the fiber actually got its name; however, it has been suggested that the word "nylon" originated from an early advertised advantage of nylon stockings—"no-run." Of course, nylon *can* run, and there were concerns about the claim, so allegedly "no-run" was modified to nylon.

Polyester

Under a microscope polyester fibers appear like smooth rods (Figure 2.12). A cross section looks like a series of circles with dark markings.

In 1941, after building upon the work of Carothers, Jon Rex Whinfield and James Tennant Dickson patented the basic material used in polyesters: polyethylene terephthalate, which is also known as PET. After W.K. Birtwhistle and C.G. Ritchie joined the team, the first polyester fiber was created in 1941: Terylene. Eventually Dupont obtained the patent to produce polyester from the English organization, Calico Printers' Association.

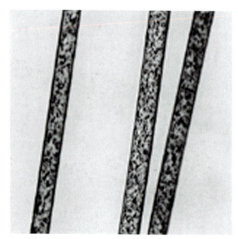

Figure 2.11 Microscopic views of nylon.

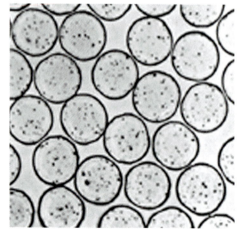

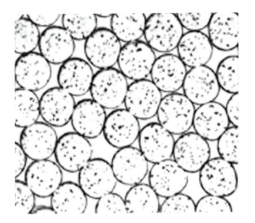

Figure 2.12 Microscopic views of polyester.

Polyester replaced nylon, rayon, and cotton in many products. In time, polyester became known for its ability to shed wrinkles yet remain rather soft when combined with cotton; however, polyester can harm the environment when blended with chlorine. The fibers are smooth and round and have excellent **wicking** properties, permitting surface water to be easily removed from the fabric.

Acrylic

Under a microscope, acrylic fibers are essentially smooth, with parallel lines extending their length (Figure 2.13). A cross section reveals circles touching, some opening to each other at the point of contact. Acrylic is produced in many varieties by changing slightly the chemical mix as found in **bicomponent fibers**. These fibers can be converted into fabrics that resist flame and the outdoor elements, making acrylic a good choice for outdoor furniture.

Acrylic polyacrytonitrile fibers are a type of plastic used to substitute for wool or silk. The first chemical acrylic composites were produced in Germany by Ch. Moreau in 1893. Further research by

H. Rein and I.G. Farbenindustrie resulted in an important publication in 1938 that described how the polymer could be successfully dissolved in a variety of aqueous solutions. Building upon this early research and the tremendous success of nylon, Wallace Carothers and his researchers at Dupont once again took the lead and developed what was first called Fiber A. Trademarked as Orlon, the first acrylic was produced in 1950.

As chemically produced fibers were growing in popularity, other companies were competing with Dupont to discover new combinations that would extend the choices already available. In Germany, Farbenfabriken introduced Pan and Dralon. The Chemstrand Corporation in the United

WICKING: The drawing up and transfer of liquid in fibers or filaments through capillary action.

BICOMPONENT FIBERS: The combining of two polymers of different chemical or physical properties similar compounds into one filament and extruding them through the same spinneret.

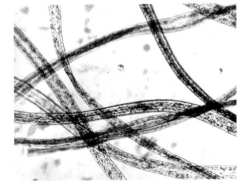

Figure 2.13 Microscopic view of Orlon.

Figure 2.14 Microscopic views of Olefin.

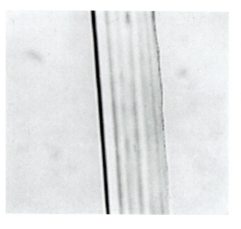

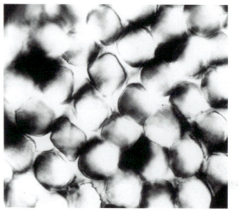

States was formed, combining Monsanto Chemical with the American Viscose Corporation. The result was Acrilian. Eventually, a host of acrilian fibers were produced, both in the United States and offshore, under names such as Zefran, Crysel, Nandel, Bi-Loft, Creslan, Dyrel, Orlon, and Zef.

Olefin

Olefin fibers originate from the paraffin (wax) family of polymers, the same family that includes polypropylene, sometimes known as polythene and used in making plastic bags, containers, and plumbing components. Under a microscope the fibers resemble glass rods (Figure 2.14), with the cross section revealing irregularly spotted circles that sometimes touch.

Early research began in England and Germany in the 1930s, with the study of pressured polymerization of polyethylene. Through the work of Karl Ziegler and the Phillips Petroleum Company in the United States, the plastic was developed that resulted in products such as plastic bottles. But it was several years later that Giulio Natta and Karl Ziegler were awarded a patent for the manufacture of polyethylene, a derivative of polypropylene. Production

began in Italy in 1951 at the Montecatini Company factory, and the product trademarked was Meraklon. The first commercially produced polypropylene resin in the United States was manufactured in 1957 by the Hercules Company and known as Herculon.

Numerous chemical improvements made to polypropylene fibers resulted in a vast array of trademarked fibers for specialty uses. Olefin, however, was the original polyethylene fiber and one of the lightest to be used in upholstery. The advantage is that more fabric can be produced from a pound of material—a pound of material can cover more surface.

UNDERSTANDING FIBER PROPERTIES AND CHARACTERISTICS

Learning how fibers and filaments perform contributes to their use in interiors. The myriad possible combinations using synthesized molecular versions of oxygen, hydrogen, carbon, and other chemicals forming larger molecules continue to evolve and grow in numbers. Confusion about the composition and performance characteristics of particular fibers can occur when an easily remembered trademark name is substituted for a name that may be more descriptive of a fiber's property based on research and chemical ingredients. There are more than 45 trademarked names for viscose rayon alone! Old names disappear and new ones surface, often leaving consumers unsure about what they are purchasing. The law requires clothing to display labels that note the generic name for the fiber found in the garment as well as how the fabric is to be cared for, but this is not necessarily true for fabrics used for interiors. Care instructions can help determine a fabric's function.

Understanding fiber properties and their functional qualities is useful in determining the placement of fabrics within a residential or commercial setting. However, from a realistic point of view, it should be noted that regardless of how practical or appropriate a fiber may appear to be for a particular installation, aesthetic issues can override what may seem to be an otherwise perfectly logical choice. The challenge is to combine the best of both aesthetic and practical considerations when choosing fabrics and to communicate the capabilities of various constructions so that a client can be guided toward most appropriate choice.

FIBER TO YARN

Fibers in usable forms with the appropriate twists and turns contribute to making fabric possible. The **American Society for Testing Materials (ASTM)** specifically defines *yarn* as a "generic term for a continuous strand of textile fibers, filaments, or

material in a form suitable for knitting, weaving, or otherwise intertwining to form a textile fabric."[1]

A yarn can be composed of many staples or filaments twisted together. The term "yarn" can mean fibers that are **single** or **plied**, loosely or tightly spun, and less processed than thread (Figure 2.15). *Thread* is typically more finished, smoother, and has a tighter twist. Thread is often used in reference to needlework and sewing, although it can be used in the mill environment when referring to warp and weft threads or "threads per inch."

The whorl and distaff were useful inventions for creating yarn, as was the

Figure 2.15 Building yarn.

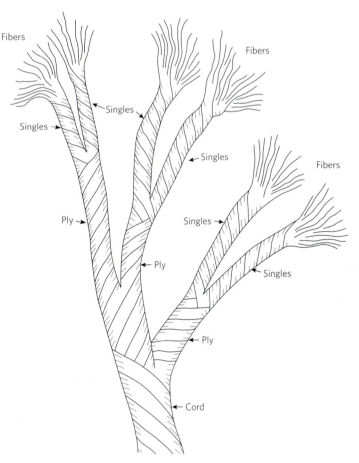

Fibers

Fibers

Fibers

Singles

Singles

Singles

Singles

Singles

Singles

Ply

Ply

Ply

Ply

Cord

spinning wheel, but in modern times, more efficient methods have emerged with the capacity to convert large quantities of fibers into twisted yarns.

Yarn Processing

There is not one standard method used to produce long, continuous yarns required for interior fabrics. Different fibers require different techniques, depending on their composition; however, the steps that cotton must pass through to create yarn provide a point of reference for other short staple fibers.

When cotton arrives at the mill, it is tightly packed and compressed in bales. The fibers must be relaxed, and any large impurities such as dirt or seeds that have remained on the bolls from the field must be removed. This is accomplished by combining several bales together in a machine named by its function: an opening.

The *picking machine* continues to fluff the fibers, but in a more refined way, while creating cotton laps, loosely compressed fiber sheets about 1 inch thick and 40 inches wide. In some modern mills the lapping phase has been omitted and the fibers are simply blown in clumps directly into the carding machine.

The carded fibers then move between two rollers, creating a thick rope called a *sliver*. The sliver is straightened further and the shortest fibers are removed by combing. During the combing process, nearly 25 percent of the fibers are removed in an effort to produce the high-quality fibers found in combed cotton. The same process is also used to create worsted wool. After combing, several slivers are combined and drawn out to create

uniformity by pulling the fibers lengthwise and over each other, thereby strengthening and improving their luster and uniformity. Roving continues the drawing process but adds a slight twist, holding the fibers together but not well enough for them to create a strong connection. The spinning phase is responsible for strengthening the bond between the fibers. There are several methods of modern spinning. Perhaps the most popular is ring spinning, which is more efficient than mule spinning, a process used primarily for wool and fine cotton thread. The ring spinning approach was invented in 1839 and is capable of twisting and winding the yarn onto *bobbins* by means of a ring or hook in one continuous motion. The ring traveler controls the twists per inch. Other methods of spinning that apply to manufactured fibers include the following (Figure 2.16):

Wet Spinning This is the oldest method of spinning manufactured fibers. Wet spinning means that the spinnerets are submerged in a chemical bath and the extruded fibers become solidified in the liquid. Examples of fibers that use this technique include rayon, aramid, acrylic, modacrylic, and spandex.

Dry Spinning Fibers in this process remain "wet" but solidify without coming in contact with a liquid that would facilitate the hardening process. Fibers produced this way include acrylic, triacetate, PBI, and spandex.

Melt Spinning The fibers that are extruded through the spinneret are melted first, then solidified through

Figure 2.16 Wet, dry, and solvent spinning.

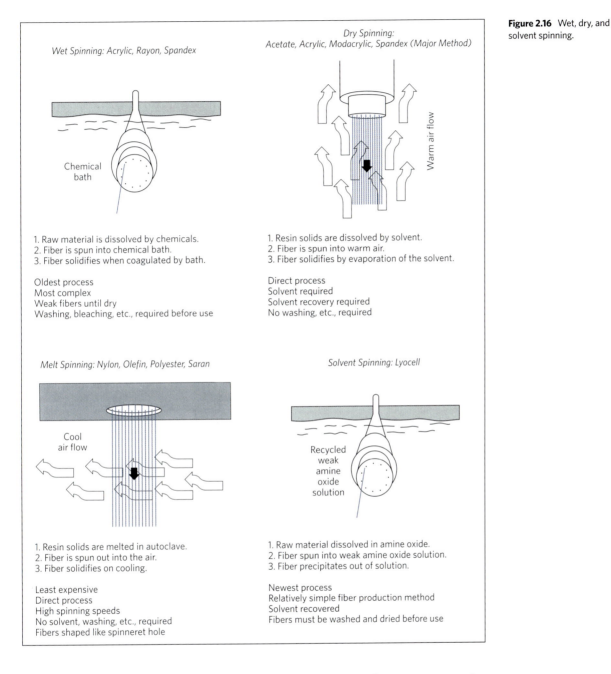

Wet Spinning: Acrylic, Rayon, Spandex

Chemical bath

1. Raw material is dissolved by chemicals.
2. Fiber is spun into chemical bath.
3. Fiber solidifies when coagulated by bath.

Oldest process
Most complex
Weak fibers until dry
Washing, bleaching, etc., required before use

Dry Spinning:
Acetate, Acrylic, Modacrylic, Spandex (Major Method)

Warm air flow

1. Resin solids are dissolved by solvent.
2. Fiber is spun into warm air.
3. Fiber solidifies by evaporation of the solvent.

Direct process
Solvent required
Solvent recovery required
No washing, etc., required

Melt Spinning: Nylon, Olefin, Polyester, Saran

Cool air flow

1. Resin solids are melted in autoclave.
2. Fiber is spun out into the air.
3. Fiber solidifies on cooling.

Least expensive
Direct process
High spinning speeds
No solvent, washing, etc., required
Fibers shaped like spinneret hole

Solvent Spinning: Lyocell

Recycled weak amine oxide solution

1. Raw material dissolved in amine oxide.
2. Fiber spun into weak amine oxide solution.
3. Fiber precipitates out of solution.

Newest process
Relatively simple fiber production method
Solvent recovered
Fibers must be washed and dried before use

exposure to air. Examples of melt spun fibers are olefin, polyester, saran, nylon, and sulfar.

Solvent or *Gel Spinning* This is a method of producing manufactured fibers where the polymer is dissolved in a solvent that forms a viscous gel. The gel is then extruded through a spinneret to form fiber strands.

To complete the production of these fibers, during the extruding process or, in some cases, after the fibers are hardened they are stretched. This operation pulls on the molecular chains to produce stronger fibers.

The final operation in creating yarn is winding, whereby the yarn is transferred from bobbins to cones. In some instances, yarns are directly wound on to **warp beams**, eliminating the need to produce cones. However, in most cases cones or yarn spools are made and attached to a **creel** to begin the formation of a warp.

Yarn Twist

In the winding process yarns are twisted. The tightness of the twist determines the yarn strength, serviceability, and texture. "Twist" refers to the number of turns that a yarn moves around its axis. Warp yarns have more twists than weft yarns because of the stress placed upon them in the weaving process. Yarns for soft-surfaced fabrics are given a slack twist, while yarns intended for smooth-surfaced fabrics are more tightly twisted. Yarns with rough, pebbly, or crinkled surfaces are given the maximum amount of twist, inhibiting the fabric from wrinkling.[2]

Yarns to be twisted can be identified as single, plied, and cord to include cable. A single or one-ply yarn is comprised of single fibers held together with a small amount of twist. A single can also be a monofilament whose denier is sufficiently sized to stand alone without twisting.

Multifilament yarns are very fine, continuous filaments numbering from 5 to 100 individual strands, twisted together to create a single. A ply yarn refers to two or more yarns (singles) twisted together. For example, three-ply yarn is composed of three singles. Ply yarns from spun fibers are produced by twisting individual strands in one direction then combining the strands and twisting them in the opposite direction. A **cord** or **cable** is made by twisting ply yarns together, creating industrial-strength fabric or rope. However, if the fiber strands are exceptionally fine, the yarn that results will produce a fine product. Yarns twisted to the left or in the counterclockwise direction produce an "S" (\\) shape design, and yarns twisted to the right or in a clockwise direction produce a "Z" (/) shape (Figure 2.17).[3]

More complex novelty yarns (also known as fancy yarns) are used to produce many different yarn shapes and textures (Figure 2.18). For example, irregularities that can appear in natural fibers or can be designed into a manufactured filament using special attachments during the spinning phase can appear as slubs. There are many kinds of special effects that can be created taking the form of flakes, loops, beads, lumps, or nubs, to name a few. The end result can be yarns with names such as boucle, ratine, and spiral.

Specialty yarns can be quite complex structures, as in the case of chenille, where fabric is produced first in the form of a **chenille** blanket that shows different patterns in different colors, and then cut between the warp yarns. These warp strips are then twisted to produce a round, caterpillar appearance.

Yarns can also be metallic. One method of achieving a metallic yarn is to laminate aluminum foil between two sheets of acetate or, preferably, polyester. Yarn can also be made by wrapping a core of natural or manufactured thread with thin layers of metal to create color.

WARP BEAMS: Wood or metal cylinders several feet long on which spools are placed to create a warp.

CREEL: A rack onto which spools are placed to create a warp. The yarns are drawn from the spools and attached to the warp/warper.

MULTIFILAMENT: Manufactured filaments composed of many fine fibers.

CORD: The result of twisting together ply yarns in a third twisting process.

CABLE: A yarn made with a cable twist as in an S/Z/S or Z/S/Z.

CHENILLE: French for "caterpillar." A soft tufted cotton, silk, or worsted yarn.

TWIST DIRECTION OF PLIED YARNS

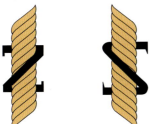

Z-twist/right-hand twist   S-twist/left-hand twist

Z-twist

S-twist

balanced twist

unbalanced twist

Yarn Twist and Direction
Simple, complex, or textured yarns are twisted to hold them together. Twist controls the cohesive characters and strength of yarn. The yarns may be twisted in a right- or left-hand manner for a minimal or maximum twisted structure.

Right-hand twist   Clockwise rotation produces a yarn strand with a "Z" torque or "Z" twist effect.
Left-hand twist   Counterclockwise rotation produces a yarn strand with a "S" torque or "S" twist effect.

Yarn twist direction allows for:
• Cohesiveness between fibers
• Utilization of either "Z" and "S" twist for simple yarns
• Combination of "Z" and "S" twist for plied yarns
• Combination of "Z" or "S" twist for durability.

Yarn twist direction produces a variation in surface appearance of fabric structure:
• Affects wear
• Facilitates processing
• Increases bulk
• Reduces picking and/or slip age

Yarn twist is also classified as balanced or unbalanced.

Balanced Yarns   Balanced yarns are twisted so that the yarn does not twist, kink, or double upon itself when suspended in a loop. Balanced yarns are used to produce smooth feeling fabrics.
Unbalanced Yarns   Unbalanced yarns will untwist and retwist in the opposite direction when suspended in a loop. Unbalanced yarns are used to produce textured and/or pebbly fabrics.

Figure 2.17 (left) Twisting yarns into "S" and "Z" configurations creates different textures.

Figure 2.18 (right) Novelty yarns can be produced to have varying surface textures.

APPLYING KNOWLEDGE OF FIBERS

Fibers and yarns in their seemingly infinite varieties point the way to end uses. The range of fibers and yarns available today spans the history of civilization. From fiber collected from a shedding vicuña to complex polymers developed in a laboratory, the search and experimentation continues for filaments that will address specific needs and, consequently, solve new problems.

Residential interiors are typically viewed as a place where more natural fibers are used, while commercial interiors, like hotels, receive the majority of manufactured fabrics. In reality, the two worlds are becoming interdependent. There is a growing trend for commercial-grade fabrics, with their special qualities and finishes, to become more a part of the home because of their functional attributes. Home offices and areas where children play, for example, are two places where manufactured fibers that are produced in appealing designs and colors make popular choices.

Identifying one yarn from another can be a challenge, especially when different yarn types are combined and included in one fabric. Interior designers need to be skillful at identifying fibers so they can recommend an appropriate selection. Clients are drawn to color, pattern, design, and sometimes the hand of the fabric—designers should go beyond these qualities and become familiar with "what's inside."

SUMMARY

Staple and filament fibers and yarn originate from nature, chemicals, and a combination of both sources. New yarns, and the ways in which they can be used, continue to evolve. History has shown that early humans relied on what could be found in their environment, including plants and animals. Minerals were used as well, and produced filaments of asbestos for protection from excessive heat.

As time progressed, fibers with natural cellulose and a mixture of chemicals were developed and evolved into fabrics such as rayon and acetate. Noncellulosic fabrics were also researched and produced, including nylon and polyester.

By understanding the properties of fabrics and the methods by which they are produced, the process of specifying fabrics becomes clearer; however, choosing fabrics tends to be an emotional process, especially for residential settings. Consequently, the final fabric choices for a room may be based more on aesthetics than on what is practical. It is the designer's responsibility to inform the client about fabrics and the consequences of choosing one fabric over another.

ACTIVITIES

1. Magnify a cotton, wool, and silk fiber filament. Compare and contrast their structures.
2. Interview an interior designer to determine the degree to which he or she uses manufactured fibers in residential settings.
3. Contact a commercial spinner such as National Spinning or the American Yarn Spinners Association. Interview a company representative about the melt spinning process. Ask your contact to contrast melt spinning with dry and wet spinning.
4. Under the supervision of your instructor, conduct a burn test for one natural fiber and one noncelluosic fiber. Contrast the results.
5. Magnify a yarn and identify the "S" and "Z" twists.

EXPAND YOUR KNOWLEDGE

1. Research two manufactured fibers in use today but not listed in the chapter. Describe their 12 characteristics.

2. Identify four yarns. Discuss your findings as they relate to the fiber characteristics noted in the chapter.

3. How are polymeric amides, such as those found in nylon, extracted from petrochemicals?

4. Why does silk continue to be a highly desired fiber?

5. Provide a detailed definition of denier. What advantage is there in being able to vary the denier of an extruded manufactured fiber?

6. Stretching manufactured fibers before or after they are hardened or dried makes them stronger. Why or how does this work?

7. Two basic yarn twists are in the shape of an "S" and a "Z." Why are two twist types necessary? Are all yarns twisted with both an "S" and a "Z"? Are there other twist configurations?

8. Is it possible to use a combination of "S" and "Z" twists to create a yarn? If so, name and detail the construction of such a yarn type.

9. Describe the construction of two fancy yarn types used today that are not mentioned in the chapter.

READ ON

Debbie Ann Gioello, *Understanding Fabrics: From Fiber to Finished Cloth*, New York: Fairchild Publications, 1982.

Katherine Paddock Hess, *Textile Fibers and Their Use*, New York: J.B. Lippincott Company, 1948.

Marjory L. Joseph, *Essentials of Textiles*, New York: Holt, Rinehart and Winston, 1976.

Sara J. Kadolph and Anna Langford, *Textiles*, 8th ed., Upper Saddle River, N.J.: Prentice Hall, 1998.

E. Kornreich, *Introduction to Fibers and Fabrics*, New York: American Elsevier Publishing Company, 1966.

Dorothy S. Lyle, *Performance of Textiles*, New York: John Wiley and Sons, 1977.

Arthur Price, Allen C. Cohen, and Ingrid Johnson, *J. J. Pizzuto's Fabric Science*, 8th ed., New York: Fairchild Publications, 2005.

Evelyn E. Stout, *Introduction to Textiles*, 3rd ed., New York: John Wiley and Sons, 1970.

Jan Yeager and Lura K. Teter-Justice, *Textiles for Residential and Commercial Interiors*, New York: Fairchild Publications, 2000.

Fabric Construction: Wovens and Nonwovens

FABRIC PRODUCTION METHODS

Fabric construction involves the conversion of fibers and yarns into cloth directed toward a particular end use. One of the most enduring methods of manufacturing fabric is weaving, accomplished by the over and under action of the warp and weft using a hand or power loom. Modern methods of weaving use high-speed looms that can produce hundreds of yards of fabric a day, especially if the construction is basic and does not use heavy yarns. Fabrics that are woven represent the most popular construction used in interior design fabrics.

Knitting is another method of producing fabric. **Knitting** occurs when one or more yarns are interlocked, with each row being drawn through and looped into the next. Like weaving, knitting has a long history—one of the earliest known discoveries was a pair of socks found in a fourth-century Egyptian tomb. The first framed knitting machine that could produce a complete row of loops at one time was developed by Reverend William Lee in 1589. The machine was capable of knitting eight loops to 1 inch of width.

Fabric can also be created by using a process whereby randomly arranged fibers or yarns are compressed, bonded, interlocked, heated (if thermoplastic), or chemically adhered to one another. This increasingly popular technique of manufacturing fiber webs, films, or bonds began in earnest around 1942 but actually predates spinning and weaving: Early humans pressed fibers together to create mats and other functional items (see Chapter 1).

THE WEAVING PROCESS

Weaving is not a static operation; rather, it is a highly coordinated, sometimes extremely rapidly moving and rhythmic process with its own set of distinct sounds. In fact, one reason mills have used wooden floors is to allow for the safe movement of the building when the machines periodi-

CHAPTER 3

KNITTING: A method of constructing fabric by interlocking series of loops of one or more yarns. Derived from the original Anglo-Saxon word *cnyttan*, meaning to weave threads by hand.

Opposite: Brocades weaving, Zoagli, Luguria, Italy.

Figure 3.1 High-speed jacquard loom.

PICKING: The movement of the weft yarns through a shed across the shuttle box.

SHUTTLE BOX: A compartment on either side of the loom used to momentarily restrain or hold the shuttle after each weft yarn is delivered.

QUILL: A tapered wooden, cardboard, fiber, or metal tube that is wrapped with yarn and encased in the shuttle.

BEATING: The final step in loom weaving. The batten beats the last weft in the shed back against preceding yarns to make a compact cloth.

REED: A comb-like device on a loom that spaces the warp ends in the desired order and also pushes succeeding weft yarns against the last weft yarn.

cally harmonize their thrashing. Without a properly constructed mill floor and building, the vibrations, especially from older machines, would shake the building over time to unsafe levels. Modern high-speed jacquard looms, shown in Figure 3.1, are usually placed on concrete floors where the thrashing sound of older looms has been replaced with a constant, high-speed "whir" sound.

In order for mills to be cost effective, they must produce considerable yardage in widths from 35 to 60 inches. There are, however, a few fabric-producing operations that continue to make smaller width fabrics, from 27 to 36 inches, as well as carpeting used in the preservation of historic site interiors or for clients who require specialized products. Providing interior design services for historic properties is an area of the profession that is often overlooked but can provide a unique opportunity to help build a career through networking with community leaders and preservation specialists.

Elements of the Loom

Fundamentally there are three operations in the weaving process (Figure 3.2). Creating a shed that "opens" or separates the warp and weft yarns from each other; **picking**, the act of propelling one or more weft or pick/filler yarns from one **shuttle box** to the next by way of the shuttle that holds the **quill** or bobbin through the shed opening; and **beating**, a process in which each weft yarn is packed against another with the help of a **reed**, thereby creating cloth.

Before the shuttle repeats its movement through the shed, some harnesses will raise and lower to weave a particular woven structure, alternating the warp and weft yarns in a predetermined pattern. The harnesses contain heddles, through which each weft yarn is drawn, keeping them aligned and lifted for the shedding

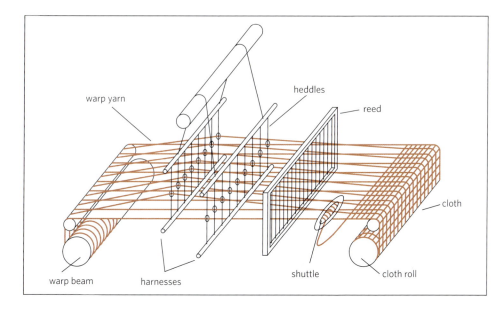

warp yarn

heddles

reed

cloth

warp beam

harnesses

shuttle

cloth roll

Figure 3.2 (left) Two-harness loom.

Figure 3.3 (below) Modern rapier mechanisms use composite materials.

process. The reed is located in front of the harnesses on the **cloth roll** side of the loom and designed to space the warp threads that come from the warp beam. The cloth roll or cloth beam appears at the front of the loom, and collects the fabric that has been produced. The reed is a comb-like device with vertical metal wires. The space between the wires is called a **dent**. The fineness of the fabric is determined by the number of dents per inch.

Modern shuttleless looms use other means for transferring picks besides noisily striking the shuttle and sending it flying back and forth from shuttle box to shuttle box. One such example is the **rapier loom,** which carries a pick via a clamp, attached to a composite or composite "profile," as shown in Figure 3.3. The composite traverses the full width of the loom or can travel half way to transfer the pick to another clamp that in turn carries it back to the other side of the loom. Composite materials are used in the mod-

ern rapier process instead of metal in order to reduce weight and increase speed. The movement of the double rapier moves very quickly and must be seen slowly to fully understand how the yarn is transferred from one clamp transfers the yarn to the other.

AIR JET LOOM: A high-speed shuttleless loom that powers the weft yarns through the shed by forced air.

WATER JET LOOM: A high-speed shuttleless loom that powers the weft yarns through the shed using forced water. Yarns must be unsized filament or nonabsorbent staple yarns that are not affected by water.

MULTIPHASED LOOMS: High-speed shuttleless looms in which several weft yarns are inserted simultaneously as multiple sheds are formed at the same time.

SELVAGE: The narrow edge of the fabric parallel to the length made with stronger yarns that are packed tightly together to protect the fabric from fraying or coming apart.

FACE: The surface of the fabric that is intended to be seen.

FINISHED: Fabric that has been processed in some way prior to sale. A fabric is said to be "converted" after it is finished.

BACK: The reverse side of the fabric's face.

Other shuttleless methods of propelling weft yarns include the **air** and **water jet looms** and the **multiphase looms**. As with all looms, the shedding, picking, and beating results in the formation of fabric that is wound on the cloth beam. This "taking up" process occurs on the front of the loom, while warp yarns are released from spools, cones, or beams that are attached to the creel and fed into the back of the loom.

During the weaving process, self-edges or a **selvage** is created on the weft edges of the fabric to keep it from coming apart, especially during the various finishing stages that the fabric can undergo. Selvages are usually stronger than the fabric produced. Several different kinds of selvages, including plain or split selvage, can be made, depending on the fabric produced. Selvages can also be dyed a particular color to ensure a coordinated connection between fabric and selvage.

Fabric Has Direction

Fabric surfaces have a face and a back. The **face** is the side of the fabric that is intended to be seen and is determined by weave structure and finish. Structurally speaking,

the face is usually the side of the fabric where more warp or weft yarns are predominately exposed. In a satin weave, discussed later in this chapter, for example, more warp yarns appear on the face (warp satin weave), and since the weave produces a sheen, the face can be identified as the smooth, reflective side. The face of some fabrics can also be determined simply by looking at the surface and noting that the face is the side that has often been **finished**, that is, processed in a way that improves the appearance or function of the fabric. Finishing processes are described in Chapter 4. The **back** is not typically seen after installation. However, on occasions, designers have knowingly used the back as the face. Among some fabrics, either side can be used as the face.

Fabric can also have a top and bottom. The direction of the fabric is easily determined when an identifiable shape is woven or printed on the face; however, when fabric does not have such figures to serve as a guide, the top and bottom are determined by weave structure or sometimes by how the fabric is finished, using a method similar to determining the face and back. Pile fabrics, for example, are constructed to lie at an angle, causing light to reflect differently depending upon the direction from which the fabric is being viewed, as seen in Figure 3.4. A chair upholstered with pile may not deliver the desired look if the seat cushion fibers point down (bottom) and the fibers on the sides of the chair point up (top). It is the designer's responsibility to clearly indicate the face and back, top and bottom, and communicate that information to the fabricators as well as how the fabric pattern should be applied.

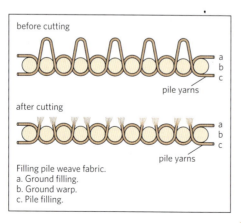

before cutting

pile yarns

after cutting

pile yarns

Filling pile weave fabric.
a. Ground filling.
b. Ground warp.
c. Pile filling.

Figure 3.4 Warp pile before and after cutting.

A few fabrics can be utilized with either side exposed because there is little or no appreciable difference; however, all fabrics must be examined carefully in order to determine which side should be exposed. Individuals who choose to acquire their own fabric, known as **Customer's Own Material (COM)**, and have it applied by themselves or by an unproven upholsterer to furniture or walls, may actually believe they are saving money by not consulting a professional designer. Unfortunately, when many yards of fabric are purchased and applied backwards or upside down, the cost quickly doubles when the client has to repurchase and reapply it the correct way.

EXAMINING WOVEN STRUCTURES

Weaving fabric involves the way fibers, threads or yarns, and filaments interrelate. In the weaving process, the manner in which the warp yarns are lifted by the harness permitting the weft yarns to be propelled through the shed determines the type of woven structure produced. These structures can be seen more clearly using a **pick glass** and a **pick needle**, whereby not only the weave structure can be determined but also the direction of the warp yarns, which in turn determine how the fabric should be cut. The vast number of woven patterns are achieved by the "lifting" capabilities of anywhere from two to many harnesses, capable of rapidly moving hundreds of warp yarns up and down.

The majority of interior fabrics originate from three basic woven structures: plain, twill, and satin. Weave types are subject to differences in production costs that can also relate to factors associated with appearance and durability. Weave types are also influenced by the type of yarns used.

There are additional woven structures, such as gauze (not to be confused with the gauze used in medical bandages) and leno weaves, that do not relate to the basic three weaves, resulting in fabric that can be used for a lightweight effect in curtains. An entire course could be built upon the intricacies of all woven structures, but that course would be best suited for fabric designers.

Plain Weave

Nearly 80 percent of all woven fabric is represented by the **plain weave**, also known as the *tabby* or *taffeta* weave. This two-harness, simple structure is created when each weft yarn travels the width of the loom, alternating over and under each warp yarn. On the shuttles' return trip, the pattern reverses. The action can be described as a *one up, one down* weave because of the movement of the yarn traveling over (up) and under (down) each warp yarn. There are several varieties of this weave, such as the *basket weave*, which can be a *two up, two down; three up, three down*, or even *four up, four down* weave. Varieties of the basket weave can also have an uneven number of "up" and "down" yarns (Figure 3.5). A plain weave is frequently used as **print cloth** because its flat, uniform surface makes it able to accept most dyes readily. The general appearance and texture of the plain weave can be modified by using heavier plied yarns and varying their degree of compactness.

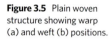

Figure 3.5 Plain woven structure showing warp (a) and weft (b) positions.

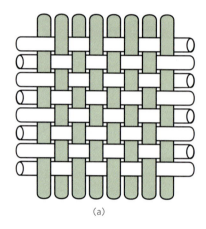

(a)   (b)

Twill Weave

The signature of a **twill weave** is its distinct diagonal rib, or *twill line*, generally slanting upward from left to right but sometimes running right to left. The latter weave is known as a *left-hand twill* and is produced when each warp yarn passes under and **floats** over at least two consecutive weft yarns but not more than four, with each weft yarn "side stepping" to the left or right, forming the diagonal. On the back of the fabric the line travels in the opposite direction. A *herringbone twill* or *broken twill* (*houndstooth*) alternates the direction of the weave from right hand to left hand, creating the distinctive chevron pattern.

An even twill pattern has the same number of warp and weft yarns showing on the surface; however, most twills are uneven. When the warp threads are exposed, the fabric is known as a *warp-faced twill* (Figure 3.6a) and is a stronger weave. When more weft yarns appear, the weave is a *filling-faced twill* (Figure 3.6b).

Satin Weave

A derivative of the twill is the **satin weave**, which is generally more dense, smoother, and heavier than a plain or twill weave and is produced with the use of five to ten or sometimes more harnesses. The weave is often made in silk or a manufactured fiber. The satin weave is usually warp

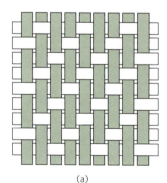

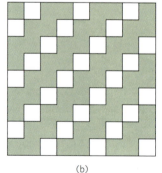

Figure 3.6 Right- and left-hand twill.   (a)   (b)

Figure 3.7 Satin weave.

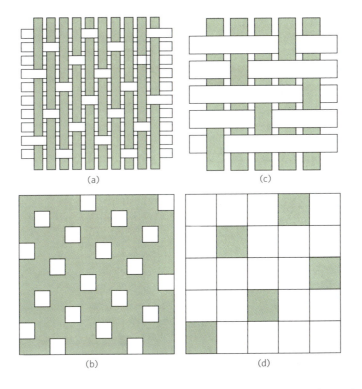

(a)   (c)

(b)   (d)

faced but can be weft faced as well. When a greater number of warp yarns appear on the face than on the back of the fabric, the fabric is known as a *sateen* and made using anywhere from four to eight harnesses, usually with lustrous filament yarns. The satin and sateen weaves do not show the twill effect because they are produced with long floats woven far apart. Satin is known as both a weave (Figure 3.7) and a generic reference to any fabric with a sheen or a silk-like texture.

Pile

A **pile** weave is produced by introducing at least one additional warp or weft yarn to the **ground** of a sometimes plain or twill weave that loops and can be either uncut or cut. The loops are formed by pulling the extra yarn away from the surface of the fabric, with wires that can be tipped with cutting blades. When the extra yarn is a loop warp yarn, the cloth is known as a warp pile with examples being terry (uncut), carpeting (uncut or cut), and **plush** (uncut or cut). When the extra yarn is a weft yarn, the result is a filling pile. Examples are velvet and velveteen (cut) and corduroy (uncut or cut). A variety of pile effects can be achieved by regulating the tension of the warp yarns or producing stronger and heavier velvets while maintaining the fine quality by utilizing a double cloth weave. This weaving method involves producing two layers of fabric at the same time, one on top of the other, with each fabric having its own set of warp and weft yarns. Other pile and pile-like fabrics that contain three or more yarns in the weaving process include **voided velvet, crushed velvet, velour, frieze,** and **grospoint.**

PILE: Raised loops, tufts, or other arrangements of yarns that stand away from the surface of the fabric.

GROUND: The plain base or background area of a decorative fabric.

PLUSH: A warp pile with a cut pile surface longer than velvet pile and less closely woven.

VOIDED VELVET: Velvet with the pile woven higher in some areas than in others or a fabric sheared to different lengths.

CRUSHED VELVET: Velvet pile with an irregular surface.

VELOUR: Woven, velvet-like fabric with close, dense pile laid in one direction.

FRIEZE: Heavy pile fabric with rows of uncut loops.

GROSPOINT: An upholstery fabric with uncut loop pile larger than frieze.

DOBBY WEAVE: A woven construction produced by a dobby, a mechanical part of a loom that controls harnesses to permit the weaving of small, geometric figures.

BIRD'S EYE: Plain dobby woven fabric with indentations resembling a bird's eye

JACQUARD: A system of weaving that permits the production of woven designs of considerable size and intricacy.

Dobby Weave

The **dobby weave**, sometimes known as *waffle weave*, actually refers to a mechanical device (dobby) on the side of a loom that is capable of controlling from 8 to approximately 40 harnesses or design options, resulting in small, geometric patterns with short floats, such as the **bird's eye** or *diaper weave*. This pattern is repeated throughout the fabric and is produced by combining the herringbone pattern and a reverse twill. The dobby contains plastic cylinders with punched holes for determining which harnesses are to be raised or lowered to create the desired pattern (Figure 3.8). Dobby weaves include plain, twill, or satin weaves.

Jacquard Weave

The highly versatile and intricate woven patterns of the **jacquard** weave, which include curves and large figures, are accomplished by the jacquard mechanism or jacquard head (Figure 3.9), capable of lifting more than 10,000 heddles individually. The head can be attached to any kind

Figure 3.8 (right) A dobby loom can weave different patterns, including plain, twill, andsatin.

Figure 3.9 (below) Electronic and non-electronic jacquard heads.

of loom with the weft yarns delivered from selvage to selvage using a shuttle, rapier, or air or water jet system. The jacquard process, theoretically, has the capability of making a fabric in an unlimited **repeat** size, where the same overall pattern appears repeated multiple times. The size of the pattern is associated with the number of hooks that lift the harnesses up and down and the number of warp yarns.

Traditionally, to create a jacquard weave, the desired design is transferred to **cards**, as seen in Figure 3.10, using a series of strategically placed punched holes. When a hole appears, a harness cord lifts one heddle at a time to produce the shed through which the weft yarns pass to create the pattern. Contemporary computer-operated jacquard looms can function with increased speed and efficiency over their nineteenth- and twentieth-century counterparts, thanks to advanced software programs that electronically provide for the lifting of the sheds.

Today, the artwork is conceived on a computer and scanned directly into the jacquard loom, where the pattern is translated electronically to direct the production of a particular design. Although technology has greatly improved the speed of some aspects of the jacquard process, setting up the loom remains time consuming, and therefore affects the cost of jacquard-produced fabric. Nonetheless, the jacquard method of weaving permits greater freedom to explore new design motifs and to create complex fabric patterns.

Jacquard patterns and woven structures are widely used in residential and commercial settings where a woven pattern with intricate design detail is required; however, jacquard fabrics tend to have long floats, and although they can be combined with more basic constructions that can increase their susceptibility to wear due to the threads being raised they should be specified with a good understanding of their intended end use and capabilities. Among the most well known jacquard weaves are damask, liséré, lampas, brocade, brocatelle jacquard tapestry, and jacquard matelassé.

Damask

Originally made in silk, **damask** can also be produced in nearly all of the natural and manufactured fibers. A damask can be made in one or two colors and has a dimensional quality, with the pattern appearing to stand in slight relief (Figure 3.11). The pattern design is created with one set

Figure 3.10 Modern jacquard cards.

REPEAT: The complete pattern on a fabric that can be seen over and over again.

CARDS: A rectangular piece of fiber board or plastic punched with holes used to control the lifting of one or more warp yarns.

DAMASK: A broad group of jacquard-woven fabrics introduced into Europe by way of Damascus, hence its name. Damasks are typically woven with large and elaborate floral or geometric patterns, originally in silk; however, damasks are now woven in a variety of natural and manufactured yarns.

Figure 3.11 Damask with a strie.

Figure 3.12 Liséré, front (a) and back (b).

Figure 3.13 Lampas, front (a) and back (b).

of warp yarns and one set of weft yarns. The pattern can be reversed and usually has more luster than the ground. Additional patterned effects can enhance the fabric by sometimes adding a **strie** that runs the entire length of the cloth.

Liséré

Two sets of warp yarns and one set of weft yarns are used to produce a **liséré** (Figure 3.12). One set of warp yarns typically matches the set of weft yarns, and they are woven together as the ground. The second set of warp yarns is composed of a variety of single-colored yarns brought to the surface of the fabric, resulting in loose yarns on the back that are sometimes cut. The weave is frequently made with a taffeta or **faille** ground.

Lampas

Lampas (Figure 3.13) is made with two or more warps and two or more wefts. As many as 18,000 weft yarns can be used to achieve a complex, multicolored pattern. An impressive two-toned effect is achieved when each warp color interlaces with a similar weft yarn. Usually a satin or twill weave is selected for the ground. A lampas can be woven with a brocade effect by allowing the weft yarns to float on the surface in a twill effect.

Brocade

Deriving its name from the Latin meaning "figure," **brocade** (Figure 3.14) is produced using more than one set of warp or weft yarns with the pattern usually appearing on a satin weave ground, al-

(a)

(b)

(a)

(b)

Figure 3.14 Brocade, front (a) and back (b).

(a)   (b)

though the pattern can also be on a twill or plain weave ground. The figures on a brocade appear "loose," in contrast to the pattern on a damask, where it seems flat and bound into the material. The design of the brocade fabric stands in relief only on the face. Brocades frequently appear in large floral or large figured patterns and can sometimes be reversed, but not as commonly as a damask fabric.

Brocatelle

Brocatelle is similar to a brocade, but the pattern design is further elevated, giving it a rich, two-dimensional, and somewhat weighted feel (Figure 3.15). Originally brocatelle was to replicate the look of embossed Italian and Spanish tooled leather. A brocatelle is usually produced from one set of fine warp yarns, one set of heavy warp yarns, and two sets of weft yarns. Using the double weave technique, brocatelles are often made with a silk and linen warp and a silk and linen weft, sometimes with metallic threads. The design appears tight, compact, and in high relief created by the linen weft floats. The ground is commonly made in a twill weave. The fabric usually has a firm texture and a high yarn count.

Jacquard Woven Tapestry

Jacquard woven tapestry is produced with two sets of warp yarns and two sets of weft yarns and woven the full width of the loom from selvage to selvage. With a hand woven jacquard tapestry, the weft yarns cover only the area of the pattern and must be cut around the perimeter of the design, resulting in loose yarns on the back of the fabric. A machine woven jacquard tapestry can be identified by the yarns on the back of the fabric reflecting the designs on the front. The fabric is not reversible because the long floats on the back are susceptible to snagging.

Jacquard Matelassé

The **jacquard matelassé** is named after the French term for cushioned or padded.

Figure 3.15 Brocatelle.

BROCATELLE: A jacquard fabric similar to a brocade but with designs standing in high relief.

JACQUARD WOVEN TAPESTRY: A jacquard woven fabric with two sets of warp yarns and two sets of weft yarns woven the full width of the loom.

JACQUARD MATELASSÉ: A fabric with a quilted or raised pattern made on a jacquard dobby loom. Whenever the coarser weft yarns interlace with the face fabric, it causes the remainder of the face to pucker.

WALES: A series of ribs, cords, or raised portions, usually in the fabric length.

COURSES: Rows of loops or stitches running the width of knitted fabric.

The jacquard matelassé is made with multiple sets of yarns, with one set being the coarser weft yarns that interlace and appear on the face of the fabric, causing it to stand out, pucker, or appear quilted.

Criteria for Evaluating Fabric Quality

When examining a woven fabric to determine its quality, keep several points in mind.

- *Yarn count*: the degree of yarn fineness
- *Thread count*: the number of warp and weft yarns per square inch, also known as the number of picks and ends
- *Yarn twist and ply*: the amount of twist each yarn contains, along with its thickness
- *Yarn type*: the kind of yarns used in the weaving process
- *Yarn balance*: the ratio of warp yarns to weft yarns

It is helpful to be able to name and describe the fabric types frequently used in interiors. As soon as a name comes to mind, such as a damask, so should an understanding of the woven structure that corresponds to that fabric. Clients may ask, for example, why a matelassé appears "puffy," and they may question whether the fabric is appropriate for its intended use. It would be an awkward moment indeed if a designer could not respond effectively to such questions.

NONWOVENS

Although weaving is the most popular technique for creating fabric for interior use, knitting, felting, and bonding are other important techniques that convert fibers or yarns into material.

Knitting

Knitting is the process of forming fabric by connecting yarns or threads with a series of loops using needles. The lengthwise yarn loops are called **wales** and the widthwise yarns are called **courses**. Knitted material can either be weft knitted, whereby the interlocking of loops is accomplished by the horizontal movement of yarn, or warp knitted, whereby yarns interlock in a lengthwise or vertical direction.

Knitting machines can be either flat or circular. Flat machines have needles arranged in one or two flat plates, or *needle beds* (Figure 3.16). The knitted

Figure 3.16 Flat-bed knitting machine.

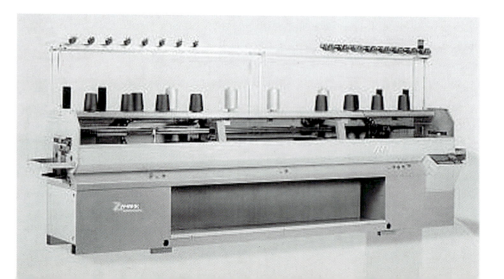

fabric drops downward through the space around the upper edges of the plate called the *throat*. Flat machines can be categorized as *latch needle*, *fine spring needle*, or *V-bed flat* machines. Typically, flatbed machines are not suitable for high volume production but are most helpful in creating original designs, because less time is required for set-up than for a circular machine. New products, therefore, can be developed faster on flatbed machines, then converted to circular machines that are capable of producing more product at a cost savings.

In circular or tubular knitting, needles are carried in grooves cut into the wall of a cylinder (Figure 3.17). The knitting process involves needles being moved through cam tracks, sliding up and down to pick up a yarn, form a new loop, then drop the loop it just created. Basically, there are four types of circular knitting: 1) run-resistant, 2) tuck stitch, 3) ribbed, and 4) double knit or interlock knitting.

Basic weft knits are *plain* or *jersey* (named after the single knit turtleneck sweater originally worn by English sailors from the Isle of Jersey), using staple yarns; *rib*; and *purl*. Examples of warp knitting are *raschel*, produced with *latch needles*; and *tricot* (from the French *tricoter*, meaning "to knit"), using *bearded* or *spring needles*. Raschel knitted products tend to be coarser than other knitted fabrics, whereas tricot flat knitted fabric that uses filament yarns has fine wales on the face that appear crosswise on the back. This form of knitting can be useful for upholstered walls, owing to its ability to conform to interior wall shapes and molding details.

Multicolored designs in weft or warp knitting configurations can be produced using the jacquard process where cards determine the selection of needles to be lifted to create the pattern. Through the years, warp, weft, and circular knitting machines have produced a host of fabrics that include car upholstery, washable pile knit, imitation fur, and fabrics that simulate cloth that can be used in interiors. New developments in circular knitting promise to provide more options for interiors.

Felt and Bonded Fabrics

Nonwoven material that does not require fibers to be processed into yarns, including felt, has existed for centuries. More than 800 years have passed since Genghis Khan constructed the walls of his yurt with yak hair!

Felt is created by interlocking natural or manufactured fibers using a combination of moisture, heat, and pressure. Unlike woven fabric, felt has no warp, weft, or selvage. Some felts are made with a combination of fibers such as cotton and adhered together to strengthen the structure. Felt is used for padding, hats, and sometimes wall insulation. Generally, though, felt is difficult to use in interiors because it lacks tensile strength and elasticity and has a tendency to tear easily. Nevertheless, felt is gaining popularity and becoming preferred by environmentally conscious designers and clients (see Chapter 6).

Nonwoven bonded fabrics are a fast-growing segment of the market, particularly since the 1950s and 1960s, when new technologies began to appear, enabling the development of an ever-increasing line of new products. As the general fabric industry

Figure 3.17 Circular knitting machine.

has decreased in production in the United States, the nonwovens have increased. For example, the so-called wipes used to collect dust, remove make-up, or make bathrooms and kitchens more sanitary increased from about $750 million in 1999 to $2.2 billion in 2004.

Nonwoven fabrics are engineered to be single use, multiuse, or durable for years of wear. Typically, nonwovens address specific functions and include properties related to strength, stretch, resilience, absorbency, flame retardancy, sterility, or a combination of these attributes. Nonwovens can be used as filler or batting between a wall and fabric used to upholster walls.

The process of manufacturing a nonwoven involves several steps. The first is to acquire fibers. Before polypropylene (used for softness), rayon was widely used and polyester (used for strength and resiliency) had entered the market in the 1970s. Other fiber blends can be used as well, including viscose, nylon, cotton, and glass fibers. After the fibers have been selected, they must be carefully aligned and closely bound together or attached to each other. **Bonding** or *binding* is a process of adhering fiber, fiber webs, or sheets together by mechanical, chemical, or thermal means. Fibers can also be warp "stitched" together by using a series of needles incorporated in the Arachne machine or laminated by using polyurethane foam. New methods of bonding are being developed at the speed of research and technology.

One important challenge to the nonwoven industry is to find more environmentally appropriate methods of disposing of the used products. The packaging of some nonwoven items such as wipes suggests that they should not be flushed down the toilet, but this is the way many of the cloths often end their service. Currently, strategies are being devised worldwide through the Association of the Nonwoven Fabrics Industry (INDA) to influence methods of proper disposal for nonwoven products.

PASSEMENTERIE

Passementerie for residential and some commercial installations can be practical as well as aesthetically pleasing. **Passementerie**, or decorative sew or trimming, is in its most basic definition a word derived from Italian, French, and Spanish roots meaning "hand," as in handwork. Although some trimmings continue to be produced using a combination of handwork and handlooms, other forms of trimming can be made on dobby looms or by using the jacquard process.

Passementerie has a long history, one that originated in fashion. Nearly every country in the world has used trimming in one form or another and has adopted its own terms for it. For example, in England passementerie was known as narrow wears, small wears, or orrice (*orris*) work, which refers to gold and silver lace used on seventeenth- and eighteenth-century ecclesiastical garments and secular costumes.

Uses of Passementerie

Today, there are three primary reasons for using decorative trims. The first is practical. Many designers consider their

BONDING: The process of adhering fiber webs or layers of fabrics together.

PASSEMENTERIE: Decorative trim of several categories usually produced in part or totally by hand and used to embellish window and bed treatments or furnishings, including pillows.

(a)

(b)

(c)

(d)

Figure 3.18 Types of passementerie: gimp (a), rosettes (b), bullion fringe (c), and tassels (d).

work incomplete or not ready for delivery unless all staples, tacks, seams, and, in some cases, zippers are covered. Also, there are drapery treatments that need to be held back by trimming to allow more light to enter a room while styling a flow of fabric to fall to the floor in a particular way.

A second purpose for specifying trimming is to recreate a historic period reflected in the architecture of a residence, historic property, or commercial establishment, such as the interior of a theater. If, for example, the date a designer is attempting to replicate is about 1820 and the interior is French, then an Empire style of trimming should be selected.

The third reason for using passementerie is to distinguish or embellish an interior. Some clients may want unique or one-of-a-kind accents to individualize or

enhance the appearance of their furnishings. And if a designer is knowledgeable about trimming and comfortable working with manipulating the various components that constitute a trim, there can be opportunities to design original pieces with the assistance of a manufacturer.

Categories of Passementerie

Trims can assume numerous shapes, styles, and color combinations, but fundamentally they can be grouped as gimps (Figure 3.18a), galloons, borders, cords and ropes, rosettes (Figure 3.18b), frogs, fringes (Figure 3.18c), tassels (Figure 3.18d), and tiebacks.[1]

Gimps are flat, narrow, woven fabric strips from $3/8$ to $1/2$ inch wide and can be plain or cut or have scalloped loops. Gimps are used to cover tacks, nail heads, and staples that hold the edges of fabric in

GIMPS: Narrow woven fabric strips used to trim the edge of window treatments or upholstered furniture. Gimps are often used to cover nail heads or to provide a transition from wood to fabric.

GALLOONS: Wide gimps.

BORDERS: Narrow fabric about 2½ to 6 inches wide sometimes woven with simple stripes, chevrons, or highly intricate designs.

CORDS: Plied and twisted yarns less than 1 inch in diameter. Ropes exceed 1 inch in diameter.

FESTOONS: Decorative swags of fabric, cord, or rope hung between two points.

ROSETTES: Gathered fabric ornaments resembling roses. Sometimes a small tassel is attached to the center.

FROGS: Decorative fabric ornaments made of wrapped vellum, cord, or silk-covered wire and formed into a series of loops.

VELLUM: Fine, transparent cotton fabric used as tracing cloth that enables a fabric designer to see a pattern through it and, using a pen or pencil, to trace over the original art, producing a facsimile of the design onto the cloth.

FRINGES: Trimmings of loose threads or cords attached to a woven header or gimp-like structure.

BULLION OR BULLION FRINGE: A series of cords attached to a woven heading or header and found, among other places, on the bottom of upholstered furniture, covering the space between the bottom frame of the furniture and the floor.

place on upholstered furniture or upholstered walls.

Galloons are similar to gimps but often wider and measure from ⅝ to 4 inches. A galloon can be patterned with cut, looped, braided, scalloped, doubled, or straight edges. Galloons are used for decorative drapery edges, table skirts, pillows, cornices, and valances.

Borders are wider than galloons and can range in width from 2½ to 6 inches. They often feature simple stripes, repeats of chevrons, or highly intricate woven designs. Borders can be applied in similar fashion to gimps and galloons.

Cords and ropes consist of plied yarns twisted together. The diameter of a

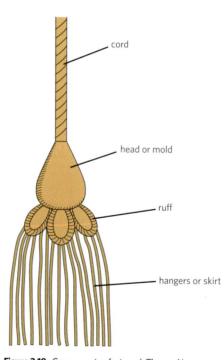

cord can be from ³⁄₁₀ to about 1 inch. When the cord exceeds 1 inch, it is referred to as a rope. Cords are used on upholstered furniture, cushions, and pillows. Often a fabric flange or tape is sewn into the cord so it can be inserted and sewn into the seam of the fabric. Cords can be used along drapery edges, at the top of valances, and as **festoons** over boarding swags.

Rosettes are typically made by hand with various components and gathered to resemble a rose. They are used on the cover of pillows and cushions. Sometimes a small tassel is attached to the center of a rosette.

Frogs are made of wrapped **vellum**, cord, or silk-covered wire and formed into a series of loops. Frogs can be as small as ¾ of an inch or as large as 5 inches in width. Some include a rosette in the center of the loop. Frogs are used in a similar manner to rosettes, and when a cord is attached, frogs can be used to hang paintings or mirrors.

Fringes can be made in many shapes and sizes and include loop, **bullion**, wood mold, tassel, and netted tassel fringe. Some of the **hangers** can be 12 inches or longer. Often the **bullion fringe** that complements the bottom of a theatre curtain is much longer than a foot in length.

Tassels are hanging ornaments that are composed of a head made of cut yarn and/or looped yarns and bullion cording that is wrapped around a wooden core, which is shaped for the desired effect (Figure 3.19). A ruff often separates the head from the hangers. Tassels are typically combined with cords to form chair

cord

head or mold

ruff

hangers or skirt

Figure 3.19 Components of a tassel. The cord is composed of twisted threads. The wooden mold shaped to form the head may be painted, covered with fabric, or have thread wound around it. The ruff is a transitional decoration between the head and skirt. The skirt may consist of cut hangers or bullions; it can be decorated with small bows or tassels.

ties and key tassels. **Tiebacks** are combined with sufficient lengths of cord to hold back a drapery treatment or curtains, and when a cord is attached, they can be used to hang paintings or mirrors. Hardware is attached to a wall or window molding so the looped ends can secure the tieback and pull the drapery away from the window.

THE MODERN MILL: MANAGEMENT AND TECHNOLOGY

The challenges of producing fabric for interiors in a present-day American mill are many. The competition that American mills confront from China, India, and other countries is well documented. The cultural, political, and economic issues in these countries that affect fabric quality and price also affect European mills.

Nevertheless, **jobbers**, a term slowly disappearing from common use, are firms that search the world for unique products appealing to designers and contribute a defined "look" for a company (see Chapter 9 for world fabric sources). For a supplier to say that a particular fabric was designed and woven in Italy or some other country continues suggests that the product has an element of implied style and quality not readily available in the U.S. Companies often use this notion to market and merchandise their products; however, American-based fabric sellers that partner with American mills can enjoy several advantages, providing the mills attend to several important issues.

Service and Innovation

Fabric suppliers require a mill to respond to their special needs. This means that as the desire for qualities, colors, and designs of woven fabrics changes, the competition increases—companies try to distinguish themselves and designers search for unique fabrics for their clients. The mill, therefore, needs to be in step with those demands and have responsive resources that communicate effectively with each other to provide the correct materials, such as a yarn with a specific density and color. When a working, integrative communication system is in place to maintain the continuity of production, service is enhanced, which is a critical part of securing and maintaining repeat business. If the mill provides frequent excuses for late deliveries, a chain reaction occurs that affects the promises that jobbers have made to their customers, eventually affecting the designer and client. Mills must welcome experimentation and be prepared to perform and meet deadlines.

Technology

Technology can have a positive impact on the speed and variety of fabric produced. However, the criteria for purchasing certain technologies should be clear. If, for example, air jet looms are used to weave fabric, they are capable of propelling weft yarns through the shed at a rate of 800 to 1,000 per minute. But these looms can weave only certain kinds of yarns and are generally less flexible than a rapier loom that passes 400 to 500 weft yarns a minute. And the electronic winding equipment (as seen in Figure 3.20) that transfers the yarns purchased by the mill onto cones

HANGERS: Individual bullions or small ornaments such as tufts that are strung on top of one another and hung on skirts of tassles or fringe.

TASSLES: Hanging fabric ornaments that are composed of a head made of cut yarns and/or looped yarns and bullion cording wrapped around usually a wooden core.

TIEBACKS: Decorative cord typically with tassles used to hold back window treatment fabric.

JOBBERS: Individuals or firms that purchase fabric from a manufacturer then sell it, in varying lengths, usually at a wholesale price. The fabric, in turn, is then sampled and sold to designers.

Figure 3.20 Modern electronic winding allows for greater flexibility, such as adjusting the tension of the yarns being wound.

Figure 3.21 Modern warp and creel.

used to create the warp (noted in Figure 3.21) should have precise tension controls so the warp can be made according to specifications. Having the flexibility to control the warp yarns, the number of warp beams, and their size and tension provides many options that relate to a fabric's quality. Modern mills are required to have the equipment to meet the needs of present-day clients.

With regard to evolving technology, one of the most important aspects of developing a new fabric is having the latest sampling equipment (as noted in Figure

3.22). The faster a sample can be made, the faster an order can be approved and generated. Although a sampling machine can cost more than $400,000, it is an essential part of responding to a fabric supplier in a timely fashion. Other technologies that can facilitate the speed of fabric production include large electronic jacquard looms that are capable of producing greatly expanded patterns. Many of these looms can be activated from the textile design studio and weave what the designer has created with a computer-aided design program.

Costing

Price is usually a consideration when purchasing product. When a fabric supplier considers purchasing fabric offshore, other issues arise: the current monetary exchange rate between the United States and other fabric-producing countries; the distance and time and language variances between countries; the weekly work and vacation/religious holiday schedules; shipping costs; and delivery times. When all of these factors are considered, producing fabric in the country of use can be con-venient and advantageous. And with environmental issues being stressed and energy costs escalating, an argument exists for all components of the fabric production process, including the application of fabric treatments such as stain repellents, to occur in close proximity to one another. The cost of producing certain fabrics in other countries may be less, but domestic fabric suppliers can gain clients by being responsive to the designers they serve and providing the assurance that a particular product will be available on time as specified.

SUMMARY

Woven and nonwoven fabric can be produced using various methods that often point to their end use. Suggesting one fabric over another for a particular installation requires knowledge of fabric composition, weave structures, and related capabilities that signal variances in quality. Knowing how to identify the face and back as well as the top and bottom of fabric helps to ensure proper application.

New fibers and nonwoven materials are being produced at a rapid pace due to technological advances and provocative marketing that encourages and promotes new ways to do old work, such as cleaning a floor or mopping up a spill. However, in the presence of such advancements, some purposeful and decorative interior details, such as passementerie, continue to be produced using techniques similar to those that have been employed for centuries.

ACTIVITIES

1. Using a pick glass or loup and a needle, count the number of weft yarns per inch in two different fabrics.
2. Using the DVD mill tour, explain the process that transforms yarns to woven fabric.
3. Obtain one fabric swatch that exemplifies each of the following weaves: plain, twill, satin, dobby, pile, and jacquard. Locate the ground, face, and pattern direction on two of the fabrics.
4. Describe and discuss several places where jacquard woven fabrics would be most suitable and places where they would not function well.
5. Acquire a full width of fabric and study the selvage to determine how its construction differs from that of the fabric itself.
6. Using the DVD mill and showroom tour segments, explain how one trimming is constructed and where it would be used.
7. Select fabrics that could be generally classified as "poor," "average," or "excellent" quality for a frequently used living room sofa. Give reasons for your selections.
8. Interview a knowledgeable employee in a fabric store. Ask the following questions:
   - What fabrics does the store sell most frequently for interiors?
   - Why are people drawn to certain kinds of fabrics and not to others?
   - What are the most common questions customers ask about fabrics?
   - What are the most common misunderstandings people have about purchasing fabric?

EXPAND YOUR KNOWLEDGE

1. How does a double rapier loom weave fabric differently from a single rapier loom?
2. Why are there different kinds of selvages?
3. How can you ensure that fabric will be applied in the proper direction with the correct side showing?
4. Does a damask have "two faces"? Explain.
5. Why is a jacquard fabric more expensive than a plain weave fabric?
6. How has technology influenced the production of fabric? What role does CAD/CAM play?
7. A lampas is made with two or more warp beams. How is this possible?
8. Why do some trims or components of trims require handwork?
9. How are nonwovens used in interiors?
10. Why must the end use of a fabric be kept in mind as selections are being considered?

READ ON

Pauline Agius, ed., *Ackermann's Regency Furniture and Interiors*, Marlborough, Wiltshire, U.K.: Crowood Press, 1984.

Herman Blum, *The Loom Has a Brain*, Littleton, N.H.: Courier Printing Company, 1970.

Francis Buresh, *Nonwoven Fabrics*, New York: Rinehold, 1962.

John Comforth, "The Art of the Trimming Maker," *Country Life* (December 1970), p. 110.

Des Dorelotiers aux Passementiers, exhibition catalog, Paris: Musée des Arts décotatifs, 1973.

Irene Emery, *The Primary Structure of Fabrics*, Washington, D.C.: The Textile Museum, 1966.

Jenny Gibbs, *Curtains and Drapes: History, Design, Inspiration*, London: Cassell, 1994.

Malcolm Gladwell, *The Tipping Point*, New York: Little, Brown & Company, 2002, pp. 175–92.

Leon Groer, *Decorative Arts in Europe, 1790–1850*, New York: Rizzoli, 1986.

Jules Labarthe, *Textiles: Origins to Usage*, New York: Macmillan, 1964.

Florence Montgomery, *Textiles in America, 1650–1850*, New York: Norton, 1984.

Amicca de Mowbray, "All the Trimmings," *Country Life* 187 (1993), pp. 66–67.

Steven Parissien, *Regency Style*, London and Washington, D.C.: Preservation Press, 1992.

Preservation, Washington, D.C.: National Trust for Historic Preservation.

Olga Raggio, James Parker, and Alice M. Zrebiec, "French Decorative Arts During the Reign of Louis XIV, 1654–1715," *Metropolitan Museum of Art Bulletin* 46 (Spring 1989), pp. 1–64.

Shuttle, Spindle, and Dyepot, Suwanee, Ga.: Handweavers Guild of America.

Dyeing, Printing, and Finishing

Understanding how light and color are perceived contributes to an appreciation of color and its application to fabric. In fabric, **dyeing** is the process whereby fibers, filaments, or **greige** goods are completely saturated with color. Fabric that has been printed carries color through the application of a thickly colored, paste-like material, usually taking the form of a design that is not woven into cloth or knitted. **Printed fabrics** can be distinguished from fiber- or filament-dyed fabrics because the color in printed material usually does not penetrate through the cloth. However, when the color does fully penetrate, as in the case of dyed sheer fabrics, an examination of individual yarns will show an inconsistent application of color.

Fabric is often subjected to treatments or processing reflecting the manner in which it is specified and to be applied. **Finishing** treatments can significantly change fiber properties through chemical, mechanical, or thermal means capable of producing different surface textures that can be seen and felt.

One purpose of the **converter** is to "convert" greige goods through dyeing, printing, and/or finishing. Converters must be knowledgeable about the fibers used in the fabrics so the appropriate treatment(s) can be applied. Some processes used in converting fabrics may cause shrinkage, making the initial yardage estimate for a particular installation incorrect. Finishing is an essential component in completing the fabric story and addresses issues related to safety and health as well.

In order to grow their business, converters have expanded their role to include commissioning fabric to be manufactured, buying fabric, and distributing product to be sold in full pieces or in 50-yard length minimums to firms such as furniture manufacturers or fabric outlets. This contrasts with companies (jobbers) who operate from design center showrooms sampling and selling fabric to designers in any

DYEING: The application of a dissolved colorant to fiber, yarn, or finished fabric.

GREIGE: French for *natural*. Fabric absent of finishing treatment; fabric just off the loom.

PRINTED FABRIC: Designs applied to fabric using color.

FINISHING: Usually a sequence of fabric treatments, excluding dye, that enhances greige goods for sale.

CONVERTER: An individual or company that finishes greige goods.

Opposite: Fabric-draped walls and ceiling in a sunroom.

lengths. The highly competitive nature of fabric sales today has contributed to blurring the lines relative to how and to whom fabric is processed, bought, and sold.

SEEING COLOR

Manipulating light and color contributes to fabric's psychological value and gives its placement purpose. Color delights the eye and attracts attention. Color can elicit an emotional response or emotions can reflect color as in "green with envy." Red is associated with emotional intensity and can stimulate heart activity, as well as hunger, and is typically only used as accents in interiors. Yellow is often seen as a cheerful, sunny color but can be strident if used concentrated a space. For example, babies have been known to cry more in yellow rooms. However, yellow has also been associated with enhancing concentration and adding focus, perhaps one reason that legal size writing pads are yellow. And in healthcare settings, color is said to support the therapeutic healing environment. Healthcare designers make a conscious effort to select appropriate colors for specific areas or rooms.

Light and Color

Gabriel D'Annunzio, the Italian poet, wrote that "color is the force of matter becoming light." Color is perceived as vibrating, radiant energy of light, distributed and reflected off an object. Where there is no light there is no color. The spectrum of electromagnetic radiation is constantly striking the earth and illuminating its various shapes and forms, making it possible to discern depth and showing the way to navigate through space. How light waves are reflected and translated visually constitutes how color is perceived.

Color theory and its application can be complex and controversial; however, there are two basic methods to achieve color, the additive method and the subtractive method.

Color achieved in the **additive** process begins with black (the absence of color) and is used to generate color through light on computer and television screens as well as in theatrical lighting. If a strong magnifying glass were to be held up to a computer monitor, a matrix of red, green, and blue pixels would emerge. It is these three colors that add light to black, creating, in their blends, new colors or wavelengths that the brain can recognize by name.

Mixing colors in the **subtractive** method results in an interaction of light similar to the additive process. It uses colored substances in printing, painting, photography, and fabric dyeing. The difference between the two methods is that the subtractive approach to developing and mixing color begins with all colors being present, resulting in a white surface, such as paper. The inks or dyes *subtract* some of the light that has been reflected. In subtractive color mixing, light reflected off a surface is what the surface does not absorb. For example, if a white surface is colored with something that absorbs red, then blue and yellow will reflect, making the surface appear green. If all colors are subtracted or absorbed, then the surface material will appear black.[1] Figure 4.1

ADDITIVE: A process of creating color using a mixture found in light. When all the colors of light blend, the result is white.

SUBTRACTIVE: Reducing or changing a color by mixing in pigment which reduces its ability to reflect specific light waves.

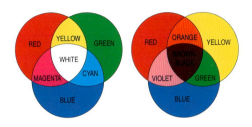

(a)

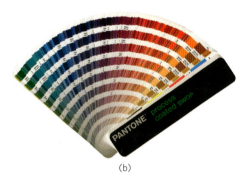

(b)

Figure 4.1 (left) Additive and subtractive mixtures of light.

Figure 4.2 (right) Munsell color tree (a) and Pantone color chart (b).

shows the combinations that produce color by the additive and subtractive methods.

Classifying Color

What becomes visual can be categorized and identified. International color systems such as **Munsell**, manufactured and marketed by GretagMacbeth Co., or **Pantone** help to standardize color using alphanumeric designations (Figure 4.2). This is especially important when manufacturing is taking place offshore and a particular color must be agreed upon. Using standard designations eliminates the ambiguity that can result from verbal labels, such as mandarin orange or royal blue, that marketers use to appeal to their customers.

As general descriptors, **hue** is the actual name of the color, such as yellow or blue. **Value** refers to the lightness or darkness of color and refers to the degree to which **incident light** is reflected off a surface. **Chroma**, or intensity, saturation, or level of strength of color describes its brightness, as in dull green or bright red. Chroma is measured on a scale from 1 to 12, where 1 is weak and 12 is strong. **Color temperature** is the apparent warmth or coolness as one color relates to another. For example, orange, red, and yellow tend to feel "warm," while violet, green, and blue feel "cool."

DYEING

In health-care and therapeutic environments, colors such as blue, green, and violet are used to calm patients, reduce blood pressure, and promote healing. Colors for such facilities reflect extensive research into determining the best colors for chronically ill patients, recovery and maternity rooms, operating rooms, as well as other spaces within health-care facilities. The examination of color and its implications has a long history.

Dyeing in the Past

The art of patterning with color and dyes is ancient. It can be traced to biblical times where, for example, Moses describes Bezaleel and Aholiab as "filled with wisdom of

MUNSELL: A color system established by Albert Munsell (1858–1918) using a three-dimensional color tree. It is often used to describe paint colors and frequently used in teaching color.

PANTONE: A color identifying and color forecasting system used in interior and fabric design, architecture, and industrial design fields. Small, numbered paper samples are used to help identify specific colors.

HUE: Name for a particular color such as yellow or red.

VALUE: Lightness or darkness of color.

INCIDENT LIGHT: Available light.

CHROMA: The relative intensity or brightness of a color, as in bright green or dull red.

COLOR TEMPERATURE: A description of the distribution of the spectral energy of light translated as a "feel," as in blue feels "cool."

heart, to work all manner of work, of the engraver, and of the cunning workman, and of the embroiderer, in blue, and in purple."[2] Another reference mentions garments dyed in the blood of grapes.

Early dyes, such as blue made from **woad** leaves, were used as early as the Bronze Age (2500–800 B.C.E.) and discovered in Denmark. Yellows were drawn from the herb root of the madder plant that produces the colorant **alizarin.** Purples came from crushing bilberry or whortleberry. Even dried insects, such as **kermes,** were used to produce a crimson color— as evidenced by the discovery of dyed fibers in a Neolithic grotto of Adaouste at Bouches du Rhone, France. Use of this dye was recorded in 1727 B.C.E.[3]

The application of color has been an important element in personal decoration through the centuries. Even before berries, roots, or colorants from rocks were applied to garments, color was added by attaching natural items such as shells, feathers, flowers, nuts, and fur to cloth. And during the Paleolithic Age, pieces of gold, silver, or bronze were incorporated onto fabric in an effort to embellish a garment and differentiate it from that of another person. But to make color last when it was not already implanted by nature on found objects was an ongoing problem. Some colorants, for example, could withstand emersion in water but would fade when exposed to light. The complex process of determining how to sustain hue over time began with early attempts using a mixture of blood, saliva, and resins from various trees as binding agents; hence, the early stages of *mordants* that eventually included alum, baking soda, and salt.

The history of dyeing can be traced through all the cultures of the world, for example, in an individual act of applying squid sepia or the formation of guilds of craftsmen, perhaps first noted by Geoffrey Chaucer in the prose and poetry of *The Canterbury Tales,* collected in Middle English between 1387 and 1400. However, one of the events in dyeing history that revolutionized the art and ushered in the science of dyeing occurred in 1856. During an Easter vacation, an 18-year-old Englishman, William Perkin, discovered by accident the artificial substance mauveine, or mauve, named from the French term for the violet-colored mallow flower. This first manufactured **dyestuff,** which imparted color when made soluble, was eventually produced from coal-tar and purified in 1862, beginning a wave of experimentation in dyes throughout Europe—especially in Germany—and eventually in the United States. Colorants fell into two basic categories: natural (animal, vegetable, and mineral) and manufactured.

How Does Dye Work?

Dyeing is related to the characteristics of light and how it is perceived by the human eye. As previously noted, dyes produce color in fibers or fabrics by the subtractive method, absorbing some wave lengths of white light and reflecting others. The reflected wave lengths are perceived as the color of the fiber.[4]

At the microscopic level, a **chromophore** is a carrier of color and emits color at the molecular level by way of electrons becoming agitated. The intensity of the hue depends on **auxochromes,** which also contribute to making hues

WOAD: A natural blue dye prepared by fermenting the leaves of the woad plant.

ALIZARIN: A dye (alzorine) originating from the madder root and now referring to a series of dyes.

KERMES: A female insect, *Kermes vermillo,* found in evergreen oaks that provided a source for the color crimson.

DYESTUFF: A colorant that becomes molecularly dispersed when placed in contact with a substrate such as hot water.

CHROMOPHORE: A chemical structure that is colored itself or becomes colored when combined with auxochromes.

AUXOCHROMES: Atomic groups of colorants that can change their color.

water soluble. The combinations of color chromophores and auxochromes create visible color.

Preparing to Color

The preparation of the yarn or fabric to be colored, or in some cases finished, is an important first step toward assuring a desired outcome. With most colorants, fabric should be clean of impurities that can interrupt or restrict the amount of color fabrics can absorb. Wool, for example, can be up to 70 percent impure and tainted with dirt and other natural materials, while cotton has fewer impurities but must be carefully processed to increase the saturation of color. Dyes for wool are **hydrophilic** (water loving) and retain their properties in water; however, the presence of **hydrophobic** materials, or materials that do not absorb or dissolve in water, such as fats in wool, will repel dyes and prevent them from penetrating the fibers. Woven goods should be thoroughly treated with chemicals that will help the fibers absorb dye, a process referred to as **desizing**. **Bleaching** removes all color from yarns, but if it is not done properly it can lead to unevenness and faulty dyeing and introduce uneven tensions, resulting in unwanted repetitive bars or stripes across the fabric known as **barre**.[5] Some natural fibers carry natural colors, and for the intended color to be clear and consistent, the natural color should be removed.

The following processes also prepare the fabric for dyeing:

- **boiling off**, a laundering technique using detergents suitable for cotton, cotton blends, silks, and manufactured yarns;
- **carbonizing**, a technique that employs sulfuric acid to remove leaves, small twigs, and grass in wool;
- **solvent scouring**, a dry-cleaning procedure to remove oils from knitted yarns and fabric;
- **tentering**, where wet warp and weft yarns are straightened on a tenter frame and made to lay perpendicular to one another;
- **degumming**, which removes the sercin from silk;
- **fulling**, where wool is preshrunk and made to feel thicker by cleaning the fibers with soap, heat, moisture, and sometimes chemicals to compact the fibers, resulting in a felt-like material.

It is also important to ensure that excess water that has accumulated during the manufacturing stage is removed from yarns and fabric. This is accomplished by using centrifuges, vacuum suction devices, and dryers with carefully controlled temperature gauges.

Color Categories

Colorants or chemical agents are conveyed onto or into yarns or cloth through two methods: pigments and dyes. Comparisons of pigments and dyes can be seen in Table 4.1. **Pigments** are the insoluble particulates that are held onto the surface of the fabric, typically by a binding agent that is applied by mechanical means or mixed into the pigment itself. This process, which is relatively simple and widely used today for printed fabrics, can

HYDROPHILIC: Having a strong attraction to water, such as rayon.

HYDROPHOBIC: Lacking an affinity for water or repelling water, like polyester.

DESIZING: A process of converting greige goods by adding agents that are later washed away and change the shape of the yarn or fabric to better accept dyes.

BLEACHING: A process of whitening yarns by removing all natural color.

BARRE: An unintentional, repetitive pattern of continuous bars and stripes.

BOILING OFF: A process of boiling cotton fibers or cloth to remove natural waxes and gums; scouring.

CARBONIZING: A chemical process to eliminate cellulose material mixed in with wool and other animal fibers.

SOLVENT SCOURING: A method of extracting impurities from fabric using organic solvents.

TENTERING: A finishing process for holding fabric to a desired width as it dries.

DEGUMMING: A process that removes sercin gum from silk filaments or fabric by boiling it in a soap solution.

FULLING: A finishing process for woolens that compresses fibers, producing felt.

PIGMENTS: Finely ground powder colorants that become dispersed in the dyeing process and remain on the surface of yarns of fabric.

Table 4.1 Comparison of Dyes and Pigments

DYES

Bond chemically with the fiber
In general, are more colorfast than pigments
Crocking and fading are less of a problem than with
    pigments
Do not affect the texture of the fabric
Can be used on fibers, yarns, fabric, and garments
Printed colors must be aged with steam or heat
Washing and rinsing are required to remove
    chemicals and excess dye

PIGMENTS

Cheaper and more efficient to apply than dyes
May stiffen the fabric
With dark colors, cracking and loss of color in
    laundering may occur
Extensive color range is possible and any color can
    be applied to any fabric
Can be added to manufactured fibers before
    extrusion
Easier to obtain a color match because the color is
    on the surface
Can be applied only as a solid color or as a print
Excellent lightfastness
Colors must be cured

Source: V.H. Elsasser, *Textiles: Concepts and Principles*, second
edition, New York: Fairchild Publications, Inc., 2005, p. 174.

DIRECT: Dyes applied directly onto cellulose fibers in a neutral or alkaline bath without prior treatment. These dyes are known to bleed and dull in color when washed; a class of dyes.

CROCKING: Transferring dye from the surface of a dyed or printed fabric onto another surface by rubbing.

FADE: To lose the original color.

BLEED: Loss of dye (color) from fabric during a wet treatment finishing process or through washing.

COLORFASTNESS: The resistance of yarns or fabric to change in color characteristics or transfer color to another fabric.

AFFINITY: Chemical attraction as in dyes for yarns.

be applied using a **direct** method. The simplicity of this method is balanced by the high probability of fabric dye being transferred from one fabric to another, as in **crocking**. The fabric could also **fade** or possibly **bleed**, that is, lose color vibrancy in the wet finishing process. When any of these problems occurs, the permanence and clarity of the fabric color is compromised, thereby reducing its degree of **colorfastness**. Furthermore, the fabric tends to become stiff, a fact which can be attributed to the heating and curing necessary to help attach the microscopic particles to the fabric.

Chemical dyestuffs, unlike pigments, thoroughly dissolve, usually in boiling, aqueous vats that churn the water, distributing and attaching the dye evenly. This application of dyes to fabric is the most common method used to dye or color fabric. After the fabric is dyed, it must be washed in appropriate detergents and then rinsed thoroughly to avoid the weakening of fibers. Printed fabrics must be steamed or aged in order to "set" the color.

Synthetic Dyes and Colorants

The vast majority of dyes used today are synthetic, and they number in the thousands. Since the first synthetic coal-tar product was developed, the growth of various dye compounds has continually expanded in quality, particularly as they relate to colorfastness and variety of available colors. As new manufactured yarns have developed, so has the need to find new ways to color them. The art and science of the dyer is to understand the properties of each yarn or fabric being dyed so the appropriate class and subclass of colorants can be used, thereby enhancing the **affinity**, or acceptance of dye to fiber. It is also important to select synthetic dyes that are classified to address not only manufactured yarns but protein and cellulosic yarns. To aid the dyer when fabric is being dyed for a custom project, it is essential to pre-mark the face and back of the fabric. Table 4.2 shows the major classifications of dyes used today.

Color Matching

Designers should be aware of the chameleon-like characteristics of color. For example, if a fabric has been dyed and dried (fabrics are a different color when wet) on one day and a second dye bath of "the same color" has been mixed to continue the dyeing job at a later point, it is possible that the **dye lots**, or different batches of dye, will not match. It is best if the designer checks with a showroom representative to ensure that the fabric to be ordered originated from the same dye lot.

The human eye senses color in different wavelengths. Two dyed fabrics may appear the same under one light source and different under another. To avoid this problem it is important to standardize all dye formulas, as well as the temperature of dissolving liquids, time of emersion, water quality, amount of dye concentrate, and degree of agitation or movement of the liquid around the yarns or fabric being dyed. Colors that exhibit a variance from

DYE LOTS: One source of a particular dyestuff.

Table 4.2 Major Dye Classifications

CELLULOSIC FIBERS	PROTEIN FIBERS
Azoic dyes (also called *naphthol dyes*) Bright colors; good colorfastness to laundering and light, but dark shades may crock Moderate cost Used primarily on cottons, but may also be used on acetate, olefin, polyester, and nylon	**Acid dyes** Wide range of bright colors but colorfastness varies Used on nylon, some rayons, acrylics, and polyesters
Direct dyes (also called *substantive dyes*) Wide range of colors, but less intense than basic or acid dyes May lose color in laundering Used primarily on cotton and rayon	**Premetalized acid dyes** Duller colors than acid dyes but better colorfastness
Direct-developed dyes Same as direct dyes, but better colorfastness	**Chrome dyes** (also called *mordant dyes*) Not as bright and smaller color range than acid dyes May bleed Excellent for wool but may harm silk
Reactive dyes Very bright colors possible Good colorfastness Difficult to match Used on cotton, rayon, and linen, also protein fibers	**Pigment dyes** See discussion of pigments in Box 11.2
	MANUFACTURED FIBERS
Sulfur dyes* Best with dark colors such as black, brown, and navy; most widely used dye for black Good colorfastness to washing and fair colorfastness to light	**Cationic dyes** (also called *basic dyes*) Bright colors with excellent colorfastness when used on synthetics Used on acetate, polyester, nylon Tend to bleed and crock
Vat dyes* Considered the best dye for colorfastness Smaller color range than other dyes Used on cotton and rayon but also on acrylics, modacrylics, and nylon	**Disperse dyes** Good color range with good colorfastness Used on most synthetics Fume fading on acetate (shades of blue turn pink, greens turn brown)
Pigment dyes See discussion of pigments in Box 11.2	**Pigment dyes** See discussion of pigments in Box 11.2

*If they are not completely washed out, some vat and sulfur dyes may cause tendering in cotton fabrics. Tendering is the weakening of a fiber due to exposure to chemicals used in dyeing or finishing or to other degradants.

Source: V.H. Elsasser, *Textiles: Concepts and Principles*, second edition, New York: Fairchild Publications, Inc., 2005, pp. 174–75.

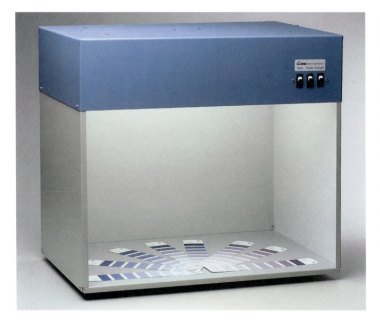

Figure 4.3 Light booths allow for examining dyed yarns under different lighting conditions.

light source to light source are called **metameric** colors. Fabric textures or variances in among woven structures can also produce metamerism. The **light booth**, as seen in Figure 4.3, is used to examine dyed yarns and fabrics under different lighting conditions, simulating daylight, incandescent, and fluorescent light to help detect metamerism.

In practice, a client may decide weeks after the drapery fabric has been purchased to install an additional feature for the window treatment, such as a **lambrequin**, a fabric-covered or upholstered over a hard surface that frames the top and sides of the window. When fabric for the lambrequin is made, it may not match the drapes. This problem could be due to a slight change in the dye lot or the position of the lambrequin relative to fixture lighting, as opposed to daylight. A slight change of color due to room lighting conditions can be understood, but two fabrics of the

same color should match when paired under the same light source. Fortunately, computerized color matching using **spectrophotometric curves** and colorimeters ensures greater speed and accuracy in matching colors. Nonetheless, inconsistencies in color can result from many factors, including dyes that have the same name but originate from different manufacturers, the degree of dye purity, the amount of fillers mixed in with the dye, or the size of the dye particles themselves. Other considerations can relate to irregularities with **dye assistants**, substances that help the dye adhere, degree of penetration, migration or solubility, and dispersion of dyes.

With regard to light, designers must be aware that light varies from region to region. For example, the fluctuations in light quality between the northeastern United States and the Caribbean can be significant, and a designer from the northeastern United States working on a project in the Caribbean would need to take these fluctuations into account. A color that appears "light" in New York City might appear "heavy" in St. Kitts.

Methods of Dyeing
Color can be applied at any stage of the fabric's development from fiber to greige goods. Dyeing methods include the following:

- **Stock dyeing** involves the dyeing of individual loose yarns after they have been cleaned of oils and dirt. Wool fibers are often stock dyed to produce **heathered** effects. The dye penetration in the yarns is thorough, and the colors produced have excellent chroma.

- **Top dyeing** is similar to stock dyeing; however, in top dyeing the long filaments are separated from the shorter ones and dyed in the sliver or roving stage of production. These longer fibers are combed out and **drafted**. Dyes are able to adhere well to these relatively loose lengths.
- **Solution dyeing**, or dope dyeing, adds color to yarns when the pigment is blended first with the liquefied manufactured material (dope), such as polyester or polyamide. This material is then extruded from the spinneret with the color inside of the filament. Solution-dyed products are excellent for interiors in part because of their colorfastness and ability to resist chemical or physical decomposition.
- **Yarn** or **skein dyeing** occurs after the spinning process has taken place. Spools of yarns or reeled hanks are immersed in dyes. This method allows controlled absorption of dyes and can be used in the production of stripes, plaids, and checks. Dyed yarn can also take the form of warp beam and package dyeing. In warp dyeing, the entire beam that has been wound with yarn is submerged in a dye vat. In package dyeing, yarn is loosely wound on perforated cylinders. Several of these packages, typically about ten, are placed on spindles and loaded into the dye vats. The dyes are under extremely high temperature and pressure and forced through perforated cylinders and around the packages.
- **Spoon dyeing** is a process whereby the dyer carefully measures and weighs the correct amount of dyestuffs and places it into large ladles. The dye material is then subjected to forced hot water and steam to liquefy the solid material. The spoon, now filled with color, is transferred to a vat of hot water and blended in to dye yarn skeins or fabric already made. The spoon-dyeing method continues to be used, but it is limited to shorter fabric runs or specialized dyeing projects.
- **Piece dyeing** is coloring a "piece" of fabric after it has been manufactured. Methods of piece dyeing include beck, jet, jig, pad, and continuous dyeing.

Beck—Fabric is sewn end-to-end to produce one continuous piece that is pulled over two cylinders then dropped into the dye bath. The fabric continues to circulate in and out of the dye until the desired color is achieved.

Jet—Fabric is sewn end-to-end and forced through a tube containing extremely hot dye. The velocity of the dye solution being forced through propels the fabric into the system. Jet dyeing is more popular than beck dyeing and uses less dyestuffs and energy.

Jig—Full-width rolled fabric is mounted to a jig above the surface of the dye. The taut fabric moves from the roll downward and into the dye bath, then surfaces to the other side to be wound onto a second roll. The process is repeated back and forth until the desired color is achieved.

Pad—Like jig dyeing, the fabric is tension-controlled. The cloth passes over a roller on the surface, then into the dye. As the dye emerges from

HEATHERED: Stock dye applied typically to wool fibers resulting in varied colors.

TOP DYEING: Dyeing yarns, especially wool, after they have been straightened and separated from the shorter fibers.

DRAFTED: When the linear density of a strand of yarn is reduced by pulling it apart.

SOLUTION DYEING: Dyeing manufactured filaments before the material is extruded.

YARN DYEING: Dyeing of yarn before weaving or knitting.

SKEIN DYEING: Dyeing of loosely wound, continuous strands of coiled yarns with a circumference of about 45 to 60 inches.

SPOON DYEING: The use of ladles or large spoons attached to long wooden handles into which dyestuffs are placed. The ladles are then submerged into an aqueous vat to dye yarn or fabric.

PIECE DYEING: Dyeing of fabric rather than dyeing yarns.

LEVEL: When dye has been moved from one area of the fabric to another to enhance the uniform distribution of color.

CROSS DYEING: Dyeing of yarns or fabric composed of two or more different yarn types to achieve a multicolored effect.

UNION DYEING: A method of dyeing to obtain one color on a fabric using different yarns.

TONE-ON-TONE DYEING: A fabric colored in lighter and darker shades of the same hue.

NANOTECHNOLOGY: The study and manipulation of atomic structures.

around the submerged roller, it is forced between padded rollers on the surface that pressures or impregnates the dye into the fabric while squeezing out excess dye material.

Continuous—When large quantities of fabric or carpeting need to be dyed the same color, the continuous method is used. Continuous dyeing is similar to pad dyeing but because of the hundreds if not thousands of yards that can pass through the rollers, it is possible that the application of color may not be level.

Dyeing for Special Effects

Competition among fabric companies and designers provides motivation to develop alternate dyeing methods that result in unique colors and color blends. Several of these techniques follow:

- **Cross dyeing** is required when two or more different yarns, such as cotton and polyester, appear in the same cloth; their affinity for accepting dyestuffs will be different. These differences in fiber makeup can create multicolored effects. When two different kinds of fibers are blended in the warp, when dyed, vertical strips can appear. And to produce what appears to be a plaid, different yarns can be used for both the warp and weft but dyed once in a mix of two different kinds of dyes.[6]
- **Union dyeing** is when yarns are colored with different dye affinities to achieve the same color. Each yarn can be dyed by a different classification of dye to achieve the same color.

- **Tone-on-tone dyeing** is used for manufactured yarns and carpeting and achieved by using one color to obtain slight tonal changes, as in light to dark. Different synthetic yarns have different affinities for dyes, so when they are subjected to the dyeing process, the effect is a shaded quality.

The future of infusing color into yarns may be in **nanotechnology**, where research in the manipulation of atomic structures measuring 1/25,400,000 of an inch or more than 1000 times narrower than the width of a human hair, is revealing methods of creating colored yarns without the use of natural or chemical colorants. Altering physical properties of fabrics, such as their level of reflectivity, will produce a change in color. It has been predicted by Mihail Roco, a senior advisor of nanotechnology at the National Science Foundation, that by 2015 more than half of all new products will originate from nanotechnology.

PRINTING: THE APPLICATION OF COLOR

From early times, fabrics were printed with designs to enhance their aesthetic appeal. Today, new printing methods have been developed for the same purpose.

Historical Impressions

The history of applying color to cloth probably developed first from hand painting fabrics. Early samples of colored fabric from centuries ago are difficult to locate because of the effects of time and weather.

Resist prints, however, can be traced to early Egyptians, while wall painting from around 2100 B.C.E. depicts colored clothing. Indonesian ikat (ee'kat), a process in which yarns are dyed *before* weaving begins, appeared in India around the fourth century B.C.E and developed much earlier in Western Asia.

Wood block and stencil methods of printing were attributed to the Chinese, but Egyptians used them too, as early as 400 C.E. Although much of the early block printing was done on paper, it eventually became transferred to woven fabric and developed into a thriving industry in Augsburg, Germany, around 1689, where the first calico print works began featuring coarse, plain woven fabrics, usually in cotton, printed in one or more colors. Block-printed fabric, as well as wallpaper and wallpaper scenics, remain available today, such as those produced since 1797 in Rixheim, France, by Zuber Cie. Block printing produces irregular effects in the design, largely due to the age of the blocks and storage conditions that often fluctuate in temperature and humidity. Such conditions contribute to cracking and some distorting of patterns. Print blocks used today can be more than 100 years old, as seen in Figure 4.4. This irregular effect, which can be aesthetically desirable, may be replicated using other methods of printing, such as screen printing.

Indian prints became popular in seventeenth-century Europe and were largely responsible for the spread of printed fabrics. The high demand for printed cloth from India provided direct competition, particularly in France, for French woolen and other fabric products. France eventu-

ally banned Indian prints: In 1686 the king of France declared that none were to be imported or manufactured in the country, and anyone seen with printed cloth from India or its imitation were literally condemned to death by hanging. As other countries, notably England and Spain, began trading with India, economic pressures were brought to bear on France, and eventually the edict was lifted, paving the way for the well-known Oberkampf print factory in Jouy, France, established in 1759. On May 1, 1760, the first toile de jouy (twahl duh jzoo-wee) was printed by the engraver and colorist Christophe-Philippe Oberkamph, initiating the production of high quality copper plate prints. The process, which he and his brother "borrowed" from England, lasted from the reign of Louis XVI to the era of Napoleon.

Figure 4.4 Wood blocks are used to print pattern and color onto cloth.

RESIST PRINTS: Prints that have designs produced by applying a paste that resists dyeing. The fabric is then submerged into a dye vat and washed. The resist material rinses away to reveal the pattern.

IKAT: A complex artistic technique used to create images on fabric. The images are dyed onto the threads before they are placed on the loom and woven into the finished product. The work *ikat* derives from the Malay word *mengikat*, meaning "to tie."

WOOD BLOCK: A hand-printing method by which designs are cut into a block of wood, color is applied to its surface, and then the block is pressed onto a piece of fabric or paper.

STENCIL: A printing technique where a design is cut into cardboard, metal, or another material and then applied to a piece of fabric or paper.

TOILE DE JOUY: A floral or scenic design printed on cotton, linen, or silk.

PRINT PASTE: A paste containing colorants and other materials.

SCREEN PRINTING: Several methods of printing using screens where the pattern is unblocked on the mesh. Print paste is applied to the screen and squeegeed across, revealing the pattern.

SUBSTRATE: A fiber or fabric to which another material, like dye, is added.

Early toile patterns, particularly from France and England, featured floral or scenic images. They took direction from regional news. For example, when a noteworthy event occurred such as the famous "Balloon Ascension," the center motif of an existing toile would be replaced by a replication of that event. It was good for business and drew attention to those who were concerned with keeping up appearances! An example of toile is shown in Figure 4.5.

Printing Techniques

Printing is the process of decorating yarns or fabric by adding colorants that can be applied using the more than 40 methods available. Dyes and pigments are typically used in conjunction with an additive of **print paste** to increase the viscosity of dyestuffs, thereby enhancing the sharpness of the image while reducing the tendency of dyes to migrate.

Numerous methods are available to apply colored patterns onto fabric, from ancient methods such as hand painting, block printing, and stenciling to newer methods such as *devor* and *cloqu*. The two

generally accepted methods of printing that remain the most commercially viable are screen printing and roller printing.

Screen Printing

Screen printing is accomplished by first making a screen framed with metal, usually aluminum. Originally, silk was used for the screen because its threads were strong and fine. Unfortunately, silk can lose its tautness, and the chemicals used to clean dye off screens contain bleach or chlorinated solvents that can destroy the silk filaments. Screens today are more likely to be made of monofilament polyester or multifilament polyester and nylon. Screens vary slightly in thread count to allow for varying amounts of dye to be transferred to the **substrate** during the printing process. Different fabrics require a different count of threads per square inch. A mesh count of approximately 200 to 260 threads per inch is used for printing fine details, but a 160- to 180-thread mesh is used for larger shapes and generally preferred for most fabric printing today.

Early screen patterns were first devised by the Japanese in the form of cut-out

Figure 4.5 Toile de Jouy.

stencils. Originally the screen was covered with film, then glued to the screen. Today, patterns are created using a photochemical process. "In preparing the stencil, the film is exposed to a positive film image in a vacuum frame. It is then developed in a solution that renders the unexposed image areas soluble in water. The solution areas are removed and the remaining film is bonded to the screen fabric."[7]

Each pattern on a printed fabric requires a different screen. It is common to see on the selvage a numbered legend that represents how many screens (colors) were used to produce the pattern. Usually the more colors, the more expensive the print will be.

The process of printing involves laying the fabric to be printed on rubberized "tables" that are prepared by applying a tacky substance so that the fabric remains in place during the printing process. A table can be 60 yards in length. In order to maintain proper **registration** so that the pattern and colors remain correctly placed, each screen locks into place using marker bars or metal brackets. The screen is laid on top of the fabric, and the color is pressed and spread across the width of the screen. The screen is then lifted, placed on the next section of fabric, and the process repeated until the color and pattern has been applied the full length of the table. Upon completing the length of the print table with one screen, the beginning point has dried and is ready to accept the second screen pattern and color.

Hand screened products can be time consuming, and they are not always cost effective, especially if larger runs are to be produced. **Hand screening** can be useful for designers and clients who require shorter runs of specialized prints. It is also somewhat easier to create a sample for examination or **strike-off** using this method.

Automated screen printing, also known as flatbed printing, is basically an acceleration of hand screening. This method involves moving the fabric (not the screen) until the full length is printed and reaches the automatic dryer. Although this method is more efficient than hand screening, it remains less efficient than **rotary screen printing**, where the screen is in the form of a cylinder instead of a flat screen.

Rotary screen printing uses hollow, perforated metal screens that are usually made from nickel. The color paste from pressurized tanks is forced through the holes in the rotating screens, producing the pattern as the fabric moves along. The rotary method of printing is the fastest of all screen printing techniques and can produce as much as 3,500 yards in a day.

Roller Printing

Machine printing, or **roller printing**, was first developed in 1785 and resembles a high-speed newspaper production system using engraved rollers that have been chemically chrome plated. This technique can print as many as 16 colors at once. Each color or design is engraved on a separate roller, and the roller is capable of yielding exceptionally fine designs, unlike rotary screen printing. Roller printing requires a great deal of preparation time before printing can begin and is cost effective only if thousands or millions of yards are printed using the same rollers. **Duplex printing** is a roller printing technique in

REGISTRATION: Alignment of pattern and/or color.

HAND SCREENING: A screen-printing process produced by physically moving screens and manually squeegeeing print paste across the screens.

STRIKE-OFF: A short test run of a fabric to determine its feasibility.

AUTOMATED SCREEN PRINTING: Screen printing using machines where fabric moves and not the screens. Separate screens are used for each color applied.

ROTARY SCREEN PRINTING: A technique using perforated metal (nickel) screens shaped into the form of hollow cylinders.

ROLLER PRINTING: A method of printing using engraved rollers or cylinders.

DUPLEX PRINTING: The technique of printing both sides of a fabric with either the same pattern or different patterns.

DIRECT PRINTING: A technique used to place a colored design on a white or light-colored ground, as opposed to resist printing.

BLOCH PRINTING: A technique where the ground cloth is completely printed with color rather than dyed. The reverse side of the fabric will be almost white.

WARP PRINTING: The printing of warp yarns before weaving.

FLOCKING: Creating a design or pattern on a fabric or wall covering using small fibers that are dropped onto or electrostatically applied to a glue pattern, sometimes with a screen.

INK-JET PRINTING: A technique using computer-controlled drops of dye that are strategically placed on fabric or carpeting.

which both sides of the fabric are printed with either the same pattern or different patterns. This method simulates a woven effect but is not often used. The same effects can be achieved with jacquard and dobby woven designs. The roller printing process is shown in Figure 4.6.

Variations

Using modified screen and roller printing techniques, additional printing effects can be produced.

- **Direct printing** is printing directly on white or light-colored ground cloth without the use of any chemical inhibitors that would etch in a design. The second application of color contains bleach and the pattern or design. When applied, the design emerges by eliminating the background color. **Bloch printing** is similar; the background color is printed, not dyed, onto the fabric, and the pattern is printed at the same time.

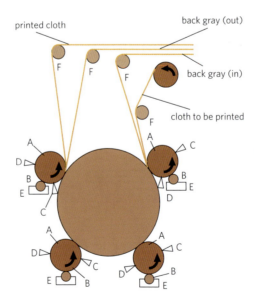

Figure 4.6 Fabric that is roller printed can be produced in large quantities, costing less than hand printed products.

- Resist printing uses a pattern paste that "resists" dyeing. The material is dyed and washed. The washing removes the dye-resist and paste, leaving a white pattern. Contrasting color can be applied by using color in the resist material, producing a two-tone effect.
- **Warp printing** (ikat) begins with dyeing the warp yarns, then weaving usually with lighter or contrasting colored weft yarns. The appearance is shadowy or nebulous.

Specialized Printing

A number of specialized printing techniques produce unique textures and effects.

- **Flocking** has existed for more than 650 years. In this process, $\frac{1}{10}$ to $\frac{1}{4}$ of an inch pieces of cotton, rayon, wool, silk, or nylon fibers called "flock" are adhered in a pattern to fabric or wall covering. The method involves applying a glue pattern on the fabric and then dropping the fibers onto the fabric. The fibers stick mechanically or adhere electrostatically. Mechanically, the fibers fall through a hopper above the cloth and drop onto the glued surface. The conveyer carrying the fabric vibrates to pack in the fibers. Electrostatically, the fibers are charged, making them stand erect on the fabric.
- **Ink-jet printing** is typically used for carpeting or pile upholstery and does not use screens or rollers. Jet printing is a highly precise, computerized method capable of shooting very small streams of color in the form of a pattern. It is possible to have more than 100 jets applying color and pattern at once.

- **Thermal transfer printing** or heat transfer printing is similar to the process used in applying decals and uses heat to transfer dyes from paper onto fabric. In the first stage, a design is printed on paper using disperse dyes; that is, finely ground dyes that are water insoluble but when ground with a dispersing agent become a good dye medium for manufactured fibers. Then the paper is pressured onto the fabric and heated to greater than 400 degrees Fahrenheit and removed. This method is best suited for nylon, acrylic, polyester, and acetate.

Setting Color

To help eliminate problems associated with color migration, crocking, fume, or **gas fading** (when dispersed dyes are exposed to oxides of nitrogen), among other difficulties, dyes need to be carefully paired with the appropriate color-setting methods.

Prints that utilize dyes are considered **wet prints**. Steam is required to set the colors and liquid is necessary to "wash" the fabric to remove excess dyes. **Dry prints** are prints that use pigments and require only heat to cure the pattern and therefore do not need to be submerged in liquid.

FABRIC FINISHES

To complete the fabric's production cycle, it is often essential to treat the cloth in ways that conform to its yarn makeup and end use. Finishes are grouped as aesthetic or functional.

Finishing can enhance the appearance of fabric as well as improve its serviceability and durability. Finishing typically refers to converted greige goods; however, chemical additives can be mixed in with the liquefied material used to manufacture yarns prior to extrusion. Whether finishing is accomplished by the dyer, printer, or companies specializing in fabric processing, many of the techniques and formulas used are carefully guarded in order to gain competitive advantage and protect one processing technique against others.

New yarn and fabric finishes are researched and developed from varied sources, such as NASA, DuPont, and universities worldwide; however, the complex process of applying treatments to fabric can change the hand or affect its performance. The challenge to address consumer demand for fabric to perform in a particular manner can be difficult to meet. For example, a fabric may be finished to feel soft but wrinkle easily or processed to be flame resistant but remain stiff. The goal is to meet end-use specifications as closely as possible while always looking to the future for finishes that meet or exceed consumer requirements for new fabrics and specialized finishes.

Retention of Finishing Material

Fabric finishes are classified according to their ability to service fabric and should be considered by the designer as part of the specification process. Fabric that receives occasional wear may only require a temporary finish; however, most fabrics are finished so they can withstand heavier use. Categories of finishes include the following:

- *Temporary* finishes can be removed or lost after one or two launderings or dry cleanings.

THERMAL TRANSFER PRINTING: A technique using a decal-like process of applying pattern by transferring dyes from paper to fabric.

GAS FADING: Fading of color, particularly with disperse dyes on acetate, caused by exposure to oxides of nitrogen. Examples are pollution from gas-fired stoves or fumes from dryers.

WET PRINTS: Prints that have been created using liquid dyes.

DRY PRINTS: Prints that have been set with heat or other means without the use of liquid.

NAPPING: A finishing process using revolving cylinders to raise yarn ends on fabric.

SHEARING: A finishing process that cuts uneven yarns mechanically.

BEETLING: A process that gives round-shaped cotton fibers a flat appearance with increased luster.

SINGEING: A finishing process for burning off protruding fibers from yarns or fabrics.

PILLING: Small tangles of fiber occurring when fabric is rubbed against itself or another material or surface.

BRUSHING: A finishing process for fabric or knit using brushes to raise the nap.

CALENDERING: A finishing process that creates a sheen on a fabric by passing it between two stainless steel or wooden rollers under regulated pressure. Sometimes the rollers are heated to a specific temperature to achieve a particular effect.

CHINTZ: A plain-woven printed or solid cotton, or cotton blend, that may be finished with a sheen applied by chemicals or by calendering.

- *Semi-durable* finishes remain on fabric for several cleanings.
- *Durable* finishes are roughly timed with the length of use of fabric—as the material wears out, so does the finish.
- *Permanent* finishes are not affected by the life of the fabric; however, the Federal Trade Commission prefers using "resistant" as a descriptor for a finish that "lasts a long time" because technically it is debatable whether any finishing treatment can be truly permanent.

Finishing Treatments

Specific processes can be used to alter the appearance and function of fabric.

Aesthetic Qualities

To attract attention to fabric and, thereby, improve its chances to be specified, several treatments are used to increase visual and tactile qualities.

- **Napping** raises the nap of fiber ends on woolens, cotton, spun silks, and spun rayon. The napper contains revolving cylinders with fine wires brushes. When the fabric passes over the wires they lift the shorter weft yarns, raising them to the surface. **Shearing** mechanically cuts the raised nap to a desired length and is used to create patterns such as stripes.
- **Beetling** provides a smooth, flat, lustrous surface on cotton and other fabrics to make them resemble linen. Beetling actually beats dampened fabric wound around an iron cylinder, hammering it with wooden mallets.
- **Singeing** or gassing is a process of removing loose fiber ends or fuzz that

has collected on the surface of the fabric. Cloth is passed over gas flame or heated copper plates just long enough to remove surface material while not burning it. In the final step, the fabric is exposed to moisture to assure that any hot surfaces will cool. Singeing helps smooth the cloth, define printed patterns, and reduce **pilling**, the formation of small fuzz balls on fabric.

- **Brushing** and *sueding* are processes that follow shearing and napping and are used to raise fibers on knits and wovens as well as remove loose threads that have accumulated after shearing. Brushing is accomplished by using bristle-covered rollers that rake the fabric. Sueding is similar to brushing, except the bristles are replaced with lightly abrasive sandpaper-like rollers. Both wovens and knits can be sueded, creating the appearance of suede. Material that is abraded using this method can lose nearly 60 percent of its tensile strength.
- **Calendering** is passing fabric through two or more cylinders made of cast iron, stainless steel, wood, or other material. As the cloth passes between the rollers, which are sometimes heated, it is pressed, usually according to pounds per square inch. Ironing produces a similar effect by creating sheen on the surface of the fabric when sufficient pressure is applied. The reflective shine can be laundered away eventually but adds appeal to many fabrics, including linens, silks, and manufactured fibers. Today, when cotton is calendered, it is often known as **chintz**.

Figure 4.7 shows the finishes achieved by calendering nonwoven fabrics. Other processes that use a calender include moiréing, schreinering, embossing, glazing, and ciréing.

- **Moiréing** (mwaah-ray'-ing) comes from French for "watered," and the surface effect on a moiré appears wavy or rippled, as shown in Figure 4.8. A moiré can be produced using engraved rollers. The light contrasting off the raised and depressed areas of the pattern gives off the watery appearance. A moiré pattern can be random and produced by pressing the fabric to be moiré against a ribbed fabric such as taffeta. As the two fabrics are pressured together between two smooth rollers, the pattern is formed. Moiré fabric is usually cotton, acetate, silk, rayon, and some ribbed synthetic fabrics. The process is permanent only for acetates and resin-treated rayons.

- **Schreinering** (shry-nuhr-ing) produces a soft luster on cotton, cotton blends, damasks, and **tricot**, a warp knitted fabric. The effect is made by the fabric passing through engraved steel rollers with 180 to 360 fine, diagonal lines per inch, barely perceptible. The pattern will be permanent if the yarns are theromoplastic.

- **Embossing** produces a raised effect in fabric by passing the cloth between heated rollers engraved with a design. Embossing can be permanent if they are thermoplastic. In other fabrics, resin finishes are used to create a high level of durability. Em-

bossing can also be used to create a **plissé** (plih-say) effect. Plissé is produced by applying a paste of sodium hydroxide, which causes part of the cloth to shrink and pucker in a manner similar to seersucker. If stretched, the puckers in a plissé will appear flat, unlike seersucker, which retains its shape. A high-speed embossing machine is shown in Figure 4.9.

Figure 4.7 (left) Nonwoven fabrics finished on a heated roll calender.

Figure 4.8 (below) Moiré patterns change their appearance as light moves and reflects off the surface.

MOIRÉING: A finishing process that produces a wavy pattern.

SCHREINERING: A finishing process that produces a high luster on fabric by using an engraved steel calender roller and a smooth roller.

TRICOT: A warp-knitted fabric, knitted flat with fine wales on the right side and more or less pronounced crosswise ribs on the back.

EMBOSSING: A finishing process that produces a raised design or pattern in relief by passing fabric between hot, engraved rollers.

PLISSÉ: A cotton fabric treated with sodium hydroxide, a caustic soda that causes the cloth to pucker or crinkle producing a stripe effect, usually in the warp direction.

Figure 4.9 High-speed embossing.

- **Glazing** is a finish that produces a reflective surface on fabric using a friction calender. Heated calender rollers rotating at different speeds cause friction between the fabric and the rollers. The fabrics are durable with this treatment, especially if they are thermoplastic or finished with resins.

- **Ciré** (see-ray), the French term for waxed, is a highly polished, wet-looking finish, similar in appearance to patent leather and produced by a friction calender. The nearly reflective or metallic shine is made through the application of heated wax or another substance to silk, rayon, cotton, or polyester.

- **Optical brighteners** or fluorescent whitening agents (FWA) are chemicals that intensify the whiteness of fabrics that are already a shade of white. The additive is a colorant that absorbs ultraviolet radiation and emits it as blue or violet light. The level of brilliance depends upon the quality of ultraviolet rays reflected off the fabric. Dimming of color may occur over time, but optical whiteners can be added during laundering if the fabric appears to be losing its luster.

- **Mercerizing**, discovered accidentally in 1844 by John Mercer, an Englishman, is a finishing process primarily for combed cotton. Mercerizing is capable of increasing the strength of cotton fibers by about 25 percent as well as increasing absorbency. Fabric can be mercerized in either the yarn or fabric stage prior to dyeing. The process involves subjecting the yarn or cloth to a 15–20 percent sodium hydroxide (caustic acid) solution, then neutralizing it. The result produces a swelling of the flat, ribbon-like fibers and causes them to contract in length. The procedure can also be used to finish linen.

Functional Qualities

Addressing practical concerns about fabric results in expanding and enhancing its usefulness. There have always been attempts to finish fabrics and to discover methods of improving its performance; however, it was not until resins were first formulated in 1929 in England by the Tootal Broadhurst Lee Co., that chemical finishes became practical to use and began literally to change the shape of fabric.

Early experimentation with resin fiber bond material involved urea formaldehyde. Formaldehyde was first produced in 1859, and urea was synthesized in 1928.

Eventually, they were combined and used to effectively control wrinkles. Because this mixture has been suspected of causing cancer, other chemical resins have been developed to perform a myriad of finishing tasks.

Resins can be used alone or combined on the face or back of fabric with an ever-increasing number of chemicals to finish not only cellulosic fibers but nearly all fiber types. Some side effects related to using finishing resins include producing overly stiff fabric, dye colors that can change hue slightly, aroma problems when wet, and creases that can be difficult to remove. Fortunately, as new chemical compositions are discovered, most difficulties with resins can be overcome.

Functional finishes aid in eliminating problems that unfinished fabrics have while adding convenience to the care and maintenance of fabric. Functional finishes, which are also applied for health and safety reasons, include the following:

- **Shrink control.** The various chemical and nonchemical processes that yarns go through to become fabric contribute to fabric shrinkage. **Relaxation shrinkage,** which refers to any change in the length or width of the fabric due to the stress of manufacturing, becomes more evident during the first laundering. Even if the fabric has been preshrunk, residual shrinkage can occur and the amount of that shrinkage needs to be stated on a label. **Progressive (residual) shrinkage** takes place each time a fabric is laundered.

  Methods that have been devised to address each kind of shrinkage include

chemical resin treatments, mechanical approaches, and the development of yarns containing shrink inhibitors. For example, the **compressive shrinkage** method is a mechanical method of preshrinking yarns using a sprayer to deliver a fine mist of water on the fabric, then compressing it against a steam-heated cylinder covered with rubber. Shrinkage of wool can be controlled using chlorine or enzymes that alter the surface scales on the fibers, consequently reducing the tendency for wool fibers to mat together. Thermoplastic fibers have a tendency to shrink almost 10 percent, but the fibers can be stabilized using a mechanical heat method.

- **Durable press.** Retaining the shape of fabric pleats and creases and ensuring durability of seams are important considerations. The multistep process involves adding resins while the fabric is wet, then drying and baking (curing) it, then applying pressure to create creases. Chemicals are often applied as a last step to improve the softness of the fabric.

- **Soil inhibitors.** Soil-resistant finishes are less likely to allow soil to penetrate fabric. Chemicals used to facilitate this action are usually silicone based. Soil-release finishes increase the level of absorbency, thereby making it easier to remove soil during laundering.

- **Waterproofing** and **water resistant** finishes. Fabric coated with vinyl can be made impervious to water. Gore-Tex uses an extremely thin layer (0.0005) of a **fluorocarbon,** chemically named polytetrafluoroethylene and trademarked by the DuPont Company as a form of Teflon to create a microporous, waterproof barrier. The treated fabric permits small heat molecules that can be produced by perspiration to escape from the fabric. But because of size, larger water molecules are not able to enter the fabric. In interiors, it provides an effective moisture barrier and is used as an upholstery fabric in health-care facilities, as well as in other commercial and residential settings. Other products containing fluorocarbons include Scotchgard and Zepel. Water-resistant fabric contains more open pores than waterproof material, allowing it to "breath" naturally. The effect water has on fabric depends on the type of yarns used and the degree of fiber compactness. For example, nylons and polyesters are hydrophobic and are less likely to absorb water.

- **Flame-resistant** finishes. Fabrics that burn rapidly when exposed to flame can contribute to death. The Flammable Fabrics Act Amendment of 1967 restricts the use of fabrics that exhibit rapid burning characteristics, although there are no restrictions on fabrics that are less flammable with the following exceptions: children's sleepwear, carpets and rugs, mattresses, and mattress pads. Various wet chemical finishes are applied to fabric to create a thermal barrier, improving their self-extinguishing qualities.

Fibers vary in their degree of flammability. Mineral fibers such as asbestos do not burn but are in limited use. Pro-

tein fibers such as silk and some thermoplastic filaments ignite slowly and remain lit for a short period of time. Other thermoplastic filaments can melt and adhere to skin. Cellulosic fibers burn and leave a residual glow that can cause new flames to ignite, depending on the amount of available oxygen. The ignition temperatures for all yarns except mineral range from 490 degrees Fahrenheit for cotton to 1,060–1,110 degrees Fahrenheit for woolen fibers. Actual burning temperatures fluctuate from 1,290–1,330 degrees Fahrenheit for polyester to 1,760 degrees Fahrenheit for acetate. Technically speaking, a flame- or fire-proof material does not exist. Even steel and concrete will distort or glassify if temperatures are high enough.

The object of flame-resistant fiber is to reduce the possibility of fire spreading, creating a major tragedy (refer to Chapter 2 for fiber and filament burning characteristics). The challenge in flame resistance is to use a chemical in its correct amount or use a process that conforms to the appropriate yarn or fabric. If the chemical dosage is too great, the fabric will exhibit undesirable effects. For example, when saline solutions were more popular and used as a fire suppressant on silk, a filament that is somewhat more flame resistant than other yarns, the salt could be drawn out of the fabric, lie on the surface, and have to be vacuumed off. This was particularly the case in humidity-controlled environments such as museums, where fabric is sometimes used to upholster walls.

- **Antibacterial/antimicrobial and anti-fungus**. Finishes that repel bacteria, microbes, and associated odors can be treated using chemicals such as pentachlorophenol that create a barrier that inhibits the formation and growth of microbes. Cellulosic yarns are particularly susceptible to breeding bacteria.
- **Anti-mildew** finishes. Fabrics used for exterior awnings and furnishings require treatment to restrict the growth of fungi that develops on fabric while curbing the aroma associated with mildew. Anti-mildew finishes such as phenol help to control the growth of mildew microorganisms.
- **Anti-static** finishes. In 1955, the *Davison's Textile Catalogue and Buyers Guide* included an ad encouraging potential buyers to purchase the Simco "Midget," a mechanical device to eliminate static, by stating that "Static is Costly! Static causes spoilage, breakage, and stoppages (of looms); it necessitates runs at reduced speeds; and it initiates fires."[8]

  Static is the result of an accumulation of negative or positive electric charges. The charges can attract or repel fabrics away from each other or machine parts. To reduce static conditions, chemicals are added to a processing stage of yarns or final cycle of wet finishing. When the fabric is dry, the chemicals attract moisture from the air, thereby reducing static electricity buildup. Biocomponent fibers consisting of two polymers that are physically or chemically different and contain carbon are naturally anti-static and

found in lingerie and carpeting. Concerns about static are especially acute in hospitals and laboratories and near computers.
- **Anti-slip** finishes. If fabrics have a relatively low yarn count, warp yarns can slide against the weft yarns, increasing friction and wear. Filament yarns slip more easily than hard-twisted fibers. Slippage can result when there are open spaces between yarns and appear as highly irregular areas on fabric. Chemical resins are usually used to control slippage and applied before weaving takes place.
- **Mothproofing**. Moths, carpet beetles, and other insects ravage hundreds of millions of dollars of fabric a year as they eat their way through wool and wool blends. Although the insects prefer to consume wool, they also cut through other fibers as they segregate the wool from other yarns. Mothproofing finishes can be applied in the fabric manufacturing stage or sprayed on. Mitin and permethrin are two chemicals used during the fabric development stage. Naphthalene mothballs and sprays can be used after fabric is produced; however, because naphthalene compounds can be harmful if ingested, they should be used with care.

Backed Fabric

The term "backed" can mean that an extra warp or weft has been woven into the structure of the cloth to give it added weight and support or that a barrier finish has been applied to extend the fabric's range of use. It is important to work with

KNIT BACKING: Cotton knit bonded to the back of a fabric.

ACRYLIC LATEX BACKING: A polymer material mixed with a by-product of rubber to prevent a fabric from slipping and to enhance its ability to be applied to walls.

WALL UPHOLSTERY BACKING: The use of multiple layers of acrylic latex coatings to prevent strike-through.

STRIKE-THROUGH: The migration of adhesives or liquid that is applied to one surface, moving through to another surface.

MOISTURE BARRIER BACKING: Fabric backing using a vinyl laminate to inhibit the strike-through of moisture.

a company that applies the backing material evenly. Examples of backed finishes include the following:

- **Knit backing** is a cotton knit bonded to the back of the fabric. Knit backing is used to reinforce silks, chenilles, and other fabrics for upholstery and prevent slippage.
- **Acrylic latex backing** prevents directional fabrics from fraying and slipping at the seams. This finish can help stabilize fabric, reduce the transmission of sound, and improve handling characteristics. Acrylic latex backing is not recommended for silks.
- **Wall upholstery backing** consists of multiple layers of acrylic latex coatings applied to the back of fabric to prevent **strike-through** or the flow-through of adhesives or other liquids. The finish can be treated to meet flammability standards while remaining flexible enough to apply.
- **Moisture barrier backing**, a vinyl laminate applied to the back of fabric, is often used to protect upholstery from spills. This type of backing is used in institutional and health-care settings to reinforce fabric while extending its life.

SUMMARY

The serendipitous methods by which early civilizations went about collecting and using some of the first colorants, such as ocher, contrast sharply with the methods employed by chemistry and technology used today. Nonetheless, the goal has remained similar: to fill the world with a color palette that is as diverse as nature itself and, possibly, to challenge the natural world with colors that have yet to be seen.

The art and science of the master dyer focuses first on fiber, then on color. Dyeing is a complex field where intervening variables, such as water quality, must be controlled in order to reach a desired and consistent effect.

Environmental concerns call attention to the proper disposal of wastewater containing toxic dye substances that can cause numerous health problems, such as asthma and upper respiratory conditions, by enforcing OSHA (Occupational Safety and Health Administration) and EPA regulations and standards.

Printed fabrics have a history that stretches back through the centuries. From monks printing fabric on the banks of the Rhine river in the eleventh century to the modern techniques of screen, roller, and jet printing, the act of applying color onto fabric enhances the fabric's appeal.

Numerous commercial techniques are used to apply dyes and pigments to yarns and fabric, and new chemical compound colorants are constantly being developed. When the appropriate dye is applied to a fabric, the color and pattern will last. When fabric is prepared before it is dyed, its ability to accept and retain color is increased.

Finishes help preserve dyes on fabric. Finishes can also change the structure of yarns, produce a soft or coarse hand, and add reflective qualities that respond to light. The various finishes can impart color topically or saturate individual yarns, and finishes can be categorized as aesthetic and functional.

Fabric finishes enhance a fabric's ability to resist flame, bacteria, and shrinkage. As new fibers and colorants are being created, new finishes are being devised to address consumer demand for fibers and fabrics that address new needs.

ACTIVITIES

1. After viewing the portion of the Mill Tour segment of the DVD on dyeing, explain spoon dyeing. What other dyeing methods are used today?
2. Test a fabric swatch to determine whether it crocks.
3. Discover what makes dyes toxic. Do all dyes produce toxins?
4. Examine a fabric swatch that has been printed and determine what defines it as a print.
5. Visit a health-care facility and report on the fabrics and the placement and use of colors.
6. Research what specifically makes a fabric antibacterial.
7. Visit a fabric store and request to examine a fabric with backing. Ask about the different kinds of backed fabrics available at the store and the applications for which they are specified.
8. Expose one colored fabric to different light conditions (for example, daylight and fluorescent light), and note any changes in color.

9. Explain how the Munsell and Pantone systems are organized and how they can be used.

EXPAND YOUR KNOWLEDGE

1. How and why is color perceived? Why must the selection of fabric take light into consideration?
2. Give examples of "warm" and "cool" colors. Where are they best used?
3. Are all fabrics finished, or are some available for use in the greige state? Under what circumstances could greige goods be used in interiors?
4. Is skein dyeing better than piece dyeing? Explain.
5. What is the role of the converter?
6. What steps must be taken to assure fabric will dye successfully? What does it mean for yarns or fabric to be properly dyed?
7. Why are both pigments *and* dyes used as colorants? Why not one or the other?
8. Why must designers be concerned about dye lots?
9. When is piece dyeing performed?
10. What role is nanotechnology research playing in the future of coloring yarns?
11. How are screens that are used in screen printing made?
12. If yarns of varying compositions are used in the construction of a fabric, what steps are taken to assure that color will be absorbed to achieve the same hue?
13. Are there permanent finishes?
14. What does mercerizing do to cotton?

15. Are there any flameproof fibers or filaments used today?
16. What are the EPA and OSHA doing to effect change in yarn processing?
17. What makes solution-dyed yarns more attractive for interior use?
18. How do modern mills dye, print, and finish fabric using the latest technology? Compare and contrast the process with the mill featured in the DVD.
19. What makes the ikat process difficult? How are ikat patterns made?

READ ON
Dyeing and Color

American Association of Textile Chemists and Colorists, *Journal of Textile Chemist and Colorant*, Research Triangle Park, North Carolina.

Encyclopedia of Textiles, by the editors of *American Fabrics Magazine*, Englewood Cliffs, N.J.: Prentice Hall, 1960.

Ralph Evans, *The Perception of Color*, New York: John Wiley, 1974.

Edith Anderson Feisner, *Color Studies*, 2nd ed., New York: Fairchild Books, 2006.

Frans Gerritsen, *Theory and Practice of Color*, New York: Van Nostrand Rinehold, 1975.

Katherine Fitz Gibbon and Andrew Hale, *Ikat: Silks of Central Asia, The Guido Goldman Collection*, London: Lawrence King Publishing, 1997.

John Gillow, *Traditional Indonesian Textiles*, London: Thames and Hudson, 1992.

R.L. Gregory, *Eye and Brain: The Psychology of Seeing*, 3rd ed., New York: McGraw-Hill, 1978.

S.V. Kalkarni et al., *Textile Dyeing Operations*, Park Ridge, N.J.: Noyes Publishing, 1986.

Jim Long and Joy Turner Luke, *The New Munsell® Student Color Set*, 2nd ed., New York: Fairchild, 2001.

David L. MacAdam, ed., *Sources of Color Science*, Cambridge, Mass.: MIT Press, 1971.

Frank H. Mahnke, *Color, Environment, and Human Response*, New York: John Wiley & Sons, 1996.

Jain Malkin, *Hospital Interior Architecture*, New York: John Wiley & Sons, 1992.

Elin Noble, *Dyes and Paints: A Hands-on Guide to Coloring Fabric*, Woodinville, Wash.: Martingale and Company, 1969.

William Partridge, *A Practical Treatise on Dyeing*, Edington, Wiltshire, England: 1973.

Ethel Rompilla, *Color for Interior Design*, New York: Harry N. Abrams, 2005.

John Shore, ed., *Colorants*, vol. 1, from The Society of Dyers and Colourists Publication, England, 1990.

http://www.fabriclink.com/University.html.

Printing

W. Clark, *An Introduction to Textile Printing*, 4th ed., New York: Halsted Press, 1974.

Jennifer Harris, ed., *Textiles: 5000 Years*, New York: Harry N. Abrams, 1993.

M. Humphries, *Fabric Printing*, Upper Saddle River, New Jersey: Prentice Hall, Inc. 1996.

R.W. James, *Printing and Dyeing of Fabrics and Plastics*, Park Ridge, N.J.: Noyes Publishing, 1974.

Lotti Lauterburg, *Fabric Printing*, New York: Rinehold Publishing Corporation, 1963.

H.L. Needles, *Textile Fibers, Dyes, Finishes, and Processes: A Concise Guide*, Park Ridge, N.J.: Noyes Publishing, 1986.

http://about.com/ For printing and dyeing processes.

Finishing

Duro Industries, http://www.duroindustries.com/

E.W. Flick, *Textile Finishing Chemicals: An Industrial Guide*, Park Ridge, N.J.: Noyes Publishing, 1990.

G. Jacobi and A. Lahr, *Detergents and Textile Washing*, New York: VCH Publications, 1987.

Schneider-Banks, Inc. at: http://www.sbifinishing.com//.

Philip E. Slade, *Handbook of Fiber Finishing Technology*, New York: Marcel Dekker, 1997.

Floor Covering: Rugs and Carpeting

DEFINING RUGS AND CARPETS

Rugs and carpets are practical, and they can be aesthetically pleasing while serving as an important foundation for designing interiors. The terms "rugs" and "carpeting" are used interchangeably or separately. When the terms are used separately, the primary difference relates to area of coverage and method of installation. **Rugs** usually cover an area of floor (or wall) and reveal floor surface around the perimeter, hence the name "area rugs." Because they are not usually attached to the floor, rugs can be moved to reorient furnishings or reversed to enhance wearability.

Carpeting is usually sold by the yard or linear foot and installed in large areas, such as hotel lobbies, or rooms in residential or commercial settings where a wall-to-wall (or *moquette*, as it was known in the nineteenth century) application would be practical. Nails and adhesives are used to attach carpet to the floor material. **Broadloom** carpet is manufactured on broad or wide looms capable of produc-

ing widths greater than 6 feet. Broadloom carpet is usually 12 feet wide but can reach 30 feet in width. **Carpet tiles** are pile floor coverings configured in predetermined shapes, usually square, and can vary in size from 12 to 36 inches but are usually 24 inches by 24 inches.

FIRST SOFT FLOOR COVERINGS

The remains of the earliest floor coverings may not exist, but the importance of floor coverings through the ages is well documented. It is difficult to trace an exact chronology for rugs because of their perishable nature; nonetheless, the use of rugs dates to before 6000 B.C.E., when pastoral nomadic tent dwellers used woven flax or hemp to soften and warm dirt floors and provide decoration.

Evidence suggests that around 6000 B.C.E., herders and nomadic hunters near the Caspian Sea used sheep, goat, and other animal fibers in spun and woven mats. Unearthed burial mounds in southern

RUGS: Area floor coverings made of any fiber, animal skin, or fur, typically without pile. Sometimes rugs are used interchangeably with carpet.

CARPETING: A tufted floor covering, usually made from natural or manufactured fibers that often cover the full width and length of an interior room. Sometimes referred to as a rug.

BROADLOOM: A carpet of various weaves, woven on a loom 12 feet wide or more.

CARPET TILES: Modular pile carpeting in various shapes, usually square, installed in rows.

Opposite: Turin Palace Hotel, Turin, Italy.

Siberia dating about 2400 B.C.E. produced animal furs, felt, leathers, and woven materials that were used as wall hangings and probably floor coverings as well. Perhaps the first "pile" rug was an animal hide.

Turkish and Persian motifs were depicted on hieroglyphic drawings and subsequently seen in Egypt in the Great Pyramids of the Giza plateau near Cairo. It appears that these early Egyptian communications spread to the Middle East, then to Mongolia and China, leading some investigators to designate Central Asia and Turkestan ("land of the Turks") as the birthplace of rugs. The discovery of once-lost manuscripts in the early 1900s by Sir Aurel Stein in Turkistan supported this belief. The independent nation of Turkmenistan has made the rug an important part of its culture. In fact, the national flag of Turkmenistan features a wide, red stripe on the left side depicting five rug *guls* (designs).

Handmade rugs are composed of a series of knots, whereas **tapestries** are basically heavily woven fabric. It could be surmised, after examining the historical progression of tapestries, that the mythical "flying carpet" piloted by Solomon was probably neither a carpet nor a rug, but rather a predominately green silk "flying tapestry."

The oldest surviving hand-knotted pile rug, excavated in 1949 from a Scythian tomb in the Pazyryk valley in Siberia, was radiocarbon dated to the fifth century B.C.E. The carpet embodies a high degree of development, and most experts believe that it indicates at least 1,000 years of *previous* experience in carpet weaving.

Patterns in the rug depict stylized lotus buds and fallow deer. The carpet is exhibited in the State Hermitage Museum in St. Petersburg, Russia.

Many of the first rugs were embedded with symbolic messages. Their designs communicated their religious, tribal, or philosophical beliefs. The rugs were colored using vegetable dyes, and the chroma varied along with the chemicals in the water and the color of found dyestuffs as the nomadic people moved from place to place. A red in one area may appear bright pink in another area. Some modern textile designers have attempted to replicate these variances in dye color to create the look of early hand-knotted nomadic rugs. An analysis of dyes can be helpful in dating rugs.

RUGS

A comparison of traditional hand-knotted **Oriental rugs** with machine-made rugs that have Oriental designs helps to clarify an important category of decorative floor covering. Designers who understand the similarities and differences can select rugs that suit their clients' tastes and budgets.

The Geography of Oriental Rugs

Present-day interiors rely on rugs to provide design value, color, comfort, and sound absorption for residential and commercial spaces. One of the more popular—and sometimes confusing—categories of rugs is Oriental.

The highly regarded, true Oriental rugs are handmade from wool (usually sheep, goat, or camel), silk, cotton, linen, hemp, or jute. The most widely used ma-

TAPESTRIES: Heavy, hand-woven fabrics with decorative designs usually depicting historical scenes.

ORIENTAL RUGS: Handmade floor coverings typically from the Middle East, Turkey, China, or Russia. The value of the rug is related, in part, to the number of knots per inch.

terial is wool, because of its strength, versatility, availability, and retention of warmth. Woolen, handmade pile rugs lack the synthetic polymers, synthetic blends, and nylon found in the nap of other types of rugs. True Oriental rugs originate from Afghanistan, China, India, Iran, Nepal, Pakistan, Tibet, Turkey, and some southern territories of the former Soviet Union, such as Azerbaijan and Armenia. Other sources include Romania, Albania, and a few North African countries, such as Morocco and Egypt.

Variety among Indigenous Rugs

The handwoven rugs produced by Native Americans are classified as *Navajo* rugs or *American Indian* rugs. The original Navajos, the *T'aa dine* living six or seven centuries ago, were adept at using domestic cotton grown in colors and grasses to weave rugs, belts, and garments. The rugs have reflected Navajo social and economic history for centuries, and they hold evidence of the blending of cultures. For example, the Spanish introduced the Navajos to wool.

Rya rugs, similar in construction to Persian rugs but with the knots farther apart, were used as bed coverings in Scandinavian castles. In Finland during the fourteenth century, rayas were commissioned for the bride and groom to kneel upon during the wedding ceremony. Today, shag-like rayas are used as tapestries, wall coverings, and bed throws. They are created with organic dyes and materials such as linen, cotton, wool, and dog hair.

Flokati rugs are Greek in origin and used by shepherds as clothing and beds. The rugs are a creation of nomadic Vlachs, who lived high in the Pindos Mountains during the sixth century C.E., as they do today. Flokati rugs are made of wool.

The history and culture of a particular group of people is often woven into their rugs and garments. And the environment reflects color choices and designs that become associated with materials used to produce the functional art.

Design and Structure

Most weavers of Oriental rugs work on a fixed vertical loom (as seen in Figure 5.1, the components of which are seen in Figure 5.2); however, some semi-nomadic weavers in the vicinity of Afghanistan, Turkey, and Iran continue to use a more portable, horizontal ground loom. A frequently repeated Oriental pattern is the medallion design, as noted in Figure 5.3. And a finished Kerman rug featuring the medallion design appears in Figure 5.4. These handmade rugs are produced by weaving intricate structures, as seen in

Figure 5.1 Fixed Oriental loom for weaving hand-loomed rugs.

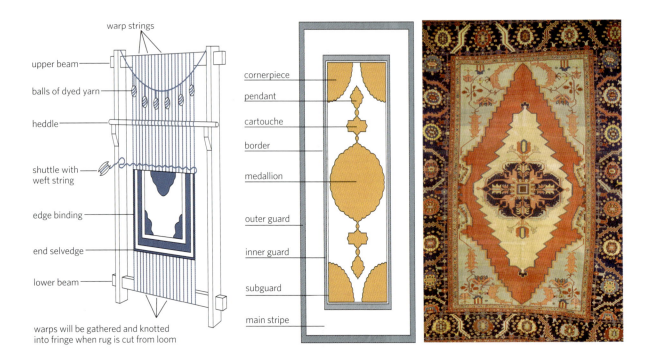

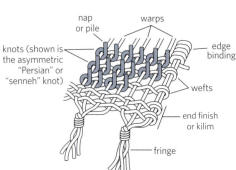

Figure 5.2 (above left)
Fixed vertical loom.

Figure 5.3 (above middle)
Medallion design on an
Oriental rug.

Figure 5.4 (above right)
Medallion design on a
Kerman rug.

Figure 5.5 (right)
Woven rug structures.

Figure 5.5. The medallion pattern appears in some of the oldest Turkish rugs. Other common overall design themes include pictorial, floral, arabesque, garden, tree compositions, and vase designs.

Differentiating between authentic Oriental rugs and rugs that resemble Orientals by borrowing design themes and yarn content from the originals can be difficult, confusing designers and clients alike. The difficulty is further compounded when

countries such as Turkey, Egypt, Romania, Albania, and Bulgaria that produce Oriental rugs in the handmade tradition also manufacture large quantities of machine-made rugs, particulary within the last 50 years. The differences between the two can be discerned using a combination of methods.

A visual examination can provide clues. Typically, the machine-made rug back appears faded and lacks clarity of design. This faded appearance is the result of overstitching across the entire back of the rug that holds the pile in place. Also, if a rug has a trademarked name on its label, it is probably not a true Oriental. Typically, handmade Oriental rugs are named for the town or village in the country where they are loomed, such as Kerman, Sarouk, Bergama, Ningxia, or Shiraz.

Another method of authenticating an Oriental rug is by examining its construction. In contrast to the overstitched pattern across the entire back of a machine-made rug, the knots in a handmade rug are visible and can be classified as Persian or Turkish, as seen in Figure 5.6. Machine-made rugs do not incorporate knots, although **hand-tufted** rugs from China and India can simulate the appearance of hand-tied knots. Likewise, the fringe on a machine-made rug has been added to the body of the carpet, whereas the fringe on a hand-made rug consists of actual warp ends that are part of the rug's construction.

Cost can be another determining factor. Some Kashan rugs contain as many as 40,000 to 50,000 knots per square foot! The finer the knots, the longer the rug takes to make—and the more the rug will cost. A skilled weaver in India can tie about 6,000 knots a day, and usually more than one person works on a rug at the same time.

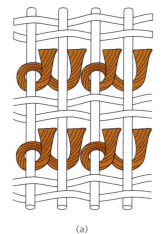

(a)

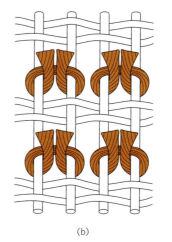

(b)

Persian Jufti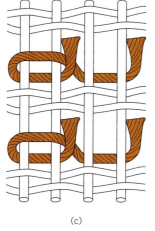

(c)

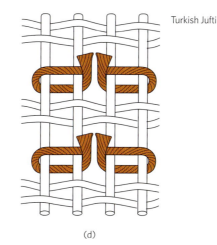

Turkish Jufti

(d)

Figure 5.6 Knots on handmade Oriental rugs may be Persian (a), which are asymmetrical, opening to the left or right, or Turkish (b), which are symmetrical. Jufti knots tie around four warps and may be either Persian (c) or Turkish (d). Jufti or "false" knots can be either Persian or Turkish style. Jufti knots are tied around *four* warps instead of the normal two. A rug made with jufti knots uses half the material and takes only half as much time to make but probably lasts half as long. It is common with some rug types such as BOKHARAS to find areas of jufti knots interspersed with regular Persian knots.

For many years, children have been used to make rugs. One reason for this, it is said, is that their small hands are better suited for manipulating fine threads such as silk and able to work intricate hand looms more efficiently. Nevertheless, most countries see child labor as a sad commentary. Initiated as a German consumer awareness movement in 1990 and eventually formalized in 1994, the nonprofit Rugmark Foundation serves to end illegal child labor and offers educational opportunities to children in India, Nepal, and Pakistan. If a rug has the Rugmark label, no children were employed in its manufacture and a portion of its purchase price will be contributed to former child weavers.

Rugs that are produced on traditional power looms rather than hand knotted can be well made and produced to withstand considerable use. They can provide a colorful addition to the overall appearance of an interior. Manufacturers of machine-made rugs using traditional Oriental motifs have sophisticated their operations in recent years, making a casual evaluation sometimes difficult. Fundamentally, machine-made Oriental designed rugs are produced from wool, cotton, or synthetics such as nylon or polypropylene (olefin) and are used decoratively in rooms or as entry mats or runners or to aid in softening floors. Modern machine-made rugs can last about 20 years, depending on use. And because of relatively new manufacturing techniques, such as heat-set polypropylene, the rugs can have a wool-like finish, translate colors clearly, resist fading, and exhibit a low rate of moisture absorption. Manufactured rugs are produced in a relatively short period of time and can be made to reflect fashionable colors of the country where they are sold, thereby changing from collection to collection. Knowing the difference between handmade and machine-made rugs becomes useful, particularly if clients ask why they should pay $12,500 for an 8 foot by 10 foot rug when they saw an "Oriental that looks just like it" for $995. Designers should be prepared to respond.

CARPETING

Carpets are made from various materials, cover floors of all compositions, and can be found in residences and commercial spaces such as offices, schools, health-care facilities, theatres, trains, airplanes, and boats, as well as on indoor/outdoor athletic fields.

The Carpet Business

Machine-made carpets occupy a sizeable portion of the residential and commercial floor covering market. According to the Carpet and Rug Institute, 1.969 billion square yards (17.721 billion square feet), valuing $12.091 billion at the mill level, was produced in 2003. The United States provides 45 percent of the world's carpet, with 80 percent being produced within a 65-mile radius of Dalton, Georgia. Carpet fiber consumption is approximately 3.5 billion pounds a year; large manufacturers use more than two million pounds a day!

Carpet and the Environment

Issues related to the health of individuals and the air quality of indoor environments have received considerable attention. The **green movement** has been, in part, an advocate of ecology, conservation, and the environment aimed at a sustainable world. The following **LEED** (Leadership in Energy and Environmental Design) protocols have been established: LEED-NC (new construction), LEED-EB (existing buildings), and LEED-CI (commercial interiors). Standards are being tested to formulate a LEED rating for new home construction. Environmental initiatives serve to alert the general public to the need for preserving the planet for future generations through conservation and the use of renewable resources.

Regarding LEED-CI, the category most related to carpeting, certain criteria address how carpeting is disposed of, reused, and recycled. Other criteria deal with construction using low-emitting products in the manufacturing process, as well as the distance traveled from the point of manufacture to installation. The carpeting component in LEED-CI is given a numerical rating that contributes to the overall score, qualifying an interior for certification. A minimum of 21 points is necessary for a LEED-CI certification. (See Chapter 6 for additional information on the environment and safety.)

Usefulness of Carpet

The production and use of carpeting have been a positive development in an otherwise diminished American fabric manufacturing story. Carpet can be listed along with other building materials in new construction, allowing it to be included in the bidding and funding process. Carpet can also be used to refurbish the floor surfaces of older buildings with minimal subfloor preparation. Carpet is also installed for the following reasons:

- Reducing airborne and floor impact sounds. Carpeting can be incorporated into wall assemblies, further reducing sound from adjacent rooms in conference centers where presentations are made simultaneously. Cut pile tends to be more effective in absorbing sound than loop pile. Higher and heavier pile also has a positive effect on sound reduction.

  The levels of acoustical transmission of sound are measured in three ways. The first is reported as an **Impact Noise Rating (INR)**, where a higher value is equated to less sound being transmitted. An INR rating of 0 or below 0 and noted as a negative number is unsatisfactory. The second method is to determine the degree of sound absorption: the **Noise Reduction Coefficient (NRC)**. The third method measures the degree of sound transparency (i.e., the amount of sound passing through walls, floors, and other barriers). It is denoted numerically as a **Sound Transmission Class (STC)**.

- Adding a decorative component to rooms and uniting other design elements, such as furnishings, or providing an atmosphere in commercial spaces to lessen the effect of a stereotypical institutional "feel."

- Adding room comfort by helping to stabilize building temperatures. This is attributed to the insulating properties of carpeting and is particularly helpful during non-use times.

GREEN MOVEMENT: A broad movement that includes concern for ecology, conservation, and the preservation of the environment.

LEADERSHIP IN ENERGY AND ENVIRONMENTAL DESIGN (LEED): An organization that has developed a rating system to identify sustainable buildings and to promote integrated, "whole building" design while raising consumer awareness about sustainable building practices.

IMPACT NOISE RATING (INR): Numerical value used to express the ability of floor covering to minimize sound.

NOISE REDUCTION COEFFICIENT (NRC): Numerical value used to express how well wall fabric and carpeting absorb sound.

SOUND TRANSMISSION CLASS (STC): Numerical value measuring the amount of sound that passes through walls.

- Eliminating the anti-reflective, hard floor surfaces in schools, where children work and play, while reducing injuries from falling.
- Reducing "floor fatigue" for individuals who spend their workday standing.

Information about carpet installation and maintenance is highlighted in Chapters 6 and 11.

MANUFACTURING METHODS

Carpet is manufactured through various methods, creating different textures to meet different needs. Understanding where a carpet will be installed helps to determine the choice of yarn content. Questions about the room's usage, including the amount of foot traffic, are important to consider. Will the carpet be used in corridors in a public building? What amount of entertaining will be done in the space? Is the room adjacent to outdoor areas? Will the carpet be exposed to constant, unfiltered daylight?

Content of Carpeting

Most carpeting is constructed to withstand considerable wear; therefore, more than 95 percent of all carpet products are constructed with synthetic fibers and filaments. The most commonly chosen include the following:

- *Nylon* Nylon is the most popular and constitutes approximately 57 percent of pile used in the United States. Nylon is resilient and resists stains. When solution-dyed, nylon is colorfast because the color is in the fibers as part of the extrusion process.
- *Olefin (polypropylene)* Olefin has many of the same properties as nylon. Additionally, olefin resists static electricity and is often used in indoor as well as outdoor settings due to its resistance to moisture, mildew, fading, and cleaning chemicals. Olefin can be used in synthetic turf for outdoor sports fields. About 36 percent of carpeting includes olefin.
- *Polyester* Generally, polyester is softer than nylon and is resistant to water-soluble stains.
- *Acrylic* Acrylic provides some of the characteristics of wool for less cost and is often used in bath mats and scatter rugs in addition to general carpeting.
- *Blends* Blends such as wool and nylon combine appearance and durability. Other blends, such as acrylic and olefin or nylon and olefin, capitalize on the individual fiber strengths.

Pile height can be a concern as well. For example, if the carpet pile is high, it should not be used in a facility for the elderly; it may be problematic, even dangerous, for the residents to move wheelchairs and walkers over the carpet. Walking can be difficult too, especially if rubber-soled shoes are worn. Carpeting in such places should be constructed in a tight weave and depress ½-inch or less. A cushion or underlayment should be used to inhibit wear on the face and back of the carpet, and scatter rugs in such places should be avoided, as well as large colorful patterns that could be distracting.

Cost is another consideration that relates to the composition of carpeting. Cost is affected by fiber content, construction, quality, design, type of cushioning, and installation. If the carpet is intended to last and remain in a high-traffic area, a higher grade of carpet should be considered. Factors such as moving furniture to accommodate the carpeting may also increase the cost and would be part of the installation expenses.

Carpet Production

In manufacturing, approximately 95 percent of carpeting uses the tufted method that evolved from producing chenille bedspreads. **Tufting** produces pile in a way similar to stiches produced by a sewing machine. Several hundred tufting needles, such as the one shown in Figure 5.7, stitch hundreds of rows of pile tufts through the backings of various compositions. The yarn is caught by loopers and held in place to produce loop pile or is cut by blades for **cut pile**; however, before the tufting procedure begins, an appropriate **backing**, called a *primary backing*, must be selected to allow the **tufting needles** to carry the pile yarns through in order to construct the carpet. Backing is usually woven or nonwoven polypropylene or polyester. A *secondary backing* or *scrim* is laminated to the primary polypropylene backing after the carpet is manufactured to reinforce and increase the carpet's dimensional stability. This backing is composed of the same material as the first backing (Figure 5.8a). Jute can also be used but is not as common as polypropylene and polyester that can withstand changes in temperature and humidity and reduce the chance of infestation. Table 5.1

TUFTING: A process in which yarns are punched through a woven or nonwoven backing material to form rows of tufts.

CUT PILE: Raised carpet loops that are cut during manufacturing by wires or a reciprocating knife blade resulting in tufts.

BACKING: In carpeting, the material that is adhered to the back of the fibers being used to hold the carpet together as it is being constructed. *Primary backing* holds the tufts in place and *secondary backing* enhances the stability of yarns being used.

TUFTING NEEDLES: The hollow needles used to punch through backing to produce tufts.

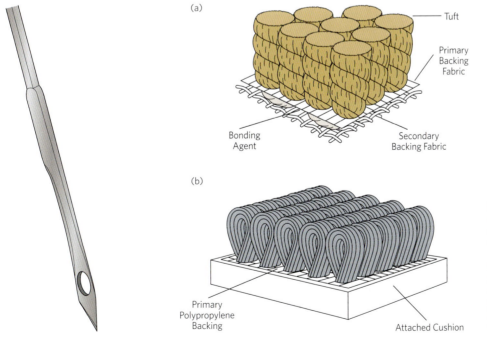

Figure 5.7 (left) Tufting needles like the one shown here stitch rows of pile tufts.

Figure 5.8 (right) Machine-made carpet backings: a system of a primary and secondary backing (a) and a cushion backing (b).

PLUSH CARPET: A smooth, cut pile finish for which individual tufts are only minimally visible and the overall visual effect is level yarn ends. The appearance is produced from brushing and shearing spun yarn singles that are set without heat.

HEAT SETTING: The use of heat in various forms to retain yarn twist.

AUTOCLAVE: A large, steam-pressured container for setting yarns.

SUPERBA®: French manufacturer and name of a continuous heat setting process for yarns using steam and pressure.

SUESSEN®: German manufacturer and name of a continuous dry heat process for setting yarns.

LATEX: A water emulsion of synthetic rubber, natural rubber, or other polymers. Almost all carpet latex consists of styrene-butadine rubber (SBR).

WOVEN OR LOOMED CARPETING: Floor covering made by traditional weaving techniques.

Table 5.1 Carpet Backing Systems

CONSTRUCTION METHOD	TYPICAL BACKING FABRICS AND/OR BACKING COMPONENTS	TYPICAL BACKCOATING CHEMICAL COMPOUNDS
Tufted	**Primary:** • woven polypropylene slit film • nonwoven, polypropylene or polyester **Secondary:** • woven leno weave polypropylene • nonwoven, polypropylene or polyester • woven jute • fiberglass reinforcement	• synthetic SBR latex • polyurethane • polyvinyl acetate • ethylene vinyl acetate • polyvinyl chloride • amorphous resins • thermoplastic polyolefin
Woven	Construction yarns may include: • cotton • jute • polypropylene • polyester • viscose rayon • blends or combinations	• Similar materials to tufted, but usually thinner coatings
Bonded	Fiberglass matting	• Polyvinyl chloride
Needlepunched	(None typically used)	• SBR latex • acrylics • ethylene vinyl acetate • SBR latex foam

Source: The Carpet and Rug Institute (www.carpet-rug.org).

reviews the backing systems for various carpet construction methods.

Yarns in cut pile are heat set, except for **plush carpet** and loop pile constructions. The process of **heat setting** contributes to yarns holding their twist, and consequently their strength, through the carpet manufacturing stage. Heat setting techniques include **autoclave, Superba,** and **Suessen.** Backing is attached with a **latex** bond. An alternative approach attaches cushion backing to add resilience, acoustical insulation, and comfort under foot, as seen in Figure 5.8b.

Woven or loomed carpeting is created on looms that simultaneously weave the face and the back, producing a complete product, as noted in Figure 5.9. Woven

Figure 5.9 The face and back of woven carpeting are loomed simultaneously.

Woven carpet is created on looms that take face and backing yarns and simultaneously weave them into a complete product. A latex back coating is usually applied for stability.

carpets are more expensive but generally are more durable than tufted carpet. Latex is often applied to the back to add stability to the yarns, and frequently a separate cushion is attached as well. Three categories of woven carpeting are velvet, Wilton, and Axminster.

- **Velvet** is inexpensive to produce and is made on a relatively uncomplicated loom without the use of a jacquard mechanism, thereby limiting the number of potential design details. Years ago only cut pile was considered velvet carpeting. Loop-pile carpeting made on the same loom was known as tapestries. Today, both cut-pile and loop pile are constructed on a velvet loom. Velvet carpets appear mostly in solid colors. The carpet is manufactured by wires that raise some of the warp yarns into loops that can vary in height. The loops can be cut or remain looped. There is typically only one row of face yarns between the warp backing yarns. The weight or bulk of a velvet carpet comes from the backing yarns and latex coating.

  One advantage of a velvet woven carpet is its pile density. This is accomplished by selecting a predetermined number of wires used to lift the yarns or by selecting a dense or heavy yarn weight. Velvets usually contain a 162, 189, or 216 **gauge** or pitch and vary from 7 to 10 wires per inch, producing 2 weft **shots** per inch.
- **Wilton** is a type of carpet construction that grew out of the mid-1880s in England. The manufacturing processes also indicate the names of towns in England where the Wilton and Axminster weaving techniques were developed and refined. William Morris, who was a proponent of connecting function and aesthetics, played an important role in the growth of the carpeting industry during this time.

Fundamentally, Wilton carpet weaving uses a jacquard mechanism to select the appropriate pile yarns to appear on the surface. The carpet design is first produced on paper and yarn colors are selected. When the jacquard cards are punched and installed, each card controls a row of tufts, thereby determining which colors will be lifted and appear on the surface of the carpet. The pile yarns that are not lifted remain "buried," warp-wise, adding weight and cushioning to the final product and making the pattern clear to see from the back. Worsted Wilton is a high-quality carpet with short pile and a tightly woven back. Wool Wilton is softer but less resilient due to the tufts being only lightly twisted. Wilton carpeting combines durability with subtlety of texture but is somewhat limited to the number of colors that can appear on the carpet. Brussels carpeting is made through a similar process, with the exception that the pile remains looped and not cut.

- **Axminster** carpet is capable of having a wide range of colors, each wound on separate loom spools. The time to prepare the loom for weaving may take several days, but a $9' \times 12'$ carpet can be woven in a few hours. No warp yarns are buried, and the thick surface pile resembles a hand-knotted rug. One

VELVET: Plain, one-color cut pile produced without a jacquard mechanism.

GAUGE: The distance between two needle points expressed in fractions of an inch: $1/10$ gauge means 10 needle points per inch.

SHOTS: In pile carpeting, the number of weft yarns per row of tufts.

WILTON: A jacquard carpet where pile yarns are raised and lowered by harnesses during weaving. When the pile appears on the carpet face, it traverses the carpet warpwise and becomes embedded in the carpet base. *Worsted Wilton* is a high-grade Wilton carpeting with short pile and a tightly woven back. *Wool Wilton* uses less twist in the yarn creating a higher pile, producing a courser product, and *brussels* carpeting is an uncut Wilton.

AXMINSTER: A jacquard carpet where tufts are formed between the warp ends by special spool-like devices that insert pile between the rows and through the loom mechanism.

FUSION BONDING:
A process where pile yarns are embedded into a vinyl compound.

NEEDLE-PUNCHED:
A type of carpeting in which downward facing barbed needles are used to force yarn through backing material. When the needles are withdrawn, enough yarn is displaced to have the yarn adhere to the base or backing.

Figure 5.10 (bottom left) A bonded tufted carpet tile shown in an installation.

Figure 5.11 (bottom right) This bonded carpet tile is designed for heavily trafficked commercial spaces, such as exhibition halls. An advantage of using carpet tiles is that if an area is worn or damaged individual tiles can be replaced without having to install new carpeting for the entire space.

unique feature of an Axminster is that it can be rolled lengthwise and folded widthwise. Axminster will always be a cut pile with the yarns appearing on one level. This is made possible because the shot of yarn traversing the face and width of the loom is actually a double shot per row. This contributes to the Axminster's dimensional stability. Axminster carpeting is produced primarily offshore in England and other locations, such as China.

Carpet manufacturing methods also include the following:

- **Fusion bonding** involves adhering sheets of pile yarns onto a backing that has been layered with adhesives, then backed with a polymetric material such as polyvinyl chloride (PVC) to provide stability (Figure 5.10). Fusion-bonded carpeting is often cut into carpet tiles and can be produced to

withstand wear in high-traffic areas (Figure 5.11). Modular carpet tiles have increased in use, in part because of their portability—especially when carpet is required in high-rise buildings or used in conjunction with floors punctuated with holes to allow for electronic cabling. The tiles can be installed around furniture with standard, releasable, or peel-off-and-stick adhesives and easily replaced. However, color-matching molecules often occur when replacing worn tiles.

- **Needle-punched** carpeting represents approximately 7 percent of all carpet manufactured. It can be used as indoor/outdoor carpet because its porous construction allows water to pass through the material. Needle-punched or needle-loomed carpeting is a nonwoven, non-pile carpeting produced largely by mechanical means. This inexpensive carpet is made using approximately 500 to 7,500 barbed needles per square

yard, traversing the width of the needle-punched machinery. The needles carry the yarn, which is forced or punched through a base of burlap, rubber, or plastic. Other applications for needle-punched products include filters, boat headliners, tennis courts, basketball courts, and fabric used in the construction of Kevlar bulletproof vests.

- **Knitted or chenille carpeting** occupies a small portion of the overall carpet market because the product lacks stability. Knitted carpet is commonly marketed as "Woven Interloc" and is installed using a direct-glue system. Knitted carpeting is produced by interlocking the backing and the pile yarns in one process. Spaces between the rows of the face yarns in the width, but not in the length, result in a product that does not unravel or come apart easily. Nevertheless, the carpet must be inspected carefully for any unusually wide spaces between the yarns. Minor imperfections can be repaired by hand using an electronic tufting gun. Custom knitted designs can also be made using the gun.
- **Flocked carpeting** is produced by electrostatically spraying manufactured fibers, or sometimes cotton and wool, onto an adhesive-coated backing. The carpet texture is velvety and resembles velour. The product is resilient and resists crushing. A secondary backing is often used to enhance the body of the carpet and to give it dimensional stability. Flocked carpeting is usually found in applications related to transportation, such as floor, seat, or sidewall coverings for airplanes, boats, and buses.

Carpet Textures and Patterns

As technology advances, so do the options. The look and feel of carpeting are enhanced, and at the same time the visible signs of soil can be reduced by varying yarn thickness, amount of twist, and pile density, and alternating the height of pile yarns. How carpet wears affects its appearance. And carpet durability depends largely on yarn length. **Bulked Continuous Filament (BCF)** wears as well as spun staple fibers. When carpet is manufactured with staple fibers, some surface shedding will appear after the installation, but it can be vacuumed away and does not reflect a flawed product or a surface that will wear poorly. Nylon and polyester can be used in either fiber or filament form. Olefin is usually BCF.

Many carpet companies now offer the option for a designer to create a carpet with custom colors, patterns, and designs using in-store CAD technology to address the specific requirements of a client. The designer should exercise caution, however, to ensure a true color match using **carpet poms** and other samples of dyed yarns that will be used to manufacture the custom carpet or rug.

Cut pile surfaces can be produced to offer different appearances, such as the following:

- **Velvet** A smooth, level-surfaced appearance achieved by applying a slight twist to the yarns. The effect is soft and plush. Velvet is a woven process as well as a descriptor for carpeting's appearance.
- **Saxony** A tighter twist to the yarns than velvet, creating a less formal

KNITTED OR CHENILLE CARPETING: A method of interlocking loops, connecting pile, backing and stitching yarns in one process.

FLOCKED CARPETING: Carpeting that is produced by electrostatically spraying fibers onto an adhesive-coated backing.

BULKED CONTINUOUS FILAMENT (BCF): Textured filament yarns that are kinked and curled by not allowing them to parallel each other during manufacturing, thereby causing them to increase loft.

CARPET POMS: Sample tufts in a wide range of colors used in custom designing custom carpet.

SAXONY: A soft, durable cut pile carpet with long pile, $1/4$ of an inch to over $1/2$ inch in length with more tip definition in the yarn ends than plush.

appearance while minimizing the track of footprints. The level yarns in a saxony vary from ¼ inch to more than ½ inch in length.

- **Friezé** Tightly twisted yarns that curl into each other in a random way, creating a textured and uneven surface. This informal appearance reduces footprints and marks left by vacuuming that would be visible in velvet pile.

By altering pile loops, different effects can be achieved.

- Tight, level loops produce a **berber** wool style that provides long-lasting carpet for high traffic areas.
- Multilevel loops that appear in two or three different levels create a slight patterned effect that can be used in a less formal setting.
- A combination of cut and loop provides a smooth surface for adding cut designs, such as sculpted squares, chevrons, and swirls.

CARPET QUALITY AND FLOOR PREPARATION

Before installation, it is useful to determine whether the carpet manufacturer includes information regarding how the carpeting should be installed and note the recommended cushion type and weight. In general, the installation of carpeting can be enhanced by following guidelines found in the Standard for Installation of Commercial Carpet, prepared by the Carpet and Rug Institute.

Performance Ratings

Selecting the appropriate carpet and preparing the floor surface prior to installation helps ensure a wearable surface. For residential settings, carpet is **Performance Rated (PR)** or carries a **Performance Appearance Rating (PAR)** number. The PR scale ranges from 1 to 5 and measures the degree to which a carpet changes appearance with use. A 5 indicates essentially no change during the first year of wear, and a 1 implies considerable change. Other scales use a 1 to 10 system where lower numbers provide wear values for areas associated with light traffic patterns and higher numbers, heavier patterns. However, not all carpet manufacturers mark their carpets with performance ratings.

Appearance retention, as measured by various scales, relates to pile density. And pile density relates to size of yarns and pile height. A wider, thicker yarn can be tufted at a wider gauge and be as dense as a fine yarn produced in a fine gauge. For areas where heavy foot traffic is the norm, dense carpet can be defined as 5,000 to 7,000 stitches per inch across the width of the carpet.

For commercial applications a carpet class system has been devised where Class I carpeting is intended for light use (private offices), Class II for medium use (classrooms and libraries), and Class III for heavy use (lobbies, airports, and healthcare facilities).

Carpet Installation

Designers are highly unlikely to install carpeting but may approve or recommend a carpet installer or provide oversight management of work in progress.

A properly installed carpet can eliminate future difficulties related to replacement or repair, disruption of business activities, loss of work hours, and the general inconvenience of having to deal with a floor covering that is not performing.

Before installation, the designer should confirm that the product that was originally specified is, in fact, the product that arrived at or near the site. Lighting conditions should be confirmed well before the order, so that issues relating to fading can be taken into consideration. It is not uncommon for carpeting to appear well before the installer or before the site is ready to accept the carpet. If the carpet is not examined early on to confirm the correct yarn composition, pattern, color, texture, and yardage, an incorrect order may go undetected for weeks, creating complications on the day when the shipping material is removed from the bolt at the job site and personnel are ready to begin the installation process. (See Chapter 7 for a schedule for carpet installation at a commercial site.)

Preparation of the Substrate

Carpeting can be installed successfully over a wide variety of substrates or subfloors, but each surface requires evaluation and preparation before the process begins. The general environment where the carpeting is to be installed needs to be considered. For example, the preferred room temperature should range from 65 to 95 degrees. Ideally, the relative humidity should be between 10 percent and 65 percent. The floor should be examined to determine if any cracks (over ⅛ inch) or protrusions (more than ¹⁄₃₂ inch) exist. Slight eruptions in flooring material will become magnified when cushioning and carpeting are installed.

If removers are to be used to facilitate the removal of floor residue and to "clean" the floor, all chemical traces of remover must be eliminated. If the floor is not clean, there is a chance that a chemical reaction will occur between the remover and the carpet adhesive, resulting in the adhesive not performing properly. Floor primers are not necessary, unless the floor surface is composed of an acoustical material or is freshly sanded or porous.

If floor surface moisture is an ongoing problem, primers will not serve as a moisture barrier and stop the influx of water. Moisture will continue to migrate, and it should be traced to its source and stopped. If used at all, primers should have a thin consistency, dry quickly, and be compatible with the adhesive being used.

When carpeting is installed over wood, the flooring areas should be structurally sound and well ventilated. Subflooring of plywood, hardwood, particle board, or other surfaces ought to be well constructed and properly installed. The subfloor should be free of contaminants such as dirt, grease, oil, or wax so the adhesives can perform well. When painted wooden floors are to be carpeted, a trial installation can be tested by covering a few feet of the surface with adhesive and carpeting and waiting approximately 72 hours to determine whether the bond is strong. If the paint does not pull up with the carpet, it will be safe to continue the carpeting installation.

Concrete surfaces need to be cured, clean, dry, and free of contaminants that may interfere with the bonding agent. Any cracks or depressions can be filled

COMPRESSIBILITY:
The degree of bulk reduction by pressing down on pile. A carpet's ability to recover its original thickness is referred to as resilience.

with a compatible latex or polymer patching compound. If powdery or porous surfaces exist, a suitable primer can be used to form a barrier between the concrete surface and the carpeting.

It is advisable not to install carpet over existing carpet or glue carpet directly to vinyl, vinyl tile, or rubber. A chemical reaction can occur between the vinyl and the adhesive, resulting in the carpeting separating from the floor surface.

If carpeting is to be installed over radiant-heated (hydronic) floors, the heat should be lowered to prevent the carpet adhesive from drying or "setting" too quickly. Also, carpeting installed over heated floors can create a reaction that may affect respiratory health. If carpet tacks or nails are used, the installer must not puncture flexible heating tubes or pipes. Carpet over heated floors should be no thicker than ⅜ inch. Cushions designed especially for this kind of installation should be considered.

It is highly desirable to place between the floor and carpet a cushion, also referred to as an underlay or pad. Benefits derived from cushioning include extending the wear of the carpet, reducing the transmission of sound, adding warmth, reducing the carpet's tendency to "crawl" or move, enhancing the ability to clean the carpet, leveling uneven floors, and improving comfort underfoot. However, improper selection of carpeting can accelerate the wear of the carpet fibers and negatively affect surface appearance. Other side effects of using the wrong cushion include wrinkling and possibly buckling of the carpet, premature seam separation, and an uncomfortable and tiring surface for walk-

ing and standing. The wrong cushion may also invalidate the carpet's warranty.

Most carpet cushioning is produced from polyurethane foam, various felted fibers, or rubber, all with varying degrees of **compressibility**. In some instances, foam or rubber cushioning is applied to the back of carpeting as part of the manufacturing process and, therefore, does not require additional cushioning. The appropriate thickness and density of the cushioning depends upon the amount of foot traffic and traffic patterns. Areas of light or moderate use such as bedrooms can use thicker and/or softer cushions. Living rooms, halls, and stairs in homes or businesses should use a firm, thin cushion. More specifically, residential cut pile, cut loop, and high-level loop carpeting require a resilient, firm cushion with a thickness of approximately ⁷⁄₁₆ inch or less. The material used for this cushioning is usually derived from polyurethane foams, including bonded foam, fiber (i.e., felt or needle-punched material), or rubber.

Berber carpet (carpet with small, tight loops) or cut pile is best cushioned with a low-flexing, stable material with cushion thickness not exceeding ⅜ inch. Because tightly looped carpeting is popular for both residential and commercial installations, the cushioning compositions listed in Table 5.2 are suggested.

Before installation, it is useful to determine whether the carpeting manufacturer includes information about how the carpeting should be installed and note the recommended cushion type and weight. In general, the installation of carpeting can be enhanced by following guidelines found in the Standard for Installation

Table 5.2 Cushioning Compositions

MATERIAL	WEIGHT AND COVERAGE
Rubberized jute	40 ounces per square yard
Felted synthetic fiber	22–28 ounces per square yard
Bonded or **rebonded polyurethane**	8 pounds per cubic foot
Prime polyurethane	2.7 pounds per cubic foot

Specification of Commercial Carpet, prepared by the Carpet and Rug Institute.

Care After Installation

After installation, it may be necessary to trim the bottom of doors if the carpet pile does not allow for clearance. Carpeting ought to be vacuumed initially to pick up excess fibers and vacuumed frequently to avoid soil grinding and cutting the carpet structure. Over time, additional changes may appear to the surface of the carpet. Some of these include:

- **Sprouting** The discovery of individual tufts extending beyond the carpet's surface. Sprouts should be cut to pile height rather than pulled.
- **Pile Shading** A color change appearing in various areas of plush carpeting caused by light that is reflected as the fibers bend. This is not a defect, but a characteristic of plush carpeting.
- **Shedding** Balls of loose surface fibers can appear and are removed with a vacuum.
- **Indentations** Places where furniture legs depress the carpet pile. Pile depressions can be raised by dampening the area and working the fibers upward, then drying them, possibly with a hair dryer.
- **Fading and Yellowing** A slight reduction or change in color can be the result of airborne residue from heating fuels,

household cleaning agents, pesticides, changes in the air alkalinity, and atmospheric or environmental contaminants.

Planning properly for the carpet installation and detailing floor surfaces can positively affect the quality and comfort of the carpeting.

SUMMARY

Rugs and carpeting are widely used as decorative and functional elements in interior design. They vary considerably in the way they are made or manufactured. They also vary in color, design, and method of installation. In order to make the most appropriate choice, the designer should know the environment where a rug or carpet will be placed and understand its intended purpose.

Oriental rugs are made from natural fibers, and most are produced in western Asia, the Middle East, China, and Turkey. Machine-made rugs can simulate the effects of Oriental rugs, but their construction is different.

Carpeting is primarily composed of manufactured yarns. The two billion square yards of carpeting produced annually are classified by type to aid in the selection process. Carpet cushioning is an important part of the installation process and should be compatible with the flooring substrate and the carpeting selected. To enhance a carpet's appearance and function, floor surfaces must be prepared and ready to accept adhesives or carpeting tacks and nails. Newly installed carpeting may exhibit a variety of characteristics, such as shedding and fading.

REBONDED POLYURETHANE: Bonded granulated urethane foam, fabricated to create porous sheets (usually six feet wide) and used for carpet cushioning.

PRIME POLYURETHANE: A family of cushion material that includes conventional prime, grafted prime, and densified prime. Conventional prime is produced by mixing conventional polyols with isocyantes and water.

SPROUTING: A minor defect caused by protruding tufts on the surface of carpeting.

PILE SHADING: A slight change in the color of plush carpeting due to the pile being slanted in opposing directions, causing light to reflect off the surface.

SHEDDING: The appearance of short fibers that work their way to the surface in newly installed carpet and can be vacuumed away.

INDENTATIONS: Depressions in rugs or carpeting caused by weight being pressed against the yarns.

FADING AND YELLOWING: A change in carpet color due to airborne chemicals, fumes, or cleaning agents.

ACTIVITIES

1. Visit a business where quality rugs are sold and determine whether any hand-knotted rugs are available. Compare and contrast hand-knotted rugs with brand-name manufactured rugs. Compare the prices.

2. Trace the geographic and historical evolution of hand-made rugs.

3. Examine a broadloom carpet in a carpet store and discuss with a salesperson its characteristics in terms of fiber content and method of manufacture.

4. Review all available carpet cushionings at a carpet store. Compare and contrast their method of construction. Pair cushionings with appropriate carpets.

5. Detail how the Impact Noise Rating (INR) is determined.

6. Discuss why and when manufactured fibers and filaments would be preferred over wool or other natural yarns.

7. Locate a carpet sample and remove the backing. Determine what material the backing is composed of and how it was made.

8. Explain the differences in manufacturing a woven and a tufted carpet. Provide carpet examples, if possible.

9. Locate a commercial establishment where berber carpeting is used. Discuss with management why they chose berber, and determine how well it is wearing.

10. Visit a health-care facility and report on where the carpeting is installed, why it was placed there, and the composition of yarns.

11. Contact a carpet installer and inquire about what they believe to be the most important aspect(s) of the installation process. Ask the installer to discuss the most problematic issues before, during, and after installation. What makes an installation difficult or routine?

12. Discuss carpet warranties with an installer. What is the carpet installer responsible for? What do they say the manufacturer's responsibility is? What does an installer expect from a designer?

EXPAND YOUR KNOWLEDGE

1. Is an Aubusson a rug or tapestry?

2. What are kilims, and how could they be used in interiors?

3. Where do Savonnerie rugs originate? What do their patterns look like, and how could they be classified?

4. What are Gobelins? How could they be used in interiors?

5. How is indoor/outdoor carpeting made, and what are its features?

6. Why do manufactured fibers and filaments represent the majority of yarns used in carpeting?

7. Can carpeting be considered a "building material"? If so, why?

8. What are the characteristics of a Class III carpet? Where would Class III carpeting be found?

9. What properties exist in some carpets that reduce electrostatic shock? What would be an example of a built-in static control system? How does the control system interact with carpeting yarns?

10. When is a secondary backing system used?

11. What issues must be taken into consideration if patterned carpet is to be installed?

READ ON

Oktay Aslanapa, *One Thousand Years of Turkish Carpets*, trans. and ed. William Edmonds, Istanbul: Even Press, 1988.

Ian Bennett, ed., *Rugs and Carpets of the World*, Secaucus, N.J: The Wellfleet Press, 1988.

Tradek Beutluck, *The Technique of Woven Tapestry*, New York: Watson-Guptill Publications, 1967.

David Black, ed., *The Macmillan Atlas of Rugs and Carpets*, New York: Macmillan Publishing Company, 1985.

The Carpet Information Center, http://www.carpetinfo.co.uk/pages/aboutpp/history.htm.

The Carpet and Rug Institute, http://www.carpet-rug.org.

The Carpet Specifiers Handbook, Dalton, Ga.: Carpet and Rug Institute, 1989.

The Columbia Electronic Encyclopedia, 6th ed., New York: Columbia University Press, www.cc.columbia.edu/cu/cup/.

Murray L. Eiland, *Oriental Rugs: A New Comprehensive Guide*, Boston: Little, Brown, 1990.

John Gillow and Bryan Sentence, *World Textiles*, New York: Little, Brown, 1999.

Hali: The International Magazine of Antique Carpet and Textile Art, London: Hali Publications, member of Centaur Holdings.

Jennifer Harris, *Textiles: 5,000 Years*, New York: Harry N. Abrams, 1993.

John P. Holms, ed., *Flooring 1-2-3*, Des Moines, Iowa: Home Depot Books/Meredith Books, 2003.

http://www.baneclene.com/articles/manufacturing-carpet.html, for information on BCF, carpet terms, and processes.

Jacobsen Oriental Rugs, http://www.jacobsenrugs.com.

Aram Jerrehian, *Oriental Rug Primer*, New York: Facts on File, 1980.

Lennart Larsson, Jr., *Carpets from China, Xinjiang, and Tibet*, London: Bamboo Publishing, 1988.

"Manufacturing Carpet," http://www.baneclene.com/articls/manufacturingcarpet.html

Enza Milanesi, *The Bullfinch Guide to Carpets*, trans. Jay Hyams, Boston: Little, Brown, 1992.

Oriental Rug Review, published in the United States from March 1981 to March 1996 in New Hampton, Mass.

Upham Arthur Pope, *A Survey of Persian Art from Prehistoric Times to the Present*, vol. X, New York: Oxford University Press, 1938–39.

Rug News (New York: Trade Data Reports).

Lila Shoskes, *Contract Carpeting*, New York: Whitney Library of Design/Watson-Guptill Publications, 1974.

William P. Spence, *Installing and Finishing Flooring*, New York: Sterling Publishers, 2003.

Peter Stone, *The Oriental Rug Lexicon*, Seattle: University of Washington Press, 1997.

Suessen, http//www.suessen.com/htmls/bsuessen.htm.

Superba, http://www.superba.com/GB/techno/heat.html.

Parviz Tanavoli, *Iranian Tribal Spreads and Salt Bags*, Tehran: Ketab Sara Company Publisher, 1991.

Pamela Thomas, *Oriental Rugs: A Guide to Identifying and Collecting*, New York: Smithmark Publishers, 1996.

World Atlas, New York: Darling Kindersley, 2003.

The Environment, Safety, and Codes

The relationship that humans should have with the resources provided by the earth has been and will continue to be a point for impassioned discussion. How to maintain a balance with nature and meet the needs of the ever-expanding twenty-first-century global population is a multifaceted and complex problem (Figure 6.1). One indication of the magnitude of this issue is the fact that the largest "structure" in the "built environment" has been the 2200-acre Fresh Kill Landfill on Staten Island, New York, which released methane gasses and other chemicals into the air and water since 1948. Fortunately, the site closed in 2001. Most people would agree that environmental challenges exist and that there is a need to achieve harmony with the natural world, but a comprehensive and generally agreed-upon plan remains elusive. Still, creating environmentally responsible and safe interiors is an important aspect of the professional interior designer's work.

RELATING TO THE ENVIRONMENT

Early hominids acquired necessities from what they discovered in their environment, for example, by retting flax to acquire cloth or applying their native intelligence to discover fire—a discovery that transformed how they ate and the places they lived. Much later, Native Americans connected their life to, and drew sustenance from, the earth. The Plains Indians, for example, derived their livelihood from the grazing buffalo, which numbered between 10 and 15 million in 1850, and their transportation from the horse. But with the invention of barbed wire, "the Devil's rope," the land became divided and "owned," affecting the social, political, and economic growth and development of the United States and the westward movement of enterprise.

More recently, Rachel Carson's 1962 *Silent Spring*, alerted readers to the vulnerability of natural systems and, in particular, the effects of DDT and other

Opposite: Room service with ocean view.

Figure 6.1 Smelter producing pollution near a school.

pesticides. And in 2003, Bill McKibben's *Enough: Staying Human in an Engineered Age* addressed an array of technologies that could alter the natural evolution of human life. These and other authors call attention to the need to preserve the natural world and to understand the environment as a direct link to the future health, well-being, and longevity of the human species.

Environmentalism encompasses activism to protect the environment and develop methods of improving the condition of natural resources. Environmentalism opposes pollution and aims to slow the progression of climate change, pointing to the dangers of greenhouse gasses, as reported in the Kyoto Protocol. Although environmentalists have been responsible for initiating the Clean Air Act, the Clean Water Act, and the formation of the EPA in 1970, their ideologies have been opposed by those who believe that human and industrial activities should not be heavily regulated.

Life Inside

Remaining healthy and preserving life and its quality are dependent upon the condition of the natural world and the conditions of *interior* environments, where people spend 90 percent of their time, according to the EPA.[1] Interior designers specify billions of dollars of products for residential and commercial projects each year. Designers also influence the selection of fabric and furnishings in vessels, airplanes, and public transportation systems (Figure 6.2). The safety of all occupants of interior spaces has become an increasing concern as designers attempt to strike a

(a)

(b)

Figure 6.2 Design for a VIP master bedroom on a Boeing 787 (a) and the living room of a yacht (b).

balance between the planet, people, and profit.

Each year, the potential exists for people to become ill because of inappropriately specified interior products, including fabric and floor coverings. Fatalities and injuries from flammable fabrics are a yearly occurrence. Furthermore, paints, adhesives, dyes, bleaches, and finishing chemicals used in fabric, such as chromium

ENVIRONMENTALISM: A movement to bring about social and political change aimed at protecting the environment and improving the condition of the natural world.

OCCUPATIONAL SAFETY AND HEALTH ADMINISTRATION (OSHA): The federal agency charged with protecting the health of workers in industry.

INDOOR AIR QUALITY (IAQ): The degree to which indoor air is pure of molds, spores, aromas, or unhealthy chemicals such as formaldehyde.

VOLATILE ORGANIC COMPOUNDS (VOCS): Organic compounds that evaporate from goods during and after manufacturing and contribute to air pollution.

chlorine and formaldehyde, have been shown to erode health as well.

Indoor Air Quality

According to **OSHA**, approximately 30 percent of nonindustrial buildings, or about 1.4 million buildings, may have **indoor air quality** (IAQ) problems. Elements of a building that affect IAQ are noted in Table 6.1. Productivity and financial gains from improving indoor environments are seen in Table 6.2. Although many of these difficulties are attributed to inadequate ventilation and encroaching chemicals from a variety of

sources, good interior air quality also depends upon the selection of low-emitting interior products that can reduce **volatile organic compounds** (VOCs). Insurance companies have indicated an increase in workers' compensation lawsuits due to poor IAQ. Although many of the claims are settled out of court for unpublicized amounts, there have been cases where a jury has awarded as much as $10 million.

According to the EPA, humans breathe between 2,000 and 3,000 gallons of air per day. And with interiors being 10 to 50 times more polluted than outdoor air, the ingested air, particularly in an enclosed

Table 6.1 Elements of a Building that Affect IAQ

Operation and maintenance of the building	Ventilation and comfort performance standards Ventilation system operational routines and schedules Housekeeping and cleaning Equipment maintenance, operator training
Occupants of the building and their activities	Occupant activities—occupational, educational, recreational, domestic Metabolism—activity and body characteristic dependent Personal hygiene—bathing, dental care, toilet use Occupant health status
Building contents	Equipment—HVAC, elevators Materials—emissions from building products and the materials used to clean, maintain, and resurface them Furnishings Appliances—cooking, office work
Outdoor environment	Climate, moisture Ambient air quality—particles and gases from combustion, industrial processes, plant metabolism (pollen, fungal spores, bacteria), human activities Soil—dust particles, pesticides, bacteria Water—radon, organic chemicals including solvents, pesticides, by-products of treatment process chemical reactions
Building fabric	Envelope—material emissions, infiltration, water intrusion Structure Floors and partitions

Source: Northeast Energy Efficiency Partnerships, Inc.

Table 6.2 Estimated potential productivity gains from improvements in indoor environments (Fisk and Rosenfeld, 1998)

SOURCE OF PRODUCTIVITY GAIN	STRENGTH OF EVIDENCE	U.S. ANNUAL SAVINGS OR PRODUCTIVITY GAIN (1993 $US)
Respiratory disease	Strong	$6—$19 billion
Allergies and asthma	Moderate to strong	$1—$4 billion
Sick building syndrome symptoms	Moderate to strong	$10—$20 billion
Worker performance	Moderate to strong	$12—$125 billion
Total Range		$29—$168 billion
Geometric mean		$70 billion

Source: Northeast Energy Efficiency Partnerships, Inc.

office space, can have a deleterious effect on health over time, contributing to respiratory ailments, dizziness, shortness of breath, memory loss, irritability, and other maladies, including multiple chemical sensitivity (MCS) and building related illness (BRI). Figure 6.3 shows the extent of airborne particulates that can accumulate.

Although estimates vary widely, the **National Energy Management Institute (NEMI)** reports that **sick building syndrome (SBS)** costs approximately $200 billion a year in lost productivity and increased health-care costs in the United States.[2] This is why the EPA has listed air quality as one of the top five environmental health risks. And the problem has global significance. For example, Australia estimates that health and productivity losses amounted to approximately $10 billion in 2002 due to indoor pollutants.

Efforts are being made to address the problem through national and international, commercial, institutional, and high-rise organizations such as Leadership in Energy and Environmental Design (LEED) and the **Building Research Establishment Environmental Assessment Method (BREEAM)**,[3] in addition to other groups that relate to more specific build-

(a)

(b)

Figure 6.3 Air ducts before (a) and after (b) contaminants are removed. Photographs provided by Mite-E-Ducts Inc. Air Duct Cleaning in Zionsville, Indiana.

INTERNATIONAL ORGANIZATION FOR STANDARDIZATION (ISO): An organization whose membership consists of national standard-setting bodies who unite to promote worldwide standardization of elements relating to interior and built environments.

GREEN DESIGN: A broad term in interior design, architecture, and construction based on energy-efficient design and products that work in harmony with nature.

SUSTAINABLE DESIGN: Design that supports economic, social, and ecological systems—such as creating autonomous buildings that use solar or wind power—without compromising the ability of future generations to meet their needs.

ing situations. For example, the **International Organization for Standardization (ISO)** exists to create consensus on specifications and criteria to be applied to materials that have crosscultural effects.

In the United States, the first LEED Gold-certified residential tower, the Solaire, was built in Battery Park, New York City and opened in September 2003 (Figure 6.4). This environmentally engineered structure features a wastewater recycling plant, a green roof garden, and photovoltaic panels that provide renewable energy.[4]

GREEN AND SUSTAINABLE DESIGN

Using environmentally compatible products results in lasting, energy-efficient, healthy buildings.

To Green or Sustain?

The terms **green design** and **sustainable design** are frequently used interchangeably to describe a movement that strives to reach a balance with the natural world while improving the health and safety of individuals. The notion of a design continuum that cycles product "cradle-to-cradle," as proposed by William McDonough,[5] instead of a more linear "cradle-to-grave" approach reinforces a philosophy based upon the continual renewal of resources and responds to both green and sustainable design.

When the terms are used separately, they can imply somewhat different meanings. "Green" can refer to products that are constructed from low-impact, organic materials. Furniture designers and manufacturers such as Baltix are beginning to think in terms of the three Rs: reduce, reuse, and recycle.

Sustainable design relates to the long-term effects of green products on the environment and how they affect people, their economic and social well-being, and the world as a whole. Sustainable design is also associated with the broad issues of land use, redevelopment, biodiversity, the efficient use of energy, and product life-cycle issues. Both terms point to the complexity of the environmental challenges that exist on many levels, including perceptual.

Perceptions

Some fabrics appear more eco-friendly than others. Conventionally grown cotton, for example, is responsible for approximately 20 percent of the world's pesticides, herbicides, and synthetic fertilizers, along with some defoliants. And because cotton is vulnerable to approximately 46 pests from 32 countries, new insecticides are being developed in order to remain ahead of pests that develop immunity to older chemicals. Seasonal applications of chemicals can range from two to nine times a year in the United States and as many as 20 in China.[6]

Polyester, however, is increasingly being recycled from post-consumer or post-industrial staple into fabric, fabric backing, and carpet that may have begun as soft drink containers. Arc-Com Fabrics, with its eco-tex collection (Figure 6.5), is one example of a firm using recycled polyester in upholstery fabrics. Other firms are working with natural fibers such as wool and ramie to develop more environmentally acceptable products.

Individual designers are also making strides in developing eco-friendly products. For example, the Milan-based designer Luisa Cevese and her trademarked Riedizioni collections combine yarn and fabric waste with translucent polyurethane and other resins.

Products and the Environment

In order to meet the environmental, economic, and health challenges, various industries and groups are advocates of recycling as well as the containment of chemical by-products that result from manufacturing fabric and fabric-related products.

According to the Carpet and Rug Institute, more than 4.7 billion pounds of carpets and rugs are deposited in landfills each year in the United States, representing 1 percent of the total discarded waste.

Figure 6.5 Arc-Com Fabrics' advertisement for its eco-tex collection, which uses recycled polyester.

In a plan to reduce this figure, the Carpet America Recovery Effort (CARE) has set a goal of recycling one-fourth of the carpet waste by 2012.

Carpet backing also represents a sizable portion of carpet waste. Although natural backings such as hemp, cotton, and natural rubber (latex) are used with some regularity, the carpet industry has tended to favor synthetics. However, a movement is now under way to restrict or eliminate backings produced with polyvinyl chloride (PVC).

Carpet industry leaders are also moving away from PVC products for cushioning and promoting the use of mohair, wool, camel hair, and jute. Presently, cushioning from natural products is approximately $6 to $10 a square yard more than

PVC-based materials. Recycled cushioning made of synthetic and other fibers is an additional $2 to $5 a square yard. It is anticipated that costs associated with natural and recycled carpet backing and cushioning will decrease over time as it becomes more accepted.

The notion of recycling fabric that appears on upholstered furniture is cost prohibitive. To date, no recycling programs are in operation that remove fabric from furniture and recycle it into another fabric product. Most of the emphasis is currently on the production of environmentally acceptable fabric for residential and commercial use. A sampling of companies that produce environmentally sensitive floor and fabric products include: Teppichfabrik AG, Interface, Victor Innovatex, Inc., and Crypton Green.

In the area of bedding, companies such as Green Sleep advertise mattresses such as the Sleeptek's Hevea natural mattress with an all-natural rubber core, layered with quilted silk and wool, covered in organic cotton. The Home Environment company sells a 100 percent organic cotton and Pure Grow Wool mattress that is hypoallergenic and contains no dyes or chemicals. In 2005, king mattresses ranged in price from $2,082 to $4,257.[7]

Product Certification

Without a set of criteria for evaluating products, it is difficult to determine by what means a product is more or less environmentally acceptable. Manufacturers also need to know by what standards they should be held accountable. To this end, various product certification programs have been devised. Two examples include

BIOPHILIC: Showing an appreciation of life and the living world.

GreenGuard, developed by GreenGuard Environmental Institute (GEI) and the Cradle to Cradle certification program devised by McDonough Braungart Design Chemistry (MBDC). Greenguard evaluates air quality, products, and the environment, as well as buildings. MBDC certification examines products from the perspective of materials used, material reutilization, energy, water, and social responsibility. (See Table 6.3) as global warming and environmental issues such as health of interiors and interior products gain increased attention by the general public, interior designers will be required to be aware of new products and the methods by which they are evaluated.

Inner-Connectiveness

The environmental relationship between products and humans, coupled with the idea of sustainability, appears to be a naturally compelling phenomenon. **Biophilic** research, pioneered by Edward O. Wilson, suggests that humans subconsciously seek to be connected with other life forms[7] and that "humanity is exalted not because we are so far above other living creatures, but because knowing them well elevates the very concept of life."[8] It seems, too, that even the sight of natural landscapes can reduce stress, aid in recovery from illness, enhance worker productivity, and facilitate physiological well-being. Specifying environmentally cooperative products may extend the feeling of innerconnectiveness.

If humans move away from acknowledging the significance of natural systems and from becoming stewards of the earth, future generations may not be able to reverse the damage now being enacted. The

Table 6.3 MBDC/Criteria for Evaluating Environmentally Sound Products

⬛MBDC

CRADLE TO CRADLE™ CERTIFICATION CRITERIA	TN or BN Certification	Silver	Gold	Platinum
1.0 Materials				
All material ingredients identified (down to the 100 ppm level)	•	•	•	•
Defined as biological or technical nutrient	•	•	•	•
All materials assessed based on their intended use and impact on Human/Environmental Health according to the following criteria: **Human Health:** Carcinogenicity, Endocrine Disruption, Mutagenicity, Reproductive Toxicity, Teratogenicity, Acute Toxicity, Chronic Toxicity, Irritation, Sensitization **Environmental Health:** Fish Toxicity, Algae Toxicity, Daphnia Toxicity, Persistence/Biodegradation, Bioaccumulation, Ozone Depletion/Climatic Relevance **Material Class Criteria:** Content of Organohalogens, Content of Heavy Metals	•	•	•	•
Strategy developed to optimize all remaining problematic ingredients/materials	•	•	•	•
Product formulation optimized (i.e., all problematic inputs replaced/phased out)	•		•	•
Meets Cradle to Cradle emission standards				•
2.0 Material Reutilization/Design for Environment				
Defined the appropriate cycle (i.e., Technical or Biological) for the product and developing a plan for product recovery and reutilization	•	•	•	•
Well defined plan (including scope and budget) for developing the logistics and recovery systems for this class of product			•	•
Recovering, remanufacturing or recycling the product into new product of equal or higher value				•
Product has been designed/manufactured for the technical or biological cycle and has a nutrient (re)utilization score >= 50	•	•	•	•
Product has been designed/manufactured for the technical or biological cycle and has a nutrient (re)utilization score >= 70			•	•
Product has been designed/manufactured for the technical or biological cycle and has a nutrient (re)utilization score >= 85				•
3.0 Energy				
Characterized energy use and source(s) for product manufacture/assembly		•	•	•
Developed strategy for using current solar income for product manufacture/assembly		•	•	•
Using 100% current solar income for product manufacture/assembly			•	•
Using 100% current solar income for entire product				•
4.0 Water				
Created or adopted water stewardship principles/guidelines		•	•	•
Characterized water flows associated with product manufacture			•	•
Implemented water conservation measures				•
Implemented innovative measures to improve quality of water discharges				•
5.0 Social Responsibility				
Publicly available corporate ethics and fair labor statement(s), adopted across entire company		•	•	•
Identified third party assessment system and begun to collect data for that system			•	•
Acceptable third party social responsibility assessment, accreditation, or certification				•

Source: MBDC

challenge, therefore, is to find integrative systems that blend environmental quality and social responsibility with economic success.

FABRIC STANDARDS, CODES, AND PRODUCT PERFORMANCE

Knowing where fabric is to be used and how it is to be applied contributes to the enhancement of a safe working environment. When **standards** are adopted by a governing agent within a city, such as a building department, they become **codes**. Fabric standards signify a level of acceptable industry performance and apply only to **contract** work. Codes are common to all geographic areas of the United States and can vary greatly in their content and interpretation. Formal codes at this time

STANDARDS: Statements explaining the minimum requirement related to test results used in the development of building codes and trade guidelines.

CODES: Legal regulations enacted by federal, state, or local governments or building departments to protect the safety and well-being of the general population.

CONTRACT: Related to fabric, carpeting, and furnishings intended for installation in offices, hotels, healthcare facilities, or public spaces. A contract is prepared by the client and bids are received, resulting in the awarding of the contract.

do not exist for fabric used in residential settings in the United States; however, this issue is being reviewed and may change. Other countries, such as England, do have codes that must be addressed for the home environment.

Codes are laws intended to help protect life and property and to ensure an appropriate level of product performance. The authority for enacting codes originates from various sources, such as the federal government, which regulates federal buildings; state legislatures, which regulate state-owned buildings; and cities or municipalities, which enact codes in response to local safety issues and concerns. Codes that apply where people gather in public spaces are particularly rigid, and codes are often modified for these high-risk areas. Fabric codes can also be more or less stringent depending on the application. For example, the codes for fabric applied to vertical surfaces such as wall panels, wall coverings, or upholstered walls are different from those for fabric on upholstered furniture.

Interior designers *must* become familiar with all relevant codes *before* the start of a contract or commercial project. One way a designer can begin to determine what codes need to be met is by discussing the requirements with the commercial client.

Tests on several aspects of fabric performance have been devised and conducted and include **flammability**, colorfastness to crocking, colorfastness to light, pilling, **seam slippage**, and resistance to **abrasion** as defined by the Wyzenbeek or Martindale test. When a designer does not have access to information related to code compliance or product performance or is

required to work with COM, an independent testing facility such as the Govmark Organization can be utilized to test fabric to determine its capabilities and to consult with on applicable codes.

Fire and Fabric

Building materials, furnishings, and fabric can contribute to hazardous and life-threatening conditions when subjected to flame. Fire damages or destroys, on the average, 1,700 homes, 300 apartment buildings, 61 schools, 69 businesses, and 135 industrial plants each year. On an annual basis, fires—

- claim more than 12,000 lives in the United States
- injure more than 300,000 Americans, of whom 50,000 will be confined in hospitals for 6 weeks to 2 years
- destroy $12 billion worth of property[9]

Technically speaking, no product exists that can be classified as "flameproof." Even concrete, steel, and bricks can become significantly distorted if the temperature is high enough, as witnessed in the disaster at the World Trade Center in New York City.

Deaths and injuries associated with fire result primarily from occupants inhaling super-heated fire gasses (smoke) that contain chemicals from building materials. If not properly specified, fabric can be a source of flame, emitting harmful smoke.

In 1942, for example, 492 people died and 166 were injured in the Cocoanut Grove night club fire in Boston. The ignition source originated from a match lit by an employee who intended to use the light

FLAMMABILITY: The measurement of a fabric's performance when it is exposed to specific sources of ignition.

SEAM SLIPPAGE: The movement of yarns in a fabric that occurs when it is pulled apart.

ABRASION: The surface wear of a fabric caused by rubbing and contact with another fabric.

MARTINDALE TEST: A test measuring the abrasion resistance of fabric and leather. Developed in England by James H. Heal, the test is used extensively on Europe and Australia.

WYZENBEEK TEST: A test measuring the abrasion resistance of fabric and leather. Developed by Andrew Wyzenbeek, this test is utilized extensively in the United States.

source to guide a replacement light bulb into a ceiling fixture surrounded by fabric. The fire quickly spread from the fabric to artificial palm trees and other material. And in the 1980 MGM Grand Hilton fire in Las Vegas, 82 people succumbed to smoke inhalation and an additional two died as a direct result of flames. A total of 679 were injured. An investigation revealed that of the 52 pieces of information that were discovered and connected to the start and fueling of the fire, 34 related to interior furniture and finishes.

The object is to specify fabric, carpeting, and rugs with burn rates that allow time for successful evacuation of an interior space and to reduce the chances of burning or melting fabric spreading to other flammable substances. Codes help address fire safety, among other important issues, and strive to keep pace with new products and the many ways they can be used.

Test Standards and the Application of Codes

Numerous recognized national and international organizations test products, leading to the development of standards. Regarding flammability, the **National Fire Protection Association (NFPA)** has existed since 1896 and tests a wide range of products, including fabric, to determine how materials burn. NFPA also conducts burn tests on entire pieces of furniture. NFPA has conducted tests that have led to the NFPA 101-2003: Life Safety Code that provides minimum building design, construction, operation, and maintenance requirements to protect occupants from smoke, toxic fumes, and panic. The Life Safety Code is one of the few codes that

has been adopted by most states and municipalities and has existed, in modified form, for more than 100 years.

The American Society for Testing Materials (ASTM) has developed more than 12,000 test methods leading to standards that cover products such as metals, petroleum, construction, and the environment, as well as fabric. Due to products changing and circumstances surrounding their use becoming modified over time, ASTM reviews all test methods every five years.

The **American Association of Textile Chemists and Colorists (AATCC)** is more than 70 years old and has published in excess of 175 test methods leading to standards. The AATCC works with dyers, finishers, chemists, and color scientists. The tests relate primarily to wet testing fabric to determine colorfastness, staining, laundering, and electrostatics.

Organizations and agencies also exist to create codes for various specialized areas, such as transportation. For example, the **Federal Aviation Administration (FAA)** develops codes for both general aviation and large commercial airlines. Boats of all categories, including floating casinos and cruise ships, have specially prepared codes for fabric and are regulated by the **International Maritime Organization (IMO)**. Regions of the country have specific agencies to regulate the use of fabric on their equipment, busses, trains, and furnishings. For example, in the New York City area, the Port Authority of New York and New Jersey has produced fabric specifications that address its particular requirements.

Codes are international in scope and include nonprofit organizations such as the

NATIONAL FIRE PROTECTION ASSOCIATION (NFPA): A nonprofit, international organization that advocates fire safety, developing and establishing fire test methods and standards.

AMERICAN ASSOCIATION OF TEXTILE CHEMISTS AND COLORISTS (AATCC): A nonprofit organization composed of chemists, dyers, finishers, and representatives associated with chemicals, color, its application, and affects. AATCC develops and establishes test methods.

FEDERAL AVIATION ADMINISTRATION (FAA): The national organization that regulates aircraft of nearly all categories, classes, and types. The FAA is also responsible for airspace and the advancement and safety of civilian aviation. The FAA develops and establishes tests, standards, and international codes.

INTERNATIONAL MARITIME ORGANIZATION (IMO): A nonprofit agency responsible for improving maritime safety and preventing pollution. The IMO develops flammability test methods, standards, and international codes.

INTERNATIONAL CODE COUNCIL (ICC): A nonprofit organization supporting the protection of health, safety, and welfare of people by providing standards, codes, and services for buildings.

ASSOCIATION FOR CONTRACT TEXTILES (ACT): A nonprofit organization that focuses on interests and various issues related to the contract fabric industry, such as guiding designers by offering suggested performance guidelines.

International Code Council (ICC). The ICC was founded in 1994 and is comprised of Building Officials and Code Administrators (BOCA), the International Conference of Building Officials (ICBO), and the Southern Building Code Congress International (SBCCI). One significant objective of the ICC was to combine the codes of the three groups into one comprehensive set of codes that could be applied without regard to regional limitations. These codes are directed to designers, architects, engineers, and contractors. In 2003, the International Fire Code (IFC) joined the ICC as a fourth member, pushing the ICC's membership beyond 50,000 members.

Fabric testing for commercial facilities that eventually leads to the formulation of codes takes place in certified laboratories, where temperature and humidity can be scientifically controlled. The tests use the scientific method and produce results that can be replicated. Some of the most stringent codes have been formulated by the City of Boston, the State of Massachusetts, and the City of New York. California has also developed strict codes. Because these areas of the country have been proactive and aggressive in code development, other cities and states have adopted similar codes.

At this time, no national codes have been agreed upon to address flammability of upholstery across all states. However, generally acceptable standards do exist for colorfastness to light, colorfastness to crocking, pilling, seam slippage, and resistance to abrasion.

In Compliance

The **Association for Contract Textiles** (**ACT**) has prepared contract fabric performance *guidelines* that may be used as a starting point for the investigation of minimum performance compliance. ACT member companies who distribute contract fabrics and agree with and support the general performance capabilities of contract products as indicated by the organization use the ACT icons on their product tags, indicating to designers the general performance capabilities of certain fabrics. The icons and their meanings appear in Figure 6.6. The ACT fabric guidelines appear in the appendix to this chapter. For up-to-date information re-

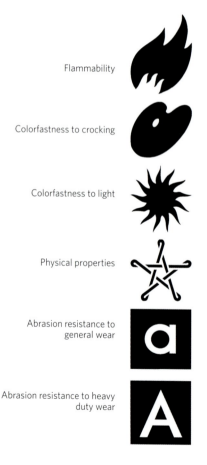

Flammability

Colorfastness to crocking

Colorfastness to light

Physical properties

Abrasion resistance to general wear

Abrasion resistance to heavy duty wear

Figure 6.6 Icons identifying ACT fabric performance features.

garding performance guidelines, visit the ACT website.

It should be noted that passing the standard required in California 117, Section E, for upholstery does not make a fabric flame retardant. This standard is a minimal standard that ACT uses when no other appropriate standard exists. Furthermore, when flammability is an issue, end use must be clearly established first; different tests apply to different applications, and compliance can be achieved only by examining each fabric installation on a case-by-case basis.

Health and Carpeting

Carpet and carpet adhesives can be a source for initiating or complicating pre-existing health problems. Some individuals can experience allergic or flu-like symptoms, headaches, respiratory ailments, or more serious physical difficulties associated with the removal, installation, or cleaning of carpeting.

Areas where carpeting is installed should be properly ventilated, and old carpet should be vacuumed before it is removed. Over years of carpet use, particulates from the outside can be tracked into spaces and build up, creating health problems, particularly if the chemicals involved are fertilizers, pesticides, or lead-based materials. The amount of lead found in dust embedded in carpet where a child plays has been found to be the best predictor of the lead level in a child's system.[10] Several studies have demonstrated that **offgassing**, the release of volatile compounds, from newly installed carpet made of natural or synthetic fibers can be a contributor to eye, nose, throat, and lung irritation in addition to dermatitis and other illnesses.

In 2004, the Carpet and Rug Institute introduced Green Label Plus. The green and white label attached to carpeting means that the product has passed independent test standards for low VOC offgassing. More specifically, Green Label Plus carpets are tested for acetaldehyde, benzene, caprolactam, 2-ethylhexanoic acid, formaldehyde, 1-methyl-2-pyrrolidinione, naphthalene, nonanal, octanal, 4-phenylcyclohexene (a source of new carpet odor), styrene, toluene, and vinyl acetate. It is generally not mandatory for carpet and rugs to be Green Label Plus certified for commercial use, although California requires new carpet specified for public places and schools to be so designated.[11] Carpets manufactured without dangerous levels of these harmful substances provide an important benefit to the occupants of buildings where they are installed (Figure 6.7).

Carpet Installation

The proper installation of new carpeting can help reduce health risks. The Building Air Quality organization suggests the following precautions:

- Speak to the carpet supplier. Ask for information on carpet emissions for the carpet to be installed.
- Ask the supplier to unroll and air out the carpet in a well-ventilated area before installation.
- Request low-emitting adhesives, if adhesives are needed.
- Consider vacating the premises during and immediately after carpet installation.

OFFGASSING: The release of volatile organic compounds into the environment.

Figure 6.7 Small children who play on carpeting are exposed to harmful particulates embedded within the fibers. Contract carpet manufacturers who eliminate these particulates have a strong selling point for such clients as designers of interiors of schools and day-care centers.

air and exhaust fumes to the outdoors, and keep them on for 48 to 72 hours after the new carpet is installed.

- Contact the carpet supplier if objectionable odors persist.

Carpet Tests and Standards

Specific tests exist for carpeting sold in the United States and installed in commercial establishments. General tests for commercial carpeting are noted in Table 6.4. Information detailing the description of some of the tests can be found on the Carpet and Rug Institute website.

Carpeting is intended for use on the floor and should not be applied to walls. Most carpet manufacturers and installers will not assume liability when carpet is installed on surfaces other than floors.

Manufacturers of adhesives are aware of the potential dangers of their products and have modified many of their solvent-containing formulas. Specialty adhesives now exist, and most adhere to EPA guidelines.

- Be sure the supplier requires the installer to follow the Carpet and Rug Institute's installation guidelines.
- Open doors and windows if possible. Increasing the amount of outside air to the space will reduce exposure to most chemicals released from the carpet. During and after installation, use fans and building mechanical systems (HVAC and exhaust) to help circulate

SUMMARY

As the population continues to grow, so does the demand for fabric products used in interiors. Many of these products that are not recycled can, over time, deplete the world's natural resources and negatively affect the symbiotic connection between humans and nature. Interior designers have an opportunity to be sensitive and responsive to environmental issues when specifying products. More environmentally cooperative products that are both useful and competitively priced are being introduced into the marketplace.

Table 6.4 Common Test Methods Used for Commercial Finished Carpet

CHARACTERISTIC	TEST METHOD/EXPLANATION	RECOMMENDED LEVELS
Average pile yarn weight (ounces/square yard)	ASTM* D-418 Method of Testing Pile Yarn Floor Covering Construction: Chemically dissolves parts of the finished carpet sample to determine the pile mass or weight. Pile mass or weight includes the pile yarn, both above the primary backing and the amount hidden or buried below the backing.	As specified
Tufts per Square Inch	ASTM* D-418 Method of Testing Pile Yarn Floor Covering Construction: Determine the gauge and multiply by the stitches per inch (SPI). ASTM D-418 offers instructions on counting the binding sites per unit length or width.	As specified
Pile Thickness/Tuft Height	ASTM* D-418 Method of Testing Pile Yarn Floor Covering Construction: Determine pile thickness for level-loop carpet or tuft height for cut-pile carpet. Accurate laboratory determination of height is important for the average pile yarn density determinations.	As specified
Average Pile YARN Density	Calculation: Measures the amount of pile fiber by weight in a given area or carpet space. Typically calculated in ounces per cubic yard. Important element in equating quality of carpet to wearability, resilience and appearance retention.	As specified
Tuft Bind	ASTM D-1335 Test Method for Tuft Bind of Pile Floor Coverings: The amount of force required to pull a single carpet from its primary backing. Determines the ability of the tufted carpet to withstand zippering and snags.	10.0 pounds of force for loop pile only is the minimum average value
Delamination strength of secondary backing	ASTM D-3936 Test Method for Delamination Strength of Secondary Backing of Pile Floor Coverings: Measures the amount of force required to strip the secondary backing from the primary carpet structure. Measured in pounds of force per inch width. Its importance is to predict the secondary delaminating due to flexing caused by traffic or heavy rolling objects.	2.5 pounds of force per inch is the minimum average value
Colorfastness to Crocking	Colorfastness to Crocking: Carpet—AATCC-165 Crockmeter Method Transfer of colorant from the surface of a carpet to another surface by rubbing. The transference of color is graded against a standardized scale ranging from 5 (no color transference) to 1 (severe transference).	Rating of 4 minimum, wet and dry, using AATCC color transference scale
Colorfastness to Light	Colorfastness to Light: Water—Cooled Xenon—Arc Lamp, Continuous Light AATCC-16, option E: Accelerated fading test using a xenon light source. After specified exposure, the specimen is graded for color loss using a 5 (no color change) to 1 (severe change) scale.	Rating of 4 minimum after 40 AATCC fading units using AATCC gray scale for color change
Electrostatic Propensity	AATCC-134 Electrostatic Propensity of Carpets: Assesses the static-generating propensity of carpets developed when a person walks across them by laboratory simulation of conditions that may be met in practice. Static generation is dependent upon humidity condition, therefore, testing is performed at 20% relative humidity. Results are expressed as kilovolts (kV). The threshold of human sensitivity is 3.5 kV, but sensitive areas may require that a lower kV product be specified.	Less than 3.5 kV for general commercial areas

(continues)

Table 6.4 (*Continued*)

CHARACTERISTIC	TEST METHOD/EXPLANATION	RECOMMENDED LEVELS
Flammability		
Methenamine pill	**FF 1-70 as found in 16 CFR 1630 and also ASTM D-2859:** Small-scale ignition test is required of all carpet for sale in the U.S.	7 passes from 8 specimens tested
Flooring Radiant Panel****	**ASTM E-648 Test Method for Critical Radiant Flux of Floor Covering Systems Using a Radiant Heat Energy Source:** Depending upon occupancy use and local, state or other building or fire codes, carpets for commercial use may require panel test classification (class I or II). Class I is considered to be a minimum rating of 0.45 watts per sq. cm; class II is considered to be 0.22 watts per sq. cm or greater. Most codes require only radiant panel testing for carpet to be installed in corridors and exit-way areas.	As per applicable local, state and federal requirements
Additional Requirements for Modular Carpet		
Tile size and Thickness	Physical Measurement	Typical tolerances are in the range of five thousandths of an inch (5 mils, 0.0005 inch)
Dimensional Stability	Machine-made Textile Floor Coverings—Determination of Dimensional Changes in Varying Moisture Conditions ISO 2551 (Aachen Test)	Within 1/32 inch of dimensional specifications ±0.2% maximum
CRI IAQ Testing Program Label	**Requirement for Indoor Air Quality** CRI IAQ Testing Program logo: Assesses emission rates of carpet product types to meet program criteria.	Total volatile organic compounds criteria not to exceed 0.5 mg/m^2 hr

*ASTM standard test methods are available from the American Society for Testing and Materials, 1916 Race Street, Philadelphia, PA 19103, Telephone 215-299-5400.
**AATCC standard test methods are available from the American Association of Textile Chemists and Colorists, P.O. Box 12215, Research Triangle Park, NC 27709, Telephone 919-549-8141.
***ISO standards are available from the American National Standards Institute, Inc., 1430 Broadway, New York, NY 10018, Telephone 212-642-4900.
****Some states or municipalities may require the Smoke Density Test. See ASTM E-662.
Source: The Carpet and Rug Institute.

Designers are obligated to contribute to the safety of those who occupy interior spaces. Codes are legal statements that need to be followed and serve to guide the work of designers toward constructing safe commercial properties. Minimum code compliance varies greatly from place to place and from situation to situation; therefore, the designer must consult the most recent regulations before fabric is considered for purchase.

Carpeting and adhesives are also subject to testing and standards. The removal and specification of carpet should be accomplished within set guidelines to avoid IAQ problems that could lead to an unhealthy interior environment.

ACTIVITIES

1. Determine where and how discarded building materials and interior products such as carpeting are disposed of in your area.
2. Research a method for measuring IAQ, and learn how it is applied to commercial interiors.
3. Visit a hotel and interview a manager to determine whether IAQ issues are addressed.
4. Contact the Cancer Society, and discover how it measures IAQ.
5. Interview a fire marshall and record his or her experiences related to fabric and flame.
6. Discover products available in your area that are environmentally cooperative. For example, do any carpet stores sell natural carpet backings? If so, how popular are they?

7. Learn what codes are enforced in your area relating to the installation of fabric in restaurants.
8. Interview a carpet installer to determine the degree to which they are aware of safe carpet removal and installation practices.
9. Locate samples of fabric that could be used for window treatments in a local hotel. What qualities make the fabric acceptable?
10. Contract a general aviation manufacturer and discuss what codes are relevant for fabric and leather used in airplane interiors.
11. Research a fabric burn test and describe how it is conducted.
12. Compare and contrast the Wyzenbeek and Martindale methods of abrasion testing.

EXPAND YOUR KNOWLEDGE

1. What circumstances need to be in place for environmentally cooperative products to have broader appeal?
2. What thinking exists that moves people away from products that are environmentally sustainable?
3. How are IAQ claims established? What evidence is collected to support a claim, and how is it obtained?
4. What is in smoke from burning fabric that makes it toxic?
5. What fibers and/or fabric treatments are preferred in office buildings in your area? Can all fabrics be made or finished to meet flammability codes?
6. Why do codes vary from locale to locale?

7. What progress is being made to develop residential fabric codes in the United States today?

8. Why do some states and cities have more stringent codes than other areas of the country?

9. How are codes defined and used in residential settings in England?

10. Why do tests conducted by various testing agencies, such as ASTM, need to be periodically reviewed?

READ ON

ASID Resource Center, Sustainable Design Information Center, http://asid.org/asid2/resource/sustainable.asp.

Penny Bonda, "Eco Design Matters: What's Green?" ISdesignNET, http://www.isdesignet.com.

Carpet and Rug Institute, http://www.carpet-rug.org.

Rachel Carson, *Silent Spring*, 40th anniversary ed., Boston: Houghton Mifflin, 2004.

Michael Crosbie, *Green Architecture: A Guide to Sustainable Design*, Rockport, Mass.: Rockport Publishers, 1994.

Green Seal, www.greenseal.org

Sharon Koomen Harmon and Katherine E. Kennon, *The Codes Guidebook for Interiors*, New York: John Wiley and Sons, 2001.

Bill McKibben, *Enough: Staying Human in an Engineered Age*, New York: Henry Holt, 2003.

Ian L. McHarg, *To Heal the Earth: Selected Writings of Ian L. McHarg*, Washington, D.C.: Island Press, 1998.

William McDonough and Michael Braungart, *Cradle to Cradle*, New York: North Point Press, 2002.

Jim Miara, "Lower Manhattan: Rebuilding, Renewing, and Remembering," *Urban Land*, 63 (9): September 2004.

Catherine Slessor, *Eco-Tech: Sustainable Architecture and High Technology*, New York: Thames and Hudson, 1997.

J. D. Spengler, J. M. Samet, and J. F. McCarthy, *Indoor Air Quality Handbook*, New York: McGraw-Hill, 2000.

Fred Still, ed., *Ecological Design Handbook: Sustainable Strategies for Architecture, Landscape Architecture, Interior Design, and Planning*, New York: McGraw-Hill, 1999.

Stephen Timms, *Responsible Products and Services: Myth or Reality?* delivered at conference entitled Making Sense of Corporate Social Responsibility, Sustainability, and Supply Chains (November 11, 2003) in Farnham, England, UK.

Concerns for Indoor Air Quality, a study conducted by the magazine *ISdesignNET*, http://www.isdesignet.com.

Consumer Product Safety Commission, *Code of Federal Regulations, Commercial Practices 16, Part 1602-1632, Subchapter D-Flammable Fabrics Act Regulations*, January 1, 2002.

Dexigner: World Design Portal, "Green Design vs. Sustainable Design," http://www.dexigner.com/product/news-g4166.html.

Dezignaré Interior Design Collective, "What Is Sustainable Design?" http://www.dezignare.com/newsletter/sustainable.html.

Eco-mall, "Carpeting, Indoor Air Quality, and the Environment," *Environmental Building News*, http://www.ecomall.com/greenshopping/ebcarpet2.htm.

European Collaborative Action 1997, "Total Volatile Organic Compounds (TVOC) in Indoor Air Quality Investigations," Report no. 19, Ispra, Italy: Joint Research Center-Environment Institute, European Commission.

Indoor Air Quality Information Clearing-house, sponsored by the U.S. EPA, Washington, D.C.

Interior Design magazine, "New Product Submissions," Spring 2003.

U.S. Department of Homeland Security, Federal Emergency Management Agency, Fire Administration, *Facts on Fire*, March 6, 2003, http://www.usfa.fema.gov/public/facts.cfm.

Specifying Residential Fabric and Trimming

Interior designers who specialize in residential design serve the public and, in doing so, are required to analyze client needs while creatively enhancing the function and quality of interior spaces.

The challenges that can confront a designer when first meeting a residential client are considerable. The designer should be prepared to discuss a wide range of issues. As with residential architecture, clients typically start with many ideas and plans that must be refined based upon cost, function, and aesthetic value while satisfying the tastes and requirements of the client. Information is garnered by being an active listener, close observer, and creative problem solver (Figure 7.1). A home, unlike a hotel, is a personal statement; often the designer needs to take into consideration emotional issues of a more personal nature. Communication is key, and relating well to clients can help transition a residential project from one stage to the next.

THE MANY FACETS OF A RESIDENTIAL PROJECT

On occasion, fabric and the manner in which it is used in residential interiors can be viewed as fashion, but for the most part, is not something to be disposed of after a brief season. In fact, many fabric patterns and qualities have been available for sale in design center showrooms for more than 50 years. Certain fabrics and patterns can define a fabric company, so when a designer needs a traditional English print, one or two companies may come to mind. See Chapter 9 for sources of residential and contract fabric.

Designing with fabric in residential settings may not always fully satisfy a designer's need to be creative, although sourcing and developing a design plan can require an inventive approach to meeting the needs of the project. For example, a client may express a desire for "environmentally friendly" rooms. This means the designer should be aware of sources for

CHAPTER 7

Opposite: Study with fabric treatment on walls and ceiling.

Figure 7.1 (right) A positive relationship between the designer and client helps facilitate the design process.

Figure 7.2 (below) Blinds made of natural fabrics such as seagrass (a) or tabac (b) provide an environmentally friendly look. Handwoven window shades by CONRAD.

natural materials such as carpeting composed of wool, sisal, or jute. Fabric for window treatments and upholstered furnishings could include linen, flax, silk, and other "natural" or recyclable fibers,

as seen in Figure 7.2. Window blinds may be composed of woven woods or natural grasses combined with fabric. Other trends in residential design favor the "safe home" or "safe home office," where the fabrics being used meet the same standards required of contract settings.

In the case of restoring and preserving a historic landmark structure, emphasis is placed on accurately reproducing or replicating the style that existed when the structure was originally designed. For example, during Queen Victoria's reign (1837–1901), fabrics on upholstered pieces included velvet, needlepoint, damask, brocade, and crewel embroidery. Ornate drapery treatments in the Victorian tradition would be embellished with valances, swags, and trimmings of tassels, cords, braids, and fringe in colors such as purple, mauve, red, and shades of green, as seen in Figure 7.3. The direction of designing

(a)

(b)

interiors indicative of historic periods is taken from existing structures, well-preserved homes, or historic reference materials. This trend of preserving history by restoring the built environment and interiors continues to grow in popularity and, as a consequence, requires knowledge of historic movements, periods, and styles.

RESIDENTIAL FABRICS APPLIED

In addition to the obvious places fabric appears in interiors, such as upholstery, fabric can also have specialized applications, such as providing a decorative separation between rooms using a **portiere** (Figure 7.4) and restricting the movement of cold air from one room to another. Creating a tent effect across the ceiling of a small room or draping fabric above a headboard to soften a wall area are other creative applications.

How fabric is applied was first understood by the wealthy, who used it to create a hierarchy of opulence—sometimes with contraband product. For example, in the 1650s England banned silk fabric im-

ports because of prevailing political circumstances, so silk brocades were secretly smuggled into England from Lyon, France. Handmade lace was more prized than gold in the eighteenth century, and allegedly it was transported to wealthy Europeans in the stomachs of dogs or in their folds of skin!

Today, concerns regarding restrictions on fabric supplies are not inhibitors to obtaining quality products of all types. Competition is strong for designers' business; and if one source does not have access to a desired fabric, another source may.

Window Treatments

Drapes and curtains are sometimes considered two separate categories, with curtains lighter in weight and feel than drapes. The expression **window treatment** is the generally preferred terminology used to describe any fabric used in association with windows, whether for curtains, drapes, or shades.

Windows of all sizes complement walls, providing views to the outside and inside. Window treatments can express formal or

PORTIERE: A length of fabric covering a doorway.

WINDOW TREATMENT: Any fabric used in association with windows, including curtains, drapes, and shades.

Figure 7.5 (above) Formal dining room window treatment.

Figure 7.6 (right) Informal window treatment.

ROMAN SHADE:
A flat, hanging window covering that forms pleats when the draw cord is pulled.

BALLOON SHADE:
A window covering with large gathers or bunches of fabric at the bottom. When the draw cord is pulled, the gathers become larger.

AUSTRIAN SHADE:
A window covering that is shirred to create lengthwise bands of horizontal folds of fabric.

informal statements, and they can be integrated and scaled into the allover room design, harmonizing with carpeting, rugs, furniture, wall treatments, and paint. Formal window treatments often rely on historical interpretations, as seen in Figure 7.5. An example of an informal treatment appears in Figure 7.6. The "undergarments" of drapes, which include supportive linings, have to be appropriately specified as well. When lining or fabric on the reverse side of drapes is visible from the outside, the color of the exterior building material should be taken into consideration as a coordinating element. Exterior views of interiors provide hints of what will follow when the door is opened. Window treatment fabric can just touch the floor surface or "pool," with additional fabric measuring from 1 to 10 inches or more. Drapery hardware contributes to shaping window fabric configurations as well. When a tieback bands around a curtain with its supporting hardware, the fabric can be made to appear relaxed or tight.

Shades can provide a more economical window treatment. A **Roman shade**, for example, appears flat and architectural and is lifted with a draw cord, creating folds as the relatively stiff fabric is pulled higher and higher, as noted in Figure 7.7. As the name implies, a **balloon shade** produces a ballooning effect as the draw cord is pulled, as seen in Figure 7.8. When the shade completely covers the window, the fabric in a balloon shade at the bottom appears as scallops and amounts to about 15 to 18 inches of gathered material. An **Austrian shade** uses at least twice the length of fabric in the treatment and, when fully lowered, gathers across the width, as noted in Figure 7.9. All three shades are constructed to operate in a similar manner, with small rings installed at the back through which cords are attached.

Upholstered Furniture

Balancing aesthetic considerations against fabrics that are highly serviceable is often a challenge for designers; however, understanding how upholstered pieces will be used helps to determine what the fabric composition will be, and in many cases, how the look and feel will be translated in the room. Heavy-use areas benefit from manufactured yarns. Blended microfibers that combine manufactured yarns with natural yarns are also desirable. Pile fabric with cut loops usually outlasts fabric with uncut loops. A balanced weave with yarns all about the same diameter will contribute to fabric wearing well, too. Fabrics with longer yarns on the surface, such as a brocade or damask, will show signs of wearing more readily. Just because a fabric is "thick" does not mean it will wear well. Some manufactured yarns resist soil but do not clean well, while natural fibers can soil more readily but tend to clean better. And, as a general rule, natural yarns tend to accept color in more subtle shades than manufactured yarns, which may also affect the choice of one fabric over another.

Fabric's application to furniture affects its appearance. For example, it is essential to identify the face of fabric properly. It is not uncommon for fabric to be placed wrong side up. Fabrics may also

Figure 7.7 (top left)
Roman shade.

Figure 7.8 (bottom left)
Balloon shade.

Figure 7.9 (top right)
Austrian shade.

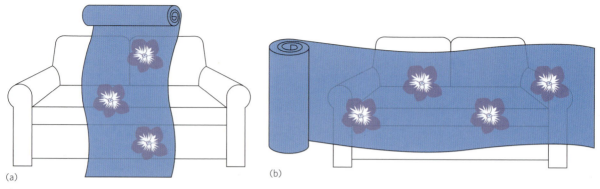

(a)   (b)

Figure 7.10 Application of fabric design and pattern using railroading and up-the-bolt orientations. (a) Fabric unrolled vertically. (b) Fabric railroaded.

RAILROADED:
A vertical pattern applied horizontally on a furnishing.

UP-THE-BOLT:
Applying fabric so the lengthwise grain runs vertically.

Figure 7.11 Coordinating wall and chair fabric.

be **railroaded** or appear **up-the-bolt**, as noted in Figure 7.10. One reason to railroad patterned fabric is to avoid showing seams. Most fabric is purchased in 54- or 60-inch widths. A designer must be careful when railroading that the desired pattern is oriented properly and approved by the client. Turning the fabric lengthwise across a sofa seat may not create seams but may change the appearance of the pattern, unless leather, vinyl, plain fabrics, or fabrics with small geometric patterns are specified. Some chenilles and velvets can also be railroaded. Other fabrics have patterns that are woven or applied and lend themselves to railroading instead of up-the-bolt, where the pattern appears widthwise, not lengthwise.

The scale of a pattern and how the fabric is applied affect the overall appearance. Large motifs should typically be centered or balanced, and stripes and geometrics usually appear in orderly lines. If a pattern is repeated, or there is considerable design appearing on the fabric, more yardage will be needed to balance the design elements on the furniture. Fabric on upholstered furniture can contrast with a drapery treatment or wall covering or integrate with it, as noted in Figure 7.11.

Wall Coverings

Fabric provides texture and design value for walls that most wallpapers and paint cannot. For direct wall applications, a backing must be applied using acrylic, vinyl, or other materials to assist in increasing the rigidity of the fabric and to provide a surface that will accept glue. Some backings are designed to be strippable and made of polypropylene fibers. A practical reason for applying fabric to walls is covering imperfections, such as cracks or pits in the plaster. This can especially be a problem if the residence is old or has soft, horsehair plaster that marks easily when old wallpaper is removed or is difficult to paint. Fabric on walls can also contribute to reducing sound and adding warmth.

Upholstered walls further reduce sound by means of **batting** made of tufted cotton or other materials being placed behind the fabric and against the wall, as seen in Figure 7.12. A wide range of fabrics can be used, because they are not glued to a wall surface. Fabrics such as a large patterned damask in a room proportionally scaled can be grand in appearance while at the same time provide a feeling of intimacy.

Bed Hangings

Like much of interior decoration, bed hangings originated long ago and grew in popularity because they solved practical problems. The notion of a baron's fourteenth-century "bed," for example, consisted of the canopy or testor; all the bed hangings, including head cloth, head and foot curtains, and base skirt; and attached appendages, such as posts, that gave structure to the furniture. Early beds and all their elaborate component parts were considered important "furniture" and often disassembled and moved from place to place.

Fabrics of varying weights surrounding many early beds were used to contain warmth and add insulation, as well as decorate a room. Side curtains also provided privacy at a time when interior architecture did not include hallways. In order to pass from room to room, it was common for people to travel through bedrooms on their way to another area of the house. Many highly ornate beds were expensive. Historically, large beds were normally the most expensive piece of furniture

Figure 7.12 Upholstered wall.

in the house. Oftentimes, wealthy families would give a newly married couple a bed as a wedding present, which was once the case in seventeenth-century France, at a cost of several thousand *livres* (French for pound, as in a pound of silver in this case).[1]

In recent times, fabric has been adapted for use on historic bed styles. The physical structure of the bed provides the first clues as to how fabric may be used. A four-poster bed is able to carry a great deal of fabric. Other bed styles, such as a half-canopy, require less (Figure 7.13). In all cases, consideration should be given to removing the dust that will collect on the surface of a canopy and bed hangings. Not unlike window treatments, a vast number of options exist to transform a bed into something elaborate, as noted in Figures 7.13 and 7.14.

Some Guidelines for Fabric Selection

There are many "rules of thumb" that apply to the selection of fabrics, but also just as many opportunities to ignore them and yield to the emotion that fabric can elicit, pulling a client in a direction that may be more about aesthetic considerations than

UPHOLSTERED WALLS: Fabric applied to walls using batting, creating a soft feel.

BATTING: Slightly matted sheets of cotton, wool, or other fibers used as padding.

(a)

(b)

Figure 7.13 (above)
Historic canopy bed
(a) and its modern-day
translation (b). The
historic example is a
daybed in the office of
Napoleon Bonaparte from
the early nineteenth
century. Note that in the
modern version, the
canopy covers the head of
a double bed and,
because of the fabric, the
look is more feminine.

Figure 7.14 (right) This
modern interpretation of
a traditional canopy
covers the entire bed.

how a product will function. One exception is reproducing the interiors of a historic home or property such as the Andrew Johnson Suite in the United States Department of Treasury, Washington, DC, where restorers are directed by findings of historical research in an effort to replicate what once existed.

Designers focus on the particular as well as the overall vision of the project, advising clients about fabric that takes into account price per yard, costs to produce a particular application, quality, comfort, style, color, and durability.

Fabric selection can be a creative process; the designer serves as the guide, but the final decision rests with the client. Numerous "shelter" magazines, historic reference materials, and "how to" books are available to stimulate designer and client alike, helping to set a stylistic direction for a room or an entire house. Nevertheless, a designer should use caution when a client is looking to adapt or replicate a room published in a magazine or book. Rarely are the ceiling heights given, and often one photo does not show the room in its entirety. Such details would provide a deeper understanding of the design and its context.

Some basic guidelines should be considered when specifying fabric. For example, brightly colored fabrics exposed to heat, sun, and humidity will fade over time. The speed and the degree to which the fading process advances depend upon several factors: the type of yarns and dyes used, the position of the house relative to the sun, and the amount of care and maintenance the fabric will receive. Window treatments with lining or **interlining** can protect colorful patterns and extend the longevity of refined fabrics, such as moiréd silk taffeta, from becoming prematurely brittle and loosing much of its **scroop**, or characteristic "crunch." **Casement fabric** can be used for decorative and practical purposes to create a fuller drapery appearance and to protect the drapery fabric. There is often a direct relationship between the weight of the window treatment fabric and the weight of the casement fabric. If, for example, a medium-weight fabric such as a damask or chintz is used, the casement could be somewhat lighter and made of cotton or a fabric of similar weight made from manufactured yarns. **Glass curtains**, which are not made of glass but made of any fabric that appears close to a glass window, can add privacy, re-

Figure 7.15 Marie-Antoinette's bed.

duce the amount of direct light entering a room, preserve fabric to be seen in the room, and add decorative value.

Knowing the clients, their living patterns, and what they typically wear in the house helps to determine what fabric should or should not be considered on upholstered pieces. If jeans with raised studs on the pockets are worn frequently, a fabric with surface floats, such as a liseré, should probably not be used because of the likelihood that the yarns will become snagged or pulled. Low-abrasion fabrics in high-use areas should be avoided.

If pets reside in the home, fabrics should be selected that are easily maintained. Shorter drapery or window treatments may be more practical, removing the temptation for pets to entertain themselves with the trailing fabric gathered on the floor.

Fabrics that will be exposed to cooking and the potential of grease layering on their surface should be finished with

INTERLINING: A fabric sewn inside drapes to provide additional structure to the treatment.

SCROOP: The sound and feel of "crunch" particular to silk and other fabrics.

CASEMENT FABRIC: Lightweight, sheer fabric used for windows.

GLASS CURTAINS: Thin, sheer window fabric hung behind drapes and close to the glass.

chemicals that will resist flames. And because smoking continues to be the number one cause of house fires, flame-resistant fabrics would add an element of safety to the rooms where smokers smoke.

Ultimately, a fabric's performance depends on the fiber selected, number of yarns per inch, weave structure, degree of colorfastness, directional stability, and finish. Fabric prices vary greatly depending on these factors; however, the most expensive products may not be the best or the most practical for a particular application. Answering questions such as where the fabrics will be used, how much use and care they will receive, and how long the client intends to live with the fabrics will facilitate the selection process.

SPECIFYING TRIMMING

Trimming is purposeful and adds a detailed finish to fabric while creating interest. By examining historic interiors, such as those depicted in Rudolph Ackermann's magazine, *The Repository of Arts, Literature, Commerce, Manufacturers, Fashion, and Politics*, published in England beginning in 1809, it becomes clear how trimming or passementerie was and is still applied today. Applications can be as simple as a narrow cord with tape connecting two edges of a sofa pillow, or as opulent as Marie-Antoinette's bedroom fabric trimmings in Versailles, as shown in Figure 7.15. Clients should be educated as to how, when, and where trimming can be used, its design possibilities, and the materials used in its composition, such as wood, wire, silk, cotton, rayon, or other yarns. Additionally, clients need information about the costs associated with applying the trim.

Purpose and Usage

Trimming is a practical element that serves many purposes as well as a vehicle to decoratively link the flow of room colors by subtly connecting rugs, fabric, wall coverings, furnishings, and paint. An example of a widely used and early form of trim is gimp, which serves several purposes, including the concealment of seams, bridging the space between the unfinished fabric edge and wood on furnishings, connecting seams on upholstered wall fabric panels, covering nail or tack heads that secure fabric to upholstery, and creating a clean transition between wall fabric and a chair rail, as seen in Figure 7.16. Narrow, plain, or ribbon gimps can be used to finish the top and bottom edge of chandelier shades. Each trim type has multiple uses.

Fringe and a small attached cord can be used to unite the leading edges of two different fabrics, as seen in the federal dining room drapes in Figure 7.17, while

Figure 7.16 Gimp between fabric wall covering and chair rail.

bullion fringe provides a means of decoratively finishing the bottom of a chair or sofa (see Figure 3.18). Frog fringe can also be used to edge drapes or pillows. Tiebacks serve as a practical solution for holding back drapery fabric to regulate light or to add privacy when released. Trimming also adds complementary colors and decoration to a room. And regarding color, trimming can match or dramatically contrast with the fabric to which it is applied. Trimming appears in many shapes, sizes, and forms to address specific uses, some more decorative than others, such as beads strung together to add a reflective quality to the edge of fabric. Other uses of trim include providing weight and decoration to swags and jabots and covering the leading edge of a **valance**, lambrequin, or **cornice**.

Considerations for Specifying Trimming

When specifying trimming for clients, several considerations should be kept in mind.

- The placement and type of trim can be discussed between the client and the designer; however, the professionals applying the trim should measure for the amount to be ordered.
- Trimming is sold by the yard.
- Trimming can feel "light" or "heavy."
- Designers can modify an existing trim, as in a **special order**, or create a completely new trim **custom order** when ordering through a supplier associated with a manufacturer. Custom trim orders usually require a 5-yard minimum.

Figure 7.17 This federal style window treatment uses a fringe to relate the two sets of drapery. The tiebacks control the amount of sunlight entering the room.

- Component parts of a special or custom-ordered trim can be dyed and configured to provide the client with a sense of what the finished product will look like.
- Special order and custom trims can take many weeks to produce, in part because of the skilled handwork needed to produce the product. Clients need to understand the time and manufacturing process involved, as well as installation issues associated with ordering trim that is not in stock.
- If considerable trimming is specified, it is best to determine what the budget will be for the room as opposed to pricing all products separately.

CHALLENGES IN SPECIFYING FABRIC

The designer coordinates the residential project and consequently is required to stay abreast of each stage of the process, from swatch selection to installation. Listening to client needs, knowing reliable fabric sources, and having available responsive individuals to apply the fabric facilitate the timely selection, delivery,

VALANCE: An overhead fabric window treatment that can be pleated, scalloped, shirred, or draped.

CORNICE: A rigid overhead window treatment mounted over drapery headings for ornamentation and to conceal drapery fixtures.

SPECIAL ORDER: A fabric or trim ordered that is not current in a collection or one that is to be changed in color or design.

CUSTOM ORDER: A fabric or trim ordered that is a new product designed and colored for a particular client.

and installation of fabrics and trimming. If the process is not monitored and managed, complications can arise.

The Client

The success of the final stages of an interior design project depends on common understandings between the designer and the client. And it is usually toward the end of a project when anxieties about schedules and money become most acute. Communication between the designer and client should be clear, so as to limit any difficulties related to the selection, approval, and installation of fabric products and furnishings.

Designers have the option of working with a client to design custom fabric, assuming the resource for such an order has manufacturing capabilities. The usual minimum for a custom fabric order is 25 yards. Any special or custom order can take months to produce, and the designer is responsible for communicating this information to the client and scheduling the work to be accomplished. If the client is willing to wait and understands that about half the cost of the order will be required before production, there should not be any difficulty in processing the work. It is essential that designers connect with reputable firms who understand the design process and who reasonably adhere to delivery schedules. Stories abound in the industry about delays, manufacturing problems, and other reasons for late shipments.

The Workroom

When fabric and trim are received by a **workroom**, they must be inspected thoroughly for flaws. It is usually the de-

signer's responsibility to inspect the fabric and confirm that it has arrived at the workroom free of imperfections. When the fabric is cut, most suppliers will *not* permit it to be returned. Many fabrics available are produced offshore. Dealing with China, for example, where the time is 12 hours ahead of Eastern Standard Time, as well as associated shipping issues, can challenge and stress the designer and client, as well as the workroom schedule. And if the product is not received within a reasonable period of time, the slot reserved for the workroom can be lost, adding further delays. The more experienced and proven a designer's resources are, the more likely a project will flow smoothly. Relationships built over time by associating with responsive, service-oriented fabric suppliers and workroom managers and staff can significantly facilitate the project and better ensure that the project will be accomplished professionally and on time. See Chapter 10, which describes the operation of the workroom.

CLASSIFYING AND UNDERSTANDING FABRIC DESIGNS

Sources of many "new" fabric designs and colors have their beginnings in early history. Knowing ways to classify fabric designs aids the designer in comprehending the breadth of fabric choices available for the end user.

Sources of Fabric Patterns and Designs

It has been said that there is "nothing new under the sun." It seems that this may be

WORKROOM: A place of business that measures, cuts, sews, fabricates, and installs fabric treatments as directed by the interior designer.

true, partly because as one age follows the next, "old" fabric designs are re-colored and adapted for a new era. Historically, early designs were first incorporated into symbols and drawings that carried messages, such as hieroglyphics on cave walls or the frescoes appearing on Pompeian walls discovered after the 79 C.E. eruption of Mount Vesuvius. Within the Western world, creativity and free expression have led to an endless mix of natural and imagined forms and colors by converting shapes originating from age-old symbols into ornament.

The primary sources of fabric designs that have developed over time are associated with archaeology, anthropology, material culture studies, ethnography, religion, psychology, and economic events. The manipulation of line, shape, color, texture, space, and repeat appears seemingly without end and, ultimately, becomes an editing challenge for the designer. Clients are usually not interested in seeing hundreds of choices. The designer must edit a manageable number in order to expedite the project so the final fabric choices can be sampled, ordered, and sent to the workroom in a timely fashion.

Design and Pattern Categories

Confidence in designing with fabric grows as knowledge increases about fabric composition and its capabilities, as well as an understanding of the broad categories of patterns, weaves, and prints available. If a client desires a South of France look, the designer should be able to freely discuss the colors, light, and general feel of that region, and the designer should be confident about how the fabrics may be used in a room and knowledgeable about where such fabrics can be purchased.

The myriad fabric choices available can make the selection process for a particular project difficult for the uninitiated. One method of grouping woven and printed fabrics is to classify them into six general categories[2] that convey different stylistic impressions. There are overlaps in the categories due, in part, to the significant role history plays. Some categories reveal literal sources of flowers, while others emerge stylized from the effects of art movements. And ethnic patterns can be shaped by circumstances related to geography, weather, and political events. The categories include—

- flora and fauna
- geometric
- novelty
- ethnic
- art movements
- historic periods

Flora and Fauna

The general category of flora is represented by grasses, nuts, pinecones, berries, trees, fruits, vegetables, and other agricultural products, as well as flowers. Fauna refers to animals, both wild and domesticated; exotic and familiar; mammals, sea creatures, birds, fish, reptiles, and so on.

Some of the very early designs reflect nature and creative interpretations derived from the natural environment. The use of designs that depict plants and animals can have particular significance in cities, where their curvaceous shapes con-

Figure 7.18 (right) City streets, avenues, and connecting buildings simulate narrow and wide interior halls.

Figure 7.19 (below) Allover design on damask.

Figure 7.20 (bottom left) The overall floral pattern in the fabric of this room in the apartment of fashion designer Carolina Herrera is nondirectional.

Figure 7.21 (bottom right) The overall floral pattern of the wallpaper has a vertical direction, while the coordinated pattern of the upholstered chair seats is nondirectional.

vide a temporary reprieve from the daily pressures of a rigid environment.

Flower designs can appear as an "allover" layout, meaning the motif covers more than half of the field or ground, as in Figure 7.19. Nondirectional patterns signify that there is no implicit top or bottom (Figure 7.20). Allover can also be a one-directional design, usually vertical (Figure 7.21). Of course, flowers and animals, as well as other motifs, can be shown in other arrangements. Scale is important to consider, too. If a client prefers a room with a traditional English country theme, small patterns and a style that combines flowers, perhaps with a traditional period selection, should be favored. A modern, open-plan apartment or home may require less pattern, especially if what appears outside, like a tree, is close enough to a window to add design value to the interior. Interiors can be complemented by outside views of a building or other architectural shapes that add to the overall line and pattern of furnishings or interior architectural elements, as noted in Figure 7.22. A Japanese garden style known as *shakkei*, meaning "borrowed view," cap-

trast with the hard, edgy squares and rectangles found in brick, concrete, and glass. In large cities, streets and avenues can appear like giant interior hallways where the amount of sky visible is determined by the height and length of the joined buildings, as seen in Figure 7.18. The shapes in nature can provide a connection with, and association to, the human form and pro-

tures a similar effect by using natural elements, such as a distant mountain, and framing it using trees, walls, or other shapes to direct the view and expand the feeling of available exterior space.

Geometric

Fabrics designed with squares, lines, hexagons, triangles, polygons, pentagons, and other geometric shapes usually appear in recurring patterns. Geometric can also be polka dots, plaids, and pinwheels in a repetitious pattern that can be taken to the point of abstraction, as in the wormy **vermicelli** design or the small-scale **diaper** pattern. Repetitive geometric shapes help to organize pattern visually and mentally and can direct the eye, creating any number of conscious or subconscious responses, as in Figure 7.23.

Universal meanings have been associated with various geometric shapes. For example, the square has been identified as a symbol for the earth and reflects a sense of equilibrium, solidness, and permanence. Corners of the square form right angles that have been associated with honor. When an oath is taken, usually the right hand is raised, creating a right angle. The subliminal messages that simple shapes convey can produce clear reactions. A distorted optical fabric inspired by the artist Victor Vasarely may evoke nervousness, while a feeling of calm may follow the consistency and predictability of the uncomplicated circles found in the **foulard** design, or the graceful, architectural arch pattern found in the **ogival** shape that appeared in sixteenth-century Turkey and Persia, or an Italian brocade.

Basic geometric shapes, such as the square, are as ancient as the structure of fabric itself reflected in the angles of the warp and weft; however, geometric designs are contemporary as well, in part because of familiar cultural symbols, as seen in the line and repeat found in high-rise buildings.

Novelty

Patterns that attract attention and are provocative, causing an almost immediate response, are considered novelty. Their life span in the marketplace may be short, unless the figure repeated on the child's printed window treatment is Mickey Mouse! Novelty fabrics often follow trends and can make strong statements in a variety of directions. For example, fabric patterns feature animals, jewels, jungle

Figure 7.22 (top) Framing an exterior view to enhance the interior.

Figure 7.23 (bottom) Geometric patterned fabric.

VERMICELLI: An overall design of usually narrow, undulating, or wiggly lines.

DIAPER: A twill weave in which three warp ends are raised, followed by a weft yarn. The pattern is then reversed.

FOULARD: A lightweight, lustrous fabric made with a two-up, two-down twill, originally in silk.

OGIVAL: A fabric pattern based on the diagonal, sometimes pointed arch or rib across a Gothic vault.

Figure 7.24 (above left) An undersea theme in a child's room is carried out in the wall mural, valence, carpeting, and bed linens.

Figure 7.25 (above right) Native American design motifs.

prints, camouflage, musical instruments, trompe l'oeil designs, cowboy themes, tropical fish or fruit, Peter Rabbit, vegetables, airplanes, and so on. Depictions of allegorical events and satirized people also can be considered novelty. Novelty fabrics provide an immediate theme in a room, from which furnishings can take direction to complete the statement, as seen in Figure 7.24.

Ethnic

Not unlike food, the varieties of ethnic fabrics are as diverse as the people who initiated the designs. Unfortunately, some cultures have been known to modify designs that, in some cases, serve to stereotype a culture or country. One example would be fabric featuring a scene from Holland, where people are oftentimes depicted wearing clogs and standing near windmills and tulips.

According to author Peter Thornton, "Anthropological theorists today con-

sider ethnicity as a subjective, dynamic concept through which groups of people determine their own distinct identities by creating boundaries between themselves and other groups through interaction. . . . Ethnicity is a creative and improvisional process, fluid and ever changing."[3] Fabrics available today are reflective of the unique heritage of each social or cultural group. For example, as seen in Figure 7.25, Native American woven designs include zigzags, feathers, animals, bows and arrows, and other iconography depicting the American Indian's life and history.

African fabrics with their well-defined colors and figures are quite different from Indonesian batiks, even though both are environmentally based. And regarding Asian interiors, Chinese designs are different from Japanese. Japanese style can be at once a contrast in extremes, where the playful exists alongside the serious, and the loud is juxtaposed with the quiet.

While these extremes exist, they are all posed in a context of a search for hidden meanings. The Chinese style is less contrasting and includes embroideries, brocades, and damasks. Patterns include peacocks, flowers, moons, religious symbols unique to Chinese culture, and hand-painted and wood block designs. An example of a room with Chinese influences appears in Figure 7.26.

Some early ethnic European styles were influenced by Asia and India. For example, the "Tree of Life" design was popular in Tudor and Elizabethan England from approximately 1485 to 1603 and continues today. The impact of Greek and Italian cultures and what was being discovered in the ruins of the late 1790s of Herculaneum became classified as neoclassicism in the 1880s and featured linearity and balance. Many European fabric styles and designs were taken from objects such as stoneware, earthenware, and porcelain.

Art Movements

An art movement usually begins as a reaction to a social, economic, or military event, or rebellion against an earlier movement. The Arts and Crafts movement, for example, began around 1860 in England as individuals, including William Morris, recognized the poor craftsmanship and style that existed during the Industrial Revolution, where nearly all things were mass produced, including art. The goal was to return to hand-fabricated products and to question the manner in which machines could be utilized in the production cycle of a product. Morris was quoted in an 1880 lecture entitled

"The Beauty of Life" as saying, "If you want a golden rule that will fit everybody, this is it: Have nothing in your home that you do not know to be useful or believe to be beautiful." The "Strawberry Thief" pattern attributed to William Morris (Figure 7.27) remains well known to this day.

Another goal of the Arts and Crafts Movement was to attempt to connect the craftsman to the artist, similar to the Bauhaus movement's merging of art and industry as a part of the Deutsche Werkbund of 1907. In contrast, Art Nouveau, French for "new art," which developed in the 1880s in Brussels, evolved from a need to create something original, aes-

Figure 7.26 (top) Inspiration from traditional Chinese designs.

Figure 7.27 (bottom) William Morris's "Strawberry Thief" design.

thetically based, free from any past constraints, and exemplified in Great Britain by the noted architect Charles Rennie Mackintosh and in America by Louis Comfort Tiffany. Popular Art Nouveau patterns consisted of writhing lilies and other "designed" plant life, mermaids, mermaid-like forms, sunflowers, and exotic birds in colors of soft brown, greens, yellows, and terra cottas.

Art Deco, or *moderne*, was a movement that originated after the First World War in France for people who wanted to express their tastes in a modern, functional style as a direct response to the involved "fussiness" of Art Nouveau. Art Deco modernized many past styles, including Middle Eastern, Far Eastern, and Greek themes. Influences came from industrial aspects of the Bauhaus as well as

the angularity of Cubism. Art Deco shapes tend to be rectilinear and symmetrical rather than asymmetrical and curvilinear, as seen in Figure 7.28. Over time, the stylized animals and Cubist shapes gave way to the somewhat cleaner lines seen in the 1930s. Art Deco was revived for a time in the 1960s, but the style is still a part of today's design vocabulary and can be seen in an array of fabrics and furnishings.

Historic Periods

A large number of fabric designs now available can be traced to, or have been adapted from, various historic periods that reveal definable characteristics. These historic period styles are closely associated with particular countries such as Greece, France, England, and the United States, or significant historical periods such as the

Figure 7.28 Art Deco bedroom.

classical Greek and Roman periods, the Middle Ages, or the Renaissance. However, there are occasions when a country such as Greece and a style like Louis XVI unite to create a unique expression of style.

Each period carries its own signature that can sometimes derive its definition from a dominant personality of the time. Examples in France include Catherine de Medici, who is associated with the use of Italian ornament during the Middle French Renaissance period (1547–89), or Napoleon I, who influenced the Empire period during his reign (1804–15) as emperor of the French and is known for incorporating symbols of his victories, like the bee that he "adopted" from the aristocratic Barberini family in Italy. And looking to England, the styles of Middle Georgian, Late Georgian, Regency, and Victorian all have their own distinctive characteristics and identifiable styles that continue today.

The history of nations and their evolution, as illustrated by designs in and on fabric, all have unique ways of telling their story by converting indigenous symbols and messages into ornament and sharing them with the world, as seen in the Rococo dining room in Figure 7.29. Museums, as guardians of artifacts and cultural pathways, have been sources for manufacturers to discover "new" fabric designs. Museums have also taken direction from their collections and created reliable revenue streams by adapting designs found on period objects. The desire to have designs that carry meaning beyond the aesthetic provides an additional level of interest, whether it is the story of a chintz, a toile, or a woven design adapted from a tapestry produced by the fifteenth-century **Gobelin** family.

GOBELIN: A family of French dyers who also became known for producing a woven tapestry fabric, mostly for royalty.

Figure 7.29 Rococo dining room.

SUMMARY

Specifying residential fabric and trim can be a daunting task because of the vast array of products available. Like other aspects of interior design, such as selecting furniture, the designer serves as editor. The work of the editor becomes clearer once the client-designer relationship has been established and the general design direction is under way.

The uses of fabric are many, and designers strengthen their position with knowledge by consulting resources such as design center showrooms, showhouses, museums, historic houses, or areas of cities where antique furniture can be seen. Fabric can stimulate an emotional response and create drama when it is applied in grand style or used in strategically small amounts, as seen in some Asian interiors.

Success in designing with residential fabric relates to understanding its possibilities for use in window treatments, upholstered furniture, walls, bed-hangings, and special applications. Working with proven resources and checking the fabric before it is cut by both the designer and the workroom helps to save time and money.

Trimming can provide a functional and aesthetically pleasing finish to a fabric installation by uniting room elements, such as color, into a cohesive fabric plan. Trimming can be elaborate or simple, expensive or relatively inexpensive, or manufactured as a special or custom order. Clients should be informed about the time involved when special or custom fabrics or trimmings are ordered.

Classifying and understanding general categories of fabrics help to orient the designer toward serving the client better. With knowledge of certain categories, such as plants and animals, geometric patterns, novelty, and art movements, and awareness of the fabrics used during different periods in world history, a designer will enjoy a more efficient use of time when viewing a project for the first time as well as specifying fabrics.

ACTIVITIES

1. Role play with a fellow student, taking turns being the residential client and the designer. Determine what the "client" requires for the interior(s), the hypothetical time constraints involved, and the budget. Attempt to convince the "client" of your knowledge of fabric and its application.

2. Select a fabric and discuss its line, shape, color, texture, and repeat. Indicate where and how the fabric could be used. Describe where it should not be used.

3. Describe the design characteristics of three fabrics reflective of an art movement and three fabrics characteristic of a historic period.

4. Research examples of ethnic fabrics and discuss how and where they could be used.

5. Study your home or your family's home. Detail how fabric and trimming, if any, are used. Discuss the style and design direction of the fabrics and their relation to the space and furnishings.

6. Determine where and why contract fabric suitable for hotel furniture could be used in the home.

7. Examine and determine the composition of strippable wall fabric backing. Learn how the wall should be prepared and how the fabric should be applied.

8. Visit a historic house and study a drapery treatment. Draw a redesign of the treatment that could be used today. Explain which design elements were eliminated and which ones remained.

9. Visit a fabric resource where trimming is sold. Compare prices, construction, and fabric composition of three different styles of trimming.

10. Examine the use of three drapery linings and their colors, as they relate to the interior and exterior color story.

11. Describe three issues involving the specification of fabric that could complicate an interior project.

4. How can exterior views seen from the interior affect decisions about window treatments?

5. What fundamental knowledge about a client would a designer need that would influence the fabric to be specified?

6. What trends or design directions now exist that relate to how fabric is used in residential spaces? From where do their influences originate?

7. What are the top five countries exporting fabric to the United States? Compare percentages of fabric manufactured in the United States to fabric produced abroad. What is the condition of companies who produce residential fabric in the United States today?

8. Why is it useful to begin fabric color selections by taking cues from existing rugs or carpets in a residence?

9. How would a designer introduce the use of trimming to a client who may be reluctant to purchase it? What arguments could be presented for its use?

EXPAND YOUR KNOWLEDGE

1. How can designers develop their professional activities so they become known for one primary design "look"?

2. How does the condition of the economy affect residential fabric usage?

3. What would the designs, patterns, or colors appear like if a new category of fabric were to be created beyond the six described in the chapter? What might the seventh category be named?

READ ON

Nicholas Barnard, *Living with Decorative Textiles*, New York: Doubleday, 1989.

Sara Bliss, *Exotic Style: Decorating Ideas from Around the World*, Gloucester, Mass.: Rockport Publishers, 2001.

Christian Brandstätter, *Wonderful Wiener Werkstätta*, U.K.: Thames & Hudson, 2003.

Tony Cohan, photos by Melba Levick and Masako Takahashi, *Mexicolor: The Spirit of Mexican Design*, Vancouver, BC: Chronical Books and Raincoast Books, 1998.

Wendy Cooper, *Classical Tastes in America 1800–1840*, New York: Abbeville Press Publishers, 1993.

Issam El-Said and Ayse Parman, *Geometric Concepts in Islamic Art*, Guilford, England: Word of Islam Festival Publishing Company, 1976.

Lucinda Ganderton, styling by Rose Hammick, photos by Catherine Gratwicke, *Vintage Fabric Style*, London/New York: Ryland, Peters & Small, 2003.

Judith Gura, the Abrams Guide to Period Styles for Interiors, New York: Harry N. Abrams, Inc., 2005.

Mark Hampton, *On Decorating*, New York: Random House, 1989.

Frank Theodore Koe, "A History Lesson," *Burke's Peerage* (Fall 1995): 42–46.

———, "Mint Condition: A Restoration of Two Suites in the U.S. Treasury Building Revives Memories of an Important Era," *Interiors* 151(7): 56–61.

———, "Preserving Our Past," *Interiors* 151(7): 48.

———, "Research Through Production: A Partnership in Preservation," *Newport Gazette,* published by the Preservation Society of Newport County, Newport, Rhode Island (Winter 1995): 2–4.

Charles McCorquodale, *The History of Interior Decoration*, London: Phaidon, 1983.

Carol Meredith, *Contemporary Interiors: Room by Room*, Gloucester, Mass.: Rockport Publishers, 2000.

Pauline C. Metcalf, "The Interiors of Ogden Codman, Jr. in Newport, Rhode Island," *Antiques* 118(3): 486–97.

Florence M. Montgomery, *Textiles in America, 1650–1870*, New York: W.W. Norton, 1984.

New York Interiors at the Turn of the Century in 131 Photographs by Joseph Byron from the Byron Collection of the Museum of the City of New York, text by Clay Lancaster, New York: Dover Publications, 1976.

Jane C. Nylander, *Fabrics for Historic Buildings,* Washington, D.C.: Preservation Press, National Trust for Historic Preservation, 1997.

Ann Stillman O'Leary, photos by Gary R. Hall, *Adirondack Style*, New York: Clarkson/Potter Publishers, 1998.

Linda Osband, *Victorian House Style: An Architectural and Interior Design Source Book*, Cincinnati, Ohio: F&W Publications, 2001.

John Pile, *A History of Interior Design*, New York: John Wiley & Sons, 2000.

Mario Praz, *An Illustrated History of Interior Decoration from Pompeii to Art Nouveau*, London: Thames and Hudson, 1994.

Paige Rense, ed., *The World of Architectural Digest Historic Interiors*, New York: Viking, 1979.

Carol Scheffler, *Great Kid's Rooms*, New York: Sterling Publishing, 2002.

Mary Schoeser, *Fabrics and Wallpaper Twentieth Century Design*, New York: E. P. Dutton, 1986.

Roderick N. Shade and Jorge S. Arango, *Harlem Style: Designing for the New Urban Aesthetic*, New York: Tabori & Chang, 2002.

Ros Byam Shaw, photos by Andrew Wood, *Naturally Modern: Creating Interiors with Wood, Stone, Leather, and Natural Fabric*, New York: Harry N. Abrams, 2000.

Jessica Strand, photos by Jennifer Levy, *Baby's Room*, San Francisco, Calif.: Chronicle Books, 2002.

Susan Sully, *New Moroccan Style: The Art of Sensual Living*, New York: Clarkson/Potter Publishers, 2003.

Kimie Tada and Geeta Metha, photos by Noboru Murata, *Japan Style: Architecture, Interiors, Design*, Singapore: Tuttle Publishing, 2005.

Andrew Weaving, *High-Rise Living*, Salt Lake City, Utah: Gibbs Smith Publisher, 2004.

Henry Wilson, *India: Decoration, Interiors, Design*, New York: Watson-Guptill Publications, 2001.

Specifying Contract Fabric and Carpeting

Specifying and selecting appropriate contract or commercial fabrics and carpeting begins with understanding local codes and specifics related to the function of a building and its occupied spaces. **Contract design** is a broad category of interior design in which designers specify significant amounts of product to facilitate the goals of a business or institution that is generally public in nature. This work has not always been carried out by interior designers. Specifying interior furnishings, including fabric, used to be largely the domain of the architect or contractor. In the case of office buildings, it was frequently the role of office managers to specify products for their workspace and employees.

INTERIOR DESIGN AND ARCHITECTURE

Today, many architectural firms have grown to understand the relationship between building structures and the complexities of interior design that include issues linked to the environment; connections between human behavior, productivity, and work performance; and the myriad product options available for the design of interiors. As a result, many of these architectural concerns staff interior design professionals who collaborate with architects on projects from their inception. The goal of a growing number of design firms is to capture the entire project, so there will be a single organization coordinating, processing, and controlling all elements of the structure and interiors. The area of contract design typically employs more designers at the start of their careers than the area of residential design.

There is no guarantee that every architectural project that a firm is awarded will include the interior design component. All projects are different; however, as an architectural firm grows in its rate of success in delivering quality buildings, the firm's chances of being awarded the interior design component of the structure increases. As clients see competent archi-

CHAPTER 8

CONTRACT DESIGN: The term applied to commercial fabric, carpeting, and furnishings intended for installation in offices, hotels, health-care facilities, and public spaces. A contract is prepared by the client and bids are received, resulting in a contract being awarded.

Opposite: A lavish ceiling treatment in a nightclub.

tects and interior designers working cooperatively together, the more logical it appears that one company should design both aspects of the project.

Because the contract field of design is so large, many firms specialize in one category or only a few subcategories.

CONTRACT CATEGORIES

Contract design encompasses many public places; however, the five most notable categories are hospitality and recreational, health care, corporate, retail, and institutional and educational. The hospitality and recreational category includes the following:

- hotels and motels
- gift shops in hotels and other facilities
- resorts
- casinos
- restaurants
- cruise ships
- airports and train and bus terminals
- country clubs and night clubs
- conference centers
- spas
- health clubs
- recreational facilities
- sports complexes
- shops in malls
- movie and stage theaters
- museums and historic sites

Health care includes the following subcategories:

- medical and dental offices
- continuing care retirement homes and "villages"

- assisted living residences
- nursing facilities
- hospitals and health maintenance group facilities
- psychiatric centers
- wellness centers
- outpatient and ambulatory facilities

The corporate category includes the following:

- offices
- conference areas
- public spaces and reception areas in office buildings
- multimedia centers and auditoriums
- financial institutions

Retail includes independent, free-standing stores and stores within transportation centers, such as railroad stations and airports.

The following are institutional and educational contract design subcategories:

- government offices
- day-care centers
- elementary and secondary public and private schools
- universities, colleges, community colleges, and technical schools
- religious institutions

Hospitality and Recreational

Each of the five major areas has its own set of general requirements, along with more specific requirements set by the client that address the particular purpose and function of each building and its spaces. For example, within the hospitality and recreational category, country clubs should have facilities where members can relax or entertain guests in an inviting environment (Figure 8.1) Hotels and all of the supporting services, such as health clubs, should be designed for comfort and prepared to greet a wide range of end users, including businesspeople as well as vacationers of all ages. Airports and other transportation centers can contribute to the appeal of their location as a tourist or business destination by providing attractive waiting areas (Figure 8.2).

Fundamentally, designers take direction from each commercial site. If fabric is being considered for recreational purposes, as in an outdoor spa, it should be able to withstand sun and possibly chlorinated pool water that collects on the seat cushions and lounge chairs. The fabrics should also be washable and mold resistant. Solution-dyed acrylic fabrics, for example, have proven successful for these applications. Products such as Avora Polyester, Trevira CS Polyester, and BASF Zeftron nylon are often specified for hospitality purposes. Additionally, fabric composed of 100 percent polyester and most rayon blends respond well to specialized treatments and can be common in hospitality settings. Fabrics within the hospitality environment must be serviceable, meaning they should be easily maintained, yet give the appearance of not being "heavy duty" (Figure 8.3).

As people participate actively in today's culture and look for new and imaginative ways to express their lifestyles, many changes have come about over time in architecture and interiors to reflect a more residential feel in public places. Hotels, for example, have expanded their

choices over the years and now provide a varied mix that contrasts with the highly uniform roadside motor inns or the high-rise, grand hotels once found in cities. Today, there are condo-hotels, conference center hotels, resort hotels, and bed and breakfast facilities that strive to address the demands of today's customers who require accessibility and connectivity. Fab-

Figure 8.1 (top) Great room in Redstone Country Club.

Figure 8.2 (bottom) Piedmont Triad Airport baggage claim waiting area.

Figure 8.3 (above) "English Is Italian" restaurant.

Figure 8.4 (above right) Residential ambiance in a guest room at the four-star Wordsworth Hotel.

Figure 8.5 (below) Dining room (a) and corridor (b) of JCA, St. Louis, Missouri. The upholstery on the chairs and the carpeting in the dining room give this health-care facility the inviting ambience of a restaurant. The carpeting in the corridor not only has an aesthetic purpose but also serves the wayfinding purpose of reinforcing the separation of the space from the common rooms, which have different flooring.

rics selected for these spaces must also meet high standards of design, color, and performance, while eliciting a level of comfort that creates a feeling of being at home while away from home. Fabrics cannot feel rigid or coarse after being treated to repel or resist everything from mildew to fire (Figure 8.4).

Modacrylic fibers made with a combination of Acrylonitrile and other mate-rials, such as vinyl chloride, vinylidene, or vinyl bromide, have proven to resist flame while maintaining a natural feel due to the flame-resistant properties built into the molecular structure of the fibers. One brand-name product that reflects these qualities is Kanecaron, produced in Japan. With only 35 percent of U.S. fire departments being able to respond to a fire within six minutes, the time smoke

(a)

(b)

(a)

(b)

Figure 8.6 Cottage living room at Hunterbrook Ridge (a) and the Seabury at Fieldhome, Yorktown Heights, New York (b).

can cause the most harm to humans, fire safety has become an increasing concern.

Restaurants often select fabric choices to conform to the cuisine being served in a country or a region of the world. If a restaurant's interior features brightly colored and printed French designs on fabric, the menu may draw inspiration from parts of France. Restaurants have many opportunities to use fabric on banquettes, window treatments, tablecloths, and at entryways, like a portiere, to lessen the effects of cold winter air entering the restaurant from the outside, especially if the interior space is small.

Health Care

Within the area of health care, it is important to specify fabric that is aesthetically pleasing, noninstitutional in appearance (Figure 8.6), durable, and easy to maintain. For some applications, it should resist stains, water damage, tearing, blood-born pathogens, incontinence, and bacteria and germs while remaining breathable. One of many fabrics and fabric finishes that has proven to be useful in health-care environments, among other places, is Crypton, which can be manufactured as a print, chenille, velvet, or woven. Its durability is

demonstrated by the fact that it can exceed 100,000 double rubs. Crypton is conceived through a multistage process that encases each fiber with a proprietary copolymer formula, P 385. Developed in 1993, Crypton is named for the husband and wife team Craig and Randy Rubin, not the comic book planet and element Krypton, and it is promoted as "the engineered fabric system." Crypton has many applications, some well beyond fabric use, such as combining it with argon gas to make Leupold rifle scopes fog- and water-resistant. Gore is another product with similar properties, appearing in a wide variety of designs and colors.

Casement fabrics, lightweight fabrics for window treatments, if specified, can be composed of flame-retardant Avora FR or Trevira CS, among other newly developed products. Wall coverings may be either vinyl, such as Boltaflex, or fabric made from treated rayon, olefin, or jute (Figure 8.7).

In the health care field of design, obsolescence can be an issue because technology usually surpasses function, not design. Interior furnishings that accommodate the necessities of life and ease of mobility compete with the rapidly changing advance-

Figure 8.7 (top) Hearth and kitchen dining room at The Green Houses at Traceway, Tupelo, Mississippi.

Figure 8.8 (bottom) Electra lobby at Warner Music Group, Burbank, California.

ments in health-care equipment and the architecture to contain and use it. Health-care aesthetics are further challenged to span the taste of several generations of end users while reflecting relationships among advancing technologies, design, and sociotechnical issues (Figure 8.8).

Corporate

Typically, individuals spend more waking hours in their offices than in their homes. Perhaps this is one reason why corporate office spaces, along with their ergonomically correct furnishings, have transcended the traditionalism of the past and can now be located in old warehouses or converted manufacturing mills or plants. The King Plow Arts Center near Atlanta is one example of a site where cultural facilities, residential spaces, and work areas merge into one structure. This site housed a farm plow manufacturing facility from 1902 to 1986. Museums have also found novel places to locate. The Bethlehem Steel Corporation's main plant, located in Bethlehem, Pennsylvania, which closed in 1995, with its massive structures and towering blast furnaces, is being converted into the National Museum of Industrial History (NMIH), a Smithsonian Institution affiliate.[1] Concerns arising from adaptive reuse architecture and interior design have challenged fabric producers to develop products, including carpeting, that meet new design, fire, and performance criteria not only for the newly constructed high-rise office building, but for older buildings as well (Figure 8.9).

Retail

Independent retail stores have a unique opportunity to individualize their operation with the assistance of fabric. Like restaurants, interior décor can reflect the mood of products being sold. Music can also work in a complementary way with fabric and furnishings to focus the consumer's attention to product offerings. Opportunities to use fabric and carpeting

Figure 8.9 (left) Curtains across fitting rooms serve as a privacy barrier for customers trying on clothes.

Figure 8.10 (right) Beaman Student Life Center/Curb Event Center at Belmont University in Nashville, Tennessee.

are numerous in retail shops and can include window treatments, curtains and panels for fitting rooms, carpeting and seating for a shoe store, and the use of fabric to enhance displays.

Fabric can signal the intent of a business to the consumer for the purpose of enhancing and growing a business. The designer must be sensitive to the goals of the retail space so that the end justifies the means. Interiors should be compatible with the purpose of the business. Interior designers may have to convince a client that their vision for an interior may not be appropriate for the function of the space. Some interiors invite people into spaces (Figure 8.10), while others are equally effective in keeping customers away.

Institutional and Educational

The rather negative or unattractive image that accompanies the notion of an "institutional setting" is rapidly changing, with more dynamic architecture and interiors being created to inspire and positively affect the social psychology of the daily work environment. Compatible fabrics selected for color and texture can trans-

form the "feel" of a space, enhancing productivity. Windows, and the natural light they provide, are no longer a privilege for top government officials or senior executives. And the relatively small work station, with its acoustical fabric dividers, is being transformed into a more open space, where carpeting can play a key role in design and function.

Fabrics used in educational settings must adhere to many of the same standards and codes of other contract interiors. In the case of preschools or day-care centers, fabric should be treated to restrict the spread of germs. Because of the physical size of young children and their proximity to the floor, soft surfaces are required for sitting and playing. Fabric blinds and screens at the windows can help darken a room during rest periods, and treated carpeting can resist spills.

Fabric in university dorms, student centers, and other common-use areas needs to be serviceable, wear well, and be of similar quality to fabrics found in hospitality environments. The potential for the stimulating use of fabrics in educational facilities is considerable (Figure 8.11).

Figure 8.11 Resource library at the Gensler resource library.

FABRIC SOURCES

The primary sources of fabric for the independent contract designer are showrooms and representatives, who visit their design offices with samples and fabric "books." In many large design firms that employ full-time interior designers, the location for product review is the in-house resource library. Corporate employees, who organize and manage product samples in the library, staff these centers and strive to collect the most current items available for examination and selection. Typically, a vast array of samples, which can number in the thousands of individual swatches and fabric books, are housed within the library. However, there are other design resource libraries that are more discerning in what they collect. Unless the products have special interest, samples are discarded about every two years or less (Figure 8.12).

There is considerable competition among the many hundreds of fabric suppliers, each vying for presentation time and library shelf space within the corporate design resource library. The needs of each design company vary, and space to store samples is limited, requiring fabric company representatives to qualify their products to the librarian and interior design department. For example, if it is important for a company to maintain a collection of fabric samples that are capable of withstanding a minimum of 50,000 double rubs and accepting specific chemical treatments, not all fabrics presented will qualify for inclusion in the library. Libraries exist to address the design specialty of the firm. Only products that perform in a certain way, have current aesthetic appeal, and can be sampled and delivered on time will occupy space in the library. Ultimately, it is the designer who must verify the appropriateness of a contract fabric selection and work with the client for final approval.

Speaking with informed design center showroom sales personnel, vendors such as **independent** and **factory representatives**, manufacturers who can produce special orders, and design library staff is a useful way to begin the fabric editing process. If time permits, it can be helpful to attend trade shows, where manufacturers introduce new products each year, such as the Neocon Market in Chicago's Merchandise Mart or the Hospitality Show in Las Vegas. Even though all contract projects are highly time-sensitive, every effort should be made to fully ensure that the selections are safe and functional for the space in which they will appear.

THE CONTRACT CLIENT

Understanding the needs of the contract client and the requirements of the project, including the time constraints and occupancy guidelines, helps facilitate the successful completion of a project.

The business of creating successful contract interiors largely depends upon meeting the wishes of the client, who is often represented by numerous owners or project stakeholders. Pleasing the client becomes more complicated as more individuals become involved in the process. In the early stages of construction, it is useful to determine who will approve fabric selections. Because of cost and personal taste, the client's desires frequently contrast with what is feasible, creating delays along the way as differences are discussed and consensus is reached. And, of course, interior designers have preferences and reasons why their fabric choices should be selected.

By the time fabric and carpeting are chosen, the project is essentially complete.

Figure 8.12 Array of KnollTextiles contract fabrics.

Pressure soon mounts to open a business or facility on time and deliver the marketing and advertising program announcing new occupancy. At this stage, building managers can rush or force the fabric and carpeting installation, leaving the interior designer little time to make adjustments. Funding too, if not properly planned, can leave resources for fabric purchasing and installation lacking. As projects move along, it is inevitable that there will be modifications and delays associated with the structure or interiors. Human nature is inclined to be more excited at the start of a new venture than toward the end, when frustration can build with each mounting problem, hastening the completion of a commercial building. One challenge is to distribute resources and emotional stamina evenly throughout a project that can take years to complete, so the finish will be as well planned and celebrated as the beginning.

CRITERIA FOR CONTRACT FABRIC SELECTIONS

In the initial stages, the designer should become completely familiar with the who, how, and where of fabric selection. Who

INDEPENDENT REPRESENTATIVE (IR): A salesperson who sells many different products, usually of one category, such as fabric. The IR can work for one multilevel company or represent many different companies.

FACTORY REPRESENTATIVE: A salesperson who represents the products of one company or factory.

will be the end users? How will they use the fabric? And where will it be applied or installed? With myriad fabric choices available, it is necessary first to allow the project to express itself and take direction from the purpose of the spaces. Mistakes can be made when knowledge of a particular project is lacking or inadequate time is allocated to fully investigate all of the spaces that will use fabric. Fabric on furniture, walls, and flooring defines and differentiates interior spaces, with fine distinctions being made between facilities, such as a continuing care retirement community (CCRC) and a geriatric clinic. For example, if little time and thought is given to the carpeting used in a long-term care facility where elderly people have serious mobility problems, the choices may impede the movement of wheelchairs and walkers through the flooring surface or carpet pile.

The challenge of selecting fabric for a particular contract installation can appear deceptively simple, but it is a rather complex process. Over-specifying can be wasteful while under-specifying can lead to premature loss of appearance and wear. No one fabric is suited for all applications and capable of wearing forever. Issues relating to trend awareness, fabric color, design and pattern, yarn composition, and code considerations are all important factors that should be taken into account. Fabric exists in a context that includes architecture, paint, wallpaper, furniture, and light, and the context needs to be acknowledged to achieve a desired effect. Other issues include general aesthetics, function, performance, and the cost associated with final fabric choices.

Aesthetics

Fabric is a sensual product, eliciting emotional responses through touch, sight, and sometimes smell. These qualities contribute to the selection of one fabric over another and help people define how they feel about being in a particular space. Fabric patterns can create tension, a sense of internal calm, or a feeling of formality (damask) or informality (burlap). Fabric styles, textures, and yarn mixes can deliver a humanizing element that contrasts with hard architectural surfaces. As fabric collections change to keep up with trends, appropriate fabric selections remain a factor in defining an area and enhancing its lasting usefulness and appearance.

Within contract settings, fabrics are often chosen for individuals who are not personally known by the designer but who will experience the interiors and finishes in places such as offices for many hours each working day. The tone and psychological feel delivered through the selection of various fabrics can have a conscious and subconscious impact on the inhabitants of the spaces, affecting mood as well as productivity.

Color is perhaps one of the more obvious elements in contributing to how a person behaves or is affected aesthetically. Human responses to color can prompt emotional feelings such as excitement or physical needs like hunger. The McDonald's arches are yellow for a reason!

Responses to color and the reactions they elicit are often connected to, and reinforced by, past experiences and associations. As author Karla J. Nielson points out, "The effect on the psyche occurs [in part] because refracted color bands of light waves are absorbed by cones and rods in the back of the eye which turn impulses sent to the pineal and pituitary glands where they are interpreted as messages, instructing these master endocrine regulators to speed up or slow down systems in the body."[2] The result is a modification in the emotional state. Pattern and texture in fabrics can stimulate similar physiological or psychological reactions. Aesthetics and the psychology of fabric color and pattern address health concerns of people in a given space. Hospitals, for example, in modern times have not always been aware of "healing colors" for walls or for fabrics, although 5,000 years ago ancient Egyptians built structures for the sick that were filled with light and color. Research has demonstrated that cycles of daylight are necessary to stimulate endocrine systems.

Unfortunately, there are no set rules for color and fabric selection in contract settings, although there have been attempts to simplify the selection process. One general rule is that a room should have one large-scale pattern, one small, one geometric, one stripe, and one or more solid fabrics with texture. It is better for designers to become familiar with each interior environment and sharpen their design instincts and product knowledge through research, experience, and critical observation than to search for rules of thumb to guide design decisions.

Fabric aesthetics carry historic and sometimes spiritual significance when designed for sites such as a historically correct Victorian bed and breakfast interior in Cape May, New Jersey, or a hotel in Beijing, China, where the depiction of bats can mean happiness, patterns of sparrows and pears are rarely seen, and the difference between a five-toed and four-toed dragon is an important distinction to make. Pattern and design can be as involved as language, and nuances should be studied in order to avoid potential misunderstandings that can result in lost projects or embarrassing situations. Being sensitive to cultural iconography and differences in world customs contributes to achieving a successful design experience while promoting positive cross-cultural relationships.

Function

Contract fabrics are selected for their functional qualities, as well as their ability to meet certain levels of abrasion wear. If the fabric is to be used for theater seats or for other stationary seating that is secured to the floor, special attention should be given to the type of padding and to the double rub test conducted from the *reverse* side. It is possible for fabric to abrade from the back to the face, instead of the reverse. Fabric on seating that moves away from users as they stand up usually receives less wear.

Elements of fabric that contribute to its longevity relate to the type and quality of the fibers being used, the number of plies and twists, density of the fibers, dimensional stability, degree of yarn slippage, type of finish, and type of backing. With the current trend of portraying some categories of contract design as residential, fabric traditionally seen on home furnishings is being specified in some hotels and assisted living environments. It must be cautioned, however, that not all residential

STANDARD TEST METHOD: A scientific, standardized method for testing, whose results can be replicated.

INTERVENING VARIABLES: In research, a variable that links independent and dependent variables. In general usage, an occurrence that is sometimes difficult to predict and can affect the results of a study or test.

MODULUS: Fabric with strength properties measured in pounds per square inch (psi), such as Kevlar produced by Dupont.

TENACITY: The quality of fabric that has a higher than normal tensile strength; the degree to which material can be pulled longitudinally without tearing it apart.

fabrics can accept the chemicals used to protect fabrics in commercial settings. Chemical processing may appear to work on select residential fabrics for a period of time but may also weaken the fibers, making them more susceptible to wear, thereby shortening their time of use before they need to be replaced. Care must be exercised if residential fabrics are to be specified for contract purposes.

Fabric provides practical solutions for coping with the natural elements. Casement fabrics can absorb, diffuse, or otherwise control light as well as reduce glare, increase privacy, or restrict an undesirable outside view. Fabric provides thermal insulating value when temperatures become cold, and fabric can block the sun and significantly reduce its penetrating radiant heat. Yarns for these purposes will typically be manufactured because of their tendency to be less susceptible to fading; otherwise, the fabric should be lined. Fabric can also be used to reduce the migration of sound from room to room or lessen the reverberation in one room. Fabric performs many functions in addition to adding general comfort and providing a soft, decorative finish to a space.

Performance

The ability of fabric to perform can be empirically measured using the **standard test method**, whereby the test findings can be replicated. Tests have been devised to set minimal standards for contract fabric. These standards, in turn, become translated into codes and should be understood by designers in order to provide a measure of safety and durability for contract installations.

In testing, every effort is made to simulate the circumstances that will occur during actual use. **Intervening variables** that link independent variables with dependent variables are difficult to control, but with newer testing methods these problems can be reduced. As noted in Chapter 6, ACT Guidelines can assist the designer in determining which minimum performance test standards fabrics should meet, thereby directing the designer toward the appropriate products.

Fabrics, as high-performance material, have their origins of discovery and refinement in places such as NASA and the aerospace industry. High-**modulus** and high-**tenacity** fibers go beyond traditional uses for contract interior purposes but may eventually find their way into public spaces as Teflon, Kevlar, and Gore-Tex have. Newer fibers developed for specialized purposes such as Nomex, with its thermal qualities and ability to resist tearing, may, in time, gain broader acceptance beyond applications that include airbags for MER Rovers and fire fighting equipment.

Composite fabrics are now in use as structural elements to complement traditional building materials. One such example is PIPD or M5, produced by Magellan Systems International. The PIPD or M5 fiber remains stable under extreme heat conditions and is resistant to ultraviolet radiation and fire. Future applications will extend to fire-protective clothing and, possibly, its use as a structural composite.[3]

Creativity, technology, and the ongoing demand for fibers that solve new design challenges serve to motivate fabric experimentation and discovery.

Cost

Determining the budget and remaining within its boundaries are essential to the success of a contract project and the reputation and longevity of a firm. Any one aspect of the project can drive the overall costs well beyond what was initially intended, creating emotional strain, delays, and cost overruns. Projects can spiral out of control quickly if costs are not kept in check. Projects may begin with very grand ideas and plans but soon become edited to what can be created practically. Bids are signed with the expectation that budget parameters will be respected.

The actual fabric material specified for contract work is only one part of the "fabric installation." All aspects should be considered, including the time needed to gather samples; the price of easy-to-operate hardware; and the labor costs for measuring and producing the fabric treatment for window or wall applications, installation, and maintenance.

The designer should select fabric that will meet or exceed the specifications for the project. Fabric that falls short of bid expectations and needs to be replaced after a few years of use only creates further costs; fabric costs actually relate to the life cycle of the yard goods. Generally, the better the quality and more durable the fabric is, the longer it will last and the more savings will be realized over time.

SPECIFYING CONTRACT CARPET

Selecting carpet for commercial spaces requires knowledge about where the carpet will be installed and what performance expectations are required for each installation. Familiarity with the properties of different carpet fibers and construction (see Chapter 5) enables the designer to specify appropriate carpeting.

Carpet is a common feature in commercial establishments such as hotels, lobbies, offices, retail locations, theaters, health-care facilities, and schools. Among the factors a designer must take into consideration as part of the specification process is compliance with the **Americans with Disabilities Act** (**ADA**), which became effective January 26, 1992. This means, in part, that ground and floor surfaces, ramps, stairs, curb ramps, and walkways should be slip-resistant, stable, and firm. Improperly installed carpeting with the incorrect pad thickness or pile height can create difficulties for individuals with disabilities who try to move through the material. Specific guidelines are published and need to applied. For example: "The maximum pile thickness shall be ½ inch. Exposed edges of carpet shall be fastened to floor surfaces and have trim along the entire length of the exposed edge. Changes in level between ¼ inch and ½ inch shall be beveled and with a slope no greater than 1:2. Changes in level greater than ½ inch shall be accomplished by means of a ramp."[4]

Carpet is typically the last interior appointment to be installed before furniture and should be scheduled carefully to eliminate delays. When carpeting arrives, the order should be checked immediately for correct color, pattern, quality, and yardage. There should be no defects observed when the carpeting is unrolled. If carpeting arrives before the scheduled

AMERICANS WITH DISABILITIES ACT (ADA): A protection of civil rights prohibiting discrimination based on disabilities from conditions affecting mobility, stamina, sight, hearing, speech, emotional illness, and learning disorders.

installation, it should be stored in a clean, dry, well ventilated location that permits ease of access. If possible, the carpeting should be unrolled to relax the fibers and backing.

Narrowing the Selection Process

Carpeting varies greatly in its general appearance and wear qualities and, therefore, should be examined thoughtfully before it is specified. Some characteristics that should be reviewed after the location of installation has been confirmed include aesthetics, appearance retention, function, and cost.

Aesthetics

Carpeting has the ability to "bring together" many interior elements that can be enhanced by selecting carpeting with compatible colors, scale of design/pattern, luster, and overall appearance. Carpet can soften the appearance of a hotel lobby or reduce psychological stress by adding a residential feel to common and private areas in a health-care facility.

Appearance Retention

Information on how a carpet wears over time and the extent of its colorfastness and color retention is helpful to know before specifying a carpet. For example, solution-dyed yarn, for which the color is combined with the melted polymers during extrusion, is increasing in popularity and facilitates cleaning. Retention of appearance in terms of carpet wearability can be determined by matching the face weight and density to the amount of anticipated foot traffic that will traverse the carpet. The content of the yarn used, pile height, size of yarn, and yarn thickness all affect how well the carpet will hold its appearance. Average yarn pile density (AYPD), or the number of pile yarns in a unit of volume, may reach approximately 4,000 yarns for normal use, while an AYPD of 6,000 may be necessary for high-traffic areas.

Function

Carpeting is subjected to various tests regarding flammability, IAQ, static control, acoustical values, and insulation. Gathering information on how a carpet wears is important, too, as defined by loss of pile density due to abrasion wear, as opposed to crushing or matting. Questions that should be raised regarding a carpet's function include the following:

- Does the carpet need to resist stains? If so, what kind of stains?
- Should the carpet be treated for moths, beetles, molds, fungus, or microbes?
- Should the carpet resist water absorption and other liquids so it can be more easily cleaned? Should it resist soiling?
- Should the carpet specified be modular or broadloom? Modular may be a preferred choice in areas that may become soiled easily and require replacement or where there is an anticipated need to service the floor under the carpeting.
- Should the adhesives be releasable in order to access wires under the floor?
- What about selecting a cushion? Cushions should be selected carefully to avoid accelerated loss of appearance, seam separation, wrinkling, and buckling.

- Does carpeting need to be specified for absorbing airborne sound or noise, or to reduce the transmission of sound or impact noise? Does carpeting need to be installed to reduce injury from falling or provide thermal insulation?
- Carpet can reduce the frequency of cleaning in some installations. Should carpeting be specified for this reason?
- Does carpeting need to be installed to offer perceived or actual "warmth"?

There are many functional reasons to consider carpeting or to dismiss it in favor of other floor finishing approaches. Each project's function, design characteristics, and bid requirements help determine whether carpeting is the best choice to specify.

Cost

Carpeting costs relate to the initial price per yard, installation, and the carpet's life cycle relative to the number of years the carpeting will be used, maintained, and cleaned. The cost of disposal is also a component part of a carpet's life cycle. Warranties are often included with the purchase of the carpet and cover items such as general wear, pattern match, static propensity, tuft binding, edge ravel, and dimensional stability. When chemically treated to resist or repel stains or other elements, a guarantee may be in force as well to protect the end user.

The manner in which carpeting is constructed and installed affects the cost. Carpet should be observed for the following details:

- number of stitches (tufts) per running inch or rows per inch in woven carpet

- type of yarn
- type of dye
- total finished weight, including all backing materials, face yarns, and topical finishes
- quality and appropriateness of backing
- amount of yarn twist
- yarn density and yarn gauge
- expenses associated with installation

A good designer should have readily available sources for products and services. Knowing a reliable carpet manufacturer or supplier and installer can help facilitate the selection, quality, and on-time delivery of carpeting.

INSTALLATION SCHEDULE OF CONTRACT CARPETING

A carefully planned schedule of specifying and installing carpeting is necessary to ensure that the opening of an office or facility is not delayed.

Nurturing and developing all the component parts of a contract project requires diligence and attention to detail. Products purchased for a site should appear in a logical order so that delays are minimal or nonexistent. When workers are stalled because the product is not on hand, money is lost.

According to the Carpet and Rug Institute, the following timeline is suggested for a client who is interested in specifying new or replacement carpet for a facility. It is useful for designers to become aware of what informed clients are thinking and what they (the clients) may expect.

120 Days Before Occupancy
- Write specifications for the carpet and installation
- Request proposals

90 Days Before Occupancy
- Review proposals
- Check references of designers, carpet companies, and installation contractors under consideration
- Select design firm and carpet provider; place order

60 Days Before Occupancy
- Confirm that the order was placed with the mill; confirm shipment date from the mill
- Review schedule of delivery and arrange for holding site for carpet to be stored before installation
- Confirm installation date

30 Days Before Occupancy
- Check correctness of shipment to include carpet style, color, pattern, and dye lot
- Check for manufacturing defects. Manufacturers will not replace carpet that has been installed
- Complete construction prior to installation to protect the new carpet
- Carpet to be installed using approved guidelines such as Carpet and Rug Institute 104/105
- Ventilate spaces during installation to protect IAQ

- Consult with designer, installer, and carpet representative to ensure that all items have been addressed[5]

Planning, selection, costing, inspection, and installation all contribute to the success of introducing carpeting into commercial spaces. The larger the project, the more time will have to be spent on each task to ensure the desired outcome.

SUMMARY
The fabric selection process is highly dependent upon the nature of the design project. Many contract design categories have their own requirements for fabrics. For example, fabric specifications for a cruise ship and the private rooms in a hospital are not the same. Knowledge of the project coupled with in-depth information on contract fabrics helps to facilitate the process of specifying.

Sources of contract fabrics include showrooms, independent and factory representatives, and resource libraries. Interior designers who are employed at large firms typically consult with the resource library, where many fabrics are catalogued by the design library staff.

Fabrics are selected for aesthetic value as well as for function, performance, cost, and availability. A balance should be maintained among all selection criteria, and the designer should also be guided by the bid proposal. A fabric that has high aesthetic value but does not perform is just as inappropriate as a fabric that meets all desired features but is not available within the time schedule designated for installation. Fabric, as one of the last interior appointments to appear, can place a project on hold, delaying the opening and consequently the revenue stream essential for the success of the project.

Contract carpeting, like fabric, is required to meet standards and codes and should be selected with the end user in mind. Issues related to aesthetics, appearance retention, function, cost, and installation are to be considered when reviewing carpeting alternatives. Examining fabric and carpeting as soon as it arrives from the mill or the distributor's warehouse is essential in order to ensure that the products are free of defects and to confirm correct color, pattern, dye lot, and style number.

ACTIVITIES

1. Determine how the fabric and carpeting in a hotel or office building in your area was specified. Interview the individuals who were responsible about the process.
2. Contact a hospital administrator and discuss how the fabrics were specified. Determine what treatments were applied to meet the standards of that facility and how the fabrics are cleaned and maintained.
3. Visit a restaurant to determine whether the fabrics specified provide clues about the style of cuisine being served.
4. Visit a day-care center and learn how and where carpeting is used.
5. Create a list of five contract fabric suppliers. Name the properties of three fabrics they sell and determine where and how they would be best used. Obtain prices.
6. Identify a company that treats carpeting to repel water and stains. Identify the stains the carpeting is said to repel and review the guarantee.
7. Identify a site where carpet tiles have been installed. Examine and report on their placement and wear.
8. Discover where carpeting has been used to accommodate individuals with disabilities. Describe the composition of the carpet.
9. Describe three carpets that meet ADA standards for safety on ramps.
10. After-market topical treatments to retard stains, static, and other undesirable qualities can be applied to carpeting. Learn whether the application of these treatments affects the carpet warranty.

EXPAND YOUR KNOWLEDGE

1. What variables are to be considered in determining how much time it will take to specify fabric for a 100-room hotel?
2. How do interior designers discover the existence of new contract fabric and carpeting collections and learn about their qualities in order to specify or recommend them for inclusion in a project?
3. How are fabrics and carpeting presented to a client for consideration?
4. How is a bid for a contract project obtained and a response submitted?

5. To what degree do "politics" influence acquiring contract products?

6. Who might be representing the hotel side of the contract decision-making team?

7. Approximately how many fabric samples should a designer present to a contract client? What variables determine the number of choices?

8. How are design, fabric quality, and color used to create the appearance of a noninstitutional look? What is meant by institutional-looking interior fabrics?

9. What fabrics would be appropriate for an outdoor spa, and where they would be placed?

10. What chemical treatments are used to aid in protecting fabric that may be exposed to hospital germs and bacteria? How are the treatments applied?

11. Interview two interior designers who recently completed commercial projects, and learn what their positive and negative experiences were. Were there any unexpected situations that had to be addressed? If so, how were they resolved?

READ ON

Paco Asensio, Editor in Chief, *Ultimate Hotel Design*, New York: teNeues Publishing Co., 2005.

Regina S. Barahan and Joseph F. Durocher, *Successful Restaurant Design*, New York: John Wiley & Sons, 2001.

George M. Beylerian, Andrew Dent, Anita Moryadas (ed.), *Material Connexion: The Global Resource of New and Innovative Materials for Architects, Artists, and Designers*, New York: Wiley, 2005.

Sarah E. Braddock Clarke and Marie O'Mahony, *Techno Textiles 2*, New York: Thames & Hudson, 2005.

Corinna Dean, *The Inspired Retail Space*, Gloucester, Mass.: Rockport Publishers, 2003.

Martin E. Dorf, *Restaurants That Work*, New York: Watson-Guptill Publications, 1992.

Brian Doyle, "Aramid, Carbon, and PBO Fibers/Yarns in Engineered Fabrics or Membranes," *Journal of Industrial Textiles* 30, no. 1 (July 2000): p. 43.

Otto Frei and Bodo Rasch, *Finding Form: Toward an Architecture of the Minimal*, Fellback, Germany: Axel Menges, 1995.

Stephen A. Kliment, ed., *Senior Living*, New York: John Wiley & Sons, 2004.

Klaus-Michael Koch, *Membrane Structures: Innovative Building with Film and Fabric*, New York: Prestel, 2004.

Lillian D. Kozloski, *Outfitting the Astronaut*, Washington, D.C.: Smithsonian Institution Press, 2003.

Cynthia Leibrock, *Design Details for Health: Making the Most of Interior Design's Healing Potential*, New York: John Wiley & Sons, 1999.

Christina Montes, ed., *New Offices*, New York: LOFT Publications, 2003.

Marie O'Mahony and Sarah Braddock, eds., *Textiles and New Technology*, London: Artemis, 1994.

Jonathan Poore, *Interior Color*, vol. 2, Gloucester, Mass.: Rockport Publishers, 2005.

Otto Riewoldt, *New Hotel Design*, New York: Watson-Gupill Publications, 2002.

Angelika Taschen, *The Hotel Book: Great Escapes South America*, ed. Christiane Reiter, London: Taschen, 2004.

Techtextil: International trade fair for technical textile and nonwovens. USA: Messe Frankfurt Inc. Germany: Messe Frankfurt GmbH, Techtextil Team http://www.techtextil.com.

Sources: Acquiring Fabric for Clients

Fabrics can be acquired from **agents**, online sites that advertise "below trade wholesale," and fabric shops. However, the professional designer may prefer to visit to-the-trade-only design centers in the United States, such as the Merchandise Mart in Chicago, Illinois (Figure 9.1). The design centers and their showrooms allow the professional designer to sample the latest products while observing industry trends, all within one facility.

DESIGN CENTERS

Design centers and marts display a wide range of new and traditional fabrics. Most centers also serve as educational and event headquarters offering **Continuing Education Unit (CEU)** and non-CEU seminars and programs to assist designers in extending their knowledge or maintaining currency after being granted membership into one or more of the following organizations: American Society of Interior Designers (ASID), Interior Design Educators Council (IDEC, in the United States), Association of Registered Interior Designers of Ontario (ARIDO, in Canada), and Colegio de Disenadores–Decoradores de Interiores (CODDI, in Puerto Rico). Seminar topics sponsored by design centers can range from exploring methods of mitigating IAQ and noise to understanding the psychology of color. There are approximately 35 design centers and marts throughout the United States and Canada (see Table 9.1).

Entrance to a design center and its various showrooms may be restricted to those who are employed by a design firm or have demonstrated a level of professionalism through formal education, practice, or both. Credentials are usually presented along with a design center application. Upon approval, some centers provide the designer a bar coded entry card.

The current trend in many U.S. design centers is to encourage and welcome the general public to visit, offering free tours

AGENTS: Individuals who represent a fabric-producing company or a firm that sells several different collections. Agents travel to designated design stores to update samples and provide sales support.

CONTINUING EDUCATION UNIT (CEU): Credit for courses, seminars, lectures, or other educational experiences approved by the educational component of an organization for content and quality. CEUs can be required for maintaining some certificates and licenses or used to extend the knowledge of the professional designer.

Opposite: Divian in the lounge of a Boeing business jet.

Figure 9.1 The Merchandise Mart design center in Chicago.

as a way of introducing the center's resources. Lists of designers are sometimes made available during the tour, and some facilities offer an introductory consultation session at no charge. Buying services associated with interior designers approved by the center exist to stimulate interest and increase the sale of products.

Usually, clients are permitted to accompany their designers into the showrooms in search of product and, in some cases, visit showrooms independently, providing they adhere to the guidelines established by the particular center. The admission policy for the Decoration & Design Building in New York City, which accepts clients, follows.

D&D Building and Showroom Admission Policy for Designers and Clients

The D&D Building is open to design trade professionals only. Admission to the showrooms (for clients) varies ac-

cording to each showroom's individual policy. Design professionals can accompany their clients during normal business hours. Clients may be admitted on their own with a current letter of introduction from a qualified design professional.

To make arrangements for a client to visit the building without a designer:

- Write a letter addressed to the D&D Building with your client's name, address, and telephone number on your company letterhead.
- Specify the showroom(s) you wish them to visit, a contact person, and the terms and services you would like the showroom(s) to provide (e.g., memo samples, tear sheets, prices, etc.)
- Specify the day your client will visit the D&D Building. If repeat showroom visits are to be made, indicate those dates in the letter. This letter must be signed by the design professional working with the client.
- Not all showrooms will allow visits by unaccompanied clients, so please check with the showroom in advance.
- Advise your client that they will be required to show a letter of introduction to every showroom they visit in the Building.
- Designers who do not give a letter of introduction to their client in advance may send it via fax to the D&D Building Marketing Department. Clients should be instructed to pick up the letter at the concierge desk in the lobby.[1]

Table 9.1 To-the-Trade Design Centers and Marts

DESIGN CENTER	WEBSITE	LOCATION	TELEPHONE
Americasmart	www.americasmart.com	240 Peachtree Street, NW Atlanta, GA 30303	404-220-3000
Architects & Designers Building	www.merchandisemart.com/kbnewyork/	150 East 58th St. New York, NY 10155	800-677-6278
Atlanta Decorative Arts Center	www.adacdesigncenter.com	349 Peachtree Hills Ave. NW Atlanta, GA 30303	404-231-1720
Back Door to the Trade	www.backdoortothetrade.com/contract.com	7301 Burnet Road Austin, TX 78757	512-420-0333
Berkeley Design Center	www.berkelydesigncenter.com	3195 Adeline St. Berkeley, CA 94703	510-652-6064
Boston Design Center	www.bostondesigncenter.com	On the Waterfront Boston, MA 02210	617-338-5062
Chicago Merchandise Mart	www.mmart.com	The Merchandise Mart Chicago, IL 60654	800-677-6278
Contract Furnishings Mart	www.cfmfloors.com/contract	915 S.E. Sandy Blvd. Portland, OR 97214	503-542-8900
Dallas Market Center	www.dallasmarketcenter.com	2100 Stemmons Freeway Dallas, TX 75207	214-655-6100
Decoration & Design Building	www.ddbuilding.com	979 Third Ave. New York, NY 10022	212-759-5408
Decorative Center Houston	www.decorativecenter.com	5120 Woodway Drive Houston, TX 77056	713-961-9292
Decorative Center Dallas	www.decorativecenterdallas.com	1400 Turtle Creek Blvd. Dallas, TX 75207	214-698-1300
Denver Design Center	www.denverdesign.com	595 S. Broadway Denver, CO 75207	303-733-2455
Design Center of the Americas (DCOTA)	www.dcota.com	1855 Griffin Road Dania Beach, FL 33004	954-920-7997
Design Center of Austin	www.designcenterofaustin.com	3601 S. Congress at Penn Field Building Austin, TX 78704	512-441-5540
Designers Walk	www.designerswalk.com	168 Bedford Road, Toronto ON M5R 2K9 Canada	416-961-1211
Gala/Crescendo	www.crescendogala@crescendogale.com	4271, Rue Saint Catherine Westmount, Montreal Quebec H3Z 1P7 Canada	514-933-0067

(*continues*)

Table 9.1 *(Continued)*

DESIGN CENTER	WEBSITE	LOCATION	TELEPHONE
Gentry Pacific Design Center	www.gentrycenter.com	560 N., Nimitz Highway Honolulu, Hawaii	808-599-8284
International Home Furnishings Center	www.ihfc.com	210 E. Commerce Ave. High Point, NC 27260	336-888-3700
International Market Square	www.imsdesignonline.com	275 Market St. Minneapolis, NM 55405	612-338-6250
L.A. Mart	www.lamart.com	1933 S. Broadway Los Angeles, CA 90007	231-763-5800
Laguna Design Center	www.lagunadesigncenter.com	23811 Aliso Creek Rd. Laguna Niguel, CA 92677	949-643-2929
Marketplace Design Center	www.marketplacedesigncenterphila.com	2400 Market St. Philadelphia, PA 19103	215-561-5000
Metro Design Center	www.metrodesigncenter.com	1206 N. Sherman St. Allentown, PA 18103	610-434-0161
Miami International Design Center	www.miamimart.net	777 N.W. 72nd Ave Miami, FL 33126	305-261-2900
Michigan Design Center	www.michigandesign.com	1700 Stutz Dr. Troy, MI 48084	248-649-4772
New York Design Center	www.nydc.com	200 Lexington Ave. New York, NY 10016	212-679-9500
Ohio Design Centre	www.ohiodesigncentre.com	23533 Mercantile Rd. Beachwood, OH 44122	216-832-1245
Pacific Design Center	www.pacificdesigncenter.com	8687 Melrose Ave. West Hollywood, CA 90069	310-657-0800
San Francisco Design Center	www.pacificdesigncenter.com	Two Henry Adams St. San Francisco, CA 94103	415-241-7958
San Francisco Mart	www.sfmart.com	1355 Market Street San Francisco, CA 94103	415-241-7958
Seattle Design Center	www.seattledesigncenter.com	5701 Sixth Ave. Seattle, WA 98108	206-762-1200
Showplace Square West	www.showplacesquarewest.com	300 D St, S.W. Washington, DC 20024	415-626-8257
The Merchandise Mart	www.kitchenbathcenter.com/dcdesigncenter/	300 D St, S.W. Washington, DC 20024	202-554-5053
World Market Center	www.lasvegasmart.com	495 South Central Parkway Las Vegas, NV 89106	888-416-8600

The depth and breadth of fabric product available in most showrooms is considerable. It is useful, therefore, for a designer and client to have a clear idea about what they are searching for *before* entering. If the search remains focused, there will be less confusion as the review of fabrics moves from showroom to showroom and samples are collected.

ACQUIRING FABRIC FROM SHOWROOMS

The showroom can be a daunting place for the uninitiated. The first step is to understand how a showroom functions and to be approved to purchase product. Knowing about a showroom's personnel and operation can facilitate a visit and contribute to ensuring that the time spent will be used effectively (Figure 9.2).

Establishing an Account

Before an interior designer can purchase product for a client, it is necessary to obtain a resale tax number or sales tax vendor identification number. Once the form is completed and approved, a certificate and a resale number are issued that will allow an individual or firm to acquire merchandise to resell. An individual or business cannot use a resale certificate to purchase merchandise it intends to use or consume in the operation of its own business. When product is sold to a client, tax is collected from the client, and the designer, in turn, pays the Internal Revenue Service when the business taxes are due. Figure 9.3 shows the New York State Application for Registration as a Sales Tax Vendor. Other states have similar forms, and many are available online. To open an account with a showroom, a designer

Figure 9.2 Lee Jofa showroom in the D&D Building, New York.

DTF-17 (6/06)   New York State Department of Taxation and Finance

Application for Registration as a Sales Tax Vendor

Please print or type

Department use only

1 Type of certificate you are applying for
(You must mark an X in one box; see instructions)   Regular ☐   Temporary ☐   Show ☐   Entertainment ☐

2 Legal name of vendor

3 Trade name or DBA *(if different from item 2)*

4 Federal employer identification number

5 Address of business location *(show entertainment or temporary vendors, use physical home address, not a P.O. box)*
Number and street | City | County | State | ZIP code | Country, if not U.S.

6a Business telephone number *(include area code)*
6b Business fax number *(include area code)*
6c Business e-mail address
7 Date you will begin business in New York State *(see instructions)*
8 Temporary vendors: Enter the date you will end business in New York

9 Mailing address, if different from business address on line 5
c/o name | Number and street | City | State | ZIP code

10 Type of organization: Individual (sole proprietor) ☐   Partnership ☐   Trust ☐   Governmental ☐   Exempt organization ☐   Corporation ☐   Limited liability partnership ☐   Limited liability company ☐   Other *(specify)* ☐

11 Reason for applying: Starting new business ☐   Acquiring all or part of existing business ☐   Adding a new location ☐   Change in organization ☐   Other *(specify)* ☐

12 Regular vendors: Will you operate more than one place of business?
☐ Yes *(mark an X in appropriate box below)*   ☐ No
☐ A Separate sales tax return will be filed for each business location. Complete a separate Form DTF-17 for each location.
☐ B One sales tax return will be filed for all business locations *(complete Form DTF-17-ATT and attach it to this application)*

13 List all owners/officers. Attach a separate sheet if necessary. All applicants must complete this section.
Name | Title | Social security number
Home address | City | State | ZIP code | Telephone number
Name | Title | Social security number
Home address | City | State | ZIP code | Telephone number
Name | Title | Social security number
Home address | City | State | ZIP code | Telephone number

14 If your business currently files New York State returns for the following taxes, check the box for the appropriate tax type and enter the identification number used on the return:
Corporation tax ☐   ID #_____   Other ☐ *(explain)* _____   ID #_____
Withholding tax ☐   ID #_____

15 If you have ever registered as a sales tax vendor with New York State, enter the information shown on the last sales tax return you filed:
Name _____   Identification number _____

16 Do you expect to **collect** any sales or use tax or **pay** any sales or use tax directly to the Department of Taxation and Finance? *(see instructions)*   Yes ☐   No ☐

17 Describe your principal business activity in New York State and enter your six-digit NAICS code:
Describe your business activity in detail *(attach a separate sheet if necessary)*
North American Industry Classification System (NAICS)

18 Are you a sidewalk vendor? .... Yes ☐ No ☐
   If Yes, do you sell food? .... Yes ☐ No ☐
19 Do you participate solely in flea markets, antique shows, or other shows? .... Yes ☐ No ☐
20 Do you intend to make retail sales of cigarettes or other tobacco products? .... Yes ☐ No ☐
21 If you withhold or will withhold New York State income tax from employees, do you need withholding tax forms or information? .... Yes ☐ No ☐
22 Do you intend to supply two-way wireless communication services to New York State customers? ..... Yes ☐ No ☐
23 Do you intend to sell new tires in New York State? .... Yes ☐ No ☐

Page 2 of 2   DTF-17 (6/06)

24 Have you been notified that you owe any New York State tax? ...... Yes ☐ No ☐
Type of tax | Amount due | Assessment number (if any) | Assessment date | Assessment currently being protested? Yes ☐ No ☐

25 Do any responsible officers, directors, partners, members, managers, or employees owe New York State or local sales and use taxes on your behalf, on behalf of another person, as a vendor of property or services, as operator of a hotel, or as recipient of amusement charges? .. Yes ☐ No ☐
Individual's name | Street address | City | State | ZIP code
Social security number | Amount due | Assessment number (if any) | Assessment date | Assessment currently being protested? Yes ☐ No ☐

26 Have you been convicted of a crime under the Tax Law during the past year? ...... Yes ☐ No ☐
Date of conviction | Court of conviction | Disposition (fine, imprisonment, probation, etc.)

27 During the past year, has any responsible officer, director, partner, member, manager, or employee of the applicant been convicted of a crime under the Tax Law? ...... Yes ☐ No ☐
Individual's name | Street address | City | State | ZIP code
Social security number | Date of conviction | Court of conviction | Disposition (fine, imprisonment, probation, etc.)

28 If previously registered as a New York State sales tax vendor, was your *Certificate of Authority* revoked or suspended during that past year?   No ☐   Yes ☐   If Yes, please indicate why _____

Questions 29, 30, and 31 apply to corporations only. If not a corporation, proceed to line 32.

29 If any shareholder owns more than half of the shares of voting stock of the applicant, has this shareholder ever owned more than half of the shares of voting stock of another corporation?   No ☐   Yes ☐   **If Yes, complete questions 30 and 31.**

30 Did this shareholder own these shares of another corporation when the corporation had a tax liability that remains unpaid? ...... Yes ☐ No ☐
Shareholder's name and SSN | Corporation name | Corporation's federal identification number
Street address | City | State | ZIP code
Type of tax | Amount due | Assessment number (if any) | Assessment date | Assessment currently being protested? Yes ☐ No ☐

31 Did this shareholder own these shares of another corporation at a time during the past year when the corporation was convicted of a crime under the Tax Law? ...... Yes ☐ No ☐
Corporation name | Federal identification number
Street address | City | State | ZIP code
Date of conviction | Court of conviction | Disposition (fine, imprisonment, probation, etc.)

32 If you acquired this business from a registered vendor, did you file Form AU-196.10, Notification of Sale, Transfer or Assignment in Bulk, with the Tax Department? Yes ☐ No ☐
Former owner's name | Address | ID #
I certify that the information in this application is true and correct. Willfully filing a false application is a misdemeanor punishable under the Tax Law. *(see instructions)*
Signature | Title | Telephone number | Date

☐ Check this box if you want your sales tax returns mailed to a tax preparer rather than the address on the front of this application. Enter preparer information in the box below:
Name of preparer | Street Address | City | State | ZIP code

This application will be returned if it is not signed or if any other information is missing.
Mail your application to: NYS Tax Department, Sales Tax Registration Unit, W A Harriman Campus, Albany NY 12227, at least 20 days (but not more than 90 days) before you begin doing business in New York State.

Figure 9.3 Application for resale tax identification number.

PROFORMA: A showroom account that requires that products are paid for in advance of their being shipped.

OPEN ACCOUNT: A showroom account where the designer or design firm has 30 days to pay for product. Products are shipped when ordered.

or design firm must present a copy of the certificate which the showroom retains on file. This procedure is followed for each showroom from which product will be purchased. After the tax certificate is reviewed and approved by the showroom manager, the designer must complete a new account application similar to the one in Figure 9.4.

Fabric company costs associated with establishing a new account range from $75 to $85. In addition, there are expenses related to maintaining the account; therefore, fabric companies prefer designers who show promise of return business. Some showrooms require a minimum dollar amount of product purchase (for example, $1,500) per year in order to maintain an active account. It is not un-common for an account to be terminated if the minimum is not maintained.

The showroom manager approves the new account application and sets the terms of purchase. Typically, a **proforma** account is established for newly approved designers. Another term meaning the same as proforma is Billed in Advance (BIA). Proforma, in this case, implies that orders must be paid before they are shipped. Terms of purchase that relate to an **open account** mean that a designer has 30 days to pay for an order. Although fabric can be sent Cash on Delivery (COD), it is rarely done. COD requires additional paperwork, and someone must be available to receive and pay for the goods.

Designers who wish to establish an account outside of their geographic area of business will usually be referred back to the showroom location near their home office. This policy helps to enhance service to those who frequent one showroom, while reducing the number of designers who may arbitrarily select a showroom, thereby creating additional and possibly unnecessary work for the staff.

Showroom Personnel

The personnel at many large or **boutique**-sized showrooms are usually knowledgeable about product and can be very helpful; however, some designers prefer to work only with a manager or company principal. These individuals can be exceptionally busy, as evidenced by the showroom manager duties, skills, and responsibilities listed below:

- conduct showroom sales
- solve customer service issues
- stimulate new business development
- manage, evaluate, and hire staff
- manage cost controls
- process computer orders and conduct follow-up activities
- communicate proficiently in Word, Excel, and Outlook
- prepare reports as needed
- maintain an esprit de corps among staff members
- write and speak effectively
- maintain showroom displays
- maintain a high level of product knowledge
- demonstrate enthusiasm and motivation for products being sold

Showroom personnel typically receive commission plus salary, so the motivation to build a strong client base is obvious. A designer may deal with only one salesperson per showroom; therefore, the showroom representative (rep) should be well chosen, competent, available, and capable of providing accurate ordering information and timely follow-up reports, if necessary. Ultimately, however, the designer is responsible for the selections that will fulfill the applications for the intended spaces. Partnering with a responsive and knowledgeable individual in the showroom who facilitates fabric requests and orders is an asset in producing the desired outcome.

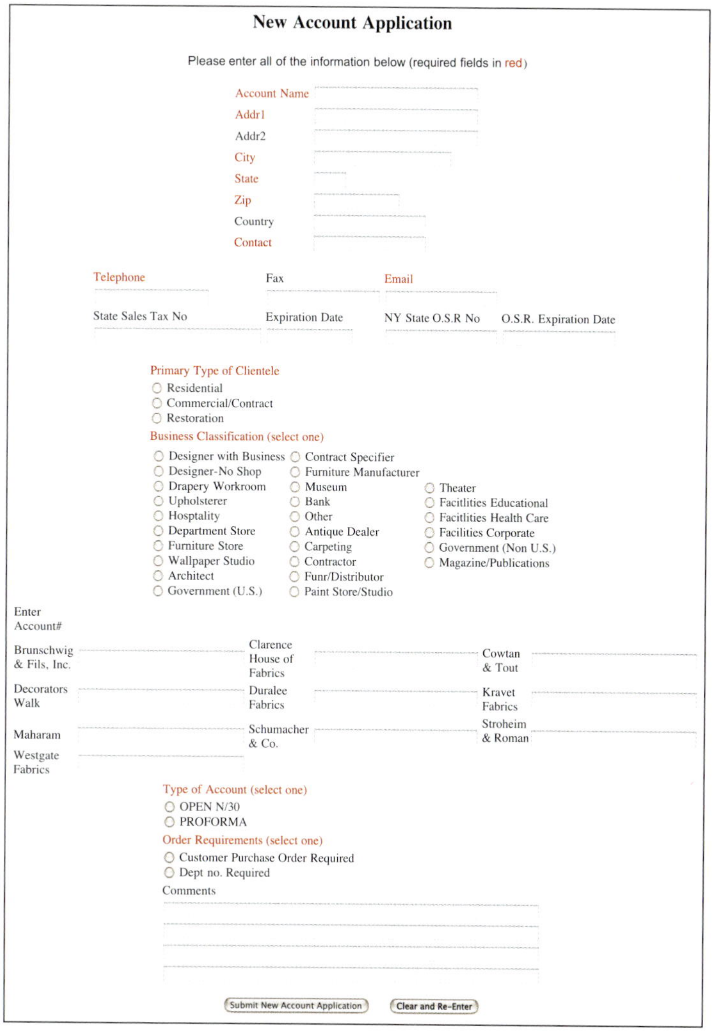
New Account Application

Please enter all of the information below (required fields in red)

Account Name
Addr1
Addr2
City
State
Zip
Country
Contact

Telephone | Fax | Email
State Sales Tax No | Expiration Date | NY State O.S.R No | O.S.R. Expiration Date

Primary Type of Clientele
Residential
Commercial/Contract
Restoration

Business Classification (select one)
Designer with Business
Designer-No Shop
Drapery Workroom
Upholsterer
Hosptality
Department Store
Furniture Store
Wallpaper Studio
Architect
Government (U.S.)
Contract Specifier
Furniture Manufacturer
Museum
Bank
Other
Antique Dealer
Carpeting
Contractor
Funr/Distributor
Paint Store/Studio
Theater
Facitlities Educational
Facitlities Health Care
Facilities Corporate
Government (Non U.S.)
Magazine/Publications

Enter Account#
Brunschwig & Fils, Inc.
Clarence House of Fabrics
Cowtan & Tout
Decorators Walk
Duralee Fabrics
Kravet Fabrics
Maharam
Schumacher & Co.
Stroheim & Roman
Westgate Fabrics

Type of Account (select one)
OPEN N/30
PROFORMA

Order Requirements (select one)
Customer Purchase Order Required
Dept no. Required

Comments

Submit New Account Application
Clear and Re-Enter

Figure 9.4 New account application.

BOUTIQUE: A small, usually specialized showroom or store.

In addition to the showroom manager and general sales personnel, specialized salespeople may use the showroom as "home base." For example, if a fabric company represents both residential and contract collections, the contract sales rep may spend considerable time visiting design or architectural firms that specialize in contract work, introducing the latest collections or explaining the capabilities of the company he or she represents. These salespeople are sometimes referred to as "outside" reps; by contrast, "inside" sales personnel remain in the showroom throughout the day. "Territory reps" spend little or no time in a showroom and travel within a given geographic region, making presentations and delivering sample products to designers, architects, and approved fabric stores located away from a design center or showroom.

A final general category of showroom personnel includes individuals who or-ganize, track, and prepare sample products in the sample department of each showroom. Fabric samples that can be seen and felt by the designer and client are an essential part of the fabric selection process (Figure 9.5).

Evaluating Fabric for Purchase

After the account is established and a member of the showroom staff is identified to assist the designer if assistance is needed, the fabric selection process begins. While reviewing potential fabric selections, the designer should learn as much as possible about each item beyond the color and pattern that may stimulate initial interest.

Considerable information about fabrics can be found on the tags attached to each showroom sample, as noted in Figure 9.6. These tags provide information that significantly contributes to determining the appropriateness and afford-

Figure 9.5 (bottom left) Fabric sample department.

Figure 9.6 (bottom right) Fabric tags reveal important information.

ability of the fabric. Fabric tags can include most, some, or all, of the information listed below.

Showroom Fabric Tag Information

- direction of pattern (usually indicated by the positioning of the tag)
- name of the fabric
- pattern number
- color of fabric or "color-way" designated as a number after a period or dash (In the number 3006-004, the fabric being considered is 3006 and the color-way is 4.)
- measurement of pattern repeat in inches and/or centimeters
- measurement of pattern width in inches and/or centimeters
- number of colors, if a print, sometimes indicated by number of screens (the more screens used, the higher the cost)
- content of fabric
- country of origin
- price
- historical source information (if any)
- care instructions
- coordinating (matching) fabric number
- companion (complementing) fabric number
- treatment applied to the fabric (if any)
- ACT guideline icons (if appropriate)

In the United States, the fabric tag may also indicate wearability information as measured by the Wyzenbeek abrasion test. This information would appear on the bottom portion of the tag. For example, "30,000 D.R." means that the fabric is durable to approximately 30,000 double rubs and implies "moderate" wear.

A tag that carries an "m" before the fabric number signifies that the fabric has been "modified" in some way. If the sample in a showroom is old or the sample was previously owned by another company, the "m" on the fabric tag could indicate that in the new production of that fabric the horizontal or vertical repeat was changed or another aspect of the design reconfigured. If a designer chooses a fabric without asking questions about the "m" number, the pattern and fabric quality may not serve the intended purpose.

In addition, questions should be asked if there is any doubt about fabric repeat. For example, are there "false selvages" that provide extra fabric to easily sew repeat widths together? What is the *usable* fabric width? If the fabric is 54 inches wide, it may be that the usable width is several inches less. Not all fabrics have easily discernable repeat patterns. The "rhythm" or flow of the pattern must be understood so it can be communicated to the workroom for proper cutting and placement on a given surface.

Understanding Pricing

Methods of pricing fabric can vary from showroom to showroom. Some fabric houses use the retail price, which is approximately one third above the net price. This pricing structure has been used, for example, in New York City showrooms. Outside New York City, the retail price may be double the net cost. In recent years it has been difficult to standardize pricing policies. The cost per yard of product is sometimes disguised using a number coding system. Pricing codes serve to discourage individuals

MEMO: A showroom sample that designers borrow for a period of usually 30 days or less to show clients initial fabric choices.

DISPLAY WINGS: Designated showroom areas where fabrics are displayed by attaching them to metal clips on movable, overhead arms that permit the wide lengths to hang freely (soft racks) or smaller samples that are attached to a firm mounting surface where fabrics can be stapled or pinned (hard racks).

CUTTING: A fabric sample cut from the source where an order will eventually be generated.

who have not been approved to purchase products. One such pricing code is the "5/10" system, which can be translated as follows: If the tag indicates that the fabric is priced at $48.60 per yard, the designer price is calculated by subtracting $5.00 from the dollar amount and $.10 from the cents amount, resulting in the designer price of $43.50 per yard. Showroom sales personnel can clarify any pricing approaches for qualified designers. These novel ways of stating prices originated because, in some instances, unqualified individuals purchased products, utilized them incorrectly, and held the

Memo-Sample / Till Cutting Requests

Designer			Date	
Address				
City				
State			Zip	
Attention				

Memo	Till Cut	Sample Number	Retail Price	Wholesale Price
☐	☐		$	$
☐	☐		$	$
☐	☐		$	$
☐	☐		$	$
☐	☐		$	$
☐	☐		$	$
☐	☐		$	$
☐	☐		$	$
☐	☐		$	$
☐	☐		$	$
☐	☐		$	$
☐	☐		$	$
☐	☐		$	$
☐	☐		$	$
☐	☐		$	$

☐ Mail to:	☐ Waiting	☐ Pickup
Name		
Address		
City	State	Zip

Figure 9.7 Showrooms provide forms for recording the fabric numbers and colorways of preliminary fabric selections.

fabric company responsible for product that allegedly did not perform well.

Selecting and Ordering Fabric

The designer should write down the fabric numbers and color-ways, as they are reviewed in the showroom, prior to collecting memo or tray samples from the sample department. Each showroom has a convenient form for this purpose, one of which is shown in Figure 9.7.

A **memo** is a fabric sample as large as 27 inches square, representative of the product seen on "hard" or "soft" **display wings** (Figure 9.8). The memo is used to show clients the direction the designer is taking for a particular space. Memos are taken to the site, where they are evaluated by the designer, client, *and* workroom to help determine how practical the fabric will be for a particular application. By contrast, a **cutting** is a small sample that usually measures about 2×3 inches. Contract cuttings can be about 8 inches square and are linked together by a chain or stored in a contract box. Fabric cuttings are usually requested after the choices have been narrowed to a few memo samples, and cuttings usually are not returned to the showroom.

Samples are taken in a variety of sizes and serve different purposes. "Flag samples" are small cuttings, about 4 inches square, attached to large showroom samples showing available color-ways. "Road samples" are carried with the traveling sales representatives. The number of samples dispersed by a company varies and depends on the level of sales generated in each showroom. Samples can be distributed based on "limited," "medium," or "full" sampling.

(a)

(b)

Figure 9.8 Hard (a) and soft (b) wings from Fabricut showroom in the D&D Building, New York.

When a fabric is about to be ordered, a **cutting for approval (CFA)** can be requested, especially when a large order is placed. Ordering a CFA will add several days to the ordering process because of the various steps required to obtain the sample from the warehouse. The CFA is a small piece of the selected fabric cut directly from the bolt or dye lot from which the order will originate. The exact number of yards for the project should be known at this point, and yardage should be verified to determine whether the order can be fulfilled from one bolt or dye lot. Variances in color from dye lot to dye lot are almost certain to occur. The CFA should be taken to the site and checked for color under existing lighting conditions. The client should provide final approval *before* the fabric is taken to the workroom. Bear in mind that older clients may see more yellow tones in fabric, resulting in a last-minute change of color. As people reach approximately 50 years of age, the eye lens that focuses light on the retina can become less elastic and cloud. This cloudiness creates a diffusion of light, producing yellowish colorings.

In addition to further clarifying the correct fabric selection before purchase, a designer or workroom may submit a fabric acknowledgement form with the CFA attached and return it to the showroom for verification of the face of the fabric, pattern direction, and whether or not the fabric can be railroaded. This form is rarely used unless the order is large. Most questions about a fabric can be answered by telephoning the showroom; however, it is better to be cautious *before* purchasing fabric than to make assumptions that may prove costly later.

Larger fabric houses spend millions of dollars each year on cutting, sewing

CUTTING FOR APPROVAL (CFA): A fabric sample cut from the same source from which the order will originate and presented to the client for review and comment.

edges, taping, tagging, packaging, tracking, and delivering samples of several different collections each year to multiple showroom locations. There are also costs associated with managing and staffing personnel within each showroom through the sample department so designers can have immediate access to sample fabrics. If memo samples are not returned or special arrangements made to extend a loan, a designer can be charged. It is the designer's responsibility to return all memo samples so they can be restocked in the sample department. The usual duration of a loan is approximately 30 days.

When a fabric is selected prior to client review, the designer may choose to "place a hold" on the yardage. This is accomplished by giving the fabric number and color-way to a showroom salesperson. While reserving product, it is useful to confirm that the total yardage to be ordered can be purchased from the same bolt and/or dye lot.

Regardless of whether the designer has daily access to a showroom or conducts business away from a design center and places orders from a sample book, a purchase order should be completed by the designer to confirm the order. The purchase order clearly identifies not only the fabric and yardage but how it is to be processed, using a **sidemark** that indicates information about the designer, client, or project (e.g., "Mrs. Smith's slipper chair— bedroom"). When designers are working on more than one project, it becomes necessary to clarify what fabric is to be used and where. It is also helpful for the workroom to see the sidemarks because the workroom processes so many orders at

one time. On-time delivery is greatly enhanced when simple written instructions or reference notes are placed on the outside of the fabric package before it is shipped from the warehouse.

Custom and Special Order Products

One way experienced designers can utilize their talents and abilities is to create a custom order fabric in close consultation with the client and fabric company. In the case of a woven fabric, yarn content, color, design, pattern, and weave structure are selected. It may take 6 to 8 weeks before the dyed skeins are ready for approval and as many as 18 weeks to receive a strike-off that, when approved, will permit the production of an order to continue to completion. Traditionally, developing a custom order fabric is an expensive undertaking and usually requires a 50 percent deposit when the order is placed. Clients can also be responsible for as much as 10 percent overage that allows for unforeseen costs or extra fabric that has to be produced to meet the minimum for a particular mill. A minimum yardage ranging from 10 to 500 yards is required for a completely new woven fabric, and at least 200 yards is required for a printed product. The number of yards depends on the complexity of the fabric and the mill producing the product. If considerable handwork is required, fewer yards can be produced, but at a greater cost. The typical special order woven fabric, where an *existing* fabric is modified, is 240 to 500 yards. Some special orders may require only a change in the weft or filler yarns, thereby reducing the cost. Other "spe-

SIDEMARK: Brief written instructions given by a designer to the company that will ship the fabric order, instructing the receiver, such as a workroom, on how or where the fabric is to be handled or used.

cials" may require treating an existing fabric in a particular way, such as adding a quilted effect.

When working with a showroom that encourages custom or special orders, it is useful for a designer to inquire whether the mill affiliated with the fabric company is a **vertical mill** or for the designer to determine the amount of experience of the subcontractors who will produce and expedite the project. Mills that produce fabric for interiors can be found throughout the world. It is essential that when fabric is specified as a custom or special order, the designer should be confident that the showroom representative will be able to expedite the order. Delays are almost certain, and clients should be prepared beforehand.

One of the most challenging aspects of designing interiors is coordinating the many facets of a project and adhering to time schedules. If the fabric arrives at the workroom on time but the trimming does not, the treatment will be placed on hold. It may be further delayed if the workroom decides to begin another project in its place, thereby further postponing the fabrication process. When the designer actively tracks all phases of a project and communicates with the showroom and workroom, the likelihood of time schedules being met increases.

THE WORLD FABRIC MARKET

The globalization of the world economy and the politics of evolving trade agreements affect how fabric is accessed, its cost, and the manner in which U.S. design centers and showrooms conduct business.

The trend in the United States to acquire fabric only from design center showrooms appears to be somewhat on the decline, in favor of a more European approach. In England, for example, design districts are established around antique or fashion centers, where fabric shops, boutiques, and salons sell fabric in a two-tier pricing arrangement. One price is for the design professional, and the other for the general public. This mix of wholesale and retail customers permits business owners to broaden their market, thereby increasing sales. Many design centers in the United States have vacancies and, in order to fill them, are looking for nontraditional showrooms or stores to occupy the empty spaces.

Realities and World Sources

Little residential or contract fabric manufacturing remains in the United States. Fabric of all qualities is produced worldwide, in places such as Belgium, China, France, Germany, Holland, India, Italy, Korea, Pakistan, South America, Southeast Asia, Spain, Switzerland, Taiwan, Thailand, and Turkey. In Turkey, for example, $3.5 billion of fabric was produced in 2005, compared with $297 million in 2003.

On the world market, business arrangements are increasingly being made with little or no input from the United States, although the decisions can have an effect on the U.S. market. One example includes the negotiations between the European Union and China to limit Chinese imports to EU countries. More specifically, the EU and China agreement of June 10, 2005, allows both to arrange the growth of fabric

VERTICAL MILL: A mill that converts raw materials into finished products, where quality and production limits are controlled on all levels.

imports in ten categories until 2008. Those relating to interiors include the importing of flax and cotton fabrics, with all other categories relating to articles of clothing.

International Fabric Fairs

International home and fabric fairs attract worldwide audiences numbering in the tens of thousands. Heimtextil sponsors international fabric fairs in Frankfurt, Germany; Moscow, Russia; and Mumbai, India. Decosit sponsors a fair in Brussels, Belgium, currently the center of the European market. Other sponsors include Intertextile Shanghai Home Textiles in Shanghai, China; Proposte in Como, Italy; and Japantex in Tokyo, Japan. And in Paris two popular shows are the La Biennale and Masion & Objet.

These shows are often attended by major fabric companies and fabric editors whose work it is to review many samples of fabrics from around the world and determine what will be purchased from the mills that attend these shows. It is important for fabric companies to have an identity as defined by the fabric they sell. It is common, therefore, for fabric editors and company executives to see a fabric that they desire for their new collection from a show, such as Proposte, and commit to purchase the pattern, thereby eliminating competition from all other companies who may want to own that product. Typically, the minimum yardages for this arrangement are several hundred yards. Because fabric for fashion can influence home furnishings, firms also frequent mill towns such as Prato, near Florence, Italy, where fashion-inspired fabric can be translated for residential use, giving firms an-

other opportunity to maintain a competitive advantage.

In recent times, fabric shows in the United States have seen fewer European and Asian visitors because what once could be seen only in the United States—new residential and contract fabrics and developments in loom technology—can now be experienced in Europe and Asia.

The Chinese Fabric Industry

China, in particular, is experiencing a building boom that has led to a sharp increase in the demand for residential and contract fabrics. In 2004, the growth was reported to be 20 percent over that of the previous year.[2] This surge was attributed to a gain in personal income and an increase in travel to the West. As the Chinese have become attracted to Western fashion and residential fabrics, "epidemic levels of counterfeiting"[3] have been reported. Western fabrics and designs produced in China eventually return to the United States and flow into the world market. As fabric production increases, costs decline, contributing to the availability of more product for less money.

It is estimated that China will "spend billions through 2015 on new buildings, renovations, and upgrading tourist facilities,"[4] billions which will affect the contract fabric market. In 2004, China imported more than $1 billion in residential fabric. The challenge for the U.S. market is to produce interior fabrics that will compete with the Chinese market in terms of price and quality or address the undervalued Chinese currency, which provides a strong competitive advantage for Chinese companies in China.

U.S. Responses to the Changing World Market

The manufacturing of woven fabrics for residential or contract use can be a labor-intensive process. Countries such as India and China, where an abundant supply of low-cost labor and high levels of productivity exist, have been successful at pressuring the U.S. market to change the way business is conducted. U.S. companies are increasingly required to be more innovative and smaller and work more efficiently, while considering the advantages of partnering with firms outside the United States. However, advances in high-tech or "smart" fibers developed in the United States and used in the medical, space program, or specialty areas help some American companies develop successful niche markets. Advanced technologies applied to manufacturing fabric and products such AutoCAD and Product-Data-Management (PDM web-enabled technologies) also contribute to the new business growth. One basic concern in the United States is to identify a labor source that will operate the equipment on a day-to-day basis.

Emerging U.S. companies, such as Adaptive Textiles, use digital technology to quickly duplicate pattern, change color, and alter scale of an existing printed fabric with no minimum yardage requirements, offering increased flexibility for the designer and client; however, design copyright laws must be respected when developing a modified print. Laser technology is also being developed and refined to expand print options and speed the process from time of design conception to delivery. The United States is known for its innovations and entrepreneurial approach to business but has difficulty sustaining a workforce to produce product on a daily basis.

Consumers are increasingly knowledgeable of where fabric originates and able to compare costs, in part because of Internet access and ease of international travel. Although the consumer may have access to more fabric of all grades, the skill to select and utilize it appropriately is the purview of the knowledgeable and creative designer. It remains the designer's task to know reliable fabric sources, be capable of evaluating quality and cost, determine what fabric is preferred for a particular space and how to coordinate and apply it, have the ability to utilize fabric in a practical and pleasing way, and possess the resources to have the design competently translated and installed in a timely fashion using the correct hardware.

SUMMARY

Design centers and marts that house showrooms remain an important source for acquiring fabric. Each center develops rules for operating and defining what it means to sell to the trade. Understanding the various roles of showroom personnel and how a fabric showroom operates can help facilitate and expedite the ordering process.

Fabric tag information reveals information about a fabric's function, design, color, quality, and price. Designers are encouraged to ask showroom employees about their fabric so the best selections can be made.

When a designer does not practice near a design center, quality fabrics can be purchased through local or regional shops and serviced by traveling agents who represent several nationally known companies and their collections. The designer should explain to the client beforehand any essential details about the fabric they are purchasing in terms of correct color, quality, and price. Fabric samples often differ from the actual order.

Offshore fabric manufacturing mills and their pricing strategies have severely reduced fabric production in the United States. Because fabric is readily available in all qualities from many sources, including the Internet, design centers are marketing their services to the general public and educating them on the benefits of working with a designer. As a result, designers are required to know more about fabric as well as other interior products.

ACTIVITIES

1. Identify three primary sources of quality fabrics in your area.
2. Tour a fabric showroom in a design center or mart. Review and report on the tag information found on one woven residential fabric and one woven contract fabric. Select products that display at least three pieces of information on each tag.
3. Interview a design center showroom manager or a manager of a store where designer fabrics can be purchased. Determine what the managers can do to help a designer.
4. Learn how to determine the Wyzenbeek number or locate information on wearability for a contract grade fabric if that information is not on the tag.
5. Determine what the trade discount would be, if any, at a fabric resource near you. Inquire how fabric is priced.
6. Visit a showroom or fabric store. Measure the horizontal and/or vertical repeat on one printed and one woven fabric to determine whether they conform to the tag information.
7. Discover how fabric is sampled when the source is not a showroom in a design center.
8. Research the residential and contract fabric production in one of the countries listed in the chapter. Determine the yarn composition (e.g., silk, cotton, wool, blends), amount of yards or meters imported per year, quality, and price. Compare a similar fabric and quality produced in the United States.
9. List the names of five fabric companies that exhibited recently at one of the international fairs noted in the chapter. Focus on one international company, and report on its latest collection of residential and/or contract fabrics.

EXPAND YOUR KNOWLEDGE

1. What are the differences, if any, between ordering fabric from a design center showroom and a fabric store serviced by an agent?
2. What is the process for canceling an order? What kind of results can be expected?
3. If a client visits a showroom without a designer, what concerns should be addressed regarding fabric selec-

tions? How would a designer prepare a client for visiting a showroom unescorted? What are some reasons a client might visit a showroom alone?

4. Why is it important to edit the number of fabrics shown to a client before a presentation?

5. Where would a fabric be used if the tag indicated 50,000 D.R.?

6. Would a universally accepted, two-tiered pricing strategy be a favorable method of costing fabric in the United States? Explain, and justify your answer.

7. What conditions would have to be met in order to revitalize the U.S. fabric manufacturing industry?

8. Price, aesthetics, quality, and location of use all contribute to fabric selection. How might a designer communicate to a residential client these issues and create a case for purchasing products that may exceed $100 a yard, net?

9. What contributes to the cost of fabric available to designers in a design center showroom?

10. What guarantees, if any, are given with a fabric purchase? What differences or similarities are there in guarantees between fabric acquired from design center showrooms, fabric stores, and Internet sources? How does a designer address a client who wants a guarantee with a fabric purchase?

11. How can a designer learn about the most recent European or Asian fabric collections without attending international fairs? How can these collections be accessed?

12. Review websites of design centers and marts for current information on their activities and a list of showrooms.

READ ON

Mary Blewett, *Last Generation: Work and Life in the Textile Mills of Lowell, Massachusetts, 1910–1960*, Amherst: University of Massachusetts Press, 1990.

Daniel Clark, *Like Night and Day: Unionization in a Southern Mill Town*, Chapel Hill: University of North Carolina Press, 1997.

Jeanette Joy Fisher, *Design Psychology: Fabrics*, http://ezinearticles.com/?Design-Psychology:-Fabrics&id=4298.

Emily Honig, *Sisters and Strangers: Women in the Shanghai Cotton Mills, 1919–1949*, Palo Alto, Calif.: Stanford University Press, 1992.

Interior Decorators' Handbook (IDH), New York: E.W. Williams Publications Company, Published semiannually.

"Introducing Decorator Fabrics," *Threads* magazine, http://www.tauton.com/threads/pages/t00015.asp.

William Moran, *The Belles of New England: The Women of the Textile Mills and the Families Whose Wealth They Wove*, New York: St. Martin's Press, 2002.

Carol Tisch, "In Brussles, They Speak Fabrics," *IsdesigNET*, http://www.isdesignet.com/Magazine/April'01/happenings.html.

The Washington, D.C., Design Center "Frequently Asked Questions," http://www.merchandisemart.com/dcdesigncenter/designcenter/_faq.html.

Inside the Workroom

Translating fabric into a useful and attractive end product requires a carefully coordinated effort between the designer, client, fabric supplier, and workroom (or the individuals who will produce the end product). Often, a full-service workroom will provide design support that begins by examining the interior architectural plans to roughly estimate fabric yardages, as seen in Figure 10.1, as well as assisting the designer in understanding what can and cannot be accomplished with certain fabric selections. On occasions workroom personnel with design experience use tracing paper over a photograph of a window or area to be addressed, helping designers explore various options, as shown in Figure 10.2; however, not all workrooms or fabricators are willing or capable of providing a comprehensive list of services.

The labor involved in fabricating a treatment requires talent and patience. Competent workroom artisans often have many years of experience sewing in varying capacities, such as in the garment industry, where delicate handwork is often required in the sewing of intricate details onto a dress. This experience carries over to detailing a window treatment, upholstering furniture, or styling other decorative fabric treatments. Some workrooms have experienced woodworkers on staff who know how chair and sofa frames are assembled and how various species of wood respond to different stains and finishes, including old wood associated with antique furniture.

THE WORK OF THE WORKROOM

The designer has, in most locations, options to exercise in completing a fabric treatment. Generally, one of three approaches, or any combination of the three, can be employed to accomplish the objectives of a fabric treatment. The option selected usually depends on the geographic location of the interior designer's

CHAPTER 10

Opposite: Candles burning on windowsill.

Figure 10.1 (left) Full-service workrooms begin by reviewing architectural plans with the designer to learn about the scope of the project and to schedule on-site measurements.

Figure 10.2 (right) Designs can be drawn on tracing paper over photos or over scaled drawings of windows.

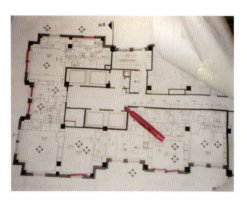

practice and the amount of funds allocated for the project.

The Full-Service Workroom

One approach is to engage a full-service workroom, if available. Full-service implies that the workroom usually has full-time professionals to consult on design concepts; estimate fabric yardages; visit a site to measure; log in and account for deliveries; and cut, sew, and produce a mock-up of the design (often in muslin) and install the final product, regardless of its domestic or foreign location. These workrooms can produce window treatments, upholstered walls, and upholstered furniture from hard wood frames they purchase or construct and move the projects through all of the stages to final completion and delivery. They may also carve their own custom wooden finials for window treatments or posts for beds in their workshop and gild or paint them to order. Many of the workrooms located in major U.S. cities can employ as many as 70 individuals in spaces exceeding 5,000 square feet. Having access to a proven, full-service workroom—and the client able to afford the services—can be convenient for the designer. All the skills and equipment necessary to complete a project successfully, regardless of its complexity, are contained in one location.

Working with Independent Artisans

The second approach requires that the designer assemble several individuals who may be talented in only one area, such as upholstering furniture, while being ever mindful of the stages that the overall project is going through. Inexperienced designers working with low-budget projects in small markets need to know competent craftspeople, who usually work independently and sometimes only in their spare time. The designer will need to qualify the individuals who can perform all the tasks a major workroom performs in-house. They will be required to source reputable people who are capable of measuring a project, cutting and sewing fabric, applying trimming, and delivering and installing the treatment or furniture. In this scenario there will probably be no one to assist in the development or modification of a design. What a designer draws to scale will be produced and installed. The designer will have to be knowledgeable about all the specifics of a particular design, choose all hardware, and offer clear instructions to those who will produce the product. If the designer wants valances to be padded, sheers made of cotton instead of polyester, or drapes interlined, those requests, along with others, will have to be made known. And if the designer cannot locate an individual who will accept the responsibility of estimating yardages or measuring, they will have to assume that task as well. Yardage estimates for various upholstered pieces can be found in the appendix to this chapter.

Additionally, some small sewing operations may not be available to receive fabric or hardware shipments because of their location or business hours. The designer may have to assume the responsibility for all deliveries, checking for imperfections and ensuring the safe arrival of all products to the fabricator. If the design project is outside the designer's usual working area, it may not be possible to convince people to travel to measure or install, necessitating the recruitment of personnel closer to the project site.

Limited Service Workrooms

Designers may also have experiences somewhere in the middle of the two scenarios noted. However, if a project is not within the vicinity of a comprehensive workroom in a medium or large market, it becomes necessary for the designer to be knowledgeable and capable of directing all operations in a timely fashion to meet client expectations.

GUIDELINES FOR CONSTRUCTING FABRIC TREATMENTS AND UPHOLSTERING FURNITURE

Producing window treatments and upholstering furniture are complex tasks. To plan and orchestrate a successful outcome, an interior designer must understand the many issues involved and keep in mind the following when dealing with a full-service workroom or individual artisians:

- Window treatment architecture and the art of applying fabric and trim to furniture often involve creating scale drawings and selecting component parts, such as wood, fabric, trim, and hardware, while remaining attentive to the budget. The actual construction process can involve frame making as well as hand and machine sewing work.

- Competent individuals must accurately measure and photograph the area or space where fabric will be installed. This task is an opportunity for the person who measures (often the installer as well) to collect information confirming whether the basic design concept will be possible to execute given the parameters of the space or area. If any construction modifications are made to the interior *after* measurements are taken (for example, if the moldings are enlarged), these changes must be communicated to the workroom without delay so the treatment can be remeasured and constructed to fit properly.

- All products sent to a workroom should be side-marked, enabling them to be carefully accounted for. Side-markings can appear on the fabric packaging and/or on the invoice that accompanies the fabric, trimming, or hardware. Workroom facilities often deal with many designers, each of whom may have multiple projects under way in different parts of the world or are working on more than one property owned by the same client. Fabric that lacks side-marking instructions can become misplaced, misdirected, lost, or used improperly. Designers and workrooms can unnecessarily spend considerable time tracking the particulars of a fabric shipment while attempting to determine its intended purpose. Even when all products are properly marked, the designer should confirm their delivery to the workroom from the supplier. Fabrics originating from foreign sources require more time to arrive at the workroom. The designer, not the workroom, is responsible for tracking all offshore products through customs and assuring their safe arrival at the workroom,

Figure 10.3 A cautionary reminder from the fabric supplier is enclosed with the fabric to indicate terms of use.

often with the help from showroom personnel. Custom fabric produced in Europe, for example, can take as long as six months to arrive at a U.S. workroom.

- Not all fabric selected for a particular installation may be suitable for the intended purpose. The arrangement of pattern or fabric weight can necessitate a change in design from what was originally conceived; or the fabric may not be usable at all, requiring another selection. Consult the individuals who cut and sew *before* a final purchase is made. When examining a small cutting or memo sample leads to doubt about a fabric's ability to perform, a few yards should be ordered so the workroom can experiment further. Once the full order has been cut, fabric cannot be returned. A cautionary note (see Figure 10.3) is enclosed with most shipments to alert the workroom and designer to the terms of use regarding the product. Conditions associated with the terms of sale of fabric are listed in Figure 10.4.

ATTENTION WORK ROOM
Please Read Carefully Before Cutting This Merchandise

Please inspect all shipments carefully upon receipt for correct color, design, and yardage BEFORE CUTTING.

Regardless of fault, all returns must be authorized by management.
No merchandise will be accepted without authorization label.
No merchandise will be accepted for credit unless specifically approved by management.
No merchandise will be accepted for credit once it has been cut into.
No merchandise will be accepted for credit after 30 days.
Please note that there will be a twenty-five percent (25%) service and handling charge for all merchandise returned, unless approved by management.
No merchandise will be accepted for credit once it has undergone a special process, such as flame-proofing, water repelling, stain resisting or piece dyeing.
No specials will be accepted for credit.
No velvets or taffetas will be accepted for credit.

NATURE'S SIGNATURES
All textile has natural characteristics that are NOT DEFECTS.
Black specks in natural fibers such as silk douppione, wool, uncombed cotton.
Foreign hairs in wool.
Broken warp threads in fine taffetas.
Color variation in various lots.
Slubs or knots in yarns.
Streaky dying due to variation of oil content in wools.

ALL DEFECTS WILL BE MARKED AT EDGE AND AMPLE YARDAGE WILL BE SHIPPED TO COVER LOSS.

Figure 10.4 Terms of sale for fabric and trimming.

PLEASE READ CAREFULLY, THESE ARE OUR TERMS OF SALE.

TERMS

Net 30 days. A service charge of 10% per month will be added to all balances over 60 days.

Each shipment made shall be considered a separate sale. Time and terms of payment are essential and if any default be made by the buyer, or if financial responsibility of the buyer shall at any time become impaired or unsatisfactory, or if any assignment for the benefit of creditors, bankruptcy, or for the appointment of a receiver for the buyer shall at any time be made or instituted, we shall have the right, at our option, to terminate all sales without notice, or to defer or discontinue further shipments until past due payments are made. If an account is placed for collection the buyer must assume all costs incurred through this action, in addition to the amounts due for merchandise.

PRICES

All quotations are exclusive of freight, special processing, or local delivery charges.

MINIMUMS

One full hide is the minimum order on all leathers. A three roll minimum is required on all wallpapers with the exception of imported papers packaged in double rolls. On these papers the minimum is two rolls.

CANCELLATIONS

Cancellation of items stocked in Europe will not be accepted after having been cut or packed.
All orders are subject to acceptance at factories.

LARGE ORDERS

A 50% deposit is required for all large orders.
Orders over $10,000.00 are not subject to cancellation once production has started.
Orders over $10,000.00 are not returnable under any circumstances.

SHIPMENT NOTES

We are not responsible for damage suffered in transit.
All shipments are made F.O.B. to our warehouse.
Complete instructions as to shipping method and route must be given at time order is placed. If no instructions are received we will ship by whatever method and route we consider the best possible way.
We shall not be liable for any delay in performance or in the delivery or shipment of merchandise herein or any damage suffered by buyer by reason of such delay when the delay is directly or indirectly caused by or in any manner arises from any causes beyond our control.

DELIVERY

Fabrics and wallpapers stocked in Europe: approximately 3 to 4 weeks. Fabrics, papers and leathers stocked in Fort Mill are shipped in approximately 48 hours. Out of stock items will be shipped in accordance with projected deliveries quoted by suppliers and manufacturers; these deliveries are subject to change without notice.

RETURNS

No merchandise can be returned for credit or exchange unless authorized by us in writing. After receipt of shipping label from our order department, returns must be sent to our warehouse.

EXAMINE GOODS BEFORE CUTTING. No allowance for any reason will be made after merchandise has been cut.

No goods returnable after 30 days from date of invoice.

Velvets, leathers, embossed fabrics, custom orders or cut yardage orders from European mills may not be returned for credit.

Less than 6 yards of fabric or trimming is not returnable.

A 25% Handling and Service charge will be applied to all items returned.

No claims are allowed if items have been treated or backed. Due to the inherent characteristics of certain natural fibers, texture and color variations may occur.

FLAMMABILITY STANDARDS

Items appearing in our price list are not intended for use in the manufacture of wearing apparel in compliance with the FLAMMABILITY FABRICS ACT as amended on May 4, 1967.
All fabrics meet the requirements of the California Bureau of Home Furnishings Technical Bulletin #117 dated February, 1975.

ABRASION TESTING

Several of our fabrics have been tested for Abrasion Resistance. Abrasion resistance is the ability of a fabric to withstand surface wear from rubbing. Fabrics which have been tested are marked with the letters **A.C.T.** (Association Contract Textiles) and their rating. A small **a** in bold means the fabric passes the **A.C.T.** standard for general contract upholstery which is 15,000 double rubs. A capital **A** in bold means the fabric passes the **A.C.T.** standard for heavy duty upholstery, which is 30,000 double rubs based on the Wyzenbeek testing method.

SPECIAL NOTES

Our materials are not guaranteed against color fading through overexposure to the sun.

We are not responsible for precise matching of color due to dye lot variations. PLEASE REQUEST CUTTING OF PRESENT STOCK.

Our materials should be dry cleaned only. They are not guaranteed against discoloration due to washing or contact with any liquid.

The suitability of a fabric for any use is entirely at the discretion of the purchaser.

Please note that certain silk fabrics, unlike man-made fibers, may contain slubs which are characteristic of their natural origin.

NO CLAIMS ALLOWED FOR LABOR UNDER ANY CONDITIONS.

Fabrics breathe and absorb moisture; according to content and construction, dimensional fluctuations of up to 3% may reasonably occur. OUR FABRICS ARE NOT GUARANTEED AGAINST SHRINKAGE.

Fabrics to be fireproofed must be tested prior to treatment. We will not be responsible for any changes caused by chemicals used in fireproofing.

This price catalogue identifies fiber content in accordance with the "Textile Fiber Products Identification Act."

We reserve the right to change the specifications and construction of the products listed herein to comply with any Government ruling or directive, or whenever we deem it necessary or advisable to make such modifications.

WELTING: A tape or covered cording sewn into a seam as reinforcement or trimming.

- Fabric should be inspected before it arrives at the workroom; however, some workrooms inspect fabric on site, using a light table to detect misweaves and other flaws. If fabric is not carefully reviewed and flaws are discovered at the time of cutting, considerable time can be lost in having to reorder new product. If the original fabric selection is not available, another choice will have to be made. Sometimes this necessitates a change in trimming, if specified, or other elements of the project, further delaying construction and installation.

- Fabric should be carefully measured. Both horizontal and vertical repeats need to be verified so that the fabric will be properly proportioned and suitably matched on window treatments or furniture arms, backs, side panels, and skirting. The primary responsibility for products arriving at the workroom in good condition lies with the company where the order originated or the designer. A significant part of the reputation of a fabric/trimming/frame hardware company rests on its ability to fulfill an order accurately and in a timely fashion. A designer's own reputation can be affected by associating with unreliable sources or sources that do not address problems.

- When fabric is cut for upholstery, large sections that fall between the repeats can be used for cushion borders, **welting**, or skirts. All welts should be cut on a bias for a better fit. Fewer seams will appear if the fabric can be cut in long lengths.

- Consider full-scale mock-ups produced in muslin, as illustrated in Figure 10.5, especially when there is a question of what the overall design is to look like and whether or not it will function. Smaller scale mock-ups can be produced with a few yards of the fabric specified to show pleating details or determine how the pattern will respond to a scaled design, as seen in Figure 10.6. A mock-up can be shown to a client, with appropriate hardware selections for approval, thereby eliminating any misunderstandings.

- If a custom chair or sofa is being constructed, designers should consider visiting the workroom with the client to test the firmness of the cushioning and the positioning of the back support. Some clients may prefer seat cushioning that extends farther outward and under the back of the knees to provide additional upper leg support. In this case, the client's leg length should be factored into the design or determined at the time of the seating.

Figure 10.5 (left) **and 10.6** (right) Mock-ups of window treatments in muslin and various fabrics help orient the designer, workroom personnel, and client to its basic appearance.

- Consider issues regarding the geographic location of a property. For example, if curtains are to be installed in a home near a body of salt water or inside a yacht, the lining and fabric should be pre-shrunk *before* arriving at the workroom site. Many fabrics can stretch or shrink up to two inches when exposed to natural elements. The amount of sun that a fabric will receive should be factored into the plan for specific kinds of linings. In certain environments, hardware should be carefully selected to ensure that it will not rust and transfer stains onto the fabric. Fabric exposed to the outdoors should be chosen to resist sun, mildew, and other elements.

- Some installations with difficult access, such as elevated window treatments located in a stairwell, out of easy reach, may require motorized equipment if they are to function. All motors, pulls, remote controls, and other hardware should be factored into the overall cost of the treatment.

- Window treatments and furnishings are often "accessorized," similarly to clothing. All trimmings and adornments must be considered as part of the design, ordered, and logged into the workroom schedule. Any delays in receiving components will postpone the production schedule and date of installation.

- All aspects of fabricating *and* installing soft furnishings require time. The more involved the treatment is, the more time it will take to successfully complete the project. A reasonable timeline should be established, incorporating the installation of other furnishings, such as carpeting. Clients should be informed about the process, costs, and schedule. Much of what constitutes a well constructed and pleasing window treatment or upholstered piece cannot be seen: The hand-sewn rings on the back of a curtain, the cured wooden support boards wrapped in compatible fabric behind a drape, a wall surface prepared to be upholstered and properly positioning, and attachment of springs with the correct tension to a chair seat and back are some of the hidden features of well-constructed and installed projects.

- For installations in commercial buildings, the hours of building access, including access to and size of freight elevators, are needed. Many commercial and residential buildings specify the service hours when contractors are permitted on the premises to do their work. Workroom personnel need to know when they can enter the building to measure and install. Additionally, the building may require a certificate of insurance in order for work to be done on the premises.

- If the project location is far from the workroom site and involves many large or heavy component pieces, a method of transport will have to be arranged. Often, moving companies are employed to pick up and deliver chairs, sofas, and various window treatments that are to be installed. The workroom should know how the finished products are to be delivered, and the client will need to be informed of any additional costs.

PICK TICKET: A work order picked up from a designer or fabric supplier that is usually delivered by hand to a workroom.

- Determine whether what is being made in the workroom will fit in the space intended. An apartment may be large, but the elevator or stairs to access it may be small. Sofas, for example, can be designed so the back can separate from the seat and arms, then be reattached on site.
- Workrooms usually collect a 50 percent deposit to initiate the project, with the remainder due before or just after installation.

CHARTING THE PROCESS: WINDOW TREATMENTS

At the moment fabric or other products arrive at a full-service workroom, a careful plan is activated to ensure that the desired end product is carefully produced and delivered on time.

Tracking fabric, trimming, and hardware through the workroom system generates a considerable amount of paperwork. Most treatments are particular to a given window or client or the specifications of a designer, showing the placement of finials and other specifics of how a treatment is intended to appear. Although the computer facilitates many operations, there is no computer program at present that permits for the individuality and range that accompany a myriad of conditions unique to each client's taste, fabric and hardware selection, and window size and location in a particular space.

Accounting for New Product Arrivals

When fabric, trimming, and hardware enter the workroom, they must be logged in and clearly accounted for, making them easy to locate later. There are different systems that account for fabric deliveries, based partly on how much activity the workroom generates. Some workrooms may receive only a few yards of fabric each week; however, busy workrooms in large markets may receive two to five deliveries a day.

When fabric, trimming, or hardware is delivered to a full-service workroom, it is opened and inspected for quantity and quality. In a fabric order, some extra material is usually included, because if flaws are discovered, it may be impossible to cut around them. Usually, a small piece of the fabric representing the order is cut and stapled or taped to work-order forms, ensuring that the correct fabric and trim has arrived (Figure 10.7). The invoice or **pick ticket** is also examined to verify the contents and to note information regarding the designer, client, fabric number including color-way, and where and how the fabric is to be applied. This information is used to complete the materials receipt form (Figure 10.8). After the form is completed, tracking labels are produced that include the designer's name, client's name, name of the product, location of product use (for example, master bath and dressing room), amount of product, company that provided the product, and date and

Figure 10.7 A small sample of the actual fabric is used to confirm fabric scale, weight, and pattern.

time of receipt of delivery, as seen in Figure 10.9. These labels are adhered onto and inside of the packaging material, then shelved to wait for their turn to be used. The invoice/pick ticket information (Figure 10.10) describing what is in the package must match the product sent. Holding bins, as seen in Figure 10.11, are where the fabric is placed. Each bin is labeled, sometimes with the designer's name. Other products are dispersed throughout the workroom to their appropriate locations. All items received in a given day are compiled and listed on a master form that includes much the same information found on the tracking labels.

The measured drawings and requirements that were agreed upon early in the process must appear in the work order. Without confirmation of all aspects of an order and all corresponding design considerations in detail, delays and confusion can complicate the fabrication process.

Materials Receipt Form

Designer

Fabric House

Fabric

Fabric Number

Client

Department

Trim

Yards Received

Date Received

Room

Item

Holding Bin

Comments:

Save   Switchboard

Figure 10.8 (left) The materials receipt form provides all relevant information about the order.

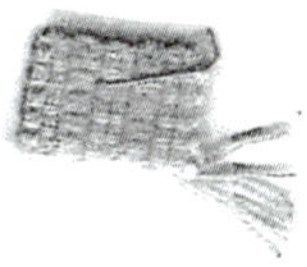

Figure 10.9 (below) In busy workrooms, tracking labels help to account for each project.

Figure 10.10 (bottom of page) The pick ticket describes the fabric or trim to package mailed from the fabric supplier.

DESIGNER
CLIENT

PORCH
CURTS.
BRUNSCHWIG & FILS   39093-028
80 Yards
DATE

26

BENNISON FABRICS INC.

THE FINE ARTS BUILDING
232 E. 59TH STREET 3rd FLOOR NY, NY 10022
TEL: (212) 223-0373   FAX: (212) 223-0655

PICK TICKET

TRANSACTION #:

DATE:

SOLD TO:

SHIP TO:

ACCOUNT #:

SIDE MARK:

PHONE #:

CUSTOMER P.O. #	SHOWROOM	SHOWROOM ORDER #	SHIP VIA	TERMS
BEN	PROFORMA			

ITEM #	DESCRIPTION	QUANTITY	LOT #	PIECE #	ON HAND ALLOWANCE
8466/330A	ZANZIBAR/FADED YELLOW/OYSTER WIDTH: 4.6" REPEAT: 24" 70% LINEN 30% COTTON	2.00			001
CFA WAIVED		2.00 L4815		2 0	6.00
				A	4.00

TABLED: When the full length of a fabric panel has been laid on a large table to ensure that the interlining and fabric are even, straight, and fitting properly.

Figure 10.11 (bottom left) Holding bins are used for product waiting to be processed.

Figure 10.12 (bottom right) (a) Fabric is carefully measured and cut to conform to a set pattern and design. (b) Fabric that is cut cannot be returned to the supplier.

Cutting and Sewing

When the time arrives to begin creating the window treatment, the fabric is delivered with the work order, which contains drawings and measurements to a section of the workroom where it is to be cut. Before the cutting begins, the fabric is carefully examined to determine its ability to be produced into the treatment as drawn. If questions arise, a mock-up will be produced or modifications to the original design will be made to accommodate the pattern and weight of the fabric. Because some fabrics can cost in excess of $300 a yard, it is essential that the plan of action is clear. After all decisions are made, the fabric is measured and cut, as seen in Figure 10.12, then forwarded to a sewing specialist. In a full-service workroom, many individuals sew. Some are experts at ma-chine sewing, as appears in Figure 10.13, and others are specialists at hand sewing, as seen in Figure 10.14. The actual design of the treatment will determine whether the cut fabric will be sewn by machine, by hand, or by a combination of both.

After the larger panels or component parts are sewn together, the fabric is **tabled**, pressed, sized, and adjusted to fit the space. If specified, linings and the layering of interlinings are added. For example, to completely darken a bedroom, the interlinings may consist of felt, black sateen, and ivory sateen over the black to restrict the dark color from shading the color of the fabric appearing outward in the room. If trimming is required, the treatment is forwarded on to individuals who sew on borders, rings, and all embellishments, as illustrated in Figures 10.15 and 10.16.

(a)

(b)

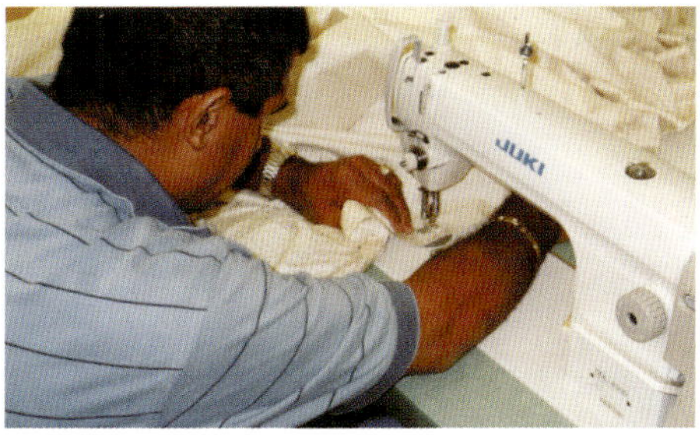

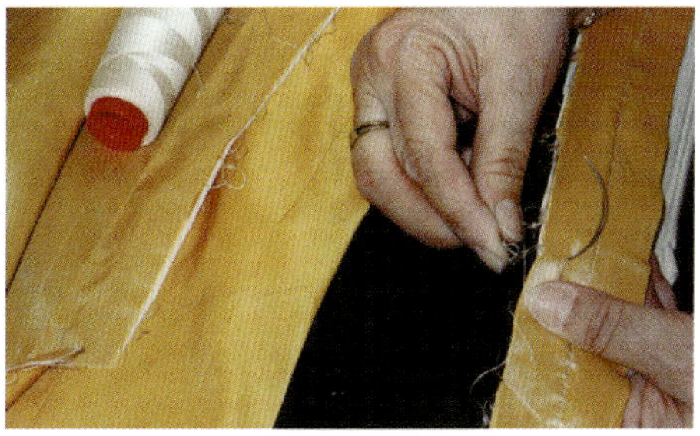

Figure 10.13 (left)
Machine stitching.

Figure 10.14 (right)
Hand stitching.

Upon completion of the window treatment, the finished product is forwarded to inspection, as seen in Figure 10.17, where it is examined for:

- loose threads left from sewing
- matching patterns
- pins remaining in the fabric folds
- correct length and width
- stains and general damage
- meeting all work-order specifications

In the case of some unusual applications, such as corner window curtains (Figure 10.18), the treatment is mounted on an inspection wall and reviewed by management to see whether the patterns (birds and leaves, in this case) align properly and the pleats are correctly placed. After the treatment is approved, it is packaged, as seen in Figure 10.19, and sent to the installation location. If the installation site is local, the installers will deliver the treatment.

CHARTING THE PROCESS: UPHOLSTERING FURNITURE

Some workrooms have the ability to manufacture frames in their shop, along with wooden accessories, such as hand-carved wooden fennels. Frame specifications for

Figure 10.15 (left) The application of hardware to a drapery treatment.

Figure 10.16 (top right) Trimming ready to be applied to a drapery treatment.

Figure 10.17 (bottom right) All completed treatments or upholstered pieces must be carefully inspected.

Figure 10.18 (top) Some window treatments are mounted to confirm the correct placement of pleats and pattern.

Figure 10.19 (bottom left) Each completed item is wrapped, and a photo of it is taped to the package to ensure proper delivery.

Figure 10.20 (bottom right) Many workrooms are able to restore old furniture.

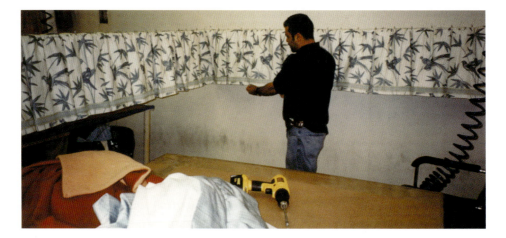

FOX EDGE: A ready-made roll, typically made of burlap and filled with jute fibers, sold by the foot. Used for seat edges and around arms and rails where soft edges are required.

JACONET DUST COVER: Cloth protecting the underneath portion of upholstered furniture.

all furniture pieces must be accurately measured, with allowances or variances accounted for, so correct fabric amounts can be specified.

One method that workrooms use to aid the designer in deciding what chairs, sofas, and other furnishings may be required by the client is to visit the workroom's showroom, if one exists. Samples include chairs, sofas, and beds that are not for sale, but serve as models sometimes covered in muslin. A designer and client have the option to choose one of the pieces and upholster it with the selected fabric or modify an existing design by changing any dimension.

Many workrooms can restore or re-upholster an existing piece owned by the client, as shown in Figure 10.20. Furniture to be recreated from an existing frame must be stripped of old glues and reinforced, with special attention placed on joint connections. Springs should also be examined and usually retied using a six- or eight-way method. Careful attention must be given to the way in which fabric and trimming was first applied before it was removed if the restoration is to be accurate. Was the edging hand stitched, or was a prefabricated **fox edge** used? Was piping applied? How was the **jaconet dust cover**, which protects the underside of the piece of furniture, attached and secured?

Knowing Client Requirements

If a workroom is to be involved in the construction of upholstered furniture for a client, the designer should know how the client plans to use the pieces and to define their notion of comfort. Specifics may include questions about how the client sits: Does the client need extra lumbar support to address a slouching posture? Does the client prefer a stiffer, more upright seat? If so, the springs will have to be stiffer and more padding will need to be added. What about the slant of the back? Some full-service workrooms have a sample chair with an adjustable back that clients can test to determine the correct position and angle of the back. What about the length of the chair or sofa? Will they need to be short, long, or somewhere in between? Does the client prefer a scoop-seating surface that cradles the body or something firmer and flatter? Chair seating for residential applications is often more personal than a sofa. Guests typically sit on sofas, whereas individual chairs tend to be fitted to those who will use them most frequently and designed to suit a particular level of comfort and/or function, such as a small bedroom chair as opposed to a chair for reading.

Building the Foundation

After the workroom management understands the particulars about the furniture piece to be produced, the work order passes on to the floor supervisor where **mechanics**, or operators, are assigned to begin the process. Specialists are involved in each phase of construction.

In creating a custom piece of furniture, staining or refinishing the legs and exposed wood is completed in a separate area of the workroom. Typically, the designer will submit small, wooden samples that reflect the desired color and finish for replication.

The first phase of upholstering is to attach jute webbing to the frame and connect the steel springs, with four-ply jute twine, as seen in Figure 10.21. Jute is used in the construction of custom furniture because of its ability to stretch slightly over time, contributing to a softer seat while retaining shape. Typically, nylon is used to tie springs in mass-produced furniture. Nylon will last longer than jute but does not provide the same comfort because of its inability to stretch when used in short lengths.

After the springs are installed and attached with jute to the webbing, a blanket

MECHANICS: Individuals who construct furniture; particularly applied to unionized shops or workrooms.

Figure 10.21 (top) New springs may need to be installed during the furniture restoration process. (bottom) Jute twine and webbing are used to contain springs and help adjust the degree of firmness of an upholstered piece.

of loosely woven burlap fabric is layered over the springs and tied together with jute cord, as appears in Figure 10.22, to keep the filling from falling onto the springs. Over the springs, a layer of what is generally called "horsehair" is applied, as in Figure 10.23.

Historically, horsehair was used to pad furniture, but today, other animal hair is used, some of which can be curled using a heat process that provides bulk to the fibers. "Horsehair fabric" for upholstery consists of varying amounts of horsehair and a mix of cotton or silk in widths from 22 to 26 inches. The blend is often 60 percent horsehair and 40 percent other fibers. The product continues to be produced in England and a few other countries. Hairs from the horse's tail are typically used in producing the woven product.

A finer grade of burlap is secured over the horsehair, and a layer of muslin is attached to the frame and burlap, as in Fig-ure 10.24. Then cotton is layered over the muslin and topped with a layer of Dacron, as seen in Figure 10.25. The cotton serves to stop the coarse hair from coming through, and the Dacron provides a smooth, consistent surface. The selected fabric is then cut and sewn onto the frame. All fibers used in producing furniture should be carefully processed to avoid allergic reactions.

Cushions are covered with muslin to reduce the pulling that the finished fabric would have to withstand if applied directly over the fillers. Because the fabric will not require excessive pulling during the upholstering process, there is a greater chance of it lasting longer. Also, with furniture covered with muslin, the designer can invite the client to the workroom to test the piece for fit and comfort. Any modifications can be easily made at this stage. In some instances, smaller workrooms may accommodate the client and designer by delivering the muslin-covered

Figure 10.22 (top left) Coarse burlap is layered over the springs and tied securely with jute cord to keep the springs in place.

Figure 10.23 (top right) Heat treated animal hair is layered over the coarse burlap and then covered with a fine grade of burlap, holding the hair in place.

Figure 10.24 (bottom left) Over the fine burlap, a cover of muslin is applied. Between the fine burlap and the muslin, the hair will not work its way to the surface during use.

Figure 10.25 (bottom right) A layer of cotton for softness and a layer of Dacron is added to provide stability and a smooth seating surface.

furniture to the client's location. This service usually enhances the relationship between all parties and provides an opportunity to review the placement and scale of the piece on site.

Upholstering

Fabric is received and accounted for in the same way that drapery fabric is processed. Fabric for upholstered pieces is temporarily stored in bins close to the upholsterers while paper templates are produced. Figure 10.26 shows how a template is made using a pointed metal stylus to perforate holes in the paper while following the line of a chair seat. Each custom-upholstered piece requires a pattern to be made of each section of the furniture before the fabric is cut. Fabric is sewn together using cotton thread, the same weight of thread used to construct window treatments. However, nylon tufting twine is used in hand sewing leathers and upholstered surfaces where more sturdy sewing is required, such as tufting.

Challenges in Upholstering

Because each fabric has inherent properties and performance characteristics based on its own set of individual "behaviors," difficulties can arise when fabric is applied to upholstery. These include:

- Fabric can stretch, especially some woven chenilles. When fabric stretches too much, it must be cut more than once before it is applied. It is not uncommon for fabric to be patterned and cut two or three times before it is sewn into place. The upholsterer must know

how much to stretch fabric so the pattern will not become distorted and affect wear. Sometimes fabric is backed when shift and stretch are likely. The designer is responsible for having the fabric backed before it arrives at the workroom. If a fabric is backed, it may become stiff and not yield easily when contouring it to chair arms and rounded furniture backs.

- Fabric patterns can pose a challenge when they are to be positioned on furniture, especially around arms and in the construction of the skirt. The upholsterer must understand symmetry and balance and apply the fabric properly.

- The application of trimming can create difficulties. If the trim is too dense, it can become difficult to sew by hand or by machine. If it is forced into the fabric, the material can pucker or pull. Other trimming selections may have to be chosen that will cause less distortion.

- Color shading in the fabric, if not discovered earlier, will require the fabric

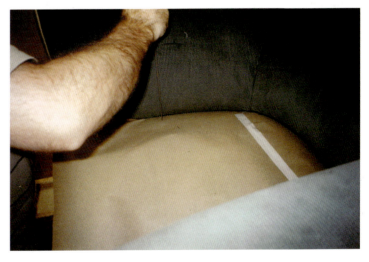

Figure 10.26 Heavy paper is used to produce a template so fabric can be cut correctly.

to be cut around the discolored area. The fabricator or mechanic will determine whether enough fabric is available to complete the work.

Fabricators have to be alert to variances in fabric and know from experience how to address each individual problem.

Inspection

When completed, furniture is inspected for many of the same problems as drapery treatments. The furniture is then photographed and wrapped in heavy paper. Furniture legs are protected using soft, padded paper. After wrapping, a photograph with the delivery information is taped onto the piece so it will be clearly identified. If the piece is being transported beyond the local area, the wrapping for shipment will be more involved.

When Things Go Wrong

Workrooms not only create fabric treatments of varying kinds and upholstered pieces from component parts, but can redo work completed by other fabricating services. The dressing table in Figure 10.27 was reconstructed with new fabric and trim because the owner noted the following problems:

- pulled sheering (Figure 10.27a)
- uneven skirt over liner (Figure 10.27b)
- selvage edge of fabric exposed on one side showing manufacturer's pin marks
- no clean finishes
- hand-stitched lining; machine-stitched skirt
- contrasting pink banding scaled too wide (Figure 10.27c)

- header not straight; slants to the right
- exposed and irregular machine-stitched lines
- Velcro on front headers do not meet, creating an open space between them (Figure 10.27c)

Part of a designer's success is directly connected to the quality of the workroom he or she employs. If a treatment is completed properly the first time, money will be saved by not having to reorder fabric and construct it a second time, or make changes that can affect the delivery schedule.

The more a designer knows about proper construction techniques; how to monitor the fabrication process; and what is aesthetically pleasing, appropriate, and practical, the fewer mistakes will be made as the project unfolds. The designer is ultimately responsible for what is delivered to a client, and it is the designer, not the workroom, to whom clients will voice their satisfaction or dissatisfaction. Whenever possible, the designer should visit the workroom to approve the finished product before it is delivered to the client.

SUMMARY

Workroom artisans transform fiber and fabric into functional and pleasing treatments and furnishings that contribute significantly to defining the quality of residential and commercial spaces. When coordinated by the designer working with the client and fabric supplier, competent workroom personnel are able to construct products that will last for

Figure 10.27 Some workrooms will repair or redo work that did not meet client expectations. This dressing table was redone because of the pulled sheering (a), the uneven skirt and overly wide pink banding (b), and the open space between the front headers (c).

(a)

(b)

(c)

many years, depending on use and how they are exposed to natural and artificial elements.

Designers have three workroom options: the full-service workroom, the workroom that provides limited or specialized services, and connecting with individual artisans who need to be identified, mobilized, and managed by the designer.

Full-service workrooms help expedite the fabricating process by measuring the site, offering design assistance, reviewing fabric to ensure its function and ability to perform, producing the fabric treatments, packing, shipping, and installing the finished product.

The designer's role in facilitating the work process is crucial. Understanding a set of guidelines can be useful in managing expectations. Knowing the process of fabrication contributes to preserving good client–designer relations by enabling the designer to justify and communicate concerns related to time, fabric selections, and costs.

Cut fabric is non-returnable, and it is generally the fabric supplier and designer who are responsible for guaranteeing the quality of the material delivered to the workroom. If all aspects of the workflow are monitored, the results will be successful and arrive in a timely fashion.

Several challenges or problems may arise as the production process unfolds, such as fabric stretching excessively, the selection of trimming that cannot be applied without affecting the appearance of the fabric, and variations in dye lots.

The process of creating quality fabric treatments and upholstered furniture is an organized, multifaceted process, and each step contributes to the completion of the final product and to the reputation of the designer.

ACTIVITIES

1. Interview an established designer in your area and ask the following questions:

   a. What are the most important qualities or skills a workroom (or individuals who produce fabric treatments) ought to possess?

   b. What was your most complex or difficult fabrication, and what made it challenging? What did you learn from the experience, and how do you apply that knowledge to installations?

   c. How do you qualify individuals to produce window treatments or upholstered furniture?

2. Contact a workroom and tour the facilities, noting the steps involved in fabricating a window treatment or an upholstered piece.

3. Compare and contrast a ready-made window treatment with one produced by a known workroom.

4. Determine three fabrics not typically suitable for window treatments. Explain why they are unsuitable.

5. Design a window treatment specifying fabric, interlining, trim, and hardware. Discuss construction methods.

6. Locate a window treatment and examine it to determine whether:

   a. the stitching has been done by hand or machine.

   b. there is interlining.

c. trimming or edges have been evenly sewn on the front and back.

d. the hem is even and unexposed.

e. hardware is attached properly and working.

f. the pattern, strie, stripe, or flow of the fabric is consistent and not pulled.

g. all surfaces are cut appropriately.

h. the treatment is even at the bottom, if it is intended to be that way.

i. the treatment appears appropriate for the space and fits the window.

j. there are any loose or pulled threads, unnecessary stitching, or over-stitching.

k. the fabric is sewn without bunching.

l. the lining or fabric against the window, as seen from outside, relates in some way to the external surface of the structure by color and/or texture.

7. Locate a sofa with an upholstered arm. Apply firm, downward pressure to the arm with your hand while standing. Determine whether the wooden frame can be felt through the padding. If wood can be felt, locate a sofa without the feel of wood. Compare and contrast prices and general construction.

8. Locate hand-carved wood on furniture and/or window treatments. Compare them to machine-made products.

9. Examine an upholstered chair produced by a workroom and compare the construction of a non–workroom-produced piece found in a furniture store.

10. Turn an upholstered chair upside down. Examine the construction and fabric finish. Describe your findings.

EXPAND YOUR KNOWLEDGE

1. What is the price range difference between a custom-made chair and one of similar size and style found in a traditional furniture store in your area? How would you justify the cost difference to a client?

2. Exactly what is "kiln-dried wood"? Explain the process. How do clients know that their furniture frames are built with dry hardwood? Why should the wood be dry? If the wood is not thoroughly dry, how could it affect upholstery?

3. How are upholstered walls constructed? What are the challenges of applying fabric?

4. What material is generally used to pad valances? What concerns should be kept in mind when applying fabric to valances?

5. What are a pelmet and a pelmet board? What is the function of a pelmet, and where is it used?

6. What is the difference between a kick pleat, box pleat, and knife pleat?

7. Over time, the length of many window treatments can shorten. What causes this to occur, and how do workrooms address the problem, if at all?

8. What effects do temperature fluctuations have on window treatments?

What temperature ranges can affect a change of shape in a treatment over time? What fabrics respond to these changes the most? What fabrics respond the least? What occurs if the treatment lining does not "move" at the same pace as the fabric visible in the room?

9. What is the approximate length of time a window treatment maintains its shape and appearance? What are some of the early signs of deterioration? Why do some treatments wear longer than others?

10. Define *Lit à la Polonaise*. What are some of the challenges a workroom would face in creating the treatment?

11. Who is responsible when a fabric treatment is poorly executed? What alternatives exist to remedy problems?

READ ON

Caroline Clifton-Mogg, photography by James Merrell, *Curtains: A Design Source Book*, New York: Stewart, Tabori & Chang, 1997.

Dinah Eastop and Kathryn Gill, *Upholstery Conservation: Principles and Practice*, London: Guild of Master Craftsmen, 1999.

David James, *Upholstery: A Beginner's Guide*, East Sussex: Guild of Master Craftsmen, 2005.

David James, *Upholstery: A Complete Course*, rev. ed., East Sussex, England: Guild of Master Craftsmen, 2004.

Chester Jones, *Colefax & Fowler: The Best in English Interior Decoration*, London: Barrie & Jenkins, 1989.

Heather Luke Krause, *Easy Upholstery: Step by Step*, Iola, Wi.: Heather Luke Krause Publications, 1993, reprinted in 2003.

Catherine Merrick and Rebecca Day, *The Encyclopedia of Curtains. Third Impression*, Lincolnshire: England: Merrick & Day, 2000.

F.A. Moreland, *The Curtain Maker's Handbook*, reprint of *F.A. Moreland's Practical Decorative Upholstery*, New York: E.F. Dutton, 1979.

Karla J. Nielson, *Window Treatments*, New York: Van Nostrand Reinhold, 1990.

Ann Sample, *Old World Charm: The Art of Elegant Interiors*, New York: McGraw-Hill, 2004.

Singer Sewing Reference Library, *Upholstery Basics*, Chanhassen, Minn., Creative Publishing International, 1997.

Dorsey Sitley and Robert D. Adler, forward by Ralph Lauren, *Swatches: A Sourcebook of Patterns with More Than 400 Fabric Designs*, New York: Tabori & Chang, 2005.

Lady Caroline Wrey, *The Complete Book of Curtains and Drapes*, Woodstock, New York: The Overlook Press, 1991.

Maintaining Fabric, Carpeting, and Rugs

Fabric is intended to be used, and, if properly cared for, it will last for many years. Depending on environmental conditions, a well-constructed window treatment can retain its appearance for 10 to 15 years. Although the initial cost of fabric for the designed interior may appear high, various installations are often replaced well before showing obvious signs of wear or becoming brittle.

But, as with living things, fabric begins to deteriorate, however slowly and imperceptibly, as soon as it is installed. It is impossible to protect it completely from all possible risks that will accrue over time. Some of these include damage caused by exposure to ultraviolet daylight or unfiltered fluorescent bulbs; abrasion; atmospheric gases (especially sulfur dioxide); liquid, solid, and dry spills; newspaper print ink; fluctuations in temperature and humidity; perspiration; animal stains and hair (Figure 11.1); tobacco smoke; burns; pests such as moths; water damage; and the effects of some dye stuffs and dry cleaning solutions that can weaken yarns.

Carpets and rugs are routinely vacuumed but furniture and window treatments traditionally do not receive the same level of attention unless a problem arises. If, for example, a spill occurs, the tendency is to immediately "clean" it with whatever may be readily available. Often this approach worsens the problem, making it more difficult to address later. And if water or water-based solvents are used on certain fabrics, spotting or shrinkage can occur, further damaging the fibers. Using appropriate cleaning products can prevent many of these problems.

ADVISING CLIENTS ABOUT FABRIC CARE AND CLEANING

It is unlikely that a designer will be called upon to clean, dust, or remove stains from fabric, but, a designer may be expected to inform clients about wear and care issues.

CHAPTER 11

Opposite: A residential interior in the city.

Figure 11.1 Pets provide challenges for maintaining a stain- and odor-free environment.

Advantages to the Designer of Being a Knowledgeable Advisor

The more information a designer imparts to clients, the more they will rely on the designer as a source for information and services. A broad understanding of cleaning and maintenance approaches will enable you to design appropriate interiors for your clients and advise them about how to maximize the service of the natural and manufactured fibers used in their spaces. Communicating the effects of natural and artificial light, for example, can influence the placement of interior fabrics and furniture and contribute to their preservation. And knowledge of what care fabric requires can lead to specifying the most appropriate product for a particular application and positioning it where it has a good chance of a long life. For example, velvet manufactured from inorganic olefin fibers would be a preferred choice in warm climates, where the growth of mildew and mold may be a concern. Or the use of a polyacryl chenille (e.g., Dolan or Dralon) or a polyacryl blend with cotton or wool that is known for shape retention, durability, and a low level of moisture absorption may be preferred over a plain cotton chenille.

Choice of Cleaning Methods

The wide range of fabric and fabric blends from which to choose complicates the selection of a cleaning method. A sofa upholstered in Crypton may require only occasional cleaning with a powdered enzyme detergent such as Tide or Cheer mixed with water,[1] while a window treatment composed of a blend of silk and linen may need to be professionally cleaned with a petroleum-based chlorinated hydrocarbon such as **perchloroethylene**, also known as **perc**—a chemical used by approximately 94 percent of all dry-cleaners worldwide that removes dirt and many stains without shrinking or discoloring fabric.

New cleaning products and responsible methods of dispersing them are emerging to respond to concerns about the environment as well as health and safety. Environmentally safe preformed enzymes are being used to clean carpets, and advances in colloidal chemistry are contributing to improve cleaning results. However, not all fabrics are easily cleaned. Restoring the shine of oxidized gold and silver threads while attempting to clean the surrounding weak yarns on an antique fabric can be difficult. And fabrics such as **Luminex** that contain optical fibers pose unique cleaning challenges as well.

Some fabric manufacturers have adopted fabric cleaning codes for spot removal and overall cleaning that were first developed in 1969. Although these codes can be helpful in determining preferred cleaning methods, the content of all fabrics should be verified first. Fabric cleaning codes were created by a consortium of furniture manufacturers to facilitate overall cleaning as well as spot removal. The coded letters may appear on fabric samples, as labels under seat cushions, or as hangtags. The fabric cleaning codes are noted below.

Fabric Cleaning Codes

Before any cleaning process begins, the fabric should be thoroughly vacuumed

PERCHLOROETHYLENE OR PERC: A highly chlorinated hydrocarbon used in dry cleaning.

LUMINEX: Fabric containing optical fibers woven with nonoptical fibers and connected to LEDs and a power source, producing a glow.

with a soft brush. A small test area should be identified and the results evaluated. In all cases, if the cleaning approach used does not yield satisfactory results, a professional cleaner should be consulted. The following codes indicate the recommended cleaners:

W (*Water-based Cleaner*) Foam from only water-based cleaning agents should be used, such as mild detergents or nonsolvent upholstery shampoos. The foam should be applied using a soft brush in a circular motion and vacuumed when dried.

S (*Solvent Cleaner*) Spot clean using a mild, water-free solvent or dry-cleaning products such as Energene, Carbona, or Renuzit. Follow directions carefully on all labels. Be sure the area is well ventilated.

WS (*Water/Solvent Cleaner*) Clean stains using a mild solvent, upholstery shampoo, foam from a mild detergent, or dry-cleaning product as noted in "S."

X (*Vacuuming or Light Brushing*) Damage such as shrinkage or staining may occur if water-based foam cleaners or solvents are used.

Codes do not appear on custom furniture or window treatments that are designed specifically for a client and produced by a workroom. The designer needs to know the content of the fabric, the composition of backings, and any applied chemical treatments to be able to recommend an appropriate schedule of maintenance to the client.

CARING FOR UPHOLSTERED FABRICS AND WINDOW TREATMENTS

Exposed upholstered surfaces, especially those positioned horizontally, and window fabrics require a regular schedule of cleaning to help maintain their condition over time. With the exception of lightweight chairs and relativity simple window treatments, upholstered furniture and walls cannot be transported for cleaning and must remain in place, necessitating periodic visits from a professional residential cleaning company. Basic on-location preventive maintenance and a schedule of cleaning can help preserve fabric. Commercial establishments usually employ professional cleaning firms that maintain a regular cleaning schedule. Smaller, independently owned businesses may be maintained by the owner or one individual hired to clean periodically.

Preventative Measures

Several approaches should be considered to help preserve the original appearance of upholstered furniture and window treatments, avoiding or delaying **restorative care** that may be costly and require professional intervention. Among these are the following:

- Addressing environmental issues that contribute to upholstered fabric being discolored or faded by light or affected by temperature fluctuations. Modern windows of quality that use metallic oxide layers and other barriers to reflect the heat and UV light of the summer sun contribute to the longevity of fabric. Windows should be evaluated before window treatment designs are planned and constructed and furniture is placed.

- Using glass curtains or other window treatments to diffuse light that enters through non-protected glass. Fine yarns in darker colors are more susceptible to fading. Heavier yarns are more sustainable in daylight.
- Incorporating interlinings to preserve window treatment fabric while restricting the flow of unfiltered daylight onto upholstery.
- Protecting window treatments from condensation that can form on glass by keeping some distance between the fabric and the glass.
- Rearranging furniture in a room to change its exposure to radiator or floor-based radiant heat and different sources of light. Lift furniture when moving it as opposed to dragging it.
- Keeping newspaper print away from fabric. Print is easily transferable and difficult to remove.
- Vacuuming upholstered pieces that receive heavy use twice a week using a soft brush. Soil and other particulates that work into the recesses of the pile can be abrasive and cut yarns over time, especially on seating areas. Special attention should be paid to upholstered arms and headrests.
- Vacuuming window treatments approximately once a month and having them professionally cleaned about once a year. Some cleaning services are able to make site visits to clean complex window treatments or heavy furniture that cannot be moved.

- Rotating cushions after vacuuming.
- Becoming aware of studs on jeans, metal belt buckles, and other hardware on clothing that may snag or pull yarn floats or puncture leather.
- Removing pets from furnishings. Pet oils, aromas, dander, and fluids, especially urine, can be difficult to remove.
- Sitting only on seat cushions, not on arms or sofa backs.
- Avoiding the use of a washing machine to clean seat covers.
- Considering the application of a topical sealer if upholstery receives frequent use. Sealed fabrics will resist stains and contribute to the ease of cleaning. Some topical conditioners, however, will affect the feel of the fabric.
- Health-care facilities, hotels and motels, and institutional dormitories as well as other public spaces require more frequent cleaning. Facility managers are usually responsible for determining who will do the cleaning and how often.

Treatments for Spills, Stains, and Burns

Many spills, stains, and burns can be satisfactorily addressed if the response is prompt by doing the following:

- Blotting (not rubbing) liquids with a noncolored tissue, paper towel, or absorbent cloth.
- Carefully removing solids with a dull blade or other instrument starting on the outside edges and working inward, and brushing away the residue from

burned or scorched fabric. Water should not be used in the removal of dry spills.

- Vacuuming dry spills, such as those from ashes or makeup.
- Using masking tape on some fabrics to aid in the lifting and removal of dry spills.

After an emergency has been treated promptly, it may be necessary to clean the spot or stain with cleaners. Before applying a commonly available fabric cleaner, it is useful to determine the yarn composition, quality and method of applied fabric dyestuffs, and whether the fabric has a protective coating or backing. Using the wrong cleaner or cleaning process can alter the overall appearance and texture of the fabric. Fine or plain-weave velvets and most knit velvets require dry-cleaning. If not cared for properly, velvet can lose pile, develop piling, appear flat, mat, and shrink. In addition, crushed velvet can lose its design value and become distorted.[2]

One popular method of treating stains is to use aerosol foam products. The danger with these products is that shrinkage can occur, especially with some rayons and cottons. Wet cleaning can also contribute to color fading and bleeding if the fabric is not tested first for colorfastness. Foams that convert into powder can be vacuumed off, but foams or synthetically neutral wet shampoos such as Orvus WA Paste, used to clean fabric as well as farm animals in the United States (Symperonic N Detergent is popular in England), need to be removed carefully with a damp sponge. If the solution is not completely lifted from the fabric after cleaning, it is possible that when it eventually dries, the area will become susceptible to rapid re-soiling.

A hot water extraction system is available for rent and can be used to clean upholstery. The equipment infuses fabric with a special detergent and water and then quickly vacuums it out with the soil. Avoid applying too much water to the fabric, and use a test area to determine the effects of the cleaning method. Water-based applications should not be used on silk, linen, or to remove oil stains but can be effective on cotton, canvas, and many treated fabrics. Acid cleaners can damage cotton and other cellulose fibers. Non-alkaline cleaners and white vinegar can be used for wool fabric.

Whenever possible, it is useful to contact the manufacturer of the fabric to learn about its composition and applied treatments, if any (such as Teflon, Zepel, or Scotchgard) to ensure that proper cleaning products will be applied. It is relatively easy to destroy fabric if precautions are not followed. For example, fabric made from glass, such as E-glass fiberglass or S-glass fabrics, should not be cleaned in a machine where the fabric tumbles. The result will be broken fibers. Commercially operated dry-cleaning machines rotate their holding baskets at 350 to 450 rpm.

Several home-based remedies exist for general cleaning. For example, one recipe combines ¼ cup of liquid dishwater detergent with one cup of warm water (Figure 11.2). This mixture is then whipped with a hand mixer until thick suds form. The suds are applied with a cloth and a spatula is used to remove the dirty suds. The area is then dried thoroughly.

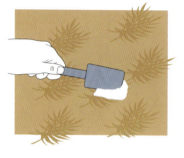

Figure 11.2 Steps in upholstery cleaning.

Dry-cleaning as a profession began in France in the mid-1800s, allegedly when turpentine accidentally spilled on a table-cloth, removing stains that could not be treated earlier. As early dry-cleaning establishments grew in popularity, it became known that laboring in one of these establishments was dangerous because of the volatility of the petroleum products being used such as kerosene, gasoline, and turpentine. Many explosions and fires were documented as a result of using these "spirits," and breathing the fumes from the products created additional health risks.

By the early 1900s, William Joseph Stoddard, an Atlanta, Georgia, dry-cleaner, developed a product known as Stoddard Solvent. This petroleum product was economical, effective, and slightly less flammable (flashpoint at about 100 degrees Fahrenheit) but was still explosive and toxic to inhale. About 30 years later, perc emerged as a nonpetroleum, nonflammable, and less toxic dry-cleaning alternative.

Dry-cleaning chemicals like perc are environmentally controversial, in part because of disposal issues related to waste sludge that collects after a dry-cleaning cycle. Vapor emissions from perc are also a source of pollution, affecting the atmosphere. Based on dry-cleaning machine test data, research shows that as much as 25 percent of perc emissions from a dry-cleaning facility with no pollution controls are due to leaks from the equipment, even though in 1993 EPA announced, under the Clean Air Act, that dry-cleaners were to use pollution controls to prevent perc leakage.[3] The aroma from perc can also be unhealthy and encourage the onset of allergies or allergic reactions. Fabric

Caution should be exercised when using grocery store products for cleaning upholstery, with *special attention given to the instructions* on the package. In some instances, cleaners can perform well, but in others, they only exacerbate the problem, creating a more complex challenge for the professional cleaner to solve.

Dry-Cleaning

The history of dry-cleaning, which actually refers to a method of cleaning that uses little or no water, dates to Pompeii and the sixth century C.E., where workers in wool, called fullers, discovered that a sedimentary clay mixed with urine, water, and **soapwart** could be used to absorb the thick oils from wool. The clay became known as fuller's clay or fuller's earth and is composed of iron oxides, silica, alumina, lime, magnesia, and water.

SOAPWART: From the Latin *sapo*, meaning *soap*. A perennial herb with coarse pink or white flowers. The leaves of the plant can serve as a detergent when mashed.

that has been dry-cleaned should be properly aired to reduce the development of health problems.

Two approaches that are potential replacements for perc are silicone-based solvents (currently expensive to use) and liquid carbon dioxide (showing inconsistent results and requiring expensive machinery).[4] A wet-cleaning process using biodegradable soap and water is also an alternative for some fabrics that carry "dry-clean only" labels. Although California plans to ban the use of perc by 2020 to help sustain the ozone layer and reduce the spread of chemical contamination, dry-cleaning and its chemicals known today continue to be an effective and popular method of cleaning many kinds of fabrics.

CARING FOR CARPETING AND RUGS

Health issues are central to carpet maintenance. Carpet, rugs, and underlayment are susceptible to collecting and holding on to dirt that supports and sustains the growth of various bacteria, mold spores, and dust mites that can lead to stimulating the onset of allergic reactions, various illnesses, and poor IAQ. In addition, the results of carpet cleaning can also initiate health-related problems. For example, there is some speculation that the cause of Kawasaki Disease or Syndrome is brought on in children under eight years old as a result of carpets being cleaned or shampooed. Additional research is required, however, to more fully investigate the relationship between this disease and carpet cleaning.

The **Children's Health Environmental Coalition (CHEC)** has been formed to increase awareness about the environment and its impact on children's health. CHEC recommends that children remain out-of-doors or away from a freshly cleaned carpet, cleaned by *any* method, for at least four hours because of the dispersion of potentially dangerous chemicals in some cleaners that include solvents, acids, mildewcides, disinfectants, and chemical propellants such as butane and propane.[5]

It is recommended that every 12 to 18 months, carpet should be deep cleaned using a wet or dry extraction method. This process will help ensure that the carpet will retain much of its original appearance while removing most spots and stains (Figure 11.3). Cleaning also extends the useful life of the carpet and, therefore, saves money.

The Carpet and Rug Institute Seal of Approval program that began in 2004 examines carpet-cleaning products and certifies only those that meet a set of per-

Figure 11.3 The successful removal of a wine stain without damaging fabric, especially after it dried, can be difficult.

formance criteria. Many products available do not perform as advertised, with some serving only to attract new soil *after* "cleaning."

Carpet and Rug Cleaning by Owner

The owner cleans more than 40 percent of residential carpet, where most commercial carpet is cleaned by professionals as part of an overall scheduled program of maintenance. To maximize the effectiveness of the cleaning process, it is essential that all instructions that accompany carpet-cleaning solutions and foams, as well as carpet-cleaning equipment, be followed. It is also important to—

- Apply chemicals and solutions in the proper dosages.
- Avoid excess water, yet properly rinse the carpet.
- Ventilate the area to aid in drying and exhaust any cleaning odors from applied solutions, especially in humid weather conditions or climates.
- Allow the carpet to completely dry before walking on it.

Cleaning products should be specified for carpet use only. If, for example, the carpet is stain resistant, appropriate products should be identified for that carpet and its filters. Ordinary soap, laundry detergent, automatic dishwashing detergent, or any strong household cleaning agents intended for use on hard surfaces such as woodwork, linoleum, or tile should not be used. Results can be enhanced by vacuuming the area to be cleaned and applying a preconditioning solution and allowing it to

activate for about ten minutes prior to cleaning.[6] Some spots and stains may require several applications of a cleaner to remove the soil completely.

Rotating fringed Oriental, Persian, or hand-loomed rugs often is recommended to reduce wear areas, and the rugs should be cleaned by an experienced specialist. If an owner plans to clean these rugs, the following steps serve as guidelines only for rugs that are *not* 100 percent silk. Silk rugs should be cleaned professionally.

- Vacuum the rug carefully and avoid the fringe being consumed by the machine. If fringe is vacuumed into the machine, turn off the cleaner and carefully remove the fringe.
- Suspend the rug and strike it with a paddle, removing embedded dirt. This act should not be done harshly or used to relieve personal stress.
- Vacuum the rug a second time.
- Test the rug in a corner for colorfastness by observing whether any color is lifted when wet-brushing it with a pH neutral cleaning solution. If color is lifted, the rug should be cleaned professionally.
- Wash the rug without scrubbing it forcefully
- Rinse with cold water
- Dry both sides thoroughly. The rug must be completely dry before anyone walks on it.

Owners can clean their own carpet at a savings but also at a risk. If they do not use cleaning solutions and procedures appropriate for the fiber composition of the carpet and underlayment material, the carpet or rug may have to be replaced, causing additional expenditures and inconvenience.

Professional Deep Cleaning Methods

The purpose of wet or dry deep cleaning is to remove imbedded dirt and stains that cannot be removed by vacuuming or using spot cleaners. The Carpet and Rug Institute lists the following five approaches used most often by professionals to deep clean carpeting after it has been thoroughly vacuumed:

- Absorbent Pad or Bonnet Method. This approach uses a machine with an absorbent pad attached similar to a floor buffer. The spinning pad contains cleaning solution. As the pad rotates, soil is absorbed into it and then rinsed out. Pads are to be replaced often so soil is not transferred back into the carpeting.
- Dry Extraction (Polymer Compound) Method. An absorbent compound saturated with detergents is brushed in and around the fibers with specially designed machines or brushes. The compound attaches to soil particles. Both the soil and the compound are removed by vacuuming.
- Dry Foam Extraction Method. A dry detergent is whipped into foam and applied to the carpet. The foam is worked into the carpet by a specially designed machine with reel-type brushes. Wet vacuuming follows. Some machines have their own extraction capabilities, while others need vacuuming after the carpet dries.

- Hot Water Extraction Method. This approach is sometimes known as steam cleaning, although no steam is emitted. Areas of heavy use are first preconditioned to suspend the embedded soil. A pressurized cleaning solution is then injected into the pile. Suspended soil and the cleaning solution are immediately extracted. Caution must be exercised to not over water the carpet surface.
- Rotary Shampoo Method. This way of cleaning carpeting uses equipment similar to the rotary bonnet method, except that a cleaning solution is injected onto the carpet before cleaning by way of specially designed brushes. A floor sander or machine designed for hard surfaces with counter-rotating brushes should not be adapted for carpeting. Pile distortion or untwisting of the fibers can result.

Engaging proven carpet-cleaning professionals is the preferred choice for ensuring the best results. Before a carpet firm is hired, it should be qualified, insured, and able to present a contract for signing that includes all work to be accomplished including the cost, if any, associated with moving furniture.

Cleaning Commercial Carpeting

Hotels, large office areas, health-care facilities, and other commercially carpeted spaces require a plan of maintenance that includes preventive as well as daily care. The approximate cost of an ongoing maintenance program should be factored into the cost of the carpet, with attention directed to the specific needs of the facil-

HIGH EFFICIENCY PARTICULATE AIR (HEPA) FILTERS: **Filters that filter very small particulates from the air. Used in homes and offices as well as the aerospace, nuclear, electronic, pharmaceutical, and medical fields.**

ity. For example, if the setting is a chronic health-care treatment center, the carpet-cleaning firm should be qualified to clean and disinfect for microbes found in blood, urine, various odors, and possibly AIDS-related bacteria. If the site is a hotel, the focus should be on eliminating food and beverage stains from hospitality areas and guest rooms, and the cleaning firm should be experienced in spot dyeing and restorative fabric and carpet repair to mask cigarette burns.

Vacuuming

In both residential and commercial spaces, the vacuum is often the first step in cleaning. Although the vacuum cleaner was patented in the United States in 1869, the evolution of the product continues with robotic models such as Tribobite, Robomaxx, and iRobot Roomba, shown in Figure 11.4. The traditional vacuum remains popular today but can be problematic. Many are susceptible to leaks from crevices in the vacuum casting material, allowing allergens, mold dust, and bacteria that were removed from one location to become airborne and redistributed back into the room.

To help contain the dust and various particulates from vacuuming, it is useful to examine the condition of the cleaning equipment and to use a specially constructed vacuum bag. For example, the **High Efficiency Particulate Air (HEPA) Filters** bag was developed in the 1940s to filter out radioactive dust contaminants from bomb shelter test sites. These filters were designed to capture particulates as small as 0.3 microns (one micron is one-thousandth of a millimeter) at efficiency ratings of 99.97 percent.[7] The filters are available for residential and commercial use and can fit vacuums of varying sizes and models. Vacuuming is an effective way to clean and maintain fabric, but only if the machine is in excellent condition and the dirt-and-dust-holding container is tightly sealed; otherwise, material that was collected will only re-circulate and contribute to poor IAQ and reactivate allergens (Figure 11.5).

For details of specific treatments for spots, stains, spills, and burns on fabric of varying types as well as carpeting and rugs, consult the references listed in the Read On! portion of this chapter.

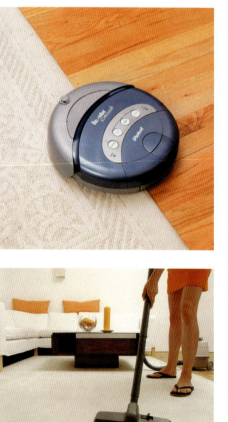

Figure 11.4 Technology is making inroads toward making vacuuming easier.

Figure 11.5 Traditional vacuum sweepers can deposit unwanted and sometimes harmful particulates in the air, spreading spores and bacteria that contribute to unhealthy conditions.

SUMMARY

Over time, window treatments, uphol-stered walls, and furniture will be exposed to a wide assortment of potentially harm-ful and life-shortening hazards. To extend the aesthetic and functional qualities of fabric, a program of care is advisable.

Understanding yarn and fabric com-positions, as well as chemical treatments and backings, helps the designer identify materials appropriate for the project and where and how these fabrics should be lo-cated in a space. The designer will also be able to develop a protocol for cleaning. Moving upholstered furniture away from unfiltered sunlight, for example, preserves fabric and influences the placement of other furnishings and objects in a room.

Owners can contribute to extending the appearance and serviceability of fab-ric by frequently vacuuming and promptly dealing with spills, potential stains, and burns. If commercially available prod-ucts are to be used, the fabric must be properly identified and instructional labels followed correctly to ensure satisfactory results. If questions arise about what treat-ment should be used, professional clean-ers should be consulted.

Carpeting, rugs, and underlayment can be a source of poor IAQ if not vacuumed and cleaned properly. Rooms should be ventilated when using carpet-cleaning chemicals. Some commercial cleaning methods can be undertaken by owners, assuming they are extremely careful to prevent injury from rented carpet clean-ing machinery and take precautions to avoid permanent damage to the carpet due to the misuse of chemicals or excess watering. Qualified professionals are best equipped to evaluate a soiled carpet and to recommend one of the five preferred methods of cleaning.

Allowances for the cost of cleaning commercial carpet should be budgeted as part of the specification process. Appro-priate carpet should be selected for the intended end use and professionals identi-fied who are competent to address stains, odors, burns, or bacteria associated with a particular commercial installation.

ACTIVITIES

1. Evaluate the condition of fabric in your home. Assess any stains or marks and determine the best way to treat them.
2. Evaluate the windows in your home. Determine whether upholstered fur-niture has changed color because of exposure to ultraviolet light. Report on the method of your findings.
3. Discover whether the vacuum cleaner you have been using is redistribut-ing dust during use.
4. Compare and contrast a typical vacuum bag with one that is spe-cially designed to capture very small particulates.
5. Interview an interior designer to de-termine how he or she generally ad-dresses fabric care issues with clients.
6. Visit a grocery store and read the con-tents of two fabric-cleaning products. Compare and contrast their ingredi-ents. Report on the proper method of using one of the products.
7. Visit a dry-cleaner and learn about the step-by-step process used to dry-clean upholstered sofa seat covers in

a blend of silk and cotton. Inquire which methods are used to evaluate fabric to determine whether it should be cleaned with water and detergent or by dry-cleaning.

8. Investigate what precautions dry-cleaning employees take, if any, to protect themselves from the side effects of dry-cleaning chemicals.

9. Interview someone who has used rented carpet-cleaning equipment and report on his or her experiences and results.

10. Interview a carpet-cleaning professional. Inquire about the methods used to clean carpeting and the process used to determine which method is most appropriate. Inquire about how carpeting underlayment is cleaned and dried.

11. Locate a company in your area that visits homes and offices to vacuum and clean fabric, carpeting, and rugs. Examine how the company works, what it charges, and what methods of cleaning it uses.

12. Research who is responsible for cleaning carpet and upholstery in a commercial establishment. Report on the schedule of maintenance.

EXPAND YOUR KNOWLEDGE

1. What is the preferred method of cleaning lamp and chandelier shades?

2. How is pet urine removed from upholstered fabric? From carpeting?

3. How would a designer respond if consulted about cleaning and repairing a 75-to-80-year-old brocade used as a portiere in a historic house?

4. What are the specific steps that a professional cleaning company would employ to clean a window treatment that includes an upholstered lambrequin?

5. Which conditions—climate, position of the sun, time of year, composition of window glass and frame, and geography—create the *worst* environment for window fabric?

6. What are the objectives of the Clean Air Act?

7. What treatment protocol is recommended to remove red wine from upholstered fabric treated with Zepel?

8. What are the dangers of an experienced homeowner using the hot water extraction method to clean carpet?

9. Obtain a copy of a contract from a professional carpet-cleaning firm. What does the contract cover? What guarantees does it offer?

10. What new dry-cleaning products and processes are being used or experimented with that can substitute for more conventional cleaning chemicals?

11. What physical symptoms may point to the need to clean carpeting or fabric in a space?

12. What treatments can be used on leather to improve its serviceability? How should a tufted leather headboard attached to a bed be cleaned?

READ ON

Don Aslette, *Do I Dust or Vacuum First?* Avon, Mass.: Adams Media, 1982.

Annie Berthold-Bond, *Clean House*, Woodstock, N.Y.: Ceres Press, 1994.

Jeff Bredenberg, *2,001 Amazing Cleaning Secrets*, Pleasantville, N.Y.: The Reader's Digest Association, 2004.

Carpet and Rug Institute, http://www.carpet-rug.org.

Linda Cobb, *Queen of Clean*, New York: Simon & Schuster, 2004.

Virginia M. Friedman, Melissa Wagner, and Nancy Armstrong, *Field Guide to Stains*, Philadelphia: Quirk Productions, Inc., 2002.

Graham and Rosemary Haley, *Haley's Hints*, New York: New American Library, 2004.

Linda Mason Hunter and Mikki Halpin, *Green Clean*, New York: Melcher Media, 2005.

http://doityourself.com/clean/upholstery.htm.

http://www.woolfurnishings.com/inforoom/stainremoval.infostain.html.

International Fabricare Institute, http://ww.ifi.org/industry/index.html.

Karen Logan, *Clean House*, New York: Pocket Books, 1997.

Cheryl Mendelson, *Home Comforts: The Art and Science of Keeping House*, New York: Scribner, 1999.

National Cleaners Association, http:/www.nca-i.com.

Yvonne Worth with Amanda Blinkhorn, *How to Clean Absolutely Everything*, Lewes, East Sussex, UK: Judy Piatkus Publishers, Ltd.: 2004.

Learning from the Professionals

It has been said that there is no substitute for experience; however, an improvement on the adage may be to supplement "experience" with a well-devised course of study. Readings and discussion that accompany the formal introduction into a subject can provide knowledge that condenses information and helps place the learner on a faster track toward the start of a successful career. Conversely, with only experience to draw from, missteps gained through "the school of hard knocks" can slow the learning process and often cost time and money due to mistakes that can affect the reputation of a new designer before he or she has an opportunity to grow and flourish.

CONNECTING ACADEMICS WITH THE PRACTICE

Typically, academic lessons provide a package of information that fits into a predetermined time period that can vary widely, depending on the administrative schedule and accrediting guidelines of an educational institution. An attempt to connect text learning with experiences from others can help balance factual knowledge with the so-called real world. Designing is much more than expressing creativity, drawing on a computer, or being engaged in one or two aspects of the design process. Successful design and the use of fabric and other materials is dependent upon maintaining the delicate balancing act of attending to financial and time constraints as well as satisfying the social, emotional, practical, and aesthetic needs of the client.

In the following pages, professional designers, fabric suppliers, and manufacturers express their opinions, experiences, and expectations in working with fabric, carpeting, and rugs.

CHAPTER 12

Opposite: A bedroom designed by Richard Keith Langham in Jackson, Mississippi.

INTERIOR DESIGN PROFESSIONALS: THE INTERVIEWS

Albert Hadley

Albert Hadley, Inc.
New York, New York

Aesthetics: Fitting fabric into the plan.

Designing with fabrics, or design in general, is very much like creating a musical composition. You have high notes and low. The designer's responsibility is to strike the right chords that produce harmonious and pleasing interiors. Delivering appropriate aesthetics is the goal of the designer. Mixing color and textures is key, as well as providing a subtle play of differences through the interactions of wovens, prints, leather, and silks taken from the vast array of available products. The challenge is not easy but very rewarding when the right balance is struck. And of course, this has to all work within the context of the client and the architecture for which the fabrics are intended.

What I mean by architecture is largely the architecture of interiors—the architecture of space. I have, on more than one occasion, insisted that a window or door be moved in a room to better accommodate the arrangement of furnishings, or to improve or enhance a view without destroying the basic plan of the property. And if glass opens to a vast panorama of sea and air, it may be better to not have any fabric at the window at all.

The importance of adhering to the original plan for interiors is important. There are so many fabrics and products of all kinds in the marketplace that it's easy for anyone to become distracted and lost, thereby moving away from what the initial plan provided. And pleasing distractions can be found everywhere to lure you off course!

One method of developing design aesthetics and the ability to edit fabrics more effectively is to observe, travel, visit museums, and take as many field trips as possible. Fabric needs to take on a tangible quality; it's difficult to *just* talk about it. Fabric should be seen, touched whenever possible, and understood in various contexts. The more one experiences, and remembers, the greater the backlog of resources there will be to select from.

Regarding rugs, some designers begin to design interiors with them, but I generally begin with the exterior and interior architecture. I think it's more important that the rug fits the room with proper proportions than to stress over the design or pattern. Of course it's important to have an attractive rug, but scale and pro-

Figure 12.1 Albert Hadley in a room he designed.

portion are crucial. It's quite possible to custom weave rugs today, but the number of high quality rugs being designed that borrow from beautiful historic patterns, consistent with all countries of the world, and appearing in a myriad of colors and sizes is staggering. It's best to shop and see what is available before adding cost and time by designing a custom rug.

Appropriateness is the most important element in creating interiors. The challenge of learning about what's new and mentally cataloging what's old and good is not easy. But with practice, a keen eye, and a hands-on perspective, appropriate and suitable design can be achieved.

Carl D'Aquino

D'Aquino Monaco, Inc.
New York, New York

Identifying clients' taste.

The process of design begins by studying the client carefully and learning about their personality and identity. If a client happens to own a special antique rug, for example, this is an excellent place to begin the discussion about a color palette for a room. Since the client has, no doubt, selected the carpet, the colors are understandably what they enjoy. Color is very important and some people cannot be saturated enough by it, while other clients prefer more neutral shades.

In an attempt to distinguish and offer a clear identity to interior spaces using neutral colors, fabrics and walls need to be treated in special ways. The question

Figure 12.2 A design by Carl D'Aquino and Francine Monaco.

becomes "how can beige be more than what it is?" It can become different by glossing walls or introducing fabrics with sheens or using other creative techniques and approaches. In this process, it becomes imperative to discover resources well beyond the confines of design centers, to be open to the suggestions that new materials may provide, such as materials used in industrial settings, while keeping perspective on the client's wishes and the overall end product.

Typically, I don't like to design a room around paintings that a client has. Sometimes this can create a look that appears overly decorated. Certainly colors from the great works of art serve as inspiration, but usually these are found in museums.

It is not my intent to impose one signature look, but rather to work with a client to discover their intrinsic design direction (which often they are unaware they have!) and help them with a unique and fitting interior that makes them comfortable.

William R. Eubanks

William R. Eubanks Interior Design, Inc.
Palm Beach, Florida

Learning clients' preferences while
educating them on possibilities.

One of the most important points in designing with fabrics is to enjoy mixing
colors. Don't shy away from color or combining tapestries, stripes, and damasks in
one room. When a variety of colors and
textures are thoughtfully grouped, the
grouping takes on a timeless quality. There
are so many fabrics of all qualities and

prices that it would be unfortunate if we,
as designers, didn't attempt to take clients
beyond the slate gray palette and show
them the range of possibilities.

It's important to listen to what clients
say and want, but it's also important to
take them outside of their comfort zone
and help them explore. To qualify you to
do this, it's necessary to get to know your
clients. Every client is different. You must
carefully observe how your clients live in
all aspects of their life—the way they
dress, their selection of art, what they do
for fun—and pull them forward, helping
them express their individuality. Determine if your clients are subtle or materi-
alistic. They will give you many clues as
to who they are and how they live if you
are prepared to receive them. And it's
important to attempt to have everyone
who lives in the house participate in the
preliminary conceptual design phase, as
well. Try to observe, as much as possible,
those who live in the space in order to understand better what direction an interior needs to take. Designers have to be
critical listeners. We need to give to our
clients our best possible work that fits
their way of life. We can't have a precon-
ceived or preplanned idea of how people
live based on a photo of a house. We have
to find an unobtrusive way to relax and
enter the minds of our clients and take
them places they thought they were not
able to go.

Regarding acquiring fabric, it's very
important to *follow-up on written and
acknowledged orders.* If you're promised
a 16-week delivery on a special order
and told after 15 weeks that it will take
an additional 8 weeks, it's best to select a

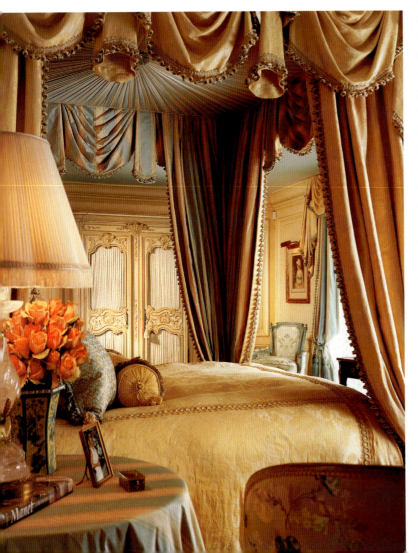

Figure 12.3 Detail of a
canopied bed from a
master bedroom.

different fabric. And dealing with reputable fabric companies is a must! Be cautious about who you do business with. Your suppliers have the ability to affect your work and reputation positively or negatively. Fewer items are stocked these days, so if a company says that you'll have to wait, you want the wait *not* to be in vain. This applies to carpet orders, as well.

When clients see a sample carpet, believe it's beautiful, and want it in a large area of their house, the designer has to take another step. He or she needs to make certain that the clients understand that scale of pattern, proportion, and lead time in ordering can affect their overall level of satisfaction. The sample that excites them in a showroom may not elicit the same level of enthusiasm when the carpet is full-size and installed. This is why a large rendering of a carpet for the client review is so important. What the clients saw earlier as a sample may have been better on stairs than on the floor in a library.

Furthermore, designers need to help clients understand something about the loom that will manufacture their carpet. If the loom produces only 27-inch-wide goods, and seams will appear every 27 inches, the client must be informed of this *before* the manufacturing process begins. Placing an order to have an expensive carpet woven and not being clear to the client exactly what the end product will look like could be disastrous! Educating and communicating with the client is an important part of being a designer; otherwise, you may literally pay for your mistakes.

Joe Nye
Joe Nye, Inc.
Los Angeles, California

Presenting fabric to residential clients.

When working with fabrics, as with design in general, it's important to focus on what's beautiful and practical. If the client wants the sofa to be "bullet proof," then consider showing them airplane fabric! It's the designer's job to edit for the client, but in order to be able to properly edit, it's important to thoroughly interview and know the client as best as you can. And when you know the client and the application of fabric, it becomes possible to preview (with the client) only a very few fabrics for each project. Typically, I show no more than three fabrics

Figure 12.4 Chairs in front of a window.

for each application. In fact, more often that not, I show only one. They are paying me to know the market and to do what they do not have time or the ability to do. It's the designer's job to know what's best, given the available resources, and to move the project along so it remains on schedule. If you're not clear about the application and expose the client to literally hundreds of fabric choices for a pillow, let's say, it will take forever before the pillows finally become covered!

I like to explore the use of all kinds of fabrics. But if the client really wants a silk on a chair that will receive a lot of use I'll have it backed, usually with acrylic. I also like to use fabrics with a combination of yarns when I believe that the room calls for heavier use.

Also regarding the fabric selection process, it's important to pay strict attention to a fabric's pattern repeat and width. It's not a good idea to have a large flower on a print cut off at the edge of the chair unless there is some sort of a plan that requires that to happen. Of course application is crucial too. Fabric for upholstered walls, for example, is usually different from fabric for soft furniture. And then there are the clients themselves that affect fabric selection. There has been a trend where both wife *and* husband are involved in the selection of interior products. Women tend to come from more of a fashion direction and men focus on comfort and practicality. The democratization of design through stores like Pottery Barn, Target, Williams-Sonoma, and Crate & Barrel has brought design directly into the mainstream of America. Everyone is exposed to varying levels of designed products and husbands realize, consciously or subconsciously, that they are affected by it. The designer should be ready and willing to accept "the man of the house" to be involved and provide his unique perspective on the desired outcomes of an interior. I'm finding that designing has become more collaborative, more interactive. Designers are hired to make informed decisions about the environment of those who will be living in the spaces and make the decisions expeditiously.

Faruk Guner
Faruk Guner Decoration
Principauté de Monaco

Design and color are important in selecting commercial carpet.

One large aspect of my work deals with floor coverings in hotels and boutiques. I prefer to work with wood, stone, or marble, but I also work with carpeting. I have recently completed the installation of carpeting in the corridors and rooms of the Metropole Hotel in Monaco.

I believe that it is important to select carpet decorations and motifs (in custom-designed carpeting) from the interior architecture and repeat them in the design of the floor covering. I think that color is important and it is imperative that the designer makes certain there is good communication with the client about color and everything else. Wrong choices can make for expensive mistakes.

Many people do not place enough emphasis on carpet borders and what they can do to connect or blend with wall col-

Figure 12.5 Fuji Restaurant interior.

ors and other colors in hallways or hotel rooms. Borders have the ability to make transitions from floors to painted walls or to tie in architectural motifs observed in rooms, halls, or common areas.

Carpet padding is also very important to a hotel. The designer must work with the client to determine how soft or firm the padding should be. People in wheelchairs must be able to move through the material too. Padding contributes to a luxurious carpet feel under foot, providing a special ambience that communicates a sense of richness and luxury. Carpeting can be made in different fiber compositions but must be flame resistant to some extent. Most recently, I have worked with carpet that is a blend of wool and synthetics.

Because I am originally from Turkey, I have most of my carpets manufactured there. I also work sometimes with English suppliers. Custom-designed carpeting is a time-consuming process with each aspect of the process requiring approval by the client. But if all goes well, the final result will be a good fit, color, and design for the space. Carpeting can bring all the elements of an area or space together and create a feeling of warmth and psychological comfort.

Greg Jordan (deceased April 2005)
Greg Jordan, Inc.
New York, New York

Narrowing choices for the client.

I like to begin designing by looking at the main rooms first and think about carpet in colors liked by the client. So much comes from a carpet or rug. You can build a room literally from the floor up that way. It's the place to start to "sell the scheme." But before the design process actually begins, it's really important to listen to what the client has to say about their space as well as what they are not saying, then try to take the client out of the box by demonstrating how various styles can be combined such as modern with European and Asian. Show clients what the ranges of options are; educate them.

Figure 12.6 Interior designed by Greg Jordan.

Eric Cohler
Eric Cohler, Inc.
New York, New York

Understanding residential space
and light prior to fabric selection.

Carpet is the foundation and fabric is the soul of an interior space. It's important to begin with the carpet, because that's what appears under and around other furnishings. Designing is about layering, and that layering begins with carpet or rugs. I've found that when specifying floor covering it's important to understand the environment where carpets or rugs will be used. For example, sisal should not be used on stairs because it can be very slippery. Often it's better to use natural fibers such as wool in a residence, because wool usually cleans better than a synthetic or synthetically blended carpet and there is less chance of off gasses being produced. When specifying carpeting for stairs, it's important to carefully select a product that will not grin. This means you don't want to expose the carpet's substrate when it bends sharply to conform to the shape of a step.

During the initial fabric meeting in a residential setting, I like to bring with me about 300 very different fabrics from which to begin to narrow down options and to scheme the entire project. This meeting will last about an hour. During this time, it's also good to try and build a verbal picture of each room with the client. I like to stretch the possibilities, then pull back to where the client feels comfortable. I look at fabric textures, color, and hand.

After I feel that I have a good idea of the direction we're moving in, I create display boards. These are *not* fancy boards. I just pin fabrics up so the client can see what I believe the scheme should be composed of. I try to do each room as though it may be a candidate for a magazine like *Architectural Digest*.

Before fabrics are selected the designer should "listen" to a room. Spaces give a designer a great deal of information. What are the ceiling heights? Where are the windows and how much light do they allow flowing into a room? What light exists in the morning and in the evening? How does the space "live" at night? What is the plasticity of the rooms? What about doors, crown moldings, fireplaces, and other interior architectural elements? What is the substrate of the space, and how does it translate structurally? Knowing these things, along with how the client lives, provides important clues as to how the design process will unfold. It's really all about accepting the challenge of transforming a series of bare boxes into a personalized home.

After the basics are known, the design process begins—which I see as an act of layering, as mentioned earlier. Armed with the knowledge of the client and the spaces that need to be addressed, I shop for fabric and usually select about 100 samples from various showrooms. I bring these to my studio and spread them out and begin the scheming process for each room, looking at color, pattern, and textures and how these will be layered and how they will respond to one another. After this process is completed, I will have discarded about 90 percent of the samples I started with. I then typically show the client only three schemes for each room. In doing the editing process, I work like a gardener who continually prunes to clear the underbrush and unnecessary plant material away, so the plants that are worthy of being viewed can be seen and appreciated without extraneous distractions.

Learning how to design well is a growth experience, but what helps is the ability to observe essentially everything. You can even understand aspects of interior design from television. By seeing reruns of *I Love Lucy*, the *Brady Bunch*, and more modern shows like *Seinfeld*, you can observe how people live in a particular era and locale. Observe how the human body moves through spaces and how motion affects design. Look at fashion and see how fabrics and their colors mirror fabric collections in design cen-

Figure 12.7 Room designed for the 2006 Kips Bay showhouse.

ters. Designers should be cross-trained and open to the wide range of possibilities that are now available, especially with carpeting, rugs, and of course, fabric.

Rina Yan
Senior Designer
FF&E Senior Designer
McLean, Virginia

Meeting contract client's needs with cost in mind.

In a hospitality application where many yards of high-end fabric are needed, it's important to understand how to get the yardage required and achieve the desired look at a good price. One way this can be achieved is by "down weaving" a fabric. More specifically, I worked on a project where 2,000 yards were needed for the corridors of a small 98-room hotel. The fabric selected was very nice and sold for $138.00 a yard. By down weaving, that is, substituting high-end yarns like silk with cotton, I was able to retain the same look, feel, color, and basic design for $9.10

Figure 12.8 Fabric
designed by Rina Yan.

a yard! Working directly with American or foreign mills, a great deal can be accomplished, assuming of course you know how to reconfigure yarn and woven structures.

I was also able to do basically the same thing with a printed fabric and reduced the cost considerably by going from 36 screens to 18 screens. I've worked with fabrics that had an original price from $88.00 to $414.00. It's interesting to realize what can be done to moderate this cost by working with mills and cooperative technical personnel.

It's also good to be aware of international mills and their capabilities. For example, I have worked with companies based in England that had mills located in Portugal and have designed carpets that were made in Turkey.

When considering fabric, it's important to consider texture, weight, and composition of yarns, as well as design. It's possible to have a nice design, but if

the colors are not compatible, the fabric won't work. All elements must be in harmony, whether the fabric is expensive or not.

I'm seeing a lot of residential-looking fabrics entering the contract market. Companies are getting better at treating fabrics to meet codes. These fabrics lend themselves to hotels and other places because of their residential touch. Trevira CS has made good strides in developing protected fabrics that have design value.

It should be kept in mind that if a special fabric is required for a particular application, clients must be prepared to wait. I once had to wait 18 months for a hand-blocked print order. Clients must be educated about the wait so there is no misunderstanding.

Susan DiMotta
Principal
Perkins Eastman
New York, New York

Fabric has helped change the look
of health-care interiors.

Hospitals, treatments centers, and senior living communities, both assisted and independent, have evolved over recent years in both architecture and interiors to resemble a hospitality environment, helping people feel more physically and psychologically comfortable. It was not long ago, while waiting to hear the results of surgery, that if the doctor took family members into a separate room to discuss the condition of a loved one, you could be almost assured that the news was going to be bad. You hoped that the conversation

Figure 12.9 A common room at The Tradition, an example of how hospitality design concepts are being introduced in a continuing care retirement community, where carpet and fabric are key elements in conveying an upscale feeling.

would be held in an open waiting area and that you would not be led off somewhere down a long hall to a private room. Today, many new hospitals have areas that are comfortably furnished where all consultations take place. When we revitalized some of the inpatient floors at Memorial Sloan-Kettering Center, it was clear that the administration wanted us to achieve a "hotel feel," where patients and those visiting would be comfortable, especially during a time of considerable stress.

Fabric and carpeting contributes a great deal to making health-care facilities feel more familiar and, consequently, more relaxing. Fortunately, products that are currently available are more pliable, better designed, and more functional, while capable of meeting fire and safety codes that have become increasingly stringent. Especially in hospitals and health-care treatment facilities, it is essential to include products such as solution-dyed nylon fabrics that are anti-microbial and backed with a moisture barrier, capable of stop-ping the flow of spills and fluids associated with incontinence. These fabrics should be *at least* 50,000 DR and capable of retaining their appearance and wear when exposed to rigorous cleaning solvents, including bleach solutions. Solution-dyed fabrics with the Gore backing system offer more design options than vinyl upholstery and can meet most hospital standards. However, at this time, the Gore application can add $10 to $12 to the cost of a yard of fabric.

In addition to upholstery fabric for seating, we also specify fabric of a lighter construction for privacy curtains and window treatments. Most of this fabric is made with polyester, Trevira CS and Avora FR, an inherently flame-resistant product that can maintain its properties even when laundered in a 160-degree wash—the temperature needed to kill most bacteria. This fabric construction should not be specified for seating.

Fabric for senior living communities usually does not have to be quite as durable or armed with as many preventive characteristics as fabrics specified for hospitals and other treatment centers. One reason for this is that bleach is not often used in the cleaning of rooms and common areas; however, fabrics specified for senior living interiors often require a moisture barrier and, of course, must comply with local codes. Another choice, other than the Gore process or vinyl upholstery, is fabric produced under Crypton guidelines, which are stain resistant and also provide a barrier to moisture. To facilitate cleaning, Crypton has developed a cleaning system that simplifies how, when, and under what conditions the fabric can be cleaned. Other fabric treatments can be specified and are considered on a case-by-case basis.

Like fabric, carpeting plays an important role in health-care settings. Carpeting in hospitals is not specified for the areas where patients are treated or around beds; however, carpeting is used in waiting and consultation areas as well as in spaces where people circulate. Pile density is always an important factor to consider when specifying carpeting for health-care interiors. Pile density formula is calculated by taking 36 times the face weight (number of ounces per yard) and dividing that number by the average pile height. A pile density of 4500 or above is acceptable for heavy commercial wear and rolling traffic. A face weight as low as 26 ounces per square yard is now possible to consider due to improved manufacturing technology.

Carpet must withstand constant cleaning; therefore, we specify a solution-dyed nylon product. In addition, the seams need to be sealed or chemically welded to ensure that no fluids will migrate under or through the carpet material. For this reason, we do not recommend carpet tiles because they cannot be properly seamed. Also, when one tile needs to be replaced due to damage, there is almost always a difference in color, creating a rather unattractive floor surface. Most of the carpet we specify is produced in 6-foot widths, however, with the availability of new backing systems for 12-foot widths, we now have additional design choices to choose from.

Many changes have come about in health-care and senior living due to pressures brought about from the general public. In order to be competitive, hospitals often conduct surveys and, as a result, improvements have been made in both hospital architecture and interiors. Furthermore, as baby boomers age, the notion of the "old folk's home" is undergoing a huge transformation that will continue well into the future.

Paul Wiseman
*The Paul Wiseman Group, Inc.
San Francisco, California*

Being aware of new products is the responsibility of the designer.

One of the lessons I learned early is to cultivate a good working relationship with fabric showroom personnel. Return the samples they loan you on time! And don't make little pillows out of them! I have to believe that one of the main reasons I was able to secure my first big project was because a fabric showroom knew me and trusted to loan me a large display sample. The client liked the fabric so much that they decided to hire me. It's important that designers take the relationships they develop with showrooms seriously and act responsibly. It costs suppliers a lot of money to sample product, and the least we can do is treat them with consideration so when we really need their assistance, they will be ready and willing to help.

Designing can be a very creative profession. Sometimes a designer may have an idea but think that it's impossible to transform the idea into something tangible and wonderful. The truth is that just about everything is possible, providing the sources are known. One thing that we're doing is selecting a fabric, like damask, and having it embroidered over certain areas of the pattern. Macondo Silks is doing some very interesting work in this area. Or explore what Sam Kaften is creating in the area of custom fabrics. It's also amazing to discover that a product like Sunbrella can be screen printed after it is ordered with a pattern you design and remain essentially weather-resistant. Speaking of outdoor fabrics, there are many advances in this area, including some impressive plastics that look like chenilles. Floor covering can take on a very special place in a room too if exceptional sources are known, such as rugs from V'Soske.

In terms of new products, there are fabric treatments that can literally help make sales. For example, Fiber Seal produces a stain- and water-resistant treatment that is guaranteed to work or the company will go to where the chair or sofa is and clean it in the room! For fami-

Figure 12.10 Detail of a seating area with a view into the adjoining library.

lies who want practical yet attractive material for their furnishings, it's a good idea to discover what is available to protect and help enhance fabric wearability. But at the other end of the scale, we have to be very conscious of the environment and the notion of green design. This is something that has captured the attention of consumers, particularly in California.

Michelle Nassopoulos
Senior Designer
The Paul Wiseman Group, Inc.
San Francisco, California

Understanding pattern repeats and the workroom.

Fabric repeat and scale are very important to know, so when dealing with workrooms the pattern will appear where it should on furniture or window treatments. It's difficult to determine sometimes how a 10-inch square showroom sample will look when it becomes 20 yards and applied to a sofa, for example.

The workroom can help determine if the selected fabric can be used in the way it was intended.

Suitability is also important. By understanding yarn composition and fabric properties, better selections can be made. When to use chenille over a silk, for example, is important to know. Finally, designers must study the nuance of color. Color and light can be complex entities to fully understand and deal with, but by consciously observing and reflecting on color choices, the skill develops.

Figure 12.11 Rendering for an apartment in the Sherry Netherland Building, New York City.

Tom Britt
Tom Britt, Inc.
New York, New York

Working with knowledgeable showroom personnel.

When dealing with showrooms it's necessary to use your good judgment and build a relationship with a *competent* showroom employee. I often make a point to engage one of the owners or the manager. In the absence of these two, I try to find the most knowledgeable person in a particular showroom. Once you've established a good relationship with someone, things go more smoothly; they become your contact and stay with you if there are problems, as well as letting you know if a fabric can be special ordered at a reasonable price.

Once, I had a very large order, around 100 yards, of printed fabric coming from overseas. Fortunately when it arrived, we checked it. It was splotchy and had many flaws. Because we waited so long and the client really wanted this particular fabric, we had to find ways to cut and work around the problems. It should be a consideration to order more yards than you might think you need. If we had to reorder the fabric we might still be waiting for it!

Harvey Herman
Harvey Herman Interior Decorating, Ltd.
Boca Raton, Florida

Follow-up is necessary to keep a project on track.

The process of designing makes up only about 20 percent, or less, of the work a designer actually does. The rest is *follow-up* and dealing with problems to make a room happen.

Fabric companies stock hundreds of samples in showrooms but have few actual fabric numbers that are available for immediate delivery. Because many of the fabrics are manufactured in China or somewhere outside the United States, complications often arise. For example, I designed a room around a large window treatment and the many yards of fabric I ordered. I even went ahead and designed and produced a rug to work with the order. After many, many weeks of waiting, I was told that the company decided not to make the fabric and discontinued it!

If you have to order fabric it will take longer than you think. A wait of 16 weeks is common now. Many companies like to gather several orders before they begin production, and this adds to the delay. New designers must ask specifics about when the fabric will be in and hold companies reasonably responsible for the dates they set. It used to be that companies would stock lots of higher-end goods, but this is rare today.

Also, sometimes the people who work in showrooms are not forthcoming with all the information you might need to facilitate a project. On one job, I needed a fabric that was, once again, discontinued. But as I probed further, I soon discovered I could *special order* 50 yards of it at about the same price it was before they stopped making it for showroom distribution. If I hadn't *asked* about their special order capabilities, I wouldn't have had the fabric the client wanted and the company would have lost a sale.

Designing is emotional, and I always plan to be with the client when products, like window treatments or furnishings, are delivered so if problems arise, they can be addressed on the spot. It's also a good idea to check and double check (when possible) the fabric for flaws *before* it is applied. Clients are paying top dollar and are very upset if they don't get what they pay for. They want it perfect. And if something is flawed, like a mark on a wooden leg of a chair, most clients will become very critical of everything else that's ordered from that point forward.

FABRIC SUPPLIERS AND MANUFACTURERS

Acquiring Fabric for Showrooms and Designers

The role of the supplier is to know the world fabric market and to make available to designers a broad range of products based upon how they see their competition and the way in which they choose to define their business.

The massive task of editing and manufacturing fabric to sell to the trade is a complicated process. Much of the fabric today is produced offshore and this, in part, challenges a company and its owners to find ways to have sufficient quantities on hand and ready for sale. Having demand for fabrics and nothing to ship will affect the growth of a business. Suppliers are challenged to educate designers on what to expect when selecting, ordering, and processing a fabric order as well as conditions related to returns and credit. The following suppliers have agreed to share their point of view.

FABRIC MANUFACTURERS AND SUPPLIERS: THE INTERVIEWS

Nina Butkin

Vice President of Design
Fabricut, S. Harris, and Vervain
Tulsa, Oklahoma

How designers should deal with clients, products, and suppliers

As a supplier and manufacturer of fabric, we encourage designers to *know their clients and understand how they live*. A fabric selected from one of our collections and inappropriately specified creates results that do not reflect favorably on the designer or us, the supplier. If 100 percent silk is selected for furniture that young children will use frequently, there's a very good chance that the fabric will not perform as intended. A well-designed product that is solution dyed and made of acrylic may be a better choice. Being knowledgeable about the properties of fibers and fabric treatments and pairing that information with the clients' lifestyle can greatly

enhance the usefulness of fabric and limit problems associated with returns. I would, however, strongly encourage designers to experiment broadly with fabric but within the context of its use. Clients need to know about aesthetics as well as wearability. And designers should be prepared to supply to clients as much information as possible about both areas.

All fabric suppliers spend a considerable amount of thought, time, and money selecting, categorizing, and delivering fabric options to designers in different forms. These tools, such as presentation books, showroom memos, or displays on showroom wings, offer varied ways designers can view and help contribute to enhancing client presentations that can translate into orders. Much can be said about how presentations impact orders.

Technology has contributed to widening the choices that are now available. However, the creation of all types of fabric is more of an art than a science, particularly when it comes to color matching and printing. Variances from color to color, for example, are judgment calls, and client expectations should be balanced against what is reasonably possible to produce. If designers become more familiar with fabric manufacturing and printing processes, tolerances can be better understood and explained.

Workrooms are an important part of transforming fabric into something useful. It's essential that designers work closely with their fabricators. If the designer does not communicate what side of a fabric should be used on a sofa, it's possible that the preferred side will not be what is seen. There are times when a designer may

Figure 12.12 The Fabricut showroom.

want to use the back of the fabric as the face. Workrooms need to be informed of that decision or any other decision about how the pattern is to be positioned on an item of furniture, window treatment, or duvet cover, for that matter. It's the responsibility of the designer to remain up to speed with what the workroom is doing so costly mistakes and delivery delays of the finished product can be avoided.

As we know, the Internet has become a convenient and highly useful tool that significantly affects the way we access information. Some fabric companies utilize the Internet to sell product. Caution must be exercised if this form of shopping is to be used. Experienced designers currently prefer to physically examine as many sample products as possible in one location and to talk directly with someone, such as a showroom representative, who may help them scheme a room. The methods of acquiring fabric through showrooms and sample books may be a more efficient method of readily exploring the many options available, especially when higher-quality fabrics are desired and several choices are needed to achieve a degree of harmony, texture, and correct color for a given space.

Lorraine Lang
Director of Design
Old World Weavers
(Division of Stark)
New York, New York

Showroom personnel and workrooms provide an important source of information. At Stark, we have four divisions: Stark Carpet, Old World Weavers, Stark Wallcovering, and Stark Fine Furniture.

Figure 12.13 The Stark showroom.

As director of design for the fabric division, I have observed recurring issues that interior designers need to be aware of. When selecting fabrics, the designer must be mindful of the appropriate application for each fabric. Fabrics that are intended for window treatments are often not suitable for upholstery. Fine fabrics that may be used in a formal living room may not wear in an active family room. Strips may be woven up the roll or railroaded. The designer must know the direction of the design in order to be certain that it will work for their intended application.

The designer should be knowledgeable about all of the attributes of the fabric before placing an order. These attributes relate to fiber content, width, cleanability, abrasion, pattern repeats, light fastness, and humidity tolerances. All of this information is available. Rather than disappoint a client and have to pay for a costly replacement, the designer should confer with his or her salesperson about how the fabric is to be used.

The designer's workroom is a valuable and knowledgeable source for information. The designer should show a sample of the fabric to be used to the workroom first to learn if the fabric can be applied appropriately. A sample backing may be suggested to enhance the stability of the fabric. If so, this information is important to know early on. Workrooms usually send a confirmation order sheet to the designer that must be reviewed, confirming the correct color, pattern, and pattern direction before the fabric is to be cut. The designer should also inform the workroom about centering, or not centering, certain motifs that will contribute to the overall design effect on a sofa or window treatment.

When calculating yardage, it is important that the workroom match motifs. This often requires additional yardage as opposed to matching a fabric with a solid pattern. Noting how the back of a sofa is to be upholstered is important too. A workroom may railroad fabric across the back to save material and labor costs; however, this may not be the desired effect, especially if the chair or sofa is to be placed more in the center of a room where the back can be seen.

Before shopping for fabric, the designer should know not only the yardage needed for the project but the size of the cuts as well. Once again, the workroom can supply this information. If the designer knows the dimensions of each area of the sofa to be upholstered, for example, it is acceptable to order fabric from stock that is in more than one piece but from the *same dye lot*. It is not always necessary to have the yardage ar-

rive at the workroom in one continuous bolt.

It is important to review all invoices to confirm the details of what was ordered. The ship to address and side mark information is particularly important. Clearly written side marked information will avoid confusion and mistakes once the fabric arrives at the workroom, where it joins many other fabric orders to be temporarily stored, waiting for its turn to be cut and sewn.

Designers should plan fabric projects well in advance, allowing enough lead-time for product that may not be in stock to be manufactured, shipped, and applied. Rushing orders often creates problems. For product to be made, at least eight weeks should be allocated. Labor-intensive fabrics can take as long as five to six *months*! But usually the wait is well worth the time spent.

Also regarding issues related to planning, it is a good idea to ask for a cutting for approval (CFA) that originates from the very same bolt or dye lot from which the full order will come. With a color-correct sample in hand, it becomes possible to more accurately coordinate other fabrics, wallcoverings, and trimmings. And as soon as the designer decides on the fabric to be ordered, it should be reserved immediately!

Designers should take advantage of new technologies and advanced yarns that are now available. For example, there are sheers that reflect harmful rays of the sun, thereby helping to cool a room and protect window treatments from fading. New fibers and fabric can also have insulating properties. Fabrics that were for outdoor use only have been refined and are now used for family rooms and spas because of their ability to be durable and repel stains, water, and mildew. Many new fabrics are also resistant to sun fading, making them popular for sunrooms and banquettes positioned close to glass windows.

It is important to visit as many showrooms as possible to see the broad spectrum of beautiful products available and to understand that there is fabric to satisfy essentially every aesthetic and fulfill every functional requirement.

Robert Bitter

Co-President
Scalamandré
New York, New York

Understanding mill capabilities helps facilitate the design project.

There are several points that designers should keep in mind as they go about the process of specifying fabric products.

1. It is usually better if a proven line item is selected rather than ordering a special product. Selecting an item we have in the collection ensures consistency of color and repeat. Nevertheless, it is very important to make certain that your end use is consistent with the fabric selected.

2. If a designer decides to acquire a fabric that is back-ordered or a special, it is necessary that the designer regularly follow up on the production schedule to know when the product will be ready to be shipped.

Figure 12.14 The Scalamandré showroom.

3. Designers need to be flexible on color. If color is absolutely critical, it is necessary to request a cutting for approval. It is costly to provide cuttings, so the designer needs to be sure they really need one for client approval.

4. Designers should remember to recycle memos by returning them to the showroom. Samples are expensive to produce and by returning them, costs for product can be kept down.

5. The industry is constantly changing and consolidating. If a pattern is modified, converted, or reproduced on a different machine or in a different mill, variances should be expected. Each fabric production run is also affected by changes in dyestuffs or dye formulas.

Interior designers must be sensitive to light issues as well that can change how a particular fabric will look in a space. With so many products available, there is usually a fabric readily available to conform to the requirements of a given project.

Christopher Hyland

Christopher Hyland, Inc.
New York, New York

Explore the variety of fabrics available.

Interior designers must learn about fabric and not hesitate about getting their hands on as many designs, colors, prints, and weaves as possible. Fabric selection should not be a casual thing. It requires a designer to spend time surveying literally hundreds and hundreds of possible choices. It's been my experience, if a designed interior embraces a wide range of fabrics, the occupants are undoubtedly broad-minded. I remember when Sharon Stone came into our showroom, she was very clear about wanting a different fabric for each chair in her house; she desired that every seated person would experience a different texture. I've also noted, in a general way, that designers who seriously consider many different fabric types in a room, tend to experience longevity in the profession as opposed to those designers whose range of selections are consistently narrow. One

who selects fabrics can look at choices with a "wide eye" or "narrow eye." A wide eye is best. Designers who restrict themselves, and consequently their clients, are doing their clients a great disservice.

I'm surprised to see how many designers do not really get into selecting fabric seriously. Many see it as a casual shopping experience. Designers really need to L-O-O-K! They need to take their time. Take their coat off. Put down their bags and consider the full range of possibilities.

Fabric and comfort go hand-in-hand and designers must learn how powerful the impact can be. Consider a dog that hops up on a favorite chair. Chances are it's upholstered. Fabric breeds familiarity and familiarity breeds comfort. Fabric is the barrier between the hard world beyond and the civilized world within. It connects one, consciously or subconsciously, with home and happiness. And it can even point us to poetry and art.

Designers must ask questions and clearly note the responses given from showroom personnel so they can accurately relate information to clients. For example, if there are only 72 yards of a particular fabric in stock and that particular fabric is woven in Malaysia only twice a year, it's possible that if the designer does not place an order quickly, they may have to wait many months to receive what they need. Communication is key to getting things done!

Designers need to know that they are responsible for fabric after purchase. Once it's cut we cannot accept the order back. Designers also need to really know their workroom to be sure that they are capable of handling fabric properly. In one in-

Figure 12.15 The Christopher Hyland showroom.

stance, fabric bolts were placed standing upright in a corner of a workroom. Every night the cleaning crew mopped the floor and dragged the dirty, wet, soapy mop loaded with cleaning chemicals against the bottom few inches of the fabric, damaging it. We cannot accept responsibility for this damage. Designers need to follow the fabric trail and be responsible for caring for their order once we have safely delivered it to the location of their choice.

Students of design, and I don't mean just young students who are working on a degree, should take time to visit major showrooms and explore what the market has available. They should travel to design centers and visit as many fabric companies as possible to see what's available and take time to study the options and consider the possibilities.

Scott Kravet, Principal

with Tony Amplo, Vice President
of Design for Portfolio
Kravet, Inc.
New York, New York

New technology enhances fabric choices.

Fabric suppliers and manufacturers are as good as their sources. Designers should be aware of what manufacturers are capable of doing for designers so their offerings to clients can be expanded.

Times are changing, and as they evolve, things are possible today that were not even considered practical in years past. For example, digital printing technology and overseas sourcing are two areas that have contributed to delivering quality products at affordable prices. Designers

Figure 12.16 The Kravet showroom.

should familiarize themselves with technology so they know what can be done. It's not necessary to understand all aspects of the Galvano engraving process and exactly how it is capable of printing fine detail, or the way a Laser Lex engraving machine works; however, understanding the basics allows a designer to expand his or her offerings by saying to a client, "If you don't like this print (or woven), I know a firm that can work with us to change some aspects of the design." Designers, particularly high-end designers, should strive to push the envelope of engravers and printers. But even before a custom design is considered, it's a good idea to work with a showroom salesperson who can make arrangements to open a company's archives, showing fabrics that were produced in the past and are easily reproducible. The options are enormous, especially when dealing with a company that has the capabilities to be a converter. Custom options usually come with yardage minimums, and designers need to know what they are; however, the issue of yardage minimums may soon be a thing of the past. There are currently digital printers costing in the neighborhood of $4 million that can print up to 1,000 yards of product a day! Once the printer is set up, any amount of fabric can be ordered at any time because of the way in which the printer stores the design and colors and reproduces the product. Ultimately, this will significantly reduce or eliminate altogether the need for warehousing fabric. Also, there will be no need for the human intervention that causes dye changes or noticeable trap lines—defects in weaving when the shed closes, "trapping" the shuttle. And there's no need to worry about the 100-degree summer temperatures and high humidity in a traditional mill affecting the results—which can happen when a rotary printing process is used.

When working with fabrics, particularly custom fabrics, designers should understand tolerances that include color and quality changes from sample to sample. Furthermore, if the knife that cuts velvet is not properly maintained, it's possible for one side of the product to be fractionally thicker than the other side. And when water is used in producing dyes, there can be minor differences between winter water and summer water, assuming the water is not filtered, as is the case from time to time when products are produced offshore. Even when silk fabric is produced on old looms in China, the weave may be slightly tighter during the morning hours and looser toward the end of the day, when the workers become tired. And, of course, the variable of light can be an issue as well. When we are developing product for the international chain of Disney hotels, it's important that we look at the strike offs or sample yardages at the location of a particular hotel.

It is necessary for a designer to understand that lead time for product development must be taken into account. It can take from six to eight weeks before screens are engraved from which a TSO (table strike off) can be reviewed. And this is only one phase of the process! Specifications should be reviewed early in the construction process of a new facility where unique products are required. Designers cannot wait until the very end and expect immediate turnaround.

Fabrics that were traditionally used in hospitality are now being used in residential settings. For example, we have a Teflon-coated, 54 percent polyacrylic and 46 percent polyester woven product appearing in contemporary designs and rated at 30,000 DR that can be used in heavy-use rooms. It's attractive, it cleans very well, and it performs for people who have pets.

One way to learn more about a company such as Kravet and its affiliates, Lee Jofa and Portfolio, is to spend time apprenticing in showrooms. If a design center showroom is not conveniently accessible, Kravet has "sub-agent showrooms" throughout the country that also provide fabric to designers. The hands-on experience will expand your knowledge and help connect you with the many options available to interior designers.

RESOURCES

The importance of staying current, recognizing the need to acquire new knowledge, and seeking new sources for product and ways to use it is central to maintaining a forward view on design.

Exploring Sources

Knowing how and where to find specific fabrics and how to apply them contributes significantly to the success of a designer. Without discovering new product sources while staying in contact with established ones, it is possible for a designer to become limited in what he or she can offer clients. More resources equals more choices. And the more choices there are, the more editing is required. Nevertheless, designing is about making informed and appropriate decisions supported by sound rationales.

The lists in the appendix to Chapter 12 do not include *all* of the organizations and fabric resources that exist. New sources for fabrics can be found all over the world, and businesses open and close all the time. Fabric suppliers must adjust to market demands based on fluctuations in the economy, and sometimes required to leave design centers where business may be less profitable. Shifts in the marketplace are inevitable as new companies start up, large companies consolidate, and big firms purchase smaller ones. Within the larger to-the-trade fabric companies, there are often smaller, boutique fabric collections that satisfy a market niche. These collections are not often widely advertised, and to see them a designer must explore. Continual monitoring is necessary to stay current with fabric collections and their continually evolving colors, designs, and fiber blends as well as the technology to create fabric for specialized uses. Experimentation with woven and nonwoven fabric using metallic yarns, for example, contin-

ues to grow. Without knowledge of the capabilities of a mill, it may be difficult to specify a custom order or to understand the construction of new combinations of materials or their ability to be converted for practical use by a workroom. Professional associations and organizations can also be useful in providing up-to-date information on many topics, such as changes in codes that relate to safety.

Because much of interior design is about developing a functioning visual product, magazines, museums (see the American Association of Museums at http://www.aam-us.org), and films—even vintage ones—can provide inspiration. If designers are aware of and open to the broad range of possibilities, sources for ideas exist almost anywhere. The designer must discover the hidden likenesses and differences in objects and fabric and provide a mix that communicates to clients and addresses their needs.

Most of the fabric firms noted in the appendix to this chapter can be found in the design centers listed in Chapter 9; however, these are not the only sources of fabric that designers can access. Some fabric shops open to the general public also have products that can be purchased by designers and used primarily in residential settings. It is not uncommon for designers to select fabric from both public and to-the-trade sources to achieve a desired effect.

SUMMARY

Thoughtful exposure to the world of design and its resources contributes to designers becoming established. Knowing where and how to access products, with the help of vendors and manufacturers who are capable of developing special order products, provides an ever-widening range of possibilities. Leading interior designers travel the world to locate products that will distinguish their spaces and help draw attention to the depth of their resources and the creative ways in which they are used.

Clients have become more knowledgeable and, as a consequence, assume that designers are well trained, experienced, and ready to introduce them to multiple possibilities and scenarios. A designer who enjoys travel and is naturally inclined to think about how fabric can be used in a space will be able to introduce clients to a range of fabric options. A designer who attends showroom events where new collections are presented will remain at the forefront of what the residential and contract markets have to offer. Likewise, a designer who visits international fabric fairs will gain knowledge of what is being produced and purchased in Europe, Asia, and other parts of the world.

Technical fabrics are evolving at a rapid pace, and new materials and combinations are being developed continually. The worlds of residential and contract fabrics are narrowing: Contract is taking on characteristics of residential, and residential is evoking the designs and functional capabilities of contract fabric. High-performance and industrial fibers are taking their place among more traditional fabrics through ongoing collaborations among designers, engineers, and manufacturing facilities. Technology is making more choices possible.

ACTIVITIES

1. Interview an interior designer and inquire about his or her—
   - method of scheduling fabric and carpet orders for a residential or commercial property
   - experiences associated with ordering and receiving fabric or carpeting
   - ideas regarding the importance of fabric color, scale, and balance as it applies to window treatment installations
   - most challenging experiences related to a fabric or carpet installation
   - showroom experiences, both good and bad
   - experiences with complications arising from special fabric or carpet orders

2. Interview someone who hired an interior designer about that experience. Evaluate the client's experience selecting fabric or rugs.

3. Contact three international sources of fabric available to designers and report on the scope of their business and available products. Determine how they compare or contrast with American fabrics in terms of price, quality, and applications.

4. Locate three businesses in your area that may be considered nontraditional sources for acquiring fabric or rugs.

5. Contact two fabric suppliers or manufacturers and determine their procedures for developing a special order fabric. Compare and contrast their methods and requirements.

6. Research one manufacturer who produces to-the-trade fabric and learn about its capabilities.

EXPAND YOUR KNOWLEDGE

1. What mistakes could an individual avoid by working with a qualified designer to specify fabric and rugs?

2. What do shelter magazines provide to designers that help them specify fabric, rugs, and carpeting? What are the dangers in transposing a room from a magazine and applying it literally to a client's space?

3. How can a designer work on more than one major project at a time? What are some of the organizational issues that confront a growing design office.

4. How can international travel contribute to expanding the vocabulary of a designer? How might a designer's visit to a European or Asian city differ from the visit of an individual who is not involved with interior design?

5. What variables should be considered in fabric selections for a private airplane? A private yacht? How would the fabric differ? What influences their difference?

6. How is technology changing the way fabric mills do business? Provide specific examples. What would be considered the "old" way of printing fabric, as opposed to the "new" way?

7. How do pets, specifically dogs and cats, affect fabric and rug selections? How and why do animals determine what an interior *can* look like? How should a designer deal with clients and their interiors where pets have become "part of the family"?

Appendixes

ACT Voluntary Performance Guidelines

ACT has developed the following voluntary Performance Guidelines to make fabric specification easier. The five symbols give architects, designers, and end-users vast useful performance information in a succinct visual way. Look for these symbols on ACT member company fabric samples to assure that the fabrics specified perform up to contract standards and pass all applicable testing.

These categories describe a material's performance features as measured by specified methods under standard laboratory conditions.

FLAMMABILITY

The measurement of a fabric's performance when it is exposed to specific sources of ignition.

Upholstery

California Technical Bulletin #117
Section E—Class 1 (Pass)

Direct Glue Wallcoverings

ASTM E 84-03
(Adhered Mounting Method)—
Class A or Class 1

Wrapped Panels and Upholstered Walls

ASTM E 84-03
(Unadhered Mounting Method)—
Class A or Class 1

Drapery

NFPA 701-89 (Small Scale)*—Pass

WET & DRY CROCKING

Transfer of dye from the surface of a dyed or printed fabric onto another surface by rubbing.

Upholstery

AATCC 8-2001
Dry Crocking, Grade 4 minimum
Wet Crocking, Grade 3 minimum

*NFPA 701-99 Test #1 is being phased in at the time of this publication, but is not yet cited in all relevant codes. Therefore, the small-scale test remains the ACT standard until further notice.

Direct Glue Wallcoverings
AATCC 8-2001
Dry Crocking, Grade 3 minimum
Wet Crocking, Grade 3 minimum

Wrapped Panels and Upholstered Walls
AATCC 8-2001
Dry Crocking, Grade 3 minimum
Wet Crocking, Grade 3 minimum

Drapery
AATCC 8-2001 (Solids)
Dry Crocking, Grade 3 minimum
Wet Crocking, Grade 3 minimum

AATCC 116-2001 (Prints)
Dry Crocking, Grade 3 minimum
Wet Crocking, Grade 3 minimum

COLORFASTNESS TO LIGHT
A material's degree of resistance to the fading effect of light.

Upholstery
AATCC 16 Option 1 or 3-2003
Grade 4 minimum at 40 hours

Direct Glue Wallcoverings
AATCC 16 Option 1 or 3-2003
Grade 4 minimum at 40 hours

Wrapped Panels and Upholstered Walls
AATCC 16 Option 1 or 3-2003
Grade 4 minimum at 40 hours

Drapery
AATCC 16 Option 1 or 3-2003
Grade 4 minimum at 60 hours

PHYSICAL PROPERTIES
ACT defines *pilling* as the formation of fuzzy balls of fiber on the surface of a fabric that remain attached to the fabric. *Breaking strength* is the measurement of stress exerted to pull a fabric apart under tension. *Seam Slippage* is the movement of yarns in a fabric that occurs when it is pulled apart at a seam.

Upholstery
Brush pill ASTM D3511-02,
    Class 3 minimum

Breaking strength ASTM D5034-95
    (2001) (Grab Test)
50 lbs. minimum in warp and weft

Seam slippage ASTM D4034
    25 lbs. minimum in warp and weft

Wrapped Panels and Upholstered Walls
Breaking strength ASTM D5034-95
    (2001) (Grab Test)
35 lbs. minimum in warp and weft

Drapery
Seam slippage ASTM D3597-02-D434-
    95 for fabrics over 6 oz./sq. yard
25 lbs. minimum in warp and weft

ABRASION
The surface wear of a fabric caused by rubbing and contact with another fabric.

General Contract Upholstery
ASTM D4157-02 (ACT approved #10
    Cotton Duck)
15,000 double rubs Wyzenbeek method

ASTM D4966-98 (12 KPa pressure)
20,000 cycles Martindale method

ASTM D4966-98 (12 KPa pressure)
40,000 cycles Martindale method

Heavy Duty Upholstery

ASTM D4157-02 (ACT approved #10
   Cotton Duck)
    30,000 double rubs Wyzenbeek method

Revised January 2005
Source: Association for Contract Textiles

Yardage Chart

These guidelines are only general estimates. Only the workroom can offer actual yardages. Yardages are based on 54-inch-wide solid color fabric. Add 1 yard for two arm covers. Add 1½ yards of fabric for extra cushions up to 30 inches wide, a chair skirt, tufting, etc.

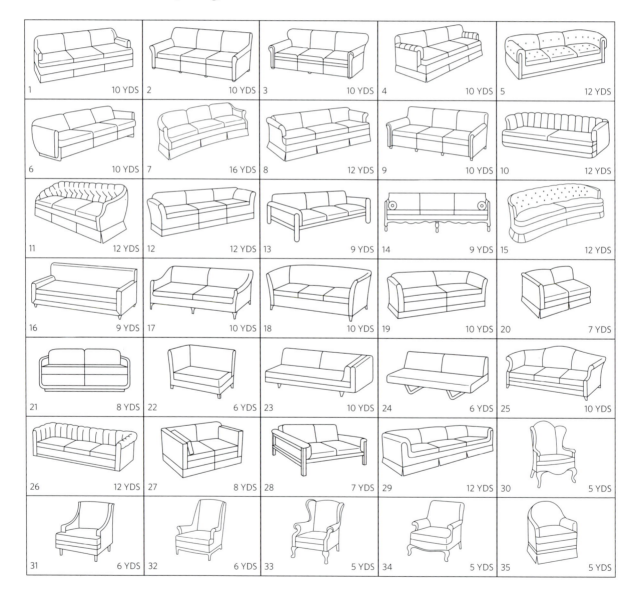

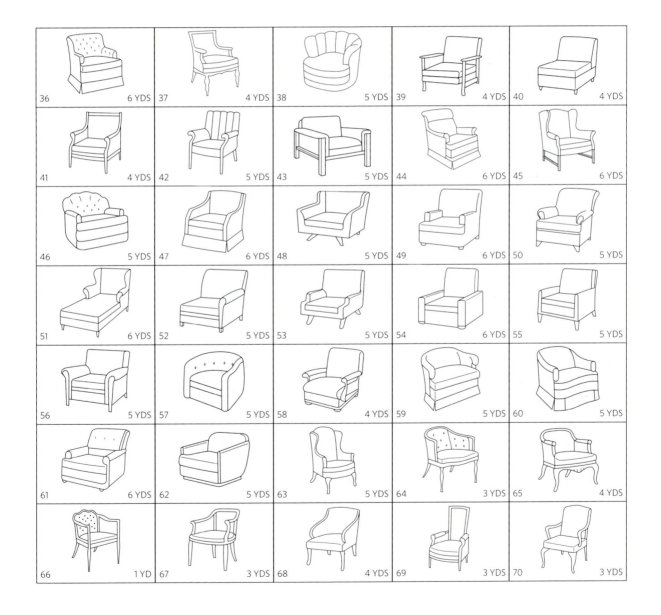

36 6 YDS	37 4 YDS	38 5 YDS	39 4 YDS	40 4 YDS
41 4 YDS	42 5 YDS	43 5 YDS	44 6 YDS	45 6 YDS
46 5 YDS	47 6 YDS	48 5 YDS	49 6 YDS	50 5 YDS
51 6 YDS	52 5 YDS	53 5 YDS	54 6 YDS	55 5 YDS
56 5 YDS	57 5 YDS	58 4 YDS	59 5 YDS	60 5 YDS
61 6 YDS	62 5 YDS	63 5 YDS	64 3 YDS	65 4 YDS
66 1 YD	67 3 YDS	68 4 YDS	69 3 YDS	70 3 YDS

Resources

TRADE DIRECTORIES

Davison's Textile Blue Book
Davison Publishing Company
http://www.davisonpublishing.com

Franklin Report
http://franklinreport.com

Industrial Fabrics Products Review
Industrial Fabrics Association International
http://www.ifai.com

Nonwovens Industry
Rodman Publications, Inc.
http://www.nonwovens-industry.com/

NATIONAL AND INTERNATIONAL TRADE GROUPS AND ORGANIZATIONS

American Society of Interior
Designers
http://www.asid.org

Association of Contract Textiles
http://contract-textiles.com

American Association of Textile
Chemists and Colorists
http://aatcc.org

American Fiber Manufacturers
Association, Inc.
http://www.fibersource.com/afma/afma.htm

American Sheep Industry Association
http://www.sheepusa.org/

American Society of Interior Design
http://www.asid.org/

American Society for Testing and
Materials
http://www.astm.org

American Textile Machinery
Association
http://www.manet.org/home.aspx

American Textile Manufactures
    Institute, Inc.
http://www.osha.gov/dcsp/alliances/
atmi/atmi/htm/

American Yarn Spinners Association
http://www.textileweb.com

Association of the Nonwoven Fabrics
    Industry
http://www.inda.org

Associazione Tessile Italiana
http://www.asstex.it/

Carpet and Rug Institute
http://www.carpet-rug.com/

Carpet Cushion Council
http://www.carpetcushion.org/

The Center for Health Design
http://www.healthdesign.org

China National Textile Industry Council
http://www.ctei.gov.cn/cntac/c_xhjj.asp

Color Association of the Unites States, Inc.
http://www.colorassociation.com/

Cotton Incorporated
http://www.cottoninc.com/

Council for Interior Design Accreditation
    (formerly Foundation for Interior
    Design Education Research)
http://www.accredit-id.org/

Decorative Fabrics Association
http://www.dfa.info/

European Council of Interior Architects
http://www.ecia.net/

Institute of Store Planners
http://www.ispo.org

Interior Design Educators Council
http://www.idec.org

Interior Design Society
http://www.interiordesignsociety.org

Interlaine
http://www.interlaine.org/

International Fabricare Institute
http://www.ifi.org/

International Facilities Management
    Association
http://www.ifma.org

International Facility Management
    Association
http://www.ifma.org

International Furnishings and Design
    Association
http://www.ifda.com/

International Home Furnishings and
    Design Association
http://www.hfia.com/

International Home Furnishings
    Representatives
http://www.ihfra.org/

International Interior Design Association
http://www.iida.org/

International Textile Manufacturers
   Federation
http://www.ifmf.org/

Knitted Textile Association
http://www.intexa.com/industry_links.htm

Leadership in Energy and Environmental
   Design
http://www.usgbc.org/LEED/

Mohair Council of America
http://www.mohairusa.com/

National Association of Decorative
   Fabrics Distributors
http://www.info@nadfd.com/

National Cleaners Association
http://www.nca-icom/nac1.cfm

National Cotton Batting Institute
http://www.natbat.com/news/cpsc01.htm

National Cotton Council of America
http://www.cotton.org/

National Council of Textile
   Organizations
http://www.ncto.org/

National Fire Protection Association, Inc.
http://www.nfpa.org/

National Home Furnishings Association
http://www.nhfa.org/

National Institute for Occupational
   Safety and Health
http://cdc.gov/niosh

National Society for Testing and Materials
http://www.engineers.his.com/collections/
astm/index.jsp

National Trust for Historic Preservation
http://www.nationaltrust.org

Occupational Safety & Health
   Administration
http://osha-slc.gov

Organization of Black Designers
http://www.core77.com/OBD/welcome.html

The Performance Textiles Association
http://www.pertexa.org.uk/

Rugmark Foundation
http://www.rugmark.org

Silk Association of India
http://www.silkassociation.com

Textile Care Allied Trades Association
http://www.tcata.org/

The Textile Institute
http://www.texi.org/

The Textile Society of America
http://www.textilesociety.org/

Upholstered Furniture Action Council
http://www.ufac.org/

U.S. Green Building Council
http://www.usgbc.org

Woolmark Co.
http://www.wool.com/

TO-THE-TRADE FABRIC SUPPLIERS

Andrew Martin
http://www.andrewmartin.com.uk/

Arc-Com
http://www.arc-com.com/

B. Berger
http://www.bberger.com/

Beacon Hill
http://www.beaconhilldesign.com/

Bergamo Fabrics, Inc.
http://www.bergamofabrics.com/
main.html

Brunschwig & Fils, Inc.
http://www.brunschwig.com/

Carleton V
http://www.jpro.com/lines/carlton_v.html

Carpet Designs
http://www.carpetdesigns.com.uk/

Chelsea Textiles
http://www.Chelsea-textiles.co.uk

Christopher Farr
http://www.cfarr.co.uk/

Christopher Hyland, Inc.
http://www.christopherhyland.com/

Christopher Norman, Inc.
http://www.christophernorman.com/

Claremont Fabrics
http://www.hanna-uk.com/claremont_htm

Clarence House
http://www.clarencehouse.com/

Collezione Cesaro
http://www.collezionecesaro.com/

Coraggio Textiles
http://www.corraggio.com/

Cortina Leather
http://www.cortinaleather.com/

Couristan, Inc.
http://www.couristan.com/

Cowtan & Tout
http://www.cowtan.com/

Decorator's Walk
http://www.decoratorswalk.com/

Designtex Group
http://www.dtex.com/

Design West
http://www.designwest.com/

Donghia
http://www.donghia.com/

Duralee
http://www.duralee.com/

Edelman Leather
http://www.edelmanleather.com

Fabricut
http://www.fabricut.com/

F. Schumacher & Company
http://www.fschumacher.com/

Fortuny, Inc.
http://www.fortuny.com/

Galbraith & Paul
http://www.galbraithandpaul.com/

Hable Textiles
http://www.thebubbly.com/The Guide/
archives/000493.html

Harsey-Fischbacher
http://www.harseyfischbacher.com/

Hinson & Company
http://www.fabricsandhome.com/

Holland & Sherry
http://www.hollandandsherry.com

Holly Hunt
http://www.hollyhunt.com/

Houles
http://www.houles.com/

JAB
http://www.jabtextile.com/

J. Robert Scott
http://www.jrobertscott.com/

Kravet, Inc.
http://www.kravet.com/

Laura Lienhard
http://www.lauralienhard.com/

Larsen
http://www.artsmia.org/larsen/fabrics/
index.cfm

Lee Jofa
http://www.leejofa.com/

KnollTextiles
http://www.knoll.com/products/
textiles_overview.jsp

Lorin Marsh
http://www.lorinmarsh.com/

Luisa Cevese
http://www.ridizioni.com/Textile.html

Madison Leathers
http://www.madisonleathers.com/

Manuel Canovas
http://www.manuelcanovas.com

Maharam
http://www.maharam.com/

Marc Phillips Decorative Rugs
http://www.marcphillipsrugs.com/

Mokum
http://www.mokumtextiles.com/

Nancy Corzine
http://www.homeportfolio.com/Product
Explorer...html?action=profile&manld=
1451

Nobilis
http://www.fabricsandhome.com

Odegard, Inc.
http://www.odegardinc.com/

Osborne & Little
http://www.osborneandlittle.com/

Passementerie, Inc.
http://www.ddbuilding.com/search/
showrooms/showrooms.asp

Patterson, Flynn & Martin/Rosecore
http://www.fschumacher.com/pfm/pfm1
.htm

Pierre Deux
http://www.pierredeux.com/

Pierre Frey
http://www.pierrefrey.com/

Pindler & Pindler, Inc.
http://www.pindler.com/

Platino International, Inc.
http://www.platinointernational.com/

Pollack
http://www.pollackassociates.com/fabrics/
fabrics.cfm

Quadrille
http://www.jprco.com/lines/quadrille
.htm

Ralph Lauren
http://www.decoratorsbest.com/
ralphlauren.com/

Renaissance Carpet & Tapestries,
   Inc.
http://www.renaissancecarpet.com/

Robert Allen
http://www.robertallendesign.com/

Rogers & Goffigon, Ltd.
http://www.ddbuilding.com/
search/showrooms/showrooms.asp

Romo
http://www.romofabrics.com/

S. Harris
http://www.sharris.com/

Saxony Carpet, Inc.
http://www.saxcarpt.com

Scalamandré
http://www.scalamandre.com/

SeaCloth
http://www.seacloth.com/

Sina Pearson
http://www.sinapearson.com/

Stanton Carpet Corp.
http://www.stantoncarpet.com/

Stark Carpet
http://www.starkcarpet.com/

Stark Fabric
http://www.old-world-weavers.com/

Stroheim
http://www.stroheim.com/

Travers
http://www.traversinc.com/view.htm

Yoma Textiles
http://www.yoma.com/

Unika-Vaev USA, Inc.
http://www.unikavaev.com/

Zimmer + Rohde
http://www.zimmer-rohde.com/

V'Soske Carpet Company
http://www.vsba.com/projects/fla_archive/
506.html

Zoffany
http://www.zoffany.co.uk/

Notes

CHAPTER 1

1. George H. Johnson, *Textile Fabrics*, New York: Harper and Brothers, 1927, xxi.
2. Adele Coulin Weibel, *Two Thousand Years of Textiles*, New York: Pantheon Books, 1952, 27.
3. Ibid, 28.
4. Kax Wilson, *A History of Textiles*, Boulder, Colo.: Westview Press, 1979.
5. Sally Fox, FoxFibers, See http://invention .about.com/library/investors/blfox.htm.
6. *American Cotton Handbook*, New York: Barnes Publishing Company, 1941, 1.
7. Herbert R. Mauersberger, ed., *Textile Fibers*, New York: Thames & Hudson, 2003, 7.
8. Mary Schoeser, *World Textiles: A Concise History*, New York: Macmillan, 1955, 4.
9. *Two Thousand Years of Textiles*, 4.
10. *A History of Textiles*, 24.
11. Norma Hollen and Jane Saddler, *Textiles*, New York: Macmillan, 1955, 40.
12. Henry Barham, "An Essay upon the Silkworm," in *The Silk Book*, Great Britain: Cowell, Ltd., 1719, 11.
13. Ethel Lewis, *The Romance of Textiles*, New York: Macmillan, 1938, 33.
14. *Two Thousand Years of Textiles*, 7.
15. Ibid, 7.
16. *A History of Textiles*, 30.
17. *Two Thousand Years of Textiles*, 13.
18. *A History of Textiles*, 39.
19. *Two Thousand Years of Textiles*, 18.

CHAPTER 2

1. American Society for Testing Materials, *Yearbook*, Part 32, 1974, 46.
2. Bernard P. Corbman, *Fiber to Fabric*, 6th ed., New York: McGraw-Hill, 1983, 43.
3. Debbie Ann Gioello, *Understanding Fabrics: From Fiber to Cloth*, New York: Fairchild Publications, 1982, 49.

CHAPTER 3

1. Diana S. Waite, *Scalamandré's Guide to Passementerie*, Ronkonkoma, N.Y., 1990.

CHAPTER 4

1. http://www.greatreality.com/ColorSub.htm.
2. *The Bible.* "Exodus" xxxv, 35.
3. Stuart Robinson, *A History of Dyed Textiles*, Hillgate, London: Studio Vista Limited, 1969, 25.
4. Patricia Lambert, Barbara Staepelaere, and Mary Fry, *Color and Fiber*, West Chester, Penn.: Shiffler Publishing, 1986, 63.
5. Joseph Rivlin, *The Dyeing of Textile Fibers: Theory and Practice*, Philadelphia: J. Rivilin Associates, 1992, 9.
6. J. J. Pizzuto, *Fabric Science*, 7th ed., Arthur Price, Allen C. Cohen, and Ingrid Johnson, New York: Fairchild Publishing, 2003, 185.
7. From Printer's National Environmental Assistance Center, "Print Process Descriptions: Screen Printing," www.pneac.org/printprocesses/screen/moreinfo17.cfm.
8. *Davison's Textile Catalogue and Buyers Guide*, Ridgewood, N.J.: Davison Publishing (November 1955): 75.

CHAPTER 7

1. L. Stephen, "The Creation and Re-creation of Ethnicity: Lessons from Zapotec and Mixtec of Oaxaca," in *Latin American Perspectives*, vol. 23, no. 2, 1966, 63–68, as quoted in Andy Storey, "Misunderstanding Ethnicity: Ancient Hatreds, False Consciousness, and Rational Choice," in *Irish Journal of Anthropology*, vol. 2, 1997, 63–8.
2. Susan Meller and Joost Elffers, *Textile Designs*, New York: Harry N. Abrams, 1991, 20.
3. Peter Thornton, *Authentic Décor: The Domestic Interior, 1620–1920*, New York: Viking Penguin, 1984, 58.

CHAPTER 8

1. Amanda Kolson Harley, "Industrial Strength," *Preservation* magazine 57 (3): 32.
2. Karla J. Nielson, "The Psychology of Fabric," *DWC Magazine*, http://www.dwcdesignet.com/DWC/March'98/designper.html.
3. Alyssa Becker, "High-Performance Fibers," in *Extreme Textiles: Designing for High Performance*. Exhibition catalogue, Matilda McQuaid, curator, Cooper-Hewitt National Design Museum, Smithsonian Institution Affiliate, New York: Princeton Architectural Press, 2005, 75.
4. "Carpet Specifications," American School and University (November 1, 1998) http://asumag.com/mag/university_carpet_specification.
5. Carpet Installation Timeline, The Carpet and Rug Institute, http://www.carpet-rug.org/drill_down_3.cfm?page=13&sub=12.

CHAPTER 9

1. New York City Decoration & Design (D&D) Building Admission Policy, www.ddbuilding.com/about_the_dd/admission_policy/admission.html.
2. Heimtextil, http://heimtextil.messefrankfurt.com.
3. *Asia Times*, http://www.atimes.com.
4. Heimtextil, http://heimtextil.messefrankfurt.com.

CHAPTER 11

1. Crypton Cleaning Instructions, http://www.butlerwoodcrafters.com/cryptoncleaning.htm.

2. A Dictionary of Cleaning Terms, New City Cleaners, http://www.newcitycleaners.com/new/dictionary/fabrics/7.html.

3. Pollution Solutions: Waste Reduction Assistance for Business, http://outreach.missouri.edu/polsol/drycln.htm.

4. ConsumerReports.org, ConsumerReports.org-Dry-cleaning alternatives2/03.

5. CHEC's HealthHouse, http://www.checnet.org/healthhouse/education/articles detail.asp?Main_ID= 443.

6. CRI (Carpet and Rug Institute), http://www.carpet-rug.org/drill_down2.cfm?page=14&sub=3&requesttimeout=350.

7. HEPA Vacuum Cleaners, http://www.aircleaners.com/hepa.phtml.

Glossary

Abrasion The surface wear of a fabric caused by rubbing and contact with another fabric. (Chapter 6)

Acrylic latex backing A polymer material mixed with a by-product of rubber to prevent a fabric from slipping and to enhance its ability to be applied to walls. (Chapter 4)

Additive A process of creating color using a mixture found in light. When all the colors of light blend, the result is white. (Chapter 4)

Affinity Chemical attraction as in dyes for yarns. (Chapter 4)

Agents Individuals who represent a fabric-producing company or a firm that sells several different collections. Agents travel to designated design stores to update samples and provide sales support. (Chapter 9)

Air jet loom A high-speed shuttleless loom that powers the weft yarns through the shed by forced air. (Chapter 3)

Alizarin A dye (alzorine) originating from the madder root and now referring to a series of dyes. (Chapter 4)

American Association of Textile Chemists and Colorists (AATCC) A nonprofit organization composed of chemists, dyers, finishers, and representatives associated with chemicals, color, its application, and affects. AATCC develops and establishes test methods. (Chapter 6)

American Society for Testing Materials (ASTM) A nonprofit organization that develops and establishes test methods for materials, products, systems, and services. (Chapter 2)

Americans with Disabilities Act (ADA) A protection of civil rights prohibiting discrimination based on disabilities from conditions affecting mobility, stamina, sight, hearing, speech, emotional illness, and learning disorders. (Chapter 8)

Antibacterial/antimicrobial and antifungus A treatment making fabric resistant to the growth of microorganisms such as molds, mildews, and rust. (Chapter 4)

Anti-mildew A treatment that inhibits the development of fungi that usually grows on fabrics in warm, moist environments. (Chapter 4)

Anti-slip A finish usually made with resin or silica to inhibit the sliding of yarns against one another. (Chapter 4)

Anti-static A chemical compound applied to fabric to reduce or eliminate the accumulation of static electricity. (Chapter 4)

Asbestos A mineral that easily separates into long, flexible fibers used in non-combustible, nonconducting, or chemically resistant material. (Chapter 1)

Association for Contract Textiles (ACT) A nonprofit organization that focuses on interests and various issues related to the contract fabric industry, such as guiding designers by offering suggested performance guidelines. (Chapter 6)

Austrian shade A window covering that is shirred to create lengthwise bands of horizontal folds of fabric. (Chapter 7)

Autoclave A large, steam-pressured container for setting yarns. (Chapter 5)

Automated screen printing Screen printing using machines where fabric moves and not the screens. Separate screens are used for each color applied. (Chapter 4)

Auxochromes Atomic groups of colorants that can change their color. (Chapter 4)

Axminster A jacquard carpet where tufts are formed between the warp ends by special spool-like devices that insert pile between the rows and through the loom mechanism. (Chapter 5)

Back The reverse side of the fabric's face. (Chapter 3)

Backing In carpeting, the material that is adhered to the back of the fibers being used to hold the carpet together as it is being constructed. *Primary backing* holds the tufts in place and *secondary backing* enhances the stability of yarns being used. (Chapter 5)

Balloon shade A window covering with large gathers or bunches of fabric at the bottom. When the draw cord is pulled, the gathers become larger. (Chapter 7)

Barre An unintentional, repetitive pattern of continuous bars and stripes. (Chapter 4)

Bast Woody material such as flax, hemp, jute, or ramie obtained from the inner cortex of the bark. (Chapter 2)

Batting Slightly matted sheets of cotton, wool, or other fibers used as padding. (Chapter 7)

Beating The final step in loom weaving. The batten beats the last weft in the shed back against preceding yarns to make a compact cloth. (Chapter 3)

Beetling A process that gives round-shaped cotton fibers a flat appearance with increased luster. (Chapter 4)

Berber A durable, low-level looped, tufted carpet usually having a pebbly texture. (Chapter 5)

Bicomponent fibers The combining of two polymers of different chemical or physical properties into one filament and extruding them through the same spinneret. (Chapter 2)

Biophilic Showing an appreciation of life and the living world. (Chapter 6)

Bird's eye Plain dobby woven fabric with indentations resembling a bird's eye. (Chapter 3)

Bleaching A process of whitening yarns by removing all natural color. (Chapter 4)

Bleed Loss of dye (color) from fabric during a wet treatment finishing process or through washing. (Chapter 4)

Bloch printing A technique where the ground cloth is completely printed with color rather than dyed. The reverse side of the fabric will be almost white. (Chapter 4)

Boiling off A process of boiling cotton fibers or cloth to remove natural waxes and gums; scouring. (Chapter 4)

Boll The seed pod of the cotton plant. The seeds vary in number and are covered with staple fibers. (Chapter 2)

Bonding The process of adhering fiber webs or layers of fabrics together. (Chapter 3)

Borders Narrow fabric about 2½ to 6 inches wide sometimes woven with simple stripes, chevrons, or highly intricate designs. (Chapter 3)

Boutique A small, usually specialized showroom or store. (Chapter 9)

Breaking strength The measurement of stress exerted to pull a fabric apart under tension. (Chapter 6)

Broadloom A carpet of various weaves, woven on a loom 12 feet wide or more. (Chapter 5)

Brocade A heavy jacquard fabric with raised floral or figured patterns emphasized by contrasting surfaces or colors. The weft yarns form the design in a double plain-weave construction. (Chapter 3)

Brocatelle A jacquard fabric similar to a brocade but with designs standing in high relief. (Chapter 3)

Brushing A finishing process for fabric or knit using brushes to raise the nap. (Chapter 4)

Building Research Establishment Environmental Assessment Method (BREEAM) A method used primarily in Great Britain to determine the environmental performance of new and existing buildings. (Chapter 6)

Bulked Continuous Filament (BCF) Textured filament yarns that are kinked and curled by not allowing them to parallel each other during manufacturing, thereby causing them to increase loft. (Chapter 5)

Bullion or bullion fringe A series of cords attached to a woven heading or header and found, among other places, on the bottom of upholstered furniture, covering the space between the bottom frame of the furniture and the floor. (Chapter 3)

Cable A yarn made with a cable twist as in an S/Z/S or Z/S/Z. (Chapter 2)

Calendering A finishing process that creates a sheen on a fabric by passing it between two stainless steel or wooden rollers under regulated pressure. Sometimes the rollers are heated to a specific temperature to achieve a particular effect. (Chapter 4)

Carbonizing A chemical process to eliminate cellulose material mixed in with wool and other animal fibers. (Chapter 4)

Carding The process of separating, distributing, and equalizing fibers to remove most impurities and some broken, short, or immature fibers. (Chapter 1)

Cards A rectangular piece of fiber board or plastic punched with holes used to control the lifting of one or more warp yarns. (Chapter 3)

Carpeting A tufted floor covering, usually made from natural or manufactured fibers that often cover the full width and length of an interior room. Sometimes referred to as a rug. (Chapter 5)

Carpet tiles Modular pile carpeting in various shapes, usually square, installed in rows. (Chapter 5)

Carpet poms Sample tufts in a wide range of colors used in custom designing carpet. (Chapter 5)

Casement fabric Lightweight, sheer fabrics used for windows. (Chapter 7)

Chenille French for "caterpillar." A soft tufted cotton, silk, or worsted yarn. (Chapter 2)

Children's Health Environmental Coalition (CHEC) A nonprofit organization dedicated to disseminating information to the public about environmental toxins that affect children's health. (Chapter 11)

Chintz A plain-woven printed or solid cotton, or cotton blend, that may be finished with a sheen applied by chemicals or by calendering. (Chapter 4)

Chroma The relative intensity or brightness of a color, as in bright green or dull red. (Chapter 4)

Chromophore A chemical structure that is colored itself or becomes colored when combined with auxochromes. (Chapter 4)

Ciré A finishing process using a hot calender and wax or other substances on silk and rayon resulting in an exceptionally high sheen. (Chapter 4)

Cloth roll The roll or cylinder at the front of a loom onto which woven fabric is collected and wound. (Chapter 3)

Codes Legal regulations enacted by federal, state, or local governments or building departments to protect the safety and well-being of the general population. (Chapter 6)

Colorfastness The resistance of yarns or fabric to change color characteristics or transfer color to another fabric. (Chapter 4)

Color temperature A description of the distribution of the spectral energy of light translated as a "feel," as in blue feels "cool." (Chapter 4)

Compressibility The degree of bulk reduction by pressing down on pile. A carpet's ability to recover original thickness is referred to as resilience. (Chapter 5)

Compressive shrinkage A mechanical method of preshrinking fabric. (Chapter 4)

Continuing Education Unit (CEU) Credit for courses, seminars, lectures, or other educational experiences approved by the educational component of an organization for content and quality. CEUs can be required for maintaining some certificates and licenses or used to extend the knowledge of the professional designer. (Chapter 9)

Contract Related to fabric, carpeting, and furnishings intended for installation in offices, hotels, health-care facilities, or public spaces. A contract is prepared by the client and bids are received, resulting in the awarding of the contract. (Chapter 6)

Contract design The term applied to commercial fabric, carpeting, and furnishings intended for installation in offices, hotels, health-care facilities, and public spaces. A contract is prepared by the client and bids are received, resulting in a contract being awarded. (Chapter 8)

Converter An individual or company that finishes greige goods. (Chapter 4)

Cord The result of twisting together ply yarns in a third twisting process. (Chapter 2)

Cords Plied and twisted yarns less than 1 inch in diameter. Ropes exceed 1 inch in diameter. (Chapter 3)

Cornice A rigid overhead window treatment mounted over drapery headings for ornamentation and to conceal drapery fixtures. (Chapter 7)

Courses Rows of loops or stitches running the width of knitted fabric. (Chapter 3)

Creel A rack onto which spools are placed to create a warp. The yarns are drawn from the spools and attached to the warp/warper. (Chapter 2)

Crocking Transferring dye from the surface of a dyed or printed fabric onto another surface by rubbing. (Chapter 4)

Cross dyeing Dyeing of yarns or fabric composed of two or more different yarn types to achieve a multicolored effect. (Chapter 4)

Crushed velvet Velvet pile with an irregular surface. (Chapter 3)

Customer's Own Material (COM) Fabric that a client has located and paid for. (Chapter 3)

Custom order A fabric or trim ordered that is a new product designed and colored for a particular client. (Chapter 7)

Cutting A fabric sample cut from the source where an order will eventually be generated. (Chapter 9)

Cutting for approval (CFA) A fabric sample cut from the same source from which the order will originate and presented to the client for review and comment. (Chapter 9)

Cut pile Raised carpet loops that are cut during manufacturing by wires or a reciprocating knife blade resulting in tufts. (Chapter 5)

Damask A broad group of jacquard-woven fabrics introduced into Europe by way of Damascus, hence its name. Damasks are typically woven with large and elaborate floral or geometric patterns, originally in silk; however, damasks are now woven in a variety of natural and manufactured yarns. (Chapter 3)

Degumming A process that removes sercin gum from silk filaments or fabric by boiling it in a soap solution. (Chapter 4)

Denier An international numbering system for describing linear densities of silk and manufactured filament. (Chapter 2)

Dent A wire in a loom reed. The number of dents per inch or in a standard width indicates the warp count of the fabric. (Chapter 3)

Desizing A process of converting greige goods by adding agents that are later washed away and change the shape of the yarn or fabric to better accept dyes. (Chapter 4)

Diaper A twill weave in which three warp ends are raised, followed by a weft yarn. The pattern is then reversed. (Chapter 7)

Direct Dyes applied directly onto cellulose fibers in a neutral or alkaline bath without prior treatment. These dyes are known to bleed and dull in color when washed; a class of dyes. (Chapter 4)

Direct printing A technique used to place a colored design on a white or light-colored ground, as opposed to resist printing. (Chapter 4)

Display wings Designated showroom areas where fabrics are displayed by attaching them to metal clips on movable, overhead arms that permit the wide lengths to hang freely (soft racks) or smaller samples that are attached to a firm mounting surface where fabrics can be stapled or pinned (hard racks). (Chapter 9)

Distaff A wooden stick about 3 feet long that holds fibers while they are twisted by hand. (Chapter 1)

Dobby weave A woven construction produced by a dobby, a mechanical part of a loom that controls harnesses to permit the weaving of small, geometric figures. (Chapter 3)

Drafted When the linear density of a strand of yarn is reduced by pulling it apart. (Chapter 4)

Dry prints Prints that have been set with heat or other means without the use of liquid. (Chapter 4)

Duplex printing The technique of printing both sides of a fabric with either the same pattern or different patterns. (Chapter 4)

Durable press A finish that contributes to the retention of pleats, creases, and seams. (Chapter 4)

Dye assistants Substances that enhance the ability of dye molecules to penetrate yarn. (Chapter 4)

Dyeing The application of a dissolved colorant to fiber, yarn, or finished fabric. (Chapter 4)

Dye lot One source of a particular dyestuff. (Chapter 4)

Dyestuff A colorant that becomes molecularly dispersed when placed in contact with a substrate such as hot water. (Chapter 4)

Embossing A finishing process that produces a raised design or pattern in relief by passing fabric between hot, engraved rollers. (Chapter 4)

Environmentalism A movement to bring about social and political change aimed at protecting the environment and improving the condition of the natural world. (Chapter 6)

Environmental Protection Agency (EPA) A government agency responsible for control and abatement of pollution of air and water by solid waste, pesticides, and radioactive and toxic substances. (Chapter 2)

Face The surface of the fabric that is intended to be seen. (Chapter 3)

Factory representative A salesperson who represents the products of one company or factory. (Chapter 8)

Fade To lose the original color. (Chapter 4)

Fading and Yellowing A change in carpet color due to airborne chemicals, fumes, or cleaning agents. (Chapter 5)

Faille A flat-ribbed fabric with a slight luster made with heavier yarns in the weft with about 36 yarns to an inch. (Chapter 3)

Federal Aviation Administration (FAA) The national organization that regulates aircraft of nearly all categories, classes, and types. The FAA is also responsible for airspace and the advancement and safety of civilian aviation. The FAA develops and establishes tests, standards, and international codes. (Chapter 6)

Felt A nonwoven sheet of matted material made from wool, hair, or certain manufactured fabrics by applying heat, moisture, and pressure. (Chapter 1)

Festoons Decorative swags of fabric, cord, or rope hung between two points. (Chapter 3)

Fiber The smallest unit of fabric capable of being spun into yarn. (Chapter 1)

Filament A fiber of extreme or indefinite length. The length permits a yarn to be made with little or no twist. (Chapter 2)

Finished Fabric that has been processed in some way prior to sale. A fabric is said to be "converted" after it is finished. (Chapter 3)

Finishing Usually a sequence of fabric treatments, excluding dye, that enhances greige goods for sale. (Chapter 4)

Flame-resistant A fabric that burns but is self-extinguishing with or without the removal of the ignition source. (Chapter 4)

Flammability The measurement of a fabric's performance when it is exposed to specific sources of ignition. (Chapter 6)

Float The portion of a yarn that rides unbound and over two or more warp or weft yarns. (Chapter 3)

Flocked carpeting Carpeting that is produced by electrostatically spraying fibers onto an adhesive-coated backing. (Chapter 5)

Flocking Creating a design or pattern on a fabric or wall covering using small fibers that are dropped onto or electrostatically applied to a glue pattern, sometimes with a screen. (Chapter 4)

Fluorocarbon A manufactured yarn formed by a long chain of synthetic polymers. (Chapter 4)

Foulard A lightweight, lustrous fabric made with a two-up, two-down twill, originally in silk. (Chapter 7)

Fox edge A ready-made roll, typically made of burlap and filled with jute fibers, sold by the foot. Used for seat edges and around arms and rails where soft edges are required. (Chapter 10)

Frieze Heavy pile fabric with rows of uncut loops. (Chapter 3)

Friezé Heavy pile carpeting made of tightly twisted yarns of uncut loops. (Chapter 5)

Fringes Trimmings of loose threads or cords attached to a woven header or gimp-like structure. (Chapter 3)

Frogs Decorative fabric ornaments made of wrapped vellum, cord, or silk-covered wire and formed into a series of loops. (Chapter 3)

Fulling A finishing process for woolens that compresses fibers, producing felt. (Chapter 4)

Fusion bonded A process where pile yarns are embedded into a vinyl compound. (Chapter 5)

Galloons Wide gimps. (Chapter 3)

Gas fading Fading of color, particularly with disperse dyes on acetate, caused by exposure to oxides of nitrogen. Examples are pollution from gas-fired stoves or fumes from dryers. (Chapter 4)

Gauge The distance between two needle points expressed in fractions of an inch: $\frac{1}{10}$ gauge means 10 needle points per inch. (Chapter 5)

Gimps Narrow woven fabric strips used to trim the edge of window treatments or upholstered furniture. Gimps are often used to cover nail heads or to provide a transition from wood to fabric. (Chapter 3)

Glass curtains   Thin, sheer window fabric hung behind drapes and close to the glass. (Chapter 7)

Glazing   A finishing process that produces a smooth, high polish on fabric using friction rollers and starch, paraffin or other materials. (Chapter 4)

Gobelin   A family of French dyers who also became known for producing a woven tapestry fabric, mostly for royalty. (Chapter 7)

Green design   A broad term in interior design, architecture, and construction based on energy-efficient design and products that work in harmony with nature. (Chapter 5)

Green movement   A broad movement that includes concern for ecology, conservation, and the preservation of the environment. (Chapter 5)

Greige   French for *natural*. Fabric absent of finishing treatment; fabric just off the loom. (Chapter 4)

Grospoint   An upholstery fabric with uncut loop pile larger than frieze. (Chapter 3)

Ground   The plain base or background area of a decorative fabric. (Chapter 3)

Hand screening   A screen-printing process produced by physically moving screens and manually squeegeeing print paste across the screens. (Chapter 4)

Hand-tufted   Having the needles inserted by hand through woven or nonwoven material to create a carpet. (Chapter 5)

Hangers   Individual bullions or small ornaments such as tufts that are strung on top of one another and hung on skirts of tassels or fringe. (Chapter 3)

Harness   A wood or metal frame that holds the heddles in position during weaving. (Chapter 1)

Heathered   Stock dye applied typically to wool fibers resulting in varied colors. (Chapter 4)

Heat setting   The use of heat in various forms to retain yarn twist. (Chapter 5)

Heddles   Cord, wire, or flat steel strips through which one or more warp threads are connected. Heddles are supported by the harness. (Chapter 1)

High Efficiency Particulate Air (HEPA) Filters   Filters that filter very small particulates from the air. Used in homes and offices as well as the aerospace, nuclear, electronic, pharmaceutical, and medical fields. (Chapter 11)

Hue   Name for a particular color such as yellow or red. (Chapter 4)

Hydrophilic   Having a strong attraction to water, such as rayon. (Chapter 4)

Hydrophobic   Lacking an affinity for water or repelling water, like polyester. (Chapter 4)

Ikat   A complex artistic technique used to create images on fabric, probably developed in western Asia. The images are dyed onto the threads before they are placed on the loom and woven into the finished product. The word *ikat* derives from the Malay word *mengikat*, meaning "to tie." (Chapter 4)

Impact Noise Rating (INR)   Numerical value used to express the ability of floor covering to minimize sound. (Chapter 5)

Incident light Available light. (Chapter 4)

Indentations Depressions in rugs or carpeting caused by weight being pressed against the yarns. (Chapter 5)

Independent representative (IR) A salesperson who sells many different products, usually of one category, such as fabric. The IR can work for one multilevel company or represent many different companies. (Chapter 8)

Indoor air quality (IAQ) The degree to which indoor air is pure of molds, spores, aromas, or unhealthy chemicals such as formaldehyde. (Chapter 6)

Interlining A fabric sewn inside drapes to provide additional structure to the treatment. (Chapter 7)

International Code Council (ICC) A nonprofit organization supporting the protection of health, safety, and welfare of people by providing standards, codes, and services for buildings. (Chapter 6)

International Maritime Organization (IMO) A nonprofit agency responsible for improving maritime safety and preventing pollution. The IMO develops flammability test methods, standards, and international codes. (Chapter 6)

International Organization for Standardization (ISO) An organization whose membership consists of national standard-setting bodies who unite to promote worldwide standardization of elements relating to interior and built environments. (Chapter 6)

Intervening variables In research, a variable that links independent and dependent variables. In general usage, an occurrence that is sometimes difficult to predict and can affect the results of a study or test. (Chapter 8)

Jaconet dust cover Cloth protecting the underneath portion of upholstered furniture. (Chapter 10)

Jacquard A system of weaving that permits the production of woven designs of considerable size and intricacy. (Chapter 3)

Jacquard matelassé A fabric with a quilted or raised pattern made on a jacquard dobby loom. Whenever the coarser weft yarns interlace with the face fabric, it causes the remainder of the face to pucker. (Chapter 3)

Jacquard mechanism A device attached to a loom using punched cards that "read" the loom like a player piano, resulting in small and large-scaled figured patterns. (Chapter 1)

Jacquard woven tapestry A jacquard woven fabric with two sets of warp yarns and two sets of weft yarns woven the full width of the loom. (Chapter 3)

Jet ink printing A technique using computer-controlled drops of dye that are strategically placed on fabric or carpeting. (Chapter 4)

Jobbers Individuals or firms that purchase fabric from a manufacturer then sell it in varying lengths, usually at a wholesale price. The fabric, in turn, is then sampled and sold to designers. (Chapter 3)

Kermes A female insect, *Kermes vermillo*, found in evergreen oaks that provided a source for the color crimson. (Chapter 4)

Knit backing Cotton knit bonded to the back of a fabric. (Chapter 4)

Knitted or chenill carpeting A method of interlocking loops, connecting pile, backing and stitching yarns in one process. (Chapter 5)

Knitting A method of constructing fabric by interlocking series of loops of one or more yarns. Derived from the original Anglo-Saxon word *cnyttan*, meaning to weave threads by hand. (Chapter 3)

Lambrequin A stiffly shaped overhead window surround covered in fabric. Unlike a cornice, a lambrequin continues down the sides of the treatment. (Chapter 4)

Lampas A jacquard fabric with a slight luster made with two sets of warp and two or more weft yarns, usually in different colors. Originally, a printed silk fabric that was made in India. (Chapter 3)

Lanolin Wool grease sometimes used in the production of ointments and cosmetics. (Chapter 1)

Latex A water emulsion of synthetic rubber, natural rubber, or other polymers. Almost all carpet latex consists of styrene-butadine rubber (SBR). (Chapter 5)

Leadership in Energy and Environmental Design (LEED) An organization that has developed a rating system to identify sustainable buildings and to promote integrated, "whole building" design while raising consumer awareness about sustainable building practices. (Chapter 5)

Level When dye has been moved from one area of the fabric to another to enhance the uniform distribution of color. (Chapter 4)

Light booth A small viewing chamber capable of producing different lighting effects. (Chapter 4)

Lincrusta Embossed wall covering made from pulp, linseed oil mixed with sawdust, plant resin, zinc oxide, and dye. Lincrusta becomes firmer with age. Similar to anaglypta. (Chapter 8)

Liners Lengths of fibrous plant tissue. (Chapter 2)

Liséré A jacquard fabric usually manufactured when a second warp beam causes the yarns to float on top, creating the pattern and leaving the yarns loose on the back. (Chapter 3)

Loft The quality of rebound or springiness in a natural or manufactured yarn. (Chapter 2)

Luminex Fabric containing optical fibers woven with nonoptical fibers and connected to LEDs and a power source, producing a glow. (Chapter 11)

Martindale test A test measuring the abrasion resistance of fabric and leather. Developed in England by James H. Heal, the test is used extensively in Europe and Australia. (Chapter 6)

Mechanics Individuals who construct furniture; particularly applied to unionized shops or workrooms. (Chapter 10)

Memo A showroom sample that designers borrow for a period of usually 30 days or less to show clients initial fabric choices. (Chapter 9)

Mercerizing A chemical treatment of cotton yarn or fabric by immersion in a strong alkali bath. Results are best with combed cotton. (Chapter 4)

Metameric A color that looks different under various light sources. (Chapter 4)

Modulus Fabric with strength properties measured in pounds per square inch (psi), such as Kevlar produced by Dupont. (Chapter 8)

Moiréing A finishing process that produces a wavy pattern. (Chapter 4)

Moisture barrier backing Fabric backing using a vinyl laminate to inhibit the strike-through of moisture. (Chapter 4)

Mothproofing Treatment of fabric with insecticides or solid chemical composites to make wool resistant to moths. (Chapter 4)

Multifilament Manufactured filaments composed of many fine fibers. (Chapter 2)

Mulitphased looms High-speed shuttleless looms in which several weft yarns are inserted simultaneously as multiple sheds are formed at the same time. (Chapter 3)

Munsell A color system established by Albert Munsell (1858–1918) using a three-dimensional color tree. It is often used to describe paint colors and frequently used in teaching color. (Chapter 4)

Nanotechnology The study and manipulation of atomic structures. (Chapter 4)

Nap Protruding fiber ends from the surface of one or both sides of a fabric, giving a fuzzy appearance and produced by brushing and elevating the fibers. (Chapter 2)

Napping A finishing process using revolving cylinders to raise yarn ends on fabric. (Chapter 4)

National Energy Management Institute (NEMI) A nonprofit organization that includes the Sheet Metal Workers' International Association (SMWIA) and the Sheet Metal and Air Conditioning Contractors' Association (SMACCA), serving to promote healthy indoor air quality and energy management systems. (Chapter 6)

National Fire Protection Association (NFPA) A nonprofit, international organization that advocates fire safety, developing and establishing fire test methods and standards. (Chapter 6)

Needle bonding A manufacturing technique where downward facing, barbed needles are used to force yarn through backing material. When the needles are withdrawn, enough yarn is displaced to have them adhere to the base/backing. (Chapter 5)

Needle-punched A type of carpeting in which downward facing barbed needles are used to force yarn through backing material. When the needles are withdrawn, enough yarn is displaced to have the yarn adhere to the base or backing. (Chapter 5)

Noise Reduction Coefficient (NRC) Numerical value used to express how well wall fabric and carpeting absorb sound. (Chapter 5)

Occupational Safety and Health Administration (OSHA) The federal agency charged with protecting the health of workers in industry. (Chapter 6)

Offgassing The release of volatile organic compounds into the environment. (Chapter 6)

Ogival A fabric pattern based on the diagonal, sometimes pointed arch or rib across a Gothic vault. (Chapter 7)

Open account A showroom account where the designer or design firm has 30 days to pay for product. Products are shipped when ordered. (Chapter 9)

Optical brighteners Agents applied to fabric that absorb ultraviolet radiation and emit it as blue or violet, making the fabric appear extra white. (Chapter 4)

Oriental rugs Handmade floor coverings typically from the Middle East, Turkey, China, or Russia. The value of the rug is related, in part, to the number of knots per inch. (Chapter 5)

Pantone A color identifying and color forecasting system used in interior and fabric design, architecture, and industrial design fields. Small, numbered paper samples are used to help identify specific colors. (Chapter 4)

Passementerie Decorative trim of several categories usually produced in part or totally by hand and used to embellish window and bed treatments or furnishings, including pillows. (Chapter 3)

Perchloroethylene or perc A highly chlorinated hydrocarbon used in dry cleaning. (Chapter 11)

Performance Appearance Rating (PAR) A rating method determining how a carpet maintains its appearance over time. (Chapter 5)

Performance Rated (PR) A rating method of determining the degree to which a carpet changes appearance over time. (Chapter 5)

Pick glass and pick needle A magnifying glass and needle used to remove usually weft yarns from a portion of fabric to analyze them or to determine the fabric's weave structure. (Chapter 3)

Picking The movement of the weft yarns through a shed across the shuttle box. (Chapter 3)

Pick ticket A work order picked up from a designer or fabric supplier that is usually delivered by hand to a workroom. (Chapter 10)

Piece dyeing Dyeing fabric rather than dying yarns. (Chapter 4)

Pigments Finely ground powder colorants that become dispersed in the dyeing process and remain on the surface of yarns and fabric. (Chapter 4)

Pile Raised loops, tufts, or other arrangements of yarns that stand away from the surface of the fabric. (Chapter 3)

Pile shading A slight change in the color of plush carpeting due to the pile being slanted in opposing directions, causing light to reflect off the surface. (Chapter 5)

Pilling Small tangles of fiber occurring when fabric is rubbed against itself or another material or surface. (Chapter 4)

Plain weave A woven structure that repeats on two warp yarns and two weft yarns. The first warp yarn passes over the first weft and under the second weft yarn. The second warp yarn reverses this action. (Chapter 3)

Plissé A cotton fabric treated with sodium hydroxide, a caustic soda that causes the cloth to pucker or crinkle producing a stripe effect, usually in the warp direction. (Chapter 4)

Plush carpet A smooth, cut pile finish for which individual tufts are only minimally visible and the overall visual effect is level yarn ends. The appearance is produced from brushing and shearing spun yarn singles that are set without heat. (Chapter 5)

Plush A warp pile with a cut pile surface longer than velvet pile and less closely woven. (Chapter 3)

Ply A yarn formed by twisting together two or more single yarns in one operation. (Chapter 2)

Polymers Substances created by the reaction of two or more monomers (simple molecular compounds) that have reactive groups allowing them to join, forming long, chain-like molecules. (Chapter 2)

Portiere A length of fabric covering a doorway. (Chapter 7)

Prime polyurethane A family of cushion material that includes conventional prime, grafted prime, and densified prime. Conventional prime is produced by mixing conventional polyols with isocyantes and water. (Chapter 5)

Print cloth A medium weight, plain weave fabric made of cotton, rayon, or blended yarns. (Chapter 3)

Printed fabric Designs applied to fabric using color. (Chapter 4)

Print paste A paste containing colorants and other materials. (Chapter 4)

Proforma A showroom account that requires that products are paid for in advance of their being shipped. (Chapter 9)

Progressive (residual) shrinkage Shrinkage each time fabric is subjected to laundering. (Chapter 4)

Quill A tapered wooden, cardboard, fiber, or metal tube that is wrapped with yarn and encased in the shuttle. (Chapter 3)

Railroaded A vertical pattern applied horizontally on a furnishing. (Chapter 7)

Rapier loom One kind of shuttleless loom using a steel tape (rapier) with a clamp on the end to deliver weft yarns. (Chapter 3)

Rebonded polyurethane Bonded granulated urethane foam, fabricated to create porous sheets (usually six feet wide) and used for carpet cushioning. (Chapter 5)

Reed A comb-like device on a loom that spaces the warp ends in the desired order and also pushes succeeding weft yarns against the last weft yarn. (Chapter 3)

Reeling Unwinding raw silk from a cocoon or unwinding yarn from bobbins or cones.

Regenerated fibers Fibers that are chemically processed from cellulose using, for example, wood chips. (Chapter 2)

Registration Alignment of pattern and/or color. (Chapter 4)

Relaxation shrinkage Shrinkage attributed to stress of manufacturing fabric. (Chapter 4)

Repeat The complete pattern on a fabric that can be seen over and over again. (Chapter 3)

Resins Organic materials that are soluble in water and used as thickeners and film-forming agents. (Chapter 4)

Resist prints Prints that have designs produced by applying a paste that resists dyeing. The fabric is then submerged into a dye vat and then washed. The resist material rinses away to reveal the pattern. (Chapter 4)

Resource library Catalogued collection of products, housed within a large design firm or independently owned. (Chapter 8)

Restorative care The most aggressive of all types of fabric and carpet care, typically involving professionals using specifically designed equipment and chemicals. (Chapter 11)

Retting Process of separating bast fibers from the natural gum and wooden matter of the plant stalk. (Chapter 2)

Roller printing A method of printing using engraved rollers or cylinders. (Chapter 4)

Roman shade A flat, hanging window covering that forms pleats when the draw cord is pulled. (Chapter 7)

Rosettes Gathered fabric ornaments resembling roses. Sometimes a small tassel is attached to the center. (Chapter 3)

Rotary screen printing   A technique using perforated metal (nickel) screens shaped into the form of hollow cylinders. (Chapter 4)

Rugs   Area floor coverings made of any fiber, animal skin, or fur, typically without pile. Sometimes rugs are used interchangeably with carpet. (Chapter 5)

Satin weave   A woven structure in which the face of the fabric is formed almost completely of warp floats produced in the repeat. (Chapter 3)

Saxony   A soft, durable cut pile carpet with long pile, ¼ of an inch to over ½ inch in length with more tip definition in the yarn ends than plush. (Chapter 5)

Schreinering   A finishing process that produces a high luster on fabric by using an engraved steel calender roller and a smooth roller. (Chapter 4)

Screen printing   Several methods of printing using screens where the pattern is unblocked on the mesh. Print paste is applied to the screen and squeegeed across, revealing the pattern. (Chapter 4)

Scroop   The sound and feel of "crunch" particular to silk and other fabrics. (Chapter 7)

Seam slippage   The movement of yarns in a fabric that occurs when it is pulled apart. (Chapter 6)

Selvage   The narrow edge of the fabric parallel to the length made with stronger yarns that are packed tightly together to protect the fabric from fraying or coming apart. (Chapter 3)

Sercin   Gum produced by the silkworm's gland. (Chapter 2)

Sericulture   The cultivation of caterpillars more commonly known as silkworms to produce raw silk. (Chapter 1)

Shearing   A finishing process that cuts uneven yarns mechanically. (Chapter 4)

Shed   The raising of some warp yarns by the harness so the shuttle can pass through. (Chapter 1)

Shedding   The appearance of short fibers that work their way to the surface in newly installed carpet and can be vacuumed away. (Chapter 5)

Shots   In pile carpeting, the number of weft yarns per row of tufts. (Chapter 5)

Shrink control   Methods for controlling the reduction in length or width of fabric. (Chapter 4)

Shuttle   A boat-shaped device that carries weft yarns through the warp shed in the weaving process. (Chapter 1)

Shuttle box   A compartment on either side of the loom used to momentarily restrain or hold the shuttle after each weft yarn is delivered. (Chapter 3)

Sick building syndrome (SBS)   The condition of a building as it relates to the health of its worker-occupants, separate from specific job-related health issues such as fatigue from working long hours or muscle aches. (Chapter 6)

Sidemark   Brief written instructions given by a designer to the company that will ship the fabric order, instructing the receiver, such as a workroom, on how the fabric is to be handled or used. (Chapter 9)

Singeing   A finishing process for burning off protruding fibers from yarns of fabrics. (Chapter 4)

Single   A continuous strand of yarn. (Chapter 2)

Sisal   A hard leaf fiber obtained from the sisal plant found in Java, East and West Africa, and Haiti. (Chapter 1)

Skein dyeing Dyeing of loosely wound, continuous strands of coiled yarns with a circumference of about 45 to 60 inches. (Chapter 4)

Slub An uneven, elongated, and somewhat thick section of a yarn considered a flaw in some fabrics such as finished satin but valued for adding texture in other fabrics. (Chapter 2)

Soapwart From the Latin *sapo*, meaning *soap*. A perennial herb with coarse pink or white flowers. The leaves of the plant can serve as a detergent when mashed. (Chapter 11)

Soil inhibitors Methods to restrict soil from entering or finishes that facilitate the release of soil from fabric. (Chapter 4)

Solution dyeing Dyeing manufactured filaments before the material is extruded. (Chapter 4)

Solvent scouring A method of extracting impurities from fabric using organic solvents. (Chapter 4)

Sound Transmission Class (STC) Numerical value measuring the amount of sound that passes through walls. (Chapter 5)

Special order A fabric or trim ordered that is not current in a collection or one that is to be changed in color or design. (Chapter 7)

Spectrophotometric curves The shapes used to analyze the spectral distribution of light energy. (Chapter 4)

Spinning The process of straightening out and twisting fibers into yarn or thread. (Chapter 1)

Spindle A round wooden stick or rod used to twist yarn in spinning. (Chapter 1)

Spinneret A nozzle with 1 to more than 1,000 holes, through which manufactured fiber material is forced, then appears as a coagulated strand. The holes are usually from 0.002 to 0.005 inch in diameter. (Chapter 2)

Spoon dyeing The use of ladles or large spoons attached to long wooden handles into which dyestuffs are placed. The ladles are then submerged into an aqueous vat to dye yarn or fabric. (Chapter 4)

Sprouting A minor defect caused by protruding tufts on the surface of carpeting. (Chapter 5)

Standards Statements explaining the minimum requirement related to test results used in the development of building codes and trade guidelines. (Chapter 6)

Standard test method A scientific, standardized method for testing, whose results can be replicated. (Chapter 8)

Staple Short fibers. Staple fibers require spinning and twisting to create a yarn. In manufactured fibers, staple fibers are cut in lengths from about 1 inch to 1½ inches from the extruded material. (Chapter 2)

Stencil A printing technique where a design is cut into cardboard, metal, or another material and then applied to a piece of fabric or paper. (Chapter 4)

Stock dyeing The process of dyeing fibers or filament after they are cleaned of foreign matter and become transformed into yarn. (Chapter 4)

Strie A fine line or narrow strip woven into the fabric. (Chapter 3)

Strike-off A short test run of a fabric to determine its feasibility. (Chapter 4)

Strike-through The migration of adhesives or liquid that is applied to one surface, moving through to another surface. (Chapter 4)

Substrate A fiber or fabric to which another material, like dye, is added. (Chapter 4)

Subtractive Reducing or changing a color by mixing in pigment which reduces its ability to reflect specific light waves. (Chapter 4)

Suessen German manufacturer and name of a continuous dry heat process for setting yarns. (Chapter 5)

Superba French manufacturer and name of a continuous heat setting process for yarns using steam and pressure. (Chapter 5)

Sustainable design Design that supports economic, social, and ecological systems such as creating autonomous buildings that use solar or wind power without compromising the ability of future generations to meet their needs. (Chapter 6)

Synthetic A term applied to any manufactured fiber other than rayon, acetate, or regenerated protein (azlon) fiber. (Chapter 2)

Tabled When the full length of a fabric panel has been laid on a large table to ensure that the interlining and fabric are even, straight, and fitting properly. (Chapter 10)

Tapa cloth Bark cloth made from beating the fibrous inner bark of certain trees, particularly the paper mulberry tree. (Chapter 1)

Tapestries Heavy, hand-woven fabrics with decorative designs usually depicting historical scenes. (Chapter 5)

Tassles Hanging fabric ornaments that are composed of a head made of

cut yarns and/or looped yarns and bullion cording wrapped around usually a wooden core. (Chapter 3)

Tenacity The quality of fabric that has a higher than normal tensile strength; the degree to which material can be pulled longitudinally without tearing it apart. (Chapter 8)

Tentering A finishing process for holding fabric to a desired width as it dries. (Chapter 4)

Thermal transfer printing A technique using a decal-like process of applying pattern by transferring dyes from paper to fabric. (Chapter 4)

Thermoplastic The capability of a yarn or filament to be softened with heat after it has hardened and cooled. (Chapter 2)

Thread A thin, continuous cord, especially strands of cotton, linen, silk, wool, or manufactured fibers often used in sewing. (Chapter 1)

Throwing The process of making a twisted yarn from reeled silk or adding an additional twist into manufactured filament. (Chapter 2)

Tiebacks Decorative cord typically with tassels used to hold back window treatment fabric. (Chapter 3)

Toile de jouy A floral or scenic design printed on cotton, linen, or silk. (Chapter 4)

Tone-on-tone dyeing A fabric colored in lighter and darker shades of the same hue. (Chapter 4)

Top dyeing Dyeing yarns, especially wool, after they have been straightened and separated from the shorter fibers. (Chapter 4)

Treadles Foot pedals used to control the opening and closing of the shed in hand-weaving. (Chapter 1)

Tricot A warp-knitted fabric, knitted flat with fine wales on the right side and more or less pronounced crosswise ribs on the back. (Chapter 4)

Tufting A process in which yarns are punched through a woven or nonwoven backing material to form rows of tufts. French from *tricoter*, meaning "to knit". (Chapter 5)

Tufting needles The hollow needles used to punch through backing to produce tufts. (Chapter 5)

Twill weave A woven structure characterized by a diagonal rib, or twill line, generally running upward from left to right. (Chapter 3)

Union dyeing A method of dyeing to obtain one color on a fabric using different yarns. (Chapter 4)

Upholstered wall covering Fabric applied to walls using batting, creating a soft feel. (Chapter 7)

Up-the-bolt Applying fabric so the lengthwise grain runs vertically. (Chapter 7)

Valance An overhead fabric window treatment that can be pleated, scalloped, shirred, or draped. (Chapter 7)

Value Lightness or darkness of color. (Chapter 4)

Vegetable dye Class of natural dyes including woad, madder, and indigo that originate from roots, bark, and berries. (Chapter 1)

Velour Woven, velvet-like fabric with close, dense pile laid in one direction. (Chapter 3)

Vellum Fine, transparent cotton fabric used as tracing cloth that enables a fabric designer to see a pattern through it and, using a pen or pencil, to trace over the original art, producing a facsimile of the design onto the cloth. (Chapter 3)

Velvet Plain, one-color cut pile produced without a jacquard mechanism. (Chapter 5)

Vermicelli An overall design of usually narrow, undulating, or wiggly lines. (Chapter 7)

Vertical mill A mill that converts raw materials into finished products, where quality and production limits are controlled on all levels. (Chapter 9)

Voided velvet Velvet with the pile woven higher in some areas than in others or a fabric sheared to different lengths. (Chapter 3)

Volatile organic compounds (VOC) Organic compounds that evaporate from goods during and after manufacturing and contribute to air pollution. (Chapter 6)

Wales A series of ribs, cords, or raised portions, usually in the fabric length. (Chapter 3)

Wall upholstery backing The use of multiple layers of acrylic latex coatings to prevent strike-through. (Chapter 4)

Warp Set of threads or yarns traveling lengthwise on the loom. Also known as ends. Warp ends interlace with weft yarns. (Chapter 1)

Warp beams Wood or metal cylinders several feet long on which spools are placed to create a warp. (Chapter 2)

Warp printing The printing of warp yarns before weaving. (Chapter 4)

Water jet loom A high-speed shuttleless loom that powers the weft yarns through the shed using forced water. Yarns must be unsized filament or nonabsorbent staple yarns that are not affected by water. (Chapter 3)

Waterproofing Preventing water from penetrating fabric, typically with the use of vinyl or linseed oil coating. (Chapter 4)

Water resistant The tendency of reducing the amount of water penetrating fabric. (Chapter 4)

Weaving The method or process of interlacing two or more sets of yarns or similar materials so that they cross each other, usually at right angles. (Chapter 1)

Weft Set of threads or yarns traveling horizontally to the warp yarns. Individual yarns are also known as picks or filling yarns and interlace with warp yarns. (Chapter 1)

Welting A tape or covered cording sewn into a seam as reinforcement or trimming. (Chapter 10)

Wet prints Prints that have been created using liquid dyes. (Chapter 4)

Whorl Small flywheel weight at the base of the spindle that keeps thread in place. (Chapter 1)

Wicking The drawing up and transfer of liquid in fibers or filaments through capillary action. (Chapter 2)

Wilton A jacquard carpet where pile yarns are raised and lowered by harnesses during weaving. When the pile appears on the carpet face, it traverses the carpet warpwise and becomes embedded in the carpet base. *Worsted Wilton* is a high-grade Wilton carpeting with short pile and a tightly woven back. *Wool Wilton* uses less twist in the yarn creating a higher pile, producing a courser product, and *brussels* carpeting is an uncut Wilton. (Chapter 5)

Window treatment Any fabric used in association with windows, including curtains, drapes, and shades. (Chapter 7)

Woad A natural blue dye prepared by fermenting the leaves of the woad plant. (Chapter 4)

Wood block A hand-printing method by which designs are cut into a block of wood, color is applied to its surface, and then the block is pressed onto a piece of fabric or paper. (Chapter 4)

Workroom A place of business that measures, cuts, sews, fabricates, and installs fabric treatments as directed by the interior designer. (Chapter 7)

Woven or loomed carpeting Floor covering made by traditional weaving techniques. (Chapter 5)

Wyzenbeek test A test measuring the abrasion resistance of fabric and leather. Developed by Andrew Wyzenbeek, this test is utilized extensively in the United States. (Chapter 6)

Yarn Two or more fibers of varying lengths, twisted together. (Chapter 1)

Yarn dyeing Dyeing of yarn before weaving or knitting. (Chapter 1)

Credits

Figure 2.15 — Illustration by Ron Carboni

Figure 2.16 — Illustration by Ron Carboni

Figure 2.17 — Illustration by Ron Carboni

Figure 2.18 — Photographs courtesy of Halcyon Yarns

CHAPTER 3

Chapter opener: Photograph © Cubo Images/Index Stock Imagery

Figure 3.1 — Photograph © Frank Theodore Koe

Figure 3.2 — Illustration by Ron Carboni

Figure 3.3 — Photograph © Frank Theodore Koe

Figure 3.4 — Illustration by Ron Carboni

Figure 3.5 — Illustration by Ron Carboni

Figure 3.6 — Illustration by Ron Carboni

Figure 3.7 — Illustration by Ron Carboni

Figure 3.8 — Photograph © Frank Theodore Koe

Figure 3.9 — Photograph © Frank Theodore Koe

Figure 3.10 — Photograph © Frank Theodore Koe

Figure 3.11 — Photograph © Frank Theodore Koe

Figure 3.12 — Photograph courtesy of Textile Fabric Consultants, Inc.

Figure 3.13 — Photograph courtesy of Textile Fabric Consultants, Inc.

Figure 3.14 — Photograph courtesy of Textile Fabric Consultants, Inc.

Figure 3.15 — Photograph courtesy of Scalamandré

Figures 3.18a–d — Photographs by Shari Amith Dunaif/High Noon Productions

Figure 3.19 — Illustration by Ron Carboni

Figure 3.20 — Photograph © Frank Theodore Koe

Figure 3.21 — Photograph © Frank Theodore Koe

Figure 3.22 — Photograph © Frank Theodore Koe

CHAPTER 4

Chapter opener: Photograph © Fernando Bengoechea/Beateworks/Corbis

Figure 4.1 — Illustration by Ron Carboni

Figures 4.2a–b — Photographs courtesy of Fairchild Publications

Figure 4.3 — Photograph courtesy of BYK-Gardner USA

Figure 4.4a — Photograph © Sue Carpenter

Figure 4.4b — Photograph courtesy of Zuber & Cie

Figure 4.5 — Photograph courtesy of Textile Fabric Consultants, Inc.

Figure 4.6 — Illustration by Ron Carboni

Figure 4.7 — Photograph courtesy of Standex Engraving, LLC

Figure 4.8 — Photograph courtesy of Textile Fabric Consultants, Inc.
Figure 4.9 — Photograph courtesy of Standex Engraving, LLC

CHAPTER 5

Chapter opener: Photograph © Matthew Hranek/Art+Commerce
Figure 5.1 — Photograph © Owen Franken/Corbis
Figure 5.2 — Illustration by Ron Carboni
Figure 5.3 — Illustration by Ron Carboni
Figure 5.4 — Photograph © Art Resource, NY
Figure 5.5 — Illustration by Ron Carboni
Figures 5.6a–d — Illustrations by Ron Carboni
Figure 5.7 — Illustration by Ron Carboni
Figures 5.8a & b — Illustrations by Ron Carboni
Figure 5.9 — Illustration by Ron Carboni
Figure 5.10 — Photograph courtesy of Armstrong
Figure 5.11 — Photograph courtesy of Armstrong

CHAPTER 6

Chapter opener: Photograph © Dan Forer/Beateworks/Corbis
Figure 6.1 — Photograph © Airphoto—Jim Wark
Figure 6.2a — Photograph © Lufthansa Technik AG
Figure 6.2 b — © Dan Forer/Beateworks/Corbis
Figure 6.3 — Photographs provided by Mite-E-Ducts Inc. Air Duct Cleaning in
               Zionsville, Indiana
Figure 6.4 — Photograph courtesy of The Solaire Building
Figure 6.5 — Photographs courtesy of Arc-Com Fabrics, Inc.
Figure 6.7 — Photograph courtesy of Lees Carpets, a division of Mohawk Industries

CHAPTER 7

Chapter opener: Photograph © Fernando Bengoechea/Beateworks/Corbis
Figure 7.1 — Photograph © image100/Alamy
Figures 7.2a–b — Handwoven window shades by CONRAD
Figure 7.3 — Photograph © Peter Aprahaman/Corbis
Figure 7.4 — Photograph by Tim Street-Porter, courtesy of The Wiseman Group
Figure 7.5 — Photograph © Nick Carter, Elizabeth Whiting & Associates/Corbis
Figure 7.6 — Photograph © Abode/Beateworks/Corbis
Figure 7.7 — Photograph by Tim Street-Porter, courtesy of The Wiseman Group

CHAPTER 8

Figure 8.10 — Photograph by Scott McDonald © Hedrich Blessing, Courtesy of Earl
        Swennson Associates, Inc.
Figures 8.11a–c — Photographs by Stephen Sullivan
Figure 8.12 — Photograph by Shari Smith Dunaif, High Noon Productions

CHAPTER 9

Chapter opener — Photograph © Manfred Schulze-Alex/Lufthansa Technik AG
Figure 9.1 — Photograph © Angelo Homak/Corbis
Figure 9.2 — Photograph by Shari Smith Dunaif/High Noon Productions
Figure 9.5 — Photograph by Shari Smith Dunaif/High Noon Productions
Figure 9.6 — Photograph by Shari Smith Dunaif/High Noon Productions
Figures 9.8a–b — Photographs by Frank Theodore Koe

CHAPTER 10

Chapter opener: Photograph © Charlie Drevstam/Canopy Photography/Veer
Figure 10.1 — Photograph by Frank Theodore Koe
Figure 10.2 — Photograph by Frank Theodore Koe
Figure 10.5 — Photograph by Frank Theodore Koe
Figure 10.6 — Photograph by Frank Theodore Koe
Figure 10.7 — Photograph by Frank Theodore Koe
Figure 10.11 — Photograph by Frank Theodore Koe
Figure 10.12 — Photograph by Frank Theodore Koe
Figure 10.13 — Photograph by Frank Theodore Koe
Figure 10.14 — Photograph by Frank Theodore Koe
Figure 10.15 — Photograph by Frank Theodore Koe
Figure 10.16 — Photograph by Frank Theodore Koe
Figure 10.17 — Photograph by Frank Theodore Koe
Figure 10.18 — Photograph by Frank Theodore Koe
Figure 10.19 — Photograph by Frank Theodore Koe
Figure 10.20 — Photograph by Frank Theodore Koe
Figure 10.21 — Photograph by Frank Theodore Koe
Figure 10.22 — Photograph by Frank Theodore Koe
Figure 10.23 — Photograph by Frank Theodore Koe
Figure 10.24 — Photograph by Frank Theodore Koe
Figure 10.25 — Photograph by Frank Theodore Koe
Figure 10.26 — Photograph by Frank Theodore Koe
Figures 10.27a–c — Photograph by Frank Theodore Koe
Chapter 10 appendix — Illustrations by Ron Carboni

CHAPTER 11

Chapter opener: Photograph © William Abranowicz/Art+Commerce

Figure 11.1 — Photograph © Jim Zuckerman/Corbis

Figure 11.2 — Illustration by Ron Carboni

Figure 11.3 — Photograph © Graeme Montgomery/Stone/Getty Images

Figure 11.4 — Photograph courtesy of iRobot Corp.

Figure 11.5 — Photograph © Royalty-Free Corbis

CHAPTER 12

Chapter opener — Photograph © Fernando Bengoechea/Beateworks/Corbis

Figure 12.1 — Photograph © Fernando Bengoechea/Beateworks/Corbis

Figure 12.2 — Designed by Carl D'Aquino & Francine Monaco
www.daquinomonaco.com, photographed by Andrew Bordwin

Figure 12.3 — Photograph courtesy of William R. Eubanks

Figure 12.4 — Photograph by John Schoenfeld

Figure 12.5 — Photograph courtesy of Faruk Guner

Figure 12.6 — Photograph courtesy of Greg Jordan

Figure 12.7 — Photograph courtesy of Eric Cohler

Figure 12.8 — Photograph courtesy of Rita Yan

Figure 12.9 — Photograph © Ed Massery

Figure 12.10 — Photograph by Tim Street-Porter, courtesy of The Wiseman Group

Figure 12.11 — Photograph by Charles Heilemann

Figure 12.12 — Photograph by Frank Theodore Koe

Figure 12.13 — Photograph by Frank Theodore Koe

Figure 12.14 — Photograph by Frank Theodore Koe

Figure 12.15 — Photograph by Frank Theodore Koe

Figure 12.16 — Photograph by Frank Theodore Koe

Index